New Directions in East Asian History

This series addresses the ways in which history influences the political, economic and social development of East Asia, a region which now plays a pivotal role in our world's multipolar international system. The series provides new perspectives on East Asia's distinctive economic and political situation through the lens of 20th century history, with a particular focus on Pre-War and Cold War periods. It argues the need to re-examine the history of East Asia and provide new historical approaches to a vibrant and constantly changing region.

Highlighting that history is at the root of many modern day conflicts in Asia, this series provides a global forum for rigorous academic research and timely debate by scholars worldwide, and showcases significant new research on East Asian history and politics in the contemporary era.

The series will appeal to specialists in the history and politics of Asia; international history; scholars of modern and contemporary Japan, Chinese and Korea as well as international relations.

NOW INDEXED ON SCOPUS!

Christopher R. Hughes · Hatsue Shinohara
Editors

East Asians in the League of Nations

Actors, Empires and Regions in Early Global Politics

palgrave
macmillan

Editors
Christopher R. Hughes
Department of International Relations
London School of Economics
London, UK

Hatsue Shinohara
Waseda University
Graduate School of Asia-Pacific Studies
Tokyo, Japan

ISSN 2522-0195 ISSN 2522-0209 (electronic)
New Directions in East Asian History
ISBN 978-981-19-7066-5 ISBN 978-981-19-7067-2 (eBook)
https://doi.org/10.1007/978-981-19-7067-2

Cover illustration: The Eastern Bureau in Singapore. The League of Nations, A Pictorial Survey. United Nations Archives at Geneva

This Palgrave Macmillan imprint is published by the registered company Springer Nature Singapore Pte Ltd.
The registered company address is: 152 Beach Road, #21-01/04 Gateway East, Singapore 189721, Singapore

Acknowledgments

The editors would like to thank the Japan Society for the Promotion of Science for its support for the workshop in Tokyo in January 2020 at which the chapters in this book were presented, as part of the project on The League of Nations in Asia and the Pacific: In Search of a New Dimension the History of the League of Nations.

Note on Romanization

The romanization of Chinese characters is always a complex problem due to the use of different systems under the Republic of China and the People's Republic of China, as well as the frequent changes of some place names in the period covered by this book. Pinyin has been used as a general rule but there are many exceptions for proper names. This is because many Chinese individuals were widely known outside China by romanized versions of their names that do not conform with either of the formal systems of romanization (such as Chiang Kai-shek) or by English names that they adopted (such as Alfred Sze). These names have been used in the main text to make it easier to identify them in the English archives and other sources. The names of such individuals in Chinese characters can be found in the Glossary.

This rule has also been used for place names when appropriate. Present-day Beijing, for example, was called Jingdu by the Chinese government until 1928 and then Peiping (Beiping) by the government that established its capital in the city of Nanjing (Nanking).

For Japanese individuals, the convention has been followed of putting the family name after the given name. Japanese versions can be found in the Glossary.

The names of Thai individuals are romanized with Thai versions provided in the glossary.

The romanized titles of all Asian language texts that are cited in the book are provided in the list of references for each chapter and in the bibliography.

Contents

Notes on Contributors

Tomoko Akami is Associate Professor (Reader) in International History at the Australian National University. Her publications include *Internationalizing the Pacific* (2002); *Japan's News Propaganda and Reuters' News Empire in Northeast Asia* (2012); *Soft Power of Japan's Total War State* (2014). Her recent works on the League of Nations have been published in *The International History Review*, *The Journal of Global History*, *The Journal of History of International Law*, as well as in various edited books. She is currently working on the project 'Towards a globalized history of international relations,' funded by the Australian Research Council (2021–2023).

Harumi Goto-Shibata is Professor at the University of Tokyo and obtained her D.Phil. in Modern History from the University of Oxford. Her publications include *The League of Nations and the East Asian Imperial Order, 1920–1946* (Palgrave Macmillan, 2020); *Japan and Britain in Shanghai, 1925–1931* (Macmillan, St Antony's series, 1995); Britain, the League of Nations and Russian Women Refugees in China in the Interwar Period, in Antony Best ed., *Britain's Retreat from Empire in East Asia, 1905–1980* (Routledge, 2017); Japanese and British Perceptions of Chinese Boycotts in Shanghai, in Kaoru Sugihara ed., *Japan, China and the Growth of the Asian International Economy, 1850–1949* (Oxford University Press, 2005). She has also published three single-authored books and two co-edited books in Japanese.

Madeleine Herren is Professor of History and Director of the Institute for European Global Studies at the University of Basel, Switzerland. She has written several books, book chapters, and journal articles on European and global history of the nineteenth and twentieth centuries, internationalism and the history of international organizations, networks in historical perspective, historiography, and intellectual history.

Publications include Gender and international relations through the lens of the League of Nations, in G. Sluga and C. Janes eds. *Women, Diplomacy and International Politics since 1500*. Abingdon: Routledge (2016); with M. Rüesch and C. Sibille, *Transnational History, Theories, Methods, Sources*. Springer (2012); *Internationale Organisationen seit 1865. Eine Globalgeschichte der internationalen Ordnung*. Darmstadt: WBG (2009). Her most recent publications include Strength through Diversity? The Paradox of Extraterritoriality and the History of the Odd Ones Out. *Journal of the History of International Law* (22) (2020); with Susanna Burghartz, *Building Paradise, a Basel Manor House and Its Residents in a Global Perspective* (forthcoming 2021).

Christopher R. Hughes is Professor Emeritus of International Relations at the LSE where he taught courses in the International Politics of the Asia Pacific, Chinese Foreign Policy, and Foreign Policy Analysis. He also served as Director of the Asia Research Centre at the LSE from 2002 to 2005. His research focuses on the Asia-Pacific with special reference to Chinese foreign policy and politics. His publications include *Taiwan and Chinese Nationalism* (Routledge 1997), *China and the Internet: Politics of the Digital Leap Forward* (edited with Gudrun Wacker, Routledge 2003), and *Chinese Nationalism in the Global Era* (Routledge 2006). He has also published numerous articles on Taiwanese and Chinese politics, International Relations theory, and foreign policy in leading academic journals.

Chang Li obtained his Ph.D. in History from National Chengchi University, Taiwan and is Adjunct Research Fellow at the Institute of Modern History, Academia Sinica and Honorary Professor at National Dong Hwa University. His major works include *International Cooperation in China: A Study of the Role of the League of Nations, 1919–1946* (in Chinese). Taibei: Zhongyang Yanjiuyuan Jindaishi Yanjiusuo (1999); Giuseppe Ros as a Scholar-Diplomat in China, 1908–1948 (in Chinese). *Institute of Modern History Bulletin* (2017); Pursuing and Attacking the Defecting

Warship *Chongqing* (in Chinese). Hong Kong: San Lian (2017); Observations and Experiences of Ambassador Wunsz King during World War II (in Chinese). Hong Kong: Chinese University of Hong Kong (2019); Recovering the Unpaid Balance on Ships Built for the United States by Jiangnan Shipyard, 1917–1936 (in Chinese). *Academia Historica Bulletin* (2019).

Lunhai Mu obtained his Ph.D. in History from Waseda University and is currently Associate Professor at Wuhan University. He is the author of *Japan's Foreign Culture Policy in the Postwar Years: Focusing on the Exploration of Reorganization from 1952 to 1972* (in Japanese). Tokyo: University of Waseda Press, 2016. His research focuses on culture, political thought, and US-Japan relations in the post-war years. He translated Hatsue Shinohara's *League of Nations* (in Japanese) into Chinese.

Takashi Saikawa obtained his Ph.D. from Ruprecht-Karls-Universität Heidelberg on *From Intellectual Co-operation to International Cultural Exchange: Japan and China in the International Committee on Intellectual Co-operation of the League of Nations, 1922–1939*. He is currently Associate Professor of Global History at Takasaki City University of Economics, Japan. His main research interests are the history of international organizations and the history of international cultural exchange. Publications include Returning to the International Community: UNESCO and Postwar Japan, 1945–1951, in Poul Duedahl ed. *A History of UNESCO: Global Actions and Impacts*, New York: Palgrave Macmillan.

Hatsue Shinohara is Professor of International Relations and History at Waseda University. She earned a Ph.D. in History (University of Chicago) under the supervision of Akira Iriye. Her major works include *US International Lawyers in the Interwar Years: Forgotten Crusade* (Cambridge: Cambridge University Press, 2012); International Law and World War One, *Diplomatic History* (38/4) (2014); Drifts toward the Empire: The Trajectory of American Reformers in the Cold War, in Marti Koskkeniemi, et al. ed., *International Law and Empire: Historical Explorations* (Oxford: Oxford University Press, 2017); Marjorie Whiteman: Not Flowers but a Medal, in Immi Tallgreen ed., *The Portrait of Women in International Law* (Oxford: Oxford University Press, forthcoming); *The League of Nations* (in Japanese) (Tokyo, 2010); Chinese translation Beijing, 2020); With Masaharu Yanagihara eds. *Adachi Mineichiro* (in Japanese) (Tokyo, 2017). She has also edited a special issue of *Kokusai Seiji* (an official journal of the Japan Association of International Relations) on International Organizations in Historical Context (in Japanese).

Teewin Suputtikun obtained his Ph.D. from Waseda University and is currently Assistant Professor in Asia-Pacific Studies at Chulalongkorn University. His published works include An Excuse for Common Goods: The Multi-purposeness of the 'Human Security' Concept in Japan's Foreign Policy. *Asian Review* (2012); Article 9 of Japan's Constitution: The History of Preservation and Evolution (in Thai) (2013); Japan's Security Strategy and the Flexibility within the Existing Framework: New Realignment and Reinterpretation of Postwar Policy Tools. *Journal of Social Sciences* (47/1) (in Thai) (2017); International Norm Localization in the Making of Japan's New Defense Policy: An Analysis of Discourses that Legitimises the Use of the Right of Collective Self-Defense (in Thai) (2018).

Rikiya Takahashi obtained his Ph.D. from Nihon University and served as an assistant legal adviser at the Permanent Mission of Japan to the United Nations before returning to academia. He is currently Associate Professor at Yokohama City University. His research traces the history of international law focusing on the League of Nations project for codifying international law during the 1920s. His publications include Nationality of Married Women in the Hague Codification Conference and Japan, *International Relations* 188 (2017) (in Japanese) and After Tachi: The Idea of 'Office of Legal Adviser' in the Ministry of Foreign Affairs in Wartime Japan, *Journal of International Law and Diplomacy* (116/3) (2017) (in Japanese).

Kayo Takuma is Professor of International Politics at Tokyo Metropolitan University. Her research interest is global health governance's origin, evolution, and challenges, with a focus on its relationship with the changing international political order. She has been engaged in several projects on this topic, including a comparative study of the G7 countries' contribution to the implementation of the International Health Regulations and health co-operation in Asia. Her major publications are (Kayo Yasuda) *Kokusai Seiji no nakano kokusai hoken jigyō* [International Health Work in International Politics: From the League of Nations Health Organisation to the WHO and UNICEF], Tokyo:

Minerva Shobō, 2014; Jinrui to Yamai: Kokusai Seiji Kara Miru Kansen Sho to Kenko Kakusa [The Mankind and Diseases: Infectious Diseases and Health Inequality in International Politics], Tokyo: Chuokoron Shinsha, 2020; Global Solidarity is Necessary to End the COVID-19 Pandemic, *Asia Pacific Review* (27/2), 2020.

Haruo Tohmatsu obtained his D.Phil in Politics and International Relations from the University of Oxford and is currently Professor at the National Defense Academy of Japan. His works in English include *The History of Anglo-Japanese Relations 1600–2000*. Palgrave McMillan (2003); *A Gathering Darkness: The Coming of War to the Far East and the Pacific, 1921–1942*. Rowman & Littlefield (2004); *Imperialism on Trial: The International Oversight of Colonial Rule*. Lexington Books (2006); *World War Zero: The Russo-Japanese War in Global Perspective*, vol. 2. Brill (2006). *The Battle for China: Essays on the Operational History of the Sino-Japanese War of 1937–1945*. Stanford University Press (2010); *Divided Memories: History Textbooks and War in Asia*. Routledge (2011); *Maritime Strategy and National Security in Britain and Japan from the Alliance to the Post-9/11 World*. Brill/Global Oriental, (2012); From the Manchurian Incident to Japan's Withdrawal from the League of Nations, in Kiyoda Tsutsui ed. *Fifteen Lectures on Showa Japan: Road to the Pacific War in Recent Historiography*. Tokyo: Japan Industry Foundation for Culture (2016); *Spain 1936: Year Zero* (Sussex Academic Press, 2018).

Abbreviations

CPDI	Committee of Experts for the Progressive Codification of International Law
FEATM	Far Eastern Association of Tropical Medicine
ICIC	International Committee on Intellectual Co-operation
ILA	International Law Association
INGO	International Non-Governmental Organisation
IO	International Organisation
JSIL	Japanese Society of International Law
LNACJ	League of Nations Advisory Committee of Jurists
LNHO	League of Nations Health Organisation
NCIC	National Committee on Intellectual Cooperation
PCIJ	Permanent Court of International Justice
ROC	Republic of China
UN	United Nations
US	United States
WHA	World Health Assembly
WHO	World Health Organisation

List of Tables

Introduction: Locating Eastern Asia and the League in Global International Relations

Christopher R. Hughes and Hatsue Shinohara

Out of a total of 54 members of the League of Nations at its zenith, only China, Japan and Siam (Thailand) were located in Eastern Asia, an area that covers the sub-regions of what are conventionally known as East and Southeast Asia in academic discourse today. By focusing on their activities, this book contributes to two emerging trajectories of research: the deconstruction of the narrative of the League as little more than a grandiose experiment in cooperation between the great powers that failed with the catastrophe of World War II; and the growing interest in how actors beyond Europe and the United States shaped the evolution of the modern international system.

C. R. Hughes (✉)
London School of Economics and Political Science, London, UK
e-mail: c.r.hughes@lse.ac.uk

H. Shinohara
Waseda University, Tokyo, Japan
e-mail: hshinohara@waseda.jp

C. R. Hughes and H. Shinohara (eds.), *East Asians in the League of Nations*, New Directions in East Asian History,
https://doi.org/10.1007/978-981-19-7067-2_1

Concerning the first of these trajectories, pioneering work by scholars such as Susan Pederson has already generated more interest in understanding how the League operated beyond Europe through policies such as the mandates system in the Middle East and the Pacific (Pederson 2007, 2015). This has been reinforced by a growing interest in how its functional organisations laid the foundations for the later development of the United Nations system and a mode of governance that addresses international issues such as labour standards, human trafficking, health and economics (Clavin and Wessels 2005; Mazower 2009). Scholars have also begun to work on particular organisations within the League, such as its Secretariat (Gram Skjoldager and Ikonomou 2017), as well as its intellectual and ideational basis (Sluga and Clavin 2014).

As for the growing interest in the evolution of the modern international political system beyond Europe and the United States, this is reflected most clearly in the growing sub-discipline of Global International Relations (Acharya 2014). There is, however, still relatively little work focusing on Eastern Asian actors and the League. The small amount of excellent work on the three states that has been done is also handicapped by a limited use of sources written in the languages of the region. This inevitably leads to a somewhat Eurocentric bias that is particularly evident in the dominance of work that has been conducted on issues that are closely connected with the fate of the League and its implications for great power politics, especially the Manchurian Crisis. The fact the League was designed to be universal in membership and not limited to developing policies and structures to promote the interests of the major Western powers is one reason among many to broaden the focus. Developments such as the institutionalisation of the principle of legal equality through the practice of one-state-one-vote in the Assembly had highly complex ramifications for international politics, such as encouraging the participation of states in Latin America and Asia and helping to consolidate the League's functional activities in Eastern Asia, which are easy to miss if too much attention is paid to the great powers.

To develop a truly Global International Relations that can analyse such innovations, it is necessary to avoid understandings of the 'global' and 'globalism' that are largely associated with Western practices and visions. Deploying theoretical concepts is, of course, indispensable. Equally important, though, is to acknowledge the significance of voices from a region like Eastern Asia by drawing on expertise in its languages, histories and cultures. Only in this way is it possible to show how the global norms diffused by the League were the outcome of an entanglement between the practices and ideas of colonial governance and those of regional actors. When this has been revealed, new light can be shed on previously studied cases and topics that have rarely been the subject of academic investigation can be brought onto the research agenda.

The contributors to this book are well qualified to take on these challengers. Taken together, they have linguistic competency in Chinese, Thai, Japanese and English and are well-versed not only in the history of the League and its period but also in the histories, cultures and societies of the three Eastern Asian states. Most originate from, or are based in, Eastern Asia, with some experts from the broader disciplines of International Relations and the history of international organisations coming from leading universities in Europe and Australia. Their research thus draws on extensive primary sources from the region and archives in Geneva and elsewhere. Some have already published pioneering research on the League and international politics more generally in English. Others are well known for extensive publications in the languages of the region and have taken this book as an opportunity to allow an English-reading audience to benefit from their extensive knowledge for the first time. There are also contributions from members of a new generation of rising scholars from the region who are well placed to take a fresh look at the primary sources from the perspective of today's academic discourse.

In terms of scope, focusing on the three Eastern Asian members of the League has obvious advantages for taking this project forward. First, looking at more than one case reduces the risk of making overly broad generalisations about the region, which can lead to stereotyping in the worst-case scenario, because each state played a distinctive role. Japan is notable as the only non-Western state to have become a permanent member of the League's Executive Council, a position that it won primarily due to the geopolitical concerns of the European powers over its ability to shape order in the 'Far East'. China presents the anomaly of a founding member of the organisation that became a crucial player in regional and world politics despite (and partly due to) being in a state of serious internal conflict and division. Siam is significant as a relatively small and weak state that could use League membership to maintain its position as the only country in Southeast Asia to have avoided colonisation.

A second reason for choosing the three Eastern Asian states is that looking at their inter-relationships makes it possible to avoid seeing the League as only concerned with relations between the major world powers.

This is not only true at the inter-state level but even more important for exploring the networks of numerous sub-state individuals and organisations that turned to the League to solve problems that were taking on increasingly international dimensions. The significance of such actors in a world dominated by empires and colonialism has been sorely overlooked in a historical narrative that has been largely pre-occupied with relations between the great powers, despite the fact that that they saw the world from a very different vantage point. That Eastern Asia escaped the carnage of World War I, for example, meant that the priorities of individuals and organisations in the region differed in important ways from those of the anti-militarist movements that promoted a liberal vision of the League in Europe and the United States (Kaiga 2021). A stronger tendency to see the organisation as a venue for practising realist strategies that promoted national interests, both in and beyond the region, is just one example of this difference.

To ensure a broad coverage of both the diversity of the region and the common themes that were faced by actors in the three states, this book is divided into our thematic sections. The first, on the League and Empires, starts with Tomoko Akami's theoretical argument for moving away from understanding the League as an organisation of states in favour of seeing its politics as structured by relations between empires, which has fascinating implications for how a concept such as 'liberal internationalism' should be understood. This is followed by Harumi Goto-Shibata's discussion of the relationship between the technical work of the League and the growth of nationalistic politics. By comparing how Japan and China engaged with this activity, it is possible to critique functionalist theories of integration and show how the political impact of cooperation depends to a large degree on the broader foreign policy priorities of the state. Both of these chapters are thus valuable contributions to the research agenda on the ideational foundations of internationalism which has been pioneered by scholars like Sluga and Clavin (Sluga and Clavin 2014).

The second section contains three chapters that explore the theme of Globalism and Inter-Civilizationism by looking at the roles played by health experts, lawyers and intellectuals in the formation of emerging international networks. Kayo Takuma thus looks at the work and legacy of the Far East Bureau of the League of Nations, based in Singapore, which was tasked with managing the spread of epidemic diseases, a problem that became increasingly international with the expansion of global contacts and the movement of troops in the two world wars. Rikiya

Takahashi examines the role played by Japan's international lawyers in the League's project to codify international law, demonstrating the tension that arose between the enthusiasm of internationalists and the demands of an increasingly nationalistic and imperialistic state. Takashi Sakawa's chapter on intellectual entanglements between the League and Eastern Asia takes an approach similar to that of Goto-Shibata by comparing the ways in which the enthusiasm of advocates of working with the League's International Committee on Intellectual Co-operation was put to the service of the very different state agendas of projecting an anti-modernist version of national identity in Japan and modernist state-building in China. All of the authors in this section thus shed light on how the need to manage global challenges created new spaces for the work of regional organisations but also raised fears of a new form of colonial domination.

The third section, on Member States, is concerned with analysing how the League provided an arena to develop diplomatic strategy and foreign policy. Through extensive research into the Thai archives, Teewin Suputtikun shows how Siam's elites saw the League as a resource for learning the arts of diplomacy with mixed degrees of success. Their painstaking strategy of omni-directional friendship and neutrality was useful for protecting their country's fragile sovereignty but had embarrassing consequences when they were unable to take a clear stand over Japan's invasion of Manchuria. Hatsue Shinohara's chapter shows how Japan's diplomats were able to play a constructive role in shaping international norms through the League Council in the 1920s but that their efforts were stymied by their government's aggressive foreign policy in the 1930s. Chang Li's chapter casts the geographical net wider by exploring how China had to face the dilemma of maintaining good relations with Italy while supporting Ethiopia as a victim of its aggression at the time of the Abyssinian crisis. These chapters all show that while League membership provided real advantages for the Eastern Asian states they were also forced to face serious dilemmas when required to take positions on thorny issues beyond their own region.

The three chapters in the fourth section take a fresh look at the Manchurian Incident. Bearing in mind that this episode has tended to dominate histories of the League because it had a direct impact on the interests of the powers and the organisation's demise, the authors show that analysis of the crisis can still yield insights into largely unexplored questions (Nish 1993; Thorne 1972). By focusing on local inputs and reactions to the drafting of the Lytton Report, they broaden out the discussion to look at how the crisis made the League an important arena in which regional actors could address complex tensions between the international system and the changing pressures of domestic politics. Haruo Tohmatsu begins by looking at the creativity involved in the consideration of applying models of international administration that had been used in Europe and the Middle East, as well as the more local idea of regional autonomy that had briefly been experimented with in China. Mu Lunhai presents an account of how the Lytton Report was received in China by analysing its coverage by leading newspapers, revealing a disjuncture between the literate population and the political elite. Christopher R. Hughes bridges the discussion by Tohmatsu and Mu by showing how China's diplomats used the League as a platform to push back against the attempts of Japan and the other imperial powers to reduce the Lytton Report to an exercise in what the International Relations theorist, Stephen Krasner, calls sovereignty as 'organised hypocrisy'.

The book finishes with a conclusion by Madeleine Herren, whose leading role in taking forward research on international organisations puts her in the best place to draw some general lessons from the contributions and to locate them in the new agenda of League studies. As she points out, Eastern Asia's engagement with the League was inevitably conditioned by the trauma of the two centuries of imperial encroachment and cultural hegemony that preceded its establishment. Yet any assumptions that Eastern Asians were passive actors have to be challenged by looking again at how state and sub-state actors shaped international norms in a world dominated by 'Western' ideas.

The purpose of undertaking a closer reading of a wide range of evidence from Eastern Asia is not, therefore, to challenge the view that the League did ultimately fail in many important respects. It is to use the League as a source of evidence, insofar as it became an institutional setting that both reflects the power hierarchy of international politics between the two world wars and provided arenas for sub-state actors from the region to seek empowerment and agency. Despite the well-documented problems that beset the organisation, it did provide a venue in which new concepts were tested and tensions between the imperial system and the ambitions of individuals and groups dedicated to recognising the values of different civilisations and cultures became more visible.

While shedding light on these complex processes is a challenging task, it is of interest not only to historians but also to all readers who are interested in developing a broader understanding of international politics and especially the origins and fate of international cooperation. This includes those who are interested in intersecting fields such as public health and international/regional cooperation. The focus on emerging norms, dissenting actors, empire and global history will also be useful for scholars and teachers and students in the field of International Relations, especially as the discipline strives towards achieving a more global outlook and the decolonisation of the curriculum.

Above all, the themes that are explored in this book resonate with many of the themes that remain central to international politics in the present day. This was made painfully aware to the contributors when the Covid-19 pandemic struck the world just as they presented their chapters to a conference at Waseda University in January 2020. Over the following two years, it quickly became clear that the centenary of the establishment of the League was also the start of the most severe global crisis since World War II. Although this inevitably posed problems for taking the project forward, requiring a higher-than-usual degree of dedication and concentration from the contributors, it was also a new source of motivation to better understand the strengths and weaknesses of international organisations. This was only further reinforced when Russia launched its invasion of Ukraine just as the final touches were being put to the book. The politicisation of health and the sight of President Zelensky of Ukraine warning the Security Council that the United Nations would be rendered obsolete if it failed to defend the integrity of his country meant that the authors hardly needed to be encouraged to draw some parallels between the findings of their research and the condition of international politics today.

References

Acharya, Amitav. 2014. Global International Relations (IR) and Regional Worlds. *International Studies Quarterly* 58: 647–659.

Chang, Li. 1999. *Guoji hezuo zai Zhongguo: lianmeng jiaose de kaocha 1919–1946* [International co-operation in China: A study on the role of the league of nations, 1919–1946]. Taibei: Zhongyang yanjiuyuan jindaishi yanjiusuo.

Chimni, B.S. 2016. International organizations, 1945-present. In J. Katz Cogan, I. Hurd, and J. Johnstone, eds. The Oxford Handbook of International Organizations. Oxford: Oxford University Press.

Clavin, Patricia and Wessels, Jens-Wihelm. 2005. Transnationalism and the league of nations: Understanding the work of its economic and financial organizations. *Contemporary European History* (14/1): 465–492.
Goto-Shibata, Harumi. 2020. *The league of nations and the East Asian imperial order, 1920–1946*. London: Palgrave Macmillan.
Gram-Skjoldager, Karen and Ikonomou Haakon A. 2017. The construction of the league of nations secretariat. Formative practices of autonomy and legitimacy in international organizations. *The International History Review* (41/2): 257–279.
Herren, Madeleine. 2016. International organizations, 1865–1945. In J. Katz Cogan, I. Hurd, and J. Johnstone, eds. The Oxford Handbook of International Organizations. Oxford: Oxford University Press. (OUP, 2016).
Kaiga, Sakiko. 2021. *Britain and intellectual origins of the league of nations, 1914–1919*. Cambridge: Cambridge University Press.
Mazower, Mark. 2009. No enchanted peace: The end of empires and the ideological origins of the United Nations. Princeton N.J: Princeton University Press.
Nish, Ian. 1993. Japan's struggle with internationalism: Japan, China and the league of nations, 1931–1933. London and New York: Kegan Paul International.
Pedersen, Susan. 2007. Back to the league of nations. *The American Historical Review* (12/4): 1091–1117. 2015.
Pederson, Susan. 2013. *Securing the world economy: The reinvention of the league of nations 1920–1940*. Oxford: Oxford University Press.
Pedersen, Susan. 2015. *The guardians: The league of nations and the crisis of empire*. Oxford: Oxford University Press.
Reinalda, Bob. 2009. *Routledge history of international organizations: From 1815 to the present day*. London: Routledge.
Sluga, Glenda, and Patricia Clavin, eds. 2014. *Internationalisms: A twentieth-century history*. Cambridge: Cambridge University Press.
Thorne, Christopher. 1972. *The limits of foreign policy: The West, the league and the far east crisis of 1931–1933*. London: Macmillan.

The League of Nations in a World of Empires

Liberal Internationalism Reconsidered: Inter-Imperialism, Liberalism, and the League of Nations in Asia and the Pacific

Tomoko Akami

Introduction

The association of the League of Nations with 'liberal internationalism' has long escaped rigorous scrutiny (Clavin 2010; Sluga and Clavin 2017; Jackson and O'Malley 2018). This is despite the existence of many alternative strands of internationalism in the inter-war period, including the communist and fascist versions (Herren 2016; Brückenhaus 2020). In this chapter, I argue that we need to address this problem by questioning the notion of liberal internationalism itself, in order to understand the nature and significance of the League and its works in 'Asia and the Pacific region'.[1] I suggest that this may also provide an answer to the question that Akira Iriye posed in 1965: what regional order came 'after imperialism' in the Pacific region, following World War I? (Iriye 1965).

T. Akami (✉)
College of Asia and the Pacific, Australian National University, Canberra, Australia
e-mail: Tomoko.Akami@anu.edu.au

C. R. Hughes and H. Shinohara (eds.), *East Asians in the League of Nations*, New Directions in East Asian History,
https://doi.org/10.1007/978-981-19-7067-2_2

Because the notion of internationalism assumes the national sovereign state as its basic unit, much of its analysis has been based on the national–international binary framework. This is even true of a significant contribution to the debate such as Glenda Sluga's 2015 book, *Internationalism in the Age of Nationalism*, which regards nationalism as constitutive of internationalism (Sluga 2015). The national–international framework continues to be dominant in analyses of the League of Nations, including even recent works which regarded the League as not only the first failed global collective security organisation, but also a harbinger of the global governing norms for the UN institutions that followed its demise (Pedersen 2007; Iriye 2004). The persistence of this binary framework is probably because most of the work on the League is focused on the Euro-American contexts, even though the analysis has shifted from politicians, diplomats, and military officers to non-state actors, such as experts and their international organisations (García et al. 2016; Pedersen 2015; Clavin 2013; Kott and Droux 2013; Borowy 2009).

International histories of the 'Pacific region' (Asia and the Pacific) between the world wars have also focused predominantly on state-centric diplomatic, security, and economic relations (see, e.g. Mori 2006). This can be seen in works on the League in the region which, until recently, have focused almost exclusively on its relations with the sovereign units of China and Japan, and to a lesser extent Siam (Osterhammel 1979; Chang 1999; Burkman 2008; Hell 2010), including those on the League during the Manchurian crisis (Thorne 1973; Nish 1993). Furthermore, the main concern of scholars has ultimately been to examine Japan's path to the war with China and then the Allied forces (Nihon kokusai seiji gakkai Taiheiyō sensō gen'in kenkyūbu 1963). The misconception has thus been created that the rest of the region did not exist, with little attention paid to colonial Asia and the Pacific islands in the Asia Pacific War until the mid-2000s (Kurasawa et al. 2005).

Scholars, however, shifted attention to the role of the League in shaping the norms of global governance and therefore the roles of experts in such norm making at international inter-governmental organisations (IOs) and international non-governmental organisation (INGOs) and their personal and institutional interactions and networks. This has exposed the problem of the exclusive focus on national sovereign units in understanding the League's work in extra-Euro-America[2] where imperial polities, not national sovereign units, dominated. Arguably, the League's most significant achievement was its role in consolidating, energising, and mobilising these experts and their institutions and networks behind the global and regional norm-making process. Moreover, in extra-Euro-America, the League utilised experts who worked not only for national sovereign states and institutions, but also for locally based colonial administrations and institutions. Some of these had already established regional networks across colonies in Asia and the Pacific before 1920, which the League came to recognise and appropriate. While many of these experts were colonial officers sent from the imperial metropoles in Europe, the US, and Japan, they also included some who were locally born and trained (Akami 2016, 2017).

These expert interactions and exchanges that were mobilised by the League created different layers of dynamics and connections in extra-Euro-America, but these actions and dynamics have been dismissed in most histories of international relations in Asia and the Pacific until recent years (on recent works on INGOs, see Davidann 1998; Akami 2002; Yasutake 2004; Paisley 2009). Below, therefore, I will use the notions of 'liberal inter-imperialism' and 'inter-colonialism' to try to show how we could incorporate diverse layers of dynamics and interactions into our understanding of how the League played a role in shaping the regional order of the inter-war period (Hanzawa 2007).

Such a critical reassessment of the 'assumed' liberal international order is increasingly important not just for analysing international politics between the world wars, but also to further our understanding of how 'liberal international' institutions are facing a growing number of serious crises in the 2020s. I hope that revealing the problems that are inherent in the League and its related 'liberal' institutions points to ways to tackle them in the way that does not erode faith in, but take us closer to achieving their fundamental ideals.

Inter-Imperialism and the Inter-Imperial Order in Asia and the Pacific in 1920–1960

I have argued elsewhere that the notions of inter-imperialism and inter-colonialism are more accurate and useful than 'internationalism' for understanding the cooperative actions initiated by the League of Nations and other non-governmental (or semi-official) organisations across polities in Asia and the Pacific region in the inter-war period (Akami 2014, 2016, 2017). This is mainly because, as Iriye pointed out in 1965, in contrast to Euro-America, empires continued to be dominant in the region after 1919 (Iriye 1965: 4). Accordingly, 'inter-imperialism' can be defined as the idea of promoting cooperative actions across the metropolitan imperial states and institutions to advance their shared interests. 'Inter-colonialism', on the other hand, is the idea of promoting cooperative actions across local colonial administrations (and other imperial polities with limited sovereign powers) and institutions to further their shared interests (Akami 2016: 3). This distinction is important because it recognises that the interests of the colonial administrations and institutions were not always identical with those of their 'parent' metropolitan imperial states and institutions (Gotō 2005: 110–121, 150–152), while it also acknowledges that they could and did work together in pursuit of their shared interests.

Building on these notions, I suggest that liberal inter-imperialism and inter-colonialism are more accurate and useful than liberal internationalism for characterising the nature of the actions and projects of the League in Asia and the Pacific in the inter-war period. The notions can also be applied to the works of the League's successors, including the United Nations Relief and Rehabilitation Administration (UNRRA) and relevant UN agencies until decolonisation became the dominant tendency in the region. By using the notion of liberal inter-imperialism, it can draw attention to the priority of the interests of the imperial states and their institutions, while not rejecting the significance of other associated layers of relationships that were occurring across the imperial polities in the region. As well as capturing the nature of the actions and projects of the League in the region, it allows us to identify and assess the broader range of diverse, yet important interactions of peoples, goods, money, and ideas across imperial polities, which have been neglected in work that assumes the national–international framework.

Re-imagining the inter-war regional order as an inter-imperial order is not particularly difficult. The four major treaties, which resulted from the Washington Conference (1921–1922) and which complemented the League's order, were in essence multilateral agreements among the empires which had colonial interests in the region to safeguard their imperial interests. To be sure, the Nine-Power Treaty included China as a signatory country and attempted to restore China's sovereign rights. Yet this effort had failed as early as 1926 (Iriye 1965). To a great extent, it amounted largely to a treaty among the concerned empires, which assured them equal access to the markets and resources of China. The disarmament conferences that were led or assisted by the League and the London

Naval Treaty of 1930 (the Treaty for the Limitation and Reduction of Naval Armaments) could be understood as inter-imperial attempts to shape international order. Even the Pact of Paris (1928), which outlawed war for the first time in human history (Hathaway and Shapiro 2017), could also be cynically understood as a pact to maintain the *status quo* of the existing interests of the empires.

Globally, the League thus had a dual nature as not only an international, but also an inter-imperial organisation. Its Assembly had a principle of one 'nation', one vote, a nation-based principle that signified the equality of sovereign states. European states acted as 'national' states for intra-European affairs, such as minority disputes; and the member states from the Americas acted as national states. Many of the members of the League Secretariat's departments and committees came predominantly from European 'nations', although they paid some attention to balancing the 'nationalities' of the staff.

At the same time, the permanent members of the Council consisted of the major empires, and certain European member states acted as 'imperial' states when addressing the issues of extra-Euro-America. These issues included: the mandates, the epidemiological intelligence service in Asia and the Pacific, dealing with 'tropical' diseases in Africa and Asia, preventing and controlling trafficking in women and children in Asia, improving rural hygiene in Asia, and labour conditions in Africa. These League's actions were shaped by inter-imperial and inter-colonial dynamics (Pedersen 2015; Jerónimo 2018; Jerónimo and Monterio 2018; Akami 2016, 2017).

For China, although the League was largely seen as an inter-imperial body, it also helped to advance a nationalist agenda. At the Paris Peace Conference, the former Allied forces sided with the Japanese empire and insisted on retaining possession of the former German concession of the Shandong Peninsula that it had occupied during the war. The League also did little to encourage the victorious empires to relinquish their *existing* privileges in China, as well as their colonies in extra-Euro-America. Despite this, however, the Beijing (Peiping) government, but especially the Nationalist government that assumed power in 1928, proactively used the League's technical committees for reforming its public health administration, financial system, and transport system and to assert its 'national' prestige and restore its sovereign rights (Kawashima 2009: 329–331; Akami 2017: 20). This was evident in China's appeal to the League against Japanese aggression in Northeast China (Manchuria) in September 1931. Yet, after a prolonged investigation, the League's Lytton Commission still upheld the pre-crisis privileges of the empires in China (Nish 1993), while condemning Japan's 'new' territorial occupation for being not only against China's national interests but also against the shared interests of the other empires.[3]

Liberal Inter-Imperialism and Inter-colonialism for the League of Nations

It is, therefore, not difficult to see the cooperative actions which the League, its supporters, and those who were involved in the various operations that it promoted in extra-Euro-America, as having been inter-imperial, rather than 'international', and that this inter-imperialism consisted of further layer(s) of the League's internationalism. I have also demonstrated elsewhere how the League mobilised expert networks across the colonial administrations in Asia and the Pacific for various projects in the 1920s and 1930s, and termed these lateral and horizontal cooperative actions across the imperial polities as 'inter-colonial' (Akami 2016: 3; 2017: 6–8). Then, is the League's inter-imperialism and inter-colonialism in Asia and the Pacific best characterised as 'liberal'?

One of the most definitive works to attach the 'liberal' label to the League and its supporters is, of course, E. H. Carr's *The Twenty Years Crisis, 1919–1939: An Introduction to the Study of International Relations*, published in 1939, shortly before the outbreak of the European part of World War II. Carr called the League and its supporters 'utopians/idealists/liberals' and criticised them on two main points. First, they relied too heavily on public opinion as *the* moral force in international politics and as *the* main means to sanction the wrong doings of states. His criticism was valid insofar as that, by the time when he completed the book, he had substantial evidence, including the case of the Manchurian crisis, that this approach did not work. Second, the League and its supporters also upheld the current international conventions and laws as being neutral, impartial, and just, while they were in fact largely the product of politics between the dominant powers (Carr 1993, first published in 1939). These laws and conventions were, therefore, 'inter-imperial'. Using 'liberal' interchangeably with 'utopian' and 'idealist', he argued that one needed to be 'realistic' about these faults of the League and its supporters.

This was to earn Carr the status of forerunner of the 'Realist' school in the discipline of International Relations (IR). Moreover, the 'debate' between the 'liberals' and 'realists' of 1919–1939, as formulated by Carr, became the first foundational debate for IR, on which theoretical frameworks such as neo-liberalism and neo-realism were then built. While this formula became standard in the pedagogy of the discipline, it was also used to describe and analyse the League and its supporters in historical works.

This rigid liberalism-realism dichotomy has been challenged by IR scholars in recent years. Having closely examined what the so-called liberals and realists had written in the inter-war period, they have concluded that such a clear division did not exist and questioned whether the 'first debate' even took place (Long and Wilson 1995; Wilson 1998; Ashworth 2002; Schmidt 2012). I have suggested elsewhere that it is best to see Carr's dichotomy as a dialectic device. He created two opposing categories, which were 'ideal' types, and framed his argument as a debate between two poles in order to make his own point. Accordingly, although he criticised the League and its supporters, Carr did not solely support a 'realist' position. Rather, he wanted the League and its supporters to realise the fallacy of adopting either of the two above-mentioned positions. His conclusion was that an ideal (or a goal) was needed in international politics because power politics would only support the *status quo* and would not provide any intellectual and practical mechanism for making necessary changes. In his view, there would always be injustice or wrongs in the existing international order, so it needed to be corrected and reformed. Such changes would only be possible, he stressed, when people had an ideal or a goal to achieve (Carr 1993: 93).

A major problem with using the term 'liberal' is that there has been no agreement on the definition of liberalism. Although the idea stemmed from the concept of 'liberty', there has been no agreed notion of liberty, and the definitions and interpretations of liberalism have changed over time (Inoue 2004: 720–721). Carr himself stressed this changing nature of liberalism, pointing out that there was a gap between the outdated strand of liberalism (*laissez faire* liberalism), which continued to be dominant in the international politics of his day, and the new strand of liberalism in various domestic contexts (Carr 1993: 27).

To compound the problem further, both in domestic and in international politics, liberalism has been a relative ideological stand against conservatism (*status quo*) and socialism/communism (revolution). In international politics since the nineteenth century, it has been reformist but ultimately anti-socialist/communist. It is most telling that experts of international law, who began to systematically consolidate their modern 'scientific' foundation of their discipline around the mid-nineteenth century (Kennedy 1996), identified its core as a loose 'liberal' consensus 'of the desirability of liberty, rights and duties, freedom of commerce, the rule of law, and sanctity of property' (Fitzmaurice 2012: 125). The same ideological stance was evident in the Fourteen Points advocated by President Woodrow Wilson in January 1918. While this document became the foundation of the post-war order and countered the ideologies of the 'autocratic' Axis powers, it also presented an ideological position against the new threat of communism that arose in Bolshevik Russia. The League of Nations took the same ideological stance in order to counter the influence of the Communist International (1919–1943), which propagated anti-capitalism, anti-imperialism, and global revolution to workers and colonial subjects around the world.

The League was, therefore, not only counter-communist, but also complicit in the perpetuation of empires and imperialism. Wilson's Fourteen Points referred to 'autonomous development' only for the nations of Europe, which would be freed from rule by the Axis empires after the war. As for the colonies, Article V stipulated: 'A free, open-minded, and absolutely impartial adjustment of all colonial claims, based upon a strict observance of the principle that in determining all such questions of sovereignty *the interests of the populations concerned must have equal weight with the equitable government* whose title is to be determined (emphasis added)'.[4] There was no mention of 'autonomous development' or 'self-determination'. Moreover, the colonies referred to were German colonies in extra-Euro-America, which were to be administered by the relevant victorious powers after the war under the League's new mandate system. The League only stood against the colonies of the Axis powers and any new colonisation, while the victorious empires maintained their own colonies.

This did not, however, mean that the League did not prompt 'reforms' under the mandates and colonial governance. Anghie suggests that its mandate system was the beginning of management of the 'Third World' by major powers (empires or former empires) in the UN era (Anghie 2005: 10 and Chapter 3). Its ultimate concern was, nonetheless, 'the well-being and development of such peoples' in the mandates, with the goal to teach them skills and develop their capacities to be able to manage self-autonomy and independence in the future. The oversight of the League's Permanent Mandate Committee (PMC) had a certain impact on the administrating powers' policies towards their mandates, such as in the area of militarisation, which was banned under the system. The Japanese empire, therefore, refrained from the fortification of its mandates in the Pacific, so long as they remained within the League (Tōmatsu 2011: Chapter 6).[5]

The oversight of the League also reached beyond the mandates. The International Labour Organization (the ILO), for example, made inquiries into forced labour practices in the mandates and the colonies (Jerónimo and Monteiro 2018: 209); the League of Nations Health Organisation (LNHO) surveyed the conditions of colonial public health administrations (Akami 2017: 19–23); the Opium Advisory Committee examined opium production in the colonies (Gotō 2005: 130); and the International Studies Conference sought data on colonial economic management and statistics.[6] These constant inquiries by the various committees and agencies of the League made the metropolitan imperial states aware of the need to pay greater attention to the governance of their mandates and colonies (Jerónimo and Monteiro 2018: 91–92; Callahan 2004: 3, 108–115, 130–132).

Can such 'oversight' by the League be characterised as 'liberal'? The answer is not easy. It could certainly put pressure on the imperial and colonial administrations to check and even reform the measures they adopted to govern their mandates and colonies. But were these reforms 'liberal', and in what sense and for whom? Scholars now agree that modern international law has served as a tool to justify colonisation and legitimise colonial rule (Fitzmaurice 2012: 122, note 1; for an alternative point, see Pitts 2021; Fitzmaurice 2012). In the inter-war period, the League (and its associated organisations, such as the ILO) pushed a 'reformist', yet counter-communist, agenda by consolidating or newly creating conventions, treaties, and legal codifications. On the one hand, countering communism meant that these 'reform' programmes had to co-opt 'progressive' elements, such as better conditions for workers. On the other hand, questions remain on whether these reforms were done for colonial management and greater economic development, and for whose interests they served, those of the colonised, those at the imperial metropole, or both.

What is clear is that the League's 'liberal' or reformist agenda was complicit in the perpetuation of empires and imperialism. This was not an aberration in extra-Euro-America, but a fundamental problem inherent in the very nature of liberalism in the imperial metropoles in the age of empires. In the mid-to-late nineteenth century, 'liberal' norms and institutions, such as parliamentary democracy, constitutionalism, and regulations and institutions to protect the liberty and rights of citizens/subjects, had developed along with bourgeois revolutions. *And* they were advanced in the imperial metropolitan centres *concurrently* with the formal colonisation of other parts of the world. Japan and the US joined the European metropolitan imperial states in this process in 1895 and 1899, respectively. This political, philosophical, and moral dilemma of the modern, formal, and democratic empire was succinctly captured by Japanese slogan, '*Uchi ni rikken, soto ni teikoku*' [internally constitution, externally empire] of the time (Matsuo 1966; Gordon 1991).

The problem of liberalism in the age of empires has begun to be scrutinised in histories of international law and international organisations in recent years (Koskenniemi 2001; Mazower 2012). Yet, it is hard to be elucidated in the works on the League which focus on Euro-America, because the problem mainly manifested in extra-Euro-American colonial contexts (Jerónimo 2018: 88, 90, 92; Akami 2016: 3; Akami 2017: 6, 8). This may explain why the problematisation of liberalism has been slower to catch on in International Relations, where many works on the intellectual history of the discipline still predominantly focus on Euro-American or, more precisely, Anglo-American texts and contexts (on Euro-centricity in IR see Hobson 2012; on racism in the discipline see Vitalis 2015).

Liberal Inter-Imperialism and the 'humanitarian' Laws of the League

The notion of 'liberal inter-imperialism' is thus useful to examine the problem of imperial metropolitan liberalism in the colonial context and helps to reveal the nature of what are presented as the 'humanitarian' laws and actions of the League in extra-Euro-America, including Asia and the Pacific. This is particularly important as the increasing number of recent new works on the role of the League in shaping the norms of global governance in fields that can broadly be categorised as 'humanitarian' affairs, such as public health, wartime conventions on the injured and prisoners of war, mandate administration, labour conditions, the trafficking in women and children, anti-slavery campaigns, and the protection of refugees.

The exploration of the relationship between humanitarianism and empire is an important development in such research. Skinner and Leste, for example, summarise Michael Barnett's *Empire of Humanity* as follows: 'It is a milestone in the questioning of both Eurocentric and presentist understanding of humanitarian intervention. It centrepieces the relationship between the extension of ***western*** concern for ***distant strangers*** and the expansion of ***western*** empires, and it challenges the conventional narrative of the non-political origins even of emergency relief' (emphasis added) (Skinner and Lester 2012: 730). Although they are mainly concerned with intra-imperial relationships, Skinner and Lester see the writing of a 'history of humanitarianism' that goes beyond the 'fundamental component of [British] imperial relations' as 'a way of bridging 'trans-imperial... approaches' (Skinner and Lester 2012: 731).

Skinner and Lester's understanding that humanitarian intervention was an extension of 'Western' empires and their concerns is problematic when analysing the League's actions in Asia and the Pacific, however. This is because the Japanese empire and region-based organisations in colonial Asia were an integral part of the inter-imperial and inter-colonial measures of the League. Moreover, characterising humanitarian intervention as an extension of the 'Western' empires' concerns with 'distant strangers' needs some qualification. Watenpaugh's work on the League's rescue of Armenian genocide survivors, for example, demonstrates that the 'distant strangers' who were worthy to save in this case were one of them (Christians) (Watenpaugh 2010). Similarly, histories of international advocacy to save the victims of trafficking in women and children demonstrate that a disproportionate degree of attention was paid to 'White Russians' in the hands of non-Europeans. This is evident in the proceedings of the League's 1937 conference on trafficking in women and children in Asia (League of Nations 1937: 63–67). In other words, the League's humanitarian actions were concerned with people 'like themselves' (Europeans). It was only in 1967 that the convention to protect and manage refugees was expanded to include non-Europeans.[7]

Judging the League's 'humanitarian' measures divides the opinions of scholars of the history of international law and the history of human rights. Some acknowledge that its attempts to codify the international conventions on the suppression of the traffic in women and children

(1921, 1933), slavery (1926), the legal status of refugees (1928, 1933), forced labour (1930), and the Geneva Convention (1929) amount to humanitarian laws, and they constituted an important part of the genealogy of the international human rights laws of the era of the UN (Sellars 2015; Limmoncelli 2010). Others, however, reject this continuity. Hoffmann and Moyn, for example, distinguish humanitarianism in the age of empires from international human rights movements after decolonisation. For Hoffmann, in 1815–1945 (or even later, the era of colonialism), rights were not universal and discussion was not about the intrinsic political and civil rights of individuals beyond political boundaries, but about the welfare afforded to them by states (Hoffmann 2011: 1–4). Moyn also stresses discontinuity and argues that only in the 1970s did the changing values and forces of social movements and other external factors make international lawyers the vanguard of the rights of human beings across political boundaries (Moyn 2010: 7).

While humanitarian elements were evident in the League's minorities treaties and the mandate system, whether these can be categorised as humanitarian laws thus remains debatable.[8] Some point out that international 'humanitarian laws', such as the League's Geneva Conventions, are misnamed, because they were actually the laws of war (van Dijk 2019). Lowe even argues that the refugee protection measures of the League were best understood as a part of the project of post-war European recovery and counter-communist schemes (Lowe 2017: 294).

In the light of such arguments, the League's 'humanitarian' actions in Asia (and other extra-Euro-American regions) could be characterised as 'inter-imperial' humanitarianism. This conceptualisation could indicate that the shared interests of empires were prioritised, not those of the suffering individuals in the colonies, while not entirely dismissing the possibility that genuine humanitarian concerns were behind the League's projects. The idea is similar to Forclaz's 'humanitarian imperialism' (Forclaz 2015), although 'inter-imperial humanitarianism' is about the nature of humanitarianism and emphasises the lateral actions of empires. High among the shared priorities was the management of transborder problems for the security of the empires and their colonies, colonial economic development and exploitation, and countering the rise of independence movements (League of Nations 1937: 27, 28–43).

Yet the possibility should not be entirely ruled out that those who were involved in making and implementing these so-called humanitarian measures were also concerned with the welfare, if not the rights, of individuals who were the victims of practices such as human trafficking. The League, for example, invited not only the colonial authorities of border security and public health, and the International Criminal Police Commission, but also concerned non-governmental organisations to the 'Conference of central authorities in eastern countries [on traffic in women and children]' that it held in Bandung in 1937. These included advocacy groups and charity organisations, which argued for the prevention of trafficking and the welfare and protection of victims, and some took care of the victims on the ground.[9] A closer examination of the motives and objectives of such actors, and the responses of the other participants is needed to determine where their priorities lay.

A similar complexity of 'inter-imperial humanitarianism' was evident in the League's rural hygiene conference on colonial Asia and Pacific in 1937. Those who gathered for the event were mainly bureaucrats from the colonial public health administrations or public health experts from the colonial universities or research institutions. There were, however, also local experts who had been born, trained, and worked in the colonies, not only colonial officers posted from the imperial metropoles. Although the conference was mainly concerned with economic development and countering independence movements, it is possible that the main concern of some of these 'colonial' experts was the welfare or right to health of the colonised (Akami 2017: 25).

Understanding the nature of the 'inter-imperial or inter-colonial humanitarianism' of the League's schemes and actions in these social fields in colonial Asia and Pacific thus requires a more detailed analysis of what drove those who shaped and implemented these projects. Interpreting the findings would not, however, be straightforward given the diverse backgrounds and different motives of the experts who were involved. Some were driven by a sense of professional mission, while for others it was just a job that had to be done; some were loyal to their imperial government and/or colonial administration, while others were more sympathetic to local independence movements. Using the term, 'inter-imperial (or inter-colonial) humanitarianism' still nonetheless allows us to recognise these complexities and ask questions about how their complex interactions defined the nature of the League's works in the colonial context.

Particularly important for conducting such research is to acknowledge the influence of a strand of welfare liberalism (as opposed to *laissez faire* liberalism) in relations to League's liberal inter-imperialism. This is because diverse strands of liberalism existed in the late nineteenth to early twentieth century as the metropolitan imperial states expanded voting rights to working-class men. In this process, these states had to develop various welfare policies to address the social and economic liberties and rights of the new voters, which would inevitably strengthen the power of the state over its citizens/subjects. In this context, policymakers and the emerging body of policy experts adopted the ideas of welfare liberalism and the welfare state beyond domestic politics. Some then argued for social imperialism which rationalised colonisation as the way for the state to gain the external resources necessary for expanding welfare measures in the imperial metropole (Semmel 1960).

It is, therefore, impossible to say that one coherent stream of liberalism drove the League's social policies in extra-Euro-America. After the Great Depression, nonetheless, a 'social medicine' approach that was influenced by welfare liberalism became dominant at the LNHO, which proposed that good health could not be achieved without the improvement of economic and social conditions (Borowy 2009; Yasuda 2014; Amrith 2006). This defined the LNHO's approach to rural hygiene, which developed from its works in rural Europe in the early 1930s and combined improving the welfare of colonial peoples with rural economic reconstruction in Asia and Africa (Akami 2017: 18, 23, 24). In this sense, the League's rural hygiene measures in colonial Asia in the late 1930s can be said to have been inter-imperial or inter-colonial projects, and were influenced by welfare liberalism.

Liberals, Public Opinion and Experts: the League and Mass-Based Democracy

Another important factor that led Carr to label the League and its supporters in the imperial metropoles as 'liberal' was their belief that public opinion was the most important moral sanction for the state's international conduct. A similar view had been articulated in the works of prominent international law experts in the mid-nineteenth century, such as *Elements of International Law* by Henry Wheaton, an influential work not only in Euro-America but also in Northeast Asia. This argued that in the age of closer interactions across civilisations, the universality of international law should be derived from a consensus among the public opinions of nations (Wheaton 1846: 43–44). The view resonated among the League's supporters as they observed the development of closer interactions and stronger democratic trends around the world. The public that the League's supporters assumed was, however, that of the age of bourgeois democracy. They were middle-class, most likely male, well-educated, newspaper reading, and rational. The problem with this was, as Walter Lippmann pointed out in 1922 and again in 1925, that politics in the imperial metropoles was moving into a new era of mass, (male)-based democracy (Lippmann 1922, 1925; Akami 2012: 115). Accordingly, the League's strategy for influencing 'public' opinion was outdated from the start (Akami 2018: 71–72).

The paramount significance that the League attached to public opinion is evident in the establishment of the Information Office within its Secretariat, and the largest allocation from its limited budget to the office. The office worked closely with members of the press, who had their own room in the League's headquarters while the major news media companies had stationed their journalists in Geneva to report on the activities of the League and the international politics which developed at the League (Akami 2018: 72–73). The office's main objective was to conduct 'peace propaganda' that emphasised the importance of peace and to publicise the League's work. While Europe was its main concern, it also tried to reach the public beyond Europe, establishing offices in Tokyo in 1926, Delhi in 1931, and Beijing in the late 1930s (Akami 2018: 71). In an attempt to communicate directly with the 'public', the League produced simple pamphlets explaining its organisation and works in several languages, to be distributed to schools and churches, as well as promotional movies for public viewing. The League of Nations Unions/Associations/Societies, which had been formed in many places, including non-member countries such as the US, helped with the dissemination of these materials to schools while church organisations also contributed to grassroots 'propaganda' activities (Akami 1995: 134). The League also started its own radio broadcasting in 1929 to disseminate peace propaganda and publicise its work.

There was, however, a distinct contrast between the League's approach to shaping public opinion and the propaganda that began to be used by political parties and military officers in the late 1920s and 1930s. This can be seen in the Information Office's devotion to the production of 'scientific and accurate' information on complex issues such as disarmament, trade deals, international sanitary conventions, media practices, or conventions on controlling the traffic in dangerous drugs. The office relied on experts to educate and enlighten the public about the complex details of such international issues and its own work. Furthermore, the office addressed members of the well-educated, middle-class (including a large portion of women and students), and other interested public who were already pro-League. This included using prominent local experts on the League or international affairs to deliver lectures organised by regional branches of the Information Office, such as the one in Tokyo (Akami 2018: 77–80). The reports of the office reveal that the League's appeal to the public was further limited. A majority of the works that the League provided for the 'public' were in fact produced by the experts and intended for policymakers or members of the policy-relevant elite, rather than the general public (Akami 2018: 73–74). At a time when politics was clearly shifting from male-middle-class democracy to male-mass-based democracy in the imperial metropoles, other than starting radio broadcasts and creating rather dull promotional pictures about the League Assembly (!), the Information Office hardly discussed the need for fundamental changes to its propaganda and dissemination methods (Akami 2018: 84–86).

In contrast, political parties, military officers, and the mass media were quick to adjust to mass-based democracy to pursue their own political and economic interests. In Japan, for example, national radio broadcasting started in 1925, as in Britain and the US, and politicians were quick to use the new medium. This was the same year in which the Japanese Diet passed the bill of universal male franchise, opening the way to the first general election based on the new law in 1928, which marked the start of the era of mass-male-based democracy. In this context, the Japanese garrison stationed along the railway lines in Manchuria (North-eastern three provinces of China) began its military aggression in September 1931, which soon resulted in its military occupation of the whole region. Educational and 'entertaining' radio programmes of the national broadcasting cooperation (NHK) contributed to build jingoistic public support for the aggression, while commercial newspapers exploited the 'incident' to boost circulation (Akami 2012: 208).

In February 1932, Prime Minister Inukai Tsuyoshi took his new caretaker government into a general election and won a landslide victory and secured a mandate from the new voters for his aggressive China policy and economic recovery (Akami 2012: 223). Several months later, the Nazis also gained the biggest vote in the German general election, paving the way for them to be elected as the governing party in 1933. Well attuned with the latest world trends and having the biggest think tank in the country, the Japanese Army quickly and competently adjusted to the emergence of mass-based democracy by equipping itself with the latest and most effective propaganda techniques (Akami 2014: 27–29). The League's Tokyo office was no match when it came to competing with the techniques, resources, and understanding of the changing political paradigm of the experts in mass propaganda at the Newspaper Section of the Japanese Army.

If the liberal core of the League depended on its belief in the moral force of public opinion, this failure to perceive and adjust to the emergence of mass-based democracy was fatal. It failed because of its assumption that the most significant part of the public was the middle-class, its dismissal or neglect of mass-based politics, and its almost exclusive reliance on experts.

Understanding the nature of the League and its actions in Asia and the Pacific more accurately, therefore, requires re-assessing the roles of its own experts and those attached to its related IOs and INGOs. They occupied the central positions in the League's Secretariat, its committees, conferences, inquiry missions, and 'technical' services. They were tasked with the three vital roles for the League's success: first, to shape the knowledge of international affairs and norms of global governance; second, to provide expert knowledge and technical details when advising politicians and diplomats; and third, to educate the public about the knowledge so that they could support peace and form the right moral judgement on international affairs. These experts also gained influence and power outside democratic institutions.

These experts, who worked for the League and its associated organisations, did not have a coherent ideological position due to several factors. First, they constituted an elite, no matter how they attained that status (birth, class, education, chance, or professional achievement). Second, although the League's projects were mainly initiated because they were thought to be contributing to 'world peace', the experts who were mobilised behind them were not 'pacifists'. Most were members of the think tanks, such as the national councils of the Institute of Pacific Relations (IPR), Chatham House or the Royal Institute of International Affairs (RIIA), and its Commonwealth branches, and the Council for Foreign Relations (CFR). Although they were supporters of the League, most did not reject war at any cost. As for Japan, only a few League supporters publicly condemned their country's aggression in Manchuria.

Some of the leading figures at the IPR and League supporters in the US, such as James Shotwell who wrote an initial draft proposal of the Pact of Paris, argued for US entry into the organisation and taking an active part in in international affairs, and this led them to advocate US entry into the war after 1939 (Accinelli 1980: 27–37).

Third, although the experts associated with the League were often assumed to be drawn from the 'liberal professions', to be representatives of 'civil society' and to be independent from the state, this was a fallacy in most cases. Many belonged to emerging policy-relevant fields of study, whether they were statisticians, economists, medical doctors, lawyers, biologists, sociologists, political scientists, or geologists. If they were not state technocrats, they often worked as governmental policy advisors or committee members. Fourth, they were not necessarily advocates for greater political participation or colonial liberation.

Perhaps the most fatal tension between the experts and what the League was supposed to stand for was their negative attitude towards 'ordinary people' or 'the masses'. The League initiated to establish the systematic academic study of international relations. Accordingly, it established the International Studies Conference (ISC) in 1928, which held annual conferences. Although the ISC became mainly concerned with the analysis of contemporary international affairs, it maintained an interest in working out how best to teach international relations at universities. By 1936, however, when an officer of the Rockefeller Foundation that funded the ISC discussed its conference in Madrid with the ISC's executive members, he felt pessimistic about the possibility of ever getting ordinary people to understand the intricacies of international affairs.[10]

The heavy reliance on elite and dismissive attitude towards the possibility of the mass-public ever being able to form the right judgement on international affairs was only reinforced, not challenged, in the US in the 1950s. As Guilhot explains, the experience of fascism of the 1930s and 1940s had effectively 'killed' the attempt to educate the public to form a sound opinion of international affairs and become the moral force in such matters after 1945. Examining the Rockefeller-sponsored conference on international relations theory in 1954, he argues that those involved agreed that it was too dangerous for the masses to decide on matters of international relations, which were best left to 'wise men' of expert knowledge (Guilhot 2011: 28).

Conclusion

Questioning the notion of liberal internationalism is a useful starting point for framing a reassessment of the League's works in Asia and the Pacific. This chapter has demonstrated that the notions of liberal inter-imperialism and inter-colonialism better capture the nature of League's works in the region. This is because these notions allow us to acknowledge and examine the complex power dynamics that took place among the experts whom the League mobilised in Asia and the Pacific and who played central roles in its projects there. On the one hand, scrutinising what 'being liberal' meant to the experts who were involved in these League projects in the area exposes the complicity of metropolitan liberalism in perpetuating the power of empires in colonial contexts. On the other hand, although these experts' liberal inter-imperialism prioritised the shared interests of imperial metropolitan states and institutions, this does not rule out the possibility that some experts were genuinely concerned with the welfare or even the rights of the people in the colonies. To explore their roles further, therefore, it is necessary to conduct more detailed analyses of the motivations and objectives which drove those involved and how they shaped the League's various 'humanitarian' schemes. The standard national–international framework does not adequately capture these complex ideas and actions of the experts involved, and here, the notions of inter-imperial and inter-colonial will be useful.

The League's heavy reliance on experts impacted its attitude on the role of 'public opinion', which its supporters regarded as the moral force in international politics, and which constituted the core of their 'liberal' belief. Despite the fact that politics in the imperial metropoles was shifting to a mass-base, the League targeted the middle classes, which it assumed were educated and rational, and would shape public opinion. This excluded significant portions of the population in the metropoles, not to mention those in polities that were under the control of empires. This problem was further exacerbated by the pessimistic and dismissive attitude of the experts towards the capacity of the general public.

Such views were not questioned but reinforced during the crucial period of defining the academic discipline of International Relations after World War II. The experience of fascism and mass-based democracy in the 1930s and the early 1940s convinced experts of international affairs in the US in the 1950s that conducting analyses on and producing the knowledge of this field needed to be left to them, not to the masses. The elitist attitude of these experts in the 1920s–1950s is not only of historical interest, but may also reveal a more fundamental problem in the way in which international organisations, both governmental and non-governmental, operate. They continue to be heavily dominated by experts, whose relationship with the majority of 'ordinary people' remains ambiguous.

Only recently have these attitudes and approaches been challenged, as the spread of the internet and SNS (Social Networking Systems) has given the 'masses' stronger voices to which policymakers and business leaders have to listen. However, certain media organisations also continue to manipulate public opinion in pursuit of profits and power, as they did before, with a detrimental impact on parliamentary democracy. Recent years have thus witnessed the worst-case scenario unfolding in front of our eyes with demagogic politicians dismissing expert knowledge and journalists' investigations as lies and fake news when they deem them to be inconvenient. As a result, some may dismiss expert knowledge, and others become confused about how to distinguish between truth and fiction (or meta-truth!), or just give up trying altogether.

Revealing the problematics of 'liberalism' from the perspectives of the inter-imperialism and inter-colonialism of the experts involved in the League's projects thus helps us to trace the origins of many of the current problems facing experts in the field of international affairs at IOs and INGOs as well as at universities. Current political problems arising from mass-based democracy are indeed not new but represent an ongoing issue which many experts and social scientists have long failed to fully engage with, because the consequences have not been as dire in the 'established' democracies as they have recently become. This chapter, I hope, prompts more works to re-examine the role of experts and the public in mass-based democracy historically and ponder its implications for the digital age during the multiple global crises of the 2020s and beyond.

Notes

1. The terminology used for the region, Asia and the Pacific, is from: Epeli Hau'ofa (1998); Matsuda (2012); Wigen (2007); Jolly (2008). For a summary of the debate, see Akami (2021). The 'Pacific region' was used until around the 1980s (Akami 2002: 36–40).

2. Euro-America here includes South America, where most states became national sovereign units by the early-to mid-nineteenth century, and for these countries, the national-international framework worked.
3. These events are discussed in greater detail in the section on the Manchurian crisis in this volume.
4. Fourteen points', 8 Jan 1918, https://avalon.law.yale.edu/20th_century/wilson14.asp. Accessed 22 July 2022.
5. On Japan's withdrawal see the chapter by Gotō-Shibata. The withdrawal became effective two years after the official announcement in 1933. Meanwhile, the Japanese government announced the abrogation of the Washington Naval Treaty of 1922 in December 1934. When this became effective in December 1936, the Japanese government began fortification in the mandate territory. However, it still continued to participate in the various technical committees of the League, including the PMC, until November 1938 when the government announced to stop all the connections with the League in response to its resolution to confirm its sanctions against Japan (based on Article 16 of the Covenant) on 30 September 1938.
6. See, for example, K.36.1935, and K.31.1936, as the materials for the ISC 1936 on 'Peaceful Change'. R4007/5B/2381/2381, League of Nations Archives, Geneva.
7. This was realised in 'Protocol relating to the status of refugees' [to the Refugee Convention of 1951], 18 Nov 1966, https://www.ohchr.org/EN/ProfessionalInterest/Pages/ProtocolStatusOfRefugees.aspx. Accessed 22 July 2022.
8. I thank Natasha Wheatley for her insights on these points.
9. These organisations were: International Missionary Council, Salvation Army, pan-pacific Women's Association, World Alliance of YMCA, World YMCA, The World Red Swastika Society of China, The China Child Welfare Association, Association for Moral and Social Hygiene (India), Association 'Ati Soetji' [Chinese Pure Heart Association] (Netherlands Indies), Indo-Europeesch-Verbond Vrouwen-Organisatie (NI), Perkoempoelan Pembasmian Perdagangan Perempoean dan Anak-anak (NI) (League of Nations 1937: 2–4)
10. Kittredge to Walker, 16 June 1936, RG 3/Ser 910/Box 7/F 60, Rockefeller Archives.

References

Accinelli, Robert D. 1980. Militant internationalists: The League of Nations Association, the Peace Movement, and US foreign policy, 1934–38. *Diplomatic History* (4/1): 19–38.

Akami, Tomoko. 1995. *The Liberal Dilemma: Internationalism and the Institute of Pacific Relations in the USA, Australia, and Japan, 1919–1942*. PhD thesis, ANU.

Akami, Tomoko. 2002. *Internationalizing the Pacific: The United States, Japan and the Institute of Pacific Relations in War and Peace, 1919–1945*. London: Routledge.

Akami, Tomoko. 2012. *Japan's News Propaganda and Reuters' News Empire in Northeast Asia, 1870–1934*. Dordrecht: Republic of Letters.

Akami, Tomoko. 2014a. Beyond Empires' Science: Inter-imperial Pacific Science Networks in the 1920s. In *Networking the International System*, ed. Madeleine Herren. New York: Springer.

Akami, Tomoko. 2014. *Soft Power of Japan's Total War State: The Board of Information and Dōmei News Agency in Foreign Policy, 1934–1945*. Dordrecht: Republic of Letters.

Akami, Tomoko. 2016. A quest to be global: The League of Nations Health Organization and inter-colonial regional governing agendas of the Far Eastern Association of Tropical Medicine, 1910–25. *The International History Review* (38/1): 1–23.

Akami, Tomoko. 2017. Imperial polities and inter-colonialism in shaping global governing norms: public health expert networks in Asia and the League of Nations Health Organization, 1908–1937. *The Journal of Global History* (12/1): 4–25.

Akami, Tomoko. 2018. The limits of peace propaganda: The Information Section of the League of Nations and its Tokyo office. In *Exorbitant Expectations: Communicating International Organizations in the 19th and 20th Centuries*, ed. Jonas Brendebach, Martin Herzer, and Heidi Tworek, 70–90. London: Routledge.

Akami, Tomoko. 2021. Understanding trans-Pacific interactions: The liberal inter-imperial order in the "Pacific" region. In *International Society in the Early Twentieth Century Asia-Pacific: Imperial Rivalries, International Organizations, and Experts*, ed. Hiroo Nakajima, 1920–1960. London: Routledge.

Amrith, Sunil S. 2006. *Decolonizing International Health: India and Southeast Asia, 1930–65*. New York: Palgrave Macmillan.

Anghie, Antony. 2005. *Imperialism, Sovereignty and the Making of International Law*. Cambridge: Cambridge University Press.

Ashworth, Lucian M. 2002. Did the realist-idealist Great Debate really happen? A revisionist history of International Relations. *International Relations* (16/1): 33–51.

Bell, Duncan. 2016. *Reordering the World: Essays on Liberalism and Empire*. Princeton: Princeton University Press.

Borowy, Iris. 2009. *Coming to Terms with World Health: The League of Nations Health Organization, 1921–1946*. Berlin: Peter Lang.

Brückenhaus, Daniel. 2020. Challenging imperialism across borders: Recent studies of twentieth century internationalist networks against empire. *Contemporary European History* (29/1): 104–115.

Burkman, Thomas. 2008. *Japan and the League of Nations: Empire and World Order, 1914–1938*. Honolulu: University of Hawai'i.

Callahan, Michael D. 2004. *A Sacred Trust: The League of Nations and Africa, 1929–1946*. Brighton: Sussex Academic Press.

Carr, E. H. 1993. *The Twenty Years' Crisis, 1919–1939*, London: Papermac. First published 1939.

Chang, Li. 1999. *Guoji hezuo zai Zhongguo: lianmeng jiaose de kaocha* 1919–1946 [International Co-operation in China: A Study on the Role of the League of Nations, 1919–1946]. Taibei: Zhongyang Yanjiuyuan Jindaishi Yanjiusuo.

Clavin, Patricia. 2010. Introduction: Conceptualizing internationalism between the World Wars. In *Internationalism Reconfigured: Transnational Ideals and Movements Between the World Wars*, ed. Daniel Laqua. London: Bloomsbury Publishing.

Clavin, Patricia. 2013. *Securing the World Economy: The Reinvention of the League of Nations, 1920–1946*. Oxford: Oxford University Press.

Davidann, Jon. 1998. *A World of Crisis and Progress: The American YMCA in Japan, 1890–1930*. Bethlehem, PA: Lehigh University Press.

Fitzmaurice, Andrew. 2012. Liberalism and empire in nineteenth century international law. *The American Historical Review* (117/1): 122–140.

Forclaz, Amalia Ribi. 2015. *Humanitarian Imperialism: The Politics of Anti-Slavery Activism, 1880–1940*. Oxford: Oxford University Press.

García, Magaly R., David Rodogno, and Liat Kozma, eds. 2016. *The League of Nations' Work on Social Issues: Visions, Endeavours and Experiments*. Geneva: United Nations.

Gordon, Andrew. 1991. *Labor and Imperial Democracy in Prewar Japan*. Berkeley: University of California Press.

Gotō, Harumi. 2005. *Ahen to Igirisu teikoku: Kokusai kisei no takamari 1906–43* [The International Control of Opium and the British Empire, 1906–1943]. Tokyo: Yamakawa shuppansha.

Guilhot, Nicholas. 2011. Introduction. In *The Invention of International Relations Theory: Realism, the Rockefeller Foundation, and the 1954 Conference on Theory*, ed. N. Guilhot. New York: Columbian University Press.

Hanzawa, Asahiko, ed. 2007. *Japan and the UN in International Politics: Historical Perspective*. Sapporo: Hokkaidō University Graduate School.

Hathaway, Oona A., and Scott J. Shapiro. 2017. *The Internationalists: And Their Plan to Outlaw War*. London: Allen Lane.

Hau'ofa, Epeli. 1998. The ocean in us. *The Contemporary Pacific* (10/2): 392–410

Hell, Stefan. 2010. *Siam and the League of Nations: Modernisation, Sovereignty and Multilateral Diplomacy, 1920–1940*. Bangkok: River Books.
Herren, Madeleine. 2016. Fascist internationalism. In *Internationalisms: A twentieth century history*, eds. Glenda Sluga and Patricia Clavin. Cambridge: Cambridge University Press.
Hobson, John. 2012. *The Eurocentric conception of world politics: Western International Theory, 1760–2010*. Cambridge: Cambridge University Press.
Hoffmann, Stefan-Ludwig. 2011. Introduction. In *Human rights in the twentieth century*, ed. S. L. Hoffmann. Cambridge: Cambridge University Press.
Inoue, Tatsuo. 2004. Jiyū shugi, Liberalism/Liberalismus/libéralisme [Liberalism]. In *Iwanami tetsugaku shisō jiten*, ed. Hiromatsu Wataru et al.. Tokyo: Iwanami shoten.
Iriye, Akira. 1965. *After imperialism: The search for a new order in the far east, 1921–1931*. Cambridge MA: Harvard University Press.
Iriye, Akira. 2004. *Global community: The role of international organizations*. Berkeley: University of California.
Jackson, Simon and Alanna O'Malley. 2018. Rocking on its hinges? The League of Nations, the United Nations and the new history of internationalism in the twentieth century. In *The institution of international order: From the League of Nations to the United Nations*, eds. S. Jackson and A. O'Malley . London: Routledge.
Jerónimo, Miguel Bandeira. 2018. A league of empires: Imperial political imagination and interwar internationalisms. In *Internationalism, Imperialism and the Formation of the Contemporary World: The Past and the Present*, eds. M. B. Jerónimo and José Pedro Monteiro. Cham: Palgrave Macmillan.
Jerónimo, Miguel Bandeiro, and José Pedro. Monteiro. 2018. Internationalism and empire: The question of "native labour" in the Portuguese Empire. In *The institution of international order: From the League of Nations to the United Nations*, ed. Jackson and O'Malley, 1919–1961. London: Routledge.
Jolly, Margaret. 2008. The South in Southern theory: Antipodean reflections on the Pacific. *Australian Humanities Review* 44: 1–20.
Kawashima, Shin. 2009. *Chūgoku kindai gaikō no keisei* [The Formation of Chinese Modern Diplomacy]. Nagoya: Nagoya daigaku shuppankai.
Kennedy, David. 1996. International Law and the Nineteenth Century: History of an Illusion. *Nordic Journal of International Law* (65/3–4): 385–420.
Koskenniemi, Martti. 2001. *The Gentle Civilizer of Nations: The Rise and Fall of International law 1870–1960*. Cambridge: Cambridge University Press.
Kott, Sandrine, and Joëlle. Droux, eds. 2013. *Globalizing Social Rights: The International Labour Organization and Beyond*. New York: Palgrave Macmillan.
Kurasawa, Aiko et al. 2005. Kankō ni attate [On Publishing This Work]. In *Ajia taiheiyō sensō*, ed. Kurasawa Aiko et al., vol. 2, Tokyo: Iwanami shoten.

League of Nations. 1937. Traffic in women and children: Work of the Bandoeng Conference [of central authorities in Eastern countries]. 20 December. Geneva C.516.M.357.1937.IV.

Limmoncelli, Stephanie A. 2010. *The Politics of Trafficking: The First International Movement to Combat the Sexual Exploitation of Women*. Stanford: Stanford University Press.

Lippmann, Walter. 1922. *Public Opinion*. New York: Harcourt, Brace & Co.

Lippmann, Walter. 1925. *The Phantom Public*. Piscataway, N.J.: Transaction Publishers.

Long, David, and Peter Wilson, eds. 1995. *Thinkers of the Twenty Years' Crisis: Inter-war Reassessed*. Oxford: Clarendon Press.

Lowe, Kimberly. 2017. Reassessing the League of Nations' humanitarian assistance regimes. In *Decades of Reconstruction: Postwar Societies, State-Building, and International Relations from the Seven Years' War to the Cold War*, ed. Ute Planert and James Retallack, 1918–1939. Cambridge: Cambridge University Press.

Matsuda, Matt. 2012. *Pacific Worlds: A History of Seas, Peoples, and Cultures*. Cambridge: Cambridge University Press.

Matsuo, Takayoshi. 1966. *Taishō demokurashi no kenkyū* [Research on Taishō Democracy]. Tokyo: Aoki shoten.

Mazower, Mark. 2012. *Governing the World: The History of an Idea*. New York: Allen Lane.

Mori, Shigeki. 2006. The "Washington system" and its aftermath: Reevaluating After Imperialism from the perspective of the Japanese historiography. *International Journal of Asian Studies* (3/2): 255–268.

Moyn, Samuel. 2010. *The Last Utopia: Human Rights in History*. Cambridge: Harvard University Press.

Nihon kokusai seiji gakkai Taiheiyō sensō gen'in kenkyūbu ed., (1963) Taiheiyō sensō e no michi: Kaisen gaikōshi, vols. 1–7, and Bekkan [Road to the Pacific War: Diplomatic History toward the War and Appendix]. Tokyo: Asahi shimbunsha (new edition in 1987–88; select English translation in 1976–1994).

Nish, Ian. 1993. *Japan's Struggle with Internationalism: Japan, China, and the League of Nations*, 1931–3. London: K. Paul International.

Osterhammel, Jürgen. 1979. "Technical Co-operation" between the League of Nations and China. *Modern Asian Studies*. (13/4): 661–680.

Paisley, Fiona. 2009. *Glamour in the Pacific: Cultural Internationalism and Race Politics in the Women's Pan Pacific*. Honolulu: University of Hawai'i Press.

Pedersen, Susan. 2007. Back to the League of Nations: review essay. *The American Historical Review* (112/4): 1091–1117.

Pedersen, Susan. 2015. *The Guardians: The League of Nations and the Crisis of Empire*. Oxford: Oxford University Press.

Pitts, Jennifer. 2012. Empire and legal universalism in the eighteenth century. *The American Historical Review*. (117/1): 92–121.

Schmidt, Brian. ed. 2012. *International Relations and the First Great Debate*. New York: Routledge.

Sellars, Kirsten. 2015. *'Crimes against Peace' and International Law*. Cambridge: Cambridge University Press.

Semmel, Bernard. 1960. *Imperialism and Social Reform*. Cambridge, Mass: Harvard University Press.

Skinner, Rob, and Alan Lester. 2012. Humanitarianism and empire: New research agendas. *The Journal of Imperial and Commonwealth History*. (40/5): 729–747.

Sluga, Glenda. 2015. *Internationalism in the Age of Nationalism*. Philadelphia: University of Pennsylvania Press.

Sluga, Glenda, and Patricia Clavin. eds. 2017. *Internationalisms: A Twentieth Century History*. Cambridge: Cambridge University Press.

Tōmatsu, Haruo. 2011. *Nihon teikoku to inin tōchi: Nanyō guntō o meguru kokusai seiji, 1914–1947*. Nagoya: Nagoya daigaku shuppankai.

van Dijk, Boyd. 2019. "The great humanitarian": The Soviet Union, the International committee of the Red Cross and the Geneva Conventions of 1949. *Law and History Review*. (37/1): 209–235.

Vitalis, Robert. 2015. *White World Order, Black Power Politics: The Birth of American International Relations*. Ithaca: Cornell University Press.

Watenpaugh, Keith David. 2010. The League of Nations' rescue of Armenian genocide survivors and the making of modern humanitarianism, 1920–1927. *The American Historical Review*. (115/5): 1315–1339.

Wheaton, Henry. 1846. *Elements of International Law*. Philadelphia: Lea and Blanchard, third edition.

Wigen, Kären. 2007. Introduction. In *Seascapes: Maritime Histories, Littoral Cultures, and Transoceanic Exchanges*, ed. Jerry H. Bentley, Renate Bridenthal, and Kären Wigen. Honolulu: University of Hawai'i Press.

Wilson, Peter. 1998. The Myth of the "First Great Debate". *Review of International Studies* (24/5): 1–16.

Yasuda, Kayo. 2014. *Kokusai seiji no nakano kokusai hoken jigyō*. Kyoto: Mineruba shobō.

Yasutake, Rumi. 2004. *Transnational Women's Activism: The United States, Japan, and Japanese Immigrant Communities in California*, 1859–1920. New York: New York University Press.

The League's Technical Work in the Years of Growing Nationalism

Harumi Goto-Shibata

The Significance of Functional Co-operation

The League of Nations was established to prevent wars. With the causes of war being so hard to predict, however, it began to address a wide range of economic, social and humanitarian issues that were only tangentially related to keeping the peace. These were initially considered to be 'technical' issues and their secondary importance is indicated by the fact that they were relegated to Article 23 of the Covenant. How they became more important during the two world wars is indicated by the recommendation of Stanley Bruce, the former Prime Minister of Australia, who used his position as chairman of a committee looking into the re-organisation of the League in 1939, to suggest using the terms 'economic and social' to denote them instead (League of Nations 1939: 5–6).

The significance of this trend for constraining the power of states to go to war was emphasised by the inventor of the functionalist theory of

H. Goto-Shibata (✉)
University of Tokyo, Tokyo, Japan
e-mail: harumigs@waka.c.u-tokyo.ac.jp

C. R. Hughes and H. Shinohara (eds.), *East Asians in the League of Nations*, New Directions in East Asian History,
https://doi.org/10.1007/978-981-19-7067-2_3

international relations, David Mitrany, who proposes that increasing transactions will reduce the destabilising dynamics of the system of sovereign states by strengthening international organisations (Mitrany 1975). This is particularly relevant for understanding the evolution of the League's work in Eastern Asia, where it began to tackle problems in the technical/functional field before it developed its political work. The number of works addressing this topic in English remains limited, however, with Tomoko Akami's research into the relationship between internationalism in Eastern Asia and the League's work in the area of public health being particularly notable (see, for example, Akami 2017).

This chapter will draw on my own work on the League's efforts to control opium and other aspects of technical co-operation between the League and China to explore how both China and Japan managed the relationship between the organisation's expanding remit and the surge of nationalism that both witnessed between the two world wars (Goto-Shibata 2020). Japan is an especially interesting case in this respect because it embraced technical work as a way to maintain involvement with the League after declaring its intention to withdraw from the organisation in March 1933 over the Manchurian Crisis. That event is covered in more detail in the chapters by Suputtikun, Mu, Tohmatsu and Hughes in this volume, and it is sufficient to note here that a wave of nationalistic reaction was triggered by the Lytton Report that was commissioned by the League, and by the recommendation of its Committee of Nineteen. It is a common misperception that Japan withdrew from the League at this point, however. Instead, it remained a full member until 26 March 1935 by taking advantage of a provision in Article 1 of the Covenant that allowed a member to withdraw two years after giving notice. More remarkable, though, is that Japan even continued to attend the League's technical commissions and committees after that date.

The second section deals with the development of technical co-operation between the League of Nations and China.[1] This officially started in 1931, just before the Manchurian Crisis. Most interesting for understanding its significance for the rising tide of nationalism in China, however, is how technical co-operation with the League continued to grow after the outbreak of the Sino-Japanese War, in July 1937. China was certainly the material beneficiary of this co-operation, but it had to

[1] The significant work on the topic is Chang Li (1999).

be carried out in a context where members of the Chinese political elite were increasingly concerned that it might infringe upon their nation's still fragile sovereignty.

Japan: Technical Co-operation in the Context of Withdrawal

Japan entered World War I as early as August 1914 on the side of the Allies. At the Paris Peace Conference of 1919, its attention was concentrated on the creation of the mandates system, tabling its proposal on racial equality and the fate of the former German interests in China's Shandong Peninsula. It was not at all prepared to deal with functional/technical issues, which it had not expected to be included in the Covenant. However, once the League was established and Japan became a permanent member of the Council, its diplomats diligently worked on many issues, not all of which were even relevant to Eastern Asia. Particularly notable, for example, is their contribution to the settlement of the status of minorities. This allowed Japan to be considered something of a model member throughout the 1920s.[2]

Japan was also a signatory to key international agreements, such as the 1928 Pact of Paris (Kellogg-Briand Pact), which attempted to outlaw the use of force to settle disputes. When former Foreign Minister Yasuya Uchida was in Europe, however, his attention was not focused on the Pact itself, because Sino-Japanese relations had drastically deteriorated after a military clash in Jinan in May that year. The priority of the Japanese government was thus to use the signing of the Pact as an opportunity to allow Uchida to negotiate with Britain over co-operation against the rise of Chinese nationalism. This was not successful, largely because Britain did not want to become the target of China's anti-foreign boycott again, as it had already been after the May Thirtieth Incident in 1925, when the Shanghai Municipal Police had opened fire on demonstrators (Goto-Shibata 1995: 91).

This instrumental approach is shown by the fact that Japan did not consider the Pact of Paris itself as amounting to anything significant. It consisted of only two articles and was almost incomplete as an international treaty. The discussion back in Japan before ratification was heated,

[2] The term was used by William Strang, looking back to the 1920s (TNA 1934a).

but it focused on whether the use of the specific phrase, 'in the name of their respective peoples', was acceptable to the country where the sovereign was the emperor. What the Pact meant to Japan's interests and security was not examined at all (Makino 2020: iii, 129).

Japan's withdrawal from the League followed the train of events after its Guandong Army initiated aggression in Manchuria, the north-eastern part of China, on 18 September 1931. After China brought the issue to the League, a report prepared by the Committee of Nineteen proclaimed in February 1933 that a settlement should observe the provisions of the Covenant, the Pact of Paris and the Nine Power Treaty of Washington and that the settlement should also observe the resolution of the League's Assembly on 11 March 1932 (Shinohara 2012: 79, 111–112). Presented with the almost unanimous adoption of the report, Japan notified the League on 27 March 1933 that it would withdraw from the organisation.

Japan's withdrawal, however, was different from Germany's. Because Article 1 of the Covenant stipulated that any member may withdraw from the League after two years' notice of declaring its intention, it remained a full member until 26 March 1935. It continued to pay financial contributions up to that date and also paid the running cost of the Eastern Bureau of the League of Nations Health Organization (Manderson 1995: 125; see also the chapter by Takuma in this book). Furthermore, Japan tried to maintain partial co-operation with the League after the two-year notice period was completed. Even After it stopped participating in the Assembly and the Council, it continued to participate in the League's technical organs. It was not until 2 November 1938, ten months before the outbreak of World War II, that Japan finally severed its relations with the League.

To explain why Japan remained partially in the League, it should be noted that the decision was only made a few days before it left the Assembly, on 24 February 1933. Yōsuke Matsuoka, who gave a speech on the day and led the Japanese delegates out, was himself a remainer. Having aimed for success inside the League, he considered that he had failed to fulfil that aim. Naotake Satō, Japan's ambassador to Belgium and one of the Japanese delegates to the League, and Yōtarō Sugimura, one of the under-Secretary-Generals of the League, were also remainers (Usui 1995: 165; Satō 1963: 338). Nobuaki Makino recorded in his diary on 27 February and 8 and 9 March that Emperor Shōwa (Hirohito) even asked whether it was really impossible to reconsider the decision to withdraw (Makino 1990: 547–548). Makino himself had been one of the Japanese representatives to the League of Nations Commission at the time of the Paris Peace Conference. In 1933, he was the Minister of the Interior, whose main role was to assist the emperor.

It should also be pointed out that even the Republic of China did not intend to expel Japan from the League at that stage. It insisted instead that Article 1 of the Covenant meant that Japan was not entitled to the right to withdraw from the League unless and until it had carried out all the resolutions and decisions of the League in respect of the Manchurian dispute.[3] This was also the opinion of Westel W. Willoughby, one of the American advisers to China, as Mu discusses in his chapter in this book.

Given this situation, why did Japan decide to withdraw from the League at all? The most plausible explanation is that it was determined to avoid the imposition of sanctions after the crisis escalated over Rehe (Jehol) Province, on the border between Manchuria, Mongolia and northern China. The Chinese considered that this had not been captured by the Japanese and sent reinforcements during the latter part of 1932. On the other hand, the authorities of Manchukuo, Japan's puppet state in Manchuria, considered Rehe to be under their control. In January 1933, the Guandong Army planned to 'maintain order' in the province, which it viewed as a police action. Other states would regard it as new aggression (Nish 1993: 202). On 16 January 1933, Emperor Hirohito told the chief of the general staff that the army should cautiously deal with the matter. The latter took this to mean that Hirohito had agreed to the attack (Katō 2007: 164).

The tension between Japan's role in the League and the rise of nationalism in its domestic politics can be seen as the crisis deepened in February. At the start of the month, the Japanese delegation was told orally that attempts at conciliation could not continue unless the threatened attack was called off (Nish 1993: 209). On 8 February, the Japanese Prime Minister, Makoto Saitō, informed the emperor that the attack was impossible from the point of the country's relations with the League, adding three days later that it might result in expulsion based on Article 12. Despite this attempt to stop the action, however, the army insisted that the emperor had already given his approval. The emperor himself was shocked to realise that this was the impact of his remark of 16 January. Although he wanted to retract it, however, his military *aide-de-camp*

[3] This document dated 28 Mar. 1933 was transmitted to the League by Wellington V. K. Koo (TNA 1933).

considered this to be impossible, insisting that only the cabinet could change the decision (Katō 2007: 165–166). The civilians in the cabinet could not control the Japanese Imperial Army, though, which vehemently insisted that it was directly accountable only to the emperor. The tragedy was that the emperor could not control the army.

Article 12 of the League's Covenant stipulates that the members of the League 'agree in no case to resort to war until three months after the award by the arbitrators or the judicial decision, or the report by the Council'. If the Guandong Army had started its aggression against Rehe after the League had made its decision, sanctions might have been put on the table for discussion based on Article 16, which states that should 'any Member of the League resort to war in disregard of its covenants under Articles 12, 13 or 15' the League would 'undertake immediately to subject it to the severance of all trade or financial relations'. Japan might then have become the first country to be expelled from the League. As Margaret Macmillan points out, honour was still an important element of politics and international affairs in pre-World War I Europe (Macmillan 2013: 236–237). Although aggression is considered illegal and dishonourable today, it is highly likely that the Japanese elite regarded sanctions or expulsion as unbearable in 1933. The Japanese Cabinet thus decided, on 20 February, that it was better for Japan's prestige to withdraw from the League if the Assembly approved the recommendation of the Committee of Nineteen (Katō 2007: 167). The Rehe campaign began just two days later.

The withdrawal from the League was thus a sudden decision, and there was no well-thought-out grand strategy behind it (Nish 1993: 206). Neither had the League decided an exact procedure for how the withdrawal should take place. Therefore, concerning the functional issues, the Japanese Cabinet decided on 28 February and 16 March 1933 that although their country would refuse to take part in the Council and the Assembly it intended to continue participating in the Disarmament Conference, the World Economic Conference, and the League's humanitarian and technical works, as well as the ILO (NGB-MJ 1933c, 351; NGB-MJ 1933d, 371; NGB-MJ 1933e, 373). The main reason for this decision was that Japan did not want its general relations with the entire world to deteriorate further (NGB-MJ 1933a, 319; NGB-MJ 1933b, 320).

Furthermore, there were several practical benefits of being a League member. First, Japan felt honoured to have a permanent seat in the

Council and several Japanese had significant positions in the League and its related organisations. One example is Mineichirō Adachi, who had been elected to be a judge of the Permanent Court of International Justice (PCIJ) in September 1930 and was serving as its president. When the election had been held, he had managed to gain 49 out of 52 votes in the Assembly and unanimous support in the Council, earning him a congratulatory telegram from Foreign Minister Kijūrō Shidehara (JACAR 1930). Japan had no desire for any drastic change to this high status in international society.

Secondly, Japan wanted to keep its mandate over the former German islands in the Pacific, north of the equator. No country raised this issue in the end, and it was not the subject of any resolutions by the Council. One reason for this is that the mandates had been conferred not by the League but by the Principal Allied and Associated Powers at the Paris Peace Conference. Article 22 of the Covenant also left open the possibility for a non-member to hold a mandate, with the United States being at one stage a strong candidate to be a mandatary over Armenia. Therefore, Japan continued to hold its mandate and submit annual administrative reports. Nobumichi Sakenobe, the retired Japanese minister to Chile, continued to take part in the Permanent Mandate Commission (Tohmatsu 2011: chap. 3; Pederson 2015: 289–291).

Thirdly, the League was the source of valuable information and knowledge. There was a Japanese Bureau for the League of Nations Affairs in Paris, which was renamed the Japanese Bureau for International Conferences in November 1933. It should be noted, however, that the office was moved to Geneva (NGB 1933a, 172; NGB 1933b, 182; NGB 1933c, 203), staying physically close to the League and avoiding isolation from the information and knowledge which it collected.

Continuing engagement with the League was driven by individuals such as Masayuki Yokoyama, who became the deputy director of the new Bureau in Geneva. Educated in a Catholic school established by French missionaries in Tokyo, the Ecole de l'Etoile de Matin, his experience and knowledge of the French language appear to have made him especially keen on international co-operation. He reported home that the League appreciated Japan's intention of partial co-operation, and that Arthur Sweetser, the American head of its Information Section, thought that it would not be difficult to have Japanese members in the various committees (NGB 1933d, 210; NGB 1934). After all, if Sweetser could be in the Secretariat, why not the Japanese? One Japanese individual who continued to work in the Secretariat was Ken Harada of the Political Section, who had started working there in 1920 as a personal assistant of Inazō Nitobe, the former Under-Secretary-General and the best-known of all Japanese internationalists.[4]

The situation, however, was not as simple as Yokoyama had reported. The opinions of some in Geneva were distinctly unfavourable towards the prospect of Japan's intentions for partial co-operation. Deputy Secretary-General of the League, Frank Walters, for example, considered that Japan could not simply withdraw under the circumstances of the Manchurian crisis. Moreover, once its withdrawal from the League did become definitive, it would have no right to participate in the activities of certain of its organisations. Much like the Chinese position, as mentioned above, he did not intend to expel Japan but hoped that it might be possible to persuade it to postpone its withdrawal for another two years (TNA 1934b).

The legal adviser of the British Foreign Office, Sir Herbert William Malkin, did not share Walters' opinion. He explained that neither he nor anybody else he had met could actually understand the meaning of the concluding words of Article 1. Besides, he could see no reason why Japan should not be treated like other non-members, including the United States (TNA 1934c). His thinking was thus very much in line with that of Sweetser.

The opinion of Joseph Avenol, the Secretary-General, was closer to that of the Chinese and Walters. This became clear in December 1933, when Japan asked whether other contracting parties of the Convention for Limiting the Manufacture and Regulating the Distribution of Narcotic Drugs would object to its ratifying the document with a reservation. This was clearly an attempt to maintain its position in the organs mentioned in the Convention, such as the Opium Advisory Committee and the Health Committee (Kamiyama 2000: 51–56). Avenol could not accept that Japan should still claim the advantages of collaboration with the League in the technical sphere as a matter of right. He considered the case of Japan, which intended to withdraw, was different from that of the United States, which had not been a member since the establishment of the League (TNA 1934d).

[4] Nitobe studied at Johns Hopkins University when Woodrow Wilson was also a student there. They even attended the same seminar (Saya 2015: 95).

Meanwhile, nationalistic opinion in Japan continued to grow further after the declaration of its intention to leave, which encouraged anti-League sentiments to become more influential in the Foreign Ministry. Mamoru Shigemitsu, who became the vice-minister in May 1933, and Kōki Hirota, who took the post of foreign minister in September, both considered that bilateral negotiations between Japan and China were more significant than the kind of intervention in Eastern Asia that could take place through international co-operation under the auspices of the League. On 17 April 1934, Eiji Amau (Amō)[5], director of the Information Bureau of the Japanese Ministry of Foreign Affairs, reflected the opinion of Shigemitsu when he made an unofficial comment on international assistance to China during a press conference (Tomizuka 2003). He argued that the intention of the powers to take common action to support China would inevitably become politicised, even if it was claimed to be only financial and technical. Many observers, including Joseph Grew, the American ambassador to Japan, considered that the growth of technical co-operation between the League and China was one of the reasons for this remark (FRUS 1934a, b). Officially starting in 1931, this had expanded under the leadership of Dr Ludwik Rajchman, the very capable director of the League of Nations Health Section. The nature of this co-operation will be discussed further in the next section.

Meanwhile, Britain and France, the mainstays of the League, by no means sympathised with Japan after the Manchurian Incident but did not think it wise to completely shut the door to its return to the organisation. Indeed, there were precedents. Although Spain had notified its intention to withdraw on 11 September 1926, it had retracted this in 1928 and remained a member. Mexico also notified its intention to withdraw by a note dated 3 December 1932 but had informed the Secretary-General on 5 May 1934, that it had changed its decision (Walters 1952: 325, 388–389; OJ 1934: 428). There was, thus, a realistic possibility that Japan might do the same, or at least postpone its decision to pull out. In February 1935, this ambiguous feeling was expressed when Roger Cambon, a counsellor of the French Embassy, brought a dispatch from Paris to the British Foreign Office that suggested orally telling the Japanese that their continued collaboration was regarded as desirable.

[5] His surname is pronounced Amō, but he spelt it Amau.

This move was related to Japan's proposed reservation on the Convention of Narcotic Drugs, mentioned above. Britain decided to adopt this procedure and the Japanese Ambassador was accordingly notified on 13 March 1935 (TNA 1935a).

On 25 April 1935, about a month after Japan's withdrawal became official, the desire to maintain a degree of Japanese co-operation was again expressed by the Chilean chair of the 14th Advisory Committee on Traffic in Women and Children. The Belgian, British, French, Italian and Polish members supported the proposal of the Danish member to ask the Council to take steps to ensure that this was facilitated. Yokoyama, feeling grateful for the suggestion made by the British member, unofficially attended the meetings of the Advisory Committee even before the Council had made any decisions on the matter (JACAR 1935).

This was repeated when the meeting of the 20th Opium Advisory Committee started on 20 May 1935. Although the Japanese representative initially refrained from taking part, most participants agreed with the British proposal that the Council should ensure that Japan would be able to continue to play a role. Even after the Chinese member made a reservation on the legal question of the representation on committees of governments that had withdrawn from the League, on 22 May, the Council decided to ensure the continued co-operation of Japan (NGB 1935; TNA 1935b).

Still, the prospect of Japan's partial co-operation was not easy. One example of the difficulties of finding a way forward arose when a Japanese judge on the PCIJ, Adachi, passed away in Amsterdam on 28 December 1934. Japan wanted to maintain this post, but when the election to fill the vacancy with Harukazu Nagaoka, Ambassador to France from 1932 to 1933, was held at the Council and the Assembly in September 1935, he only secured 35 out of 51 votes. This was 14 less than Adachi had gained five years earlier (Goto-Shibata 2017: 193–214).

Another example occurred when there was a reduction of members of the Health Committee, as part of the Council's general attempt to reform the League's technical organs that began in 1934. The committee which examined this issue recommended reducing the number from 26 to 12. Throughout 1936, Yokoyama contacted Rajchman and asked him to maintain a Japanese member. Failing to gain a favourable answer, he requested a meeting with Avenol in January 1937 and stressed that if a Japanese member could attend the committee, the co-operation between Japan and the League of Nations Health Organization would become smoother. Yokoyama's negotiations did not bear fruit, however, and Japan lost its membership of the committee when the Council met that month and was relegated to the status of a sub-member without the right to vote. The costs of attending were also to be borne by Japan (Yasuda 2014: 34, 50–51).

Meanwhile, the task of the Japanese advocates of continuing co-operation became harder when the situation in Japan deteriorated following the Young Officers' revolt in February 1936, when rebellious troops occupied the centre of Tokyo and killed several prominent officials. Although the uprising was just suppressed, this signalled the continuing rise of the power of the military as Japan's politics was in the process of being overwhelmed by hyper-nationalism. The opinions of those who supported international co-operation were becoming steadily weaker as they were removed from the decision-making process and transferred to irrelevant positions. At the end of 1936, for example, Yokoyama was moved from Geneva to be appointed Minister to Egypt. This was not a demotion, but it removed him from the centre of international co-operation.

Technical Co-operation and China's Sovereignty

The above discussion shows Japan's withdrawal from the League was not a sudden rupture in 1933, as is commonly perceived, but a more incremental process that was shaped by the determination of both the Japanese internationalists and League members to maintain links, as nationalism drove the invasion of Manchuria and began to dominate domestic politics. This section will explore how technical co-operation between the League and China interacted very differently with rising nationalism and the development of a harder understanding of sovereignty as the conflict with Japan continued to escalate.[6]

The technical co-operation between China and the League officially began in 1931 and continued until the end of 1940, well after the outbreak of the full-scale Sino-Japanese War in July 1937. The nature and scale of this co-operation were not envisaged by the League's Covenant but developed through personal initiatives. Rajchman was one of the central actors on the League side and his good relationship with T. V.

[6] There are numerous works on the Sino-Japanese War written in Japanese, including Ishijima and Kubo (2004); Nishimura, Ishijima and Tajima (2011).

Soong, the Harvard-educated brother-in-law of Chiang Kai-shek, was indispensable. The Chinese stance on the League was ambivalent at best. Even the enthusiastic Soong had thought it necessary to seek the advice of Arthur Young, an American adviser to the Republic of China, before he decided to embark on co-operation (Chang 1999: 136, 177–181). This trust in America is typical of the many members of China's governing elite (see the chapter by Hughes in this book). Many of those who had been educated there were not sure whether they could trust the League of Nations with Britain and France as its mainstays, the traditional imperial powers in Eastern Asia. Britain, it should be remembered, still dominated the Shanghai International Settlement in the inter-war period, where it owned the magnificent buildings on the riverfront that it had constructed.

Indeed, unlike the inter-state system in Europe after World War I, East and Southeast Asia continued to be what Akami describes in her chapter as 'inter-imperial'. China, Siam and Japan were the only independent states, while the rest of the region still consisted of colonies under the powers. Alongside the British and French empires were the Dutch East Indies and the Portuguese colony of Macao, while Japan occupied Taiwan and Korea. Even the United States, despite the trust of many in China, still ruled the Philippines.

Furthermore, it should be noted that China, too, had maintained something of its older imperial face. This is particularly significant for the south-western province of Yunnan, where technical co-operation with the League was carried out in 1939. Despite the description of China as 'semi-colonial' in the inter-war years, the Han Chinese from the central provinces were effectively colonisers who had started to migrate there as the Qing had expanded its overland empire in the eighteenth century. When the Republic of China inherited the territory of the former Qing Empire, the central government had only been able to exert a degree of control through indigenous leaders, much as the British maintained indirect rule in the peripheral regions of Burma that bordered on Yunnan.

It is important to bear this fragile domestic political situation in mind when assessing the nature of technical co-operation under the auspices of the League after the outbreak of the Sino-Japanese War in July 1937. Due to the hostilities, tens of thousands of people had to flee for safety and refuge. As the twenty-first-century cases of SARS, MERS and COVID-19 show only too painfully, the movement of people tends to be accompanied by the spread of diseases. China thus had little choice but to seek outside assistance for the prevention and control of epidemics and the general relief of the civilian population and refugees in the region. Among the epidemics mentioned in a memorandum submitted by Quo Tai-chi (Guo Taiqi), the Chinese representative to the League, in September 1937, are cholera, smallpox and typhus (OJ 1937). With cholera having been frequently observed in Shanghai and smallpox endemic in Hong Kong, the Chinese were particularly afraid that these illnesses might spread to other places.

Although the general relief of the population was beyond the League's financial capacity, it did decide to provide medical supplies and send experts to co-operate with the Chinese authorities to assist with the prevention of epidemic diseases, forming units of English-, French- and German-speaking experts. In 1938, the German-speaking unit worked in the city of Xi'an. Its members were Swiss and Austrian. The French-speaking unit worked in south China which bordered on French Indochina, under the leadership of Inspector-General Antoine Lasne, who had been responsible for public health in the French colonial territories. The English-speaking unit was assigned Hunan, Hubei and Jiangxi provinces. Its leader was Dr Robert Cecil Robertson, the head of the division of pathological research at the Henry Lester Institute of Medical Research in the Shanghai International Settlement. He had been in China for more than ten years. Dr E. I. B. Hawes was Robertson's assistant. He had worked at the British army hospital in Aldershot and came with his wife to Hankou, a part of Wuhan. The International Red Cross Committee of the city also assisted with the maintenance of some of the isolation hospitals. Robertson reported, in his letter to Sir Alexander Cadogan, the British under-secretary of state for foreign affairs and the former ambassador to China, that the British Relief Committee under the chairmanship of the consul-general in Hankou was generous and sympathetic to the type of work that was being carried out (TNA 1938a).

As the war dragged on into the summer of 1938, the Chinese government asked the League to continue the anti-epidemic work for a second year. Although the League was willing to do this, however, differences of opinion surfaced over what it should involve. The Chinese, as the beneficiary, were dissatisfied with the existing methods and argued that increasing their own control over the co-operation would greatly enhance efficiency (Chang 1999: 117). The League experts genuinely wanted to help but did not consider themselves to be working under the Chinese authorities. This was problematic because it assumed the attitude of a 'civilising mission' while the idea of tutelage by the civilised and powerful was considered to be patronising and condescending by those who were placed in the position of inferiority. The Chinese were acutely sensitive and opposed to any imputations that they were uncivilised or underdeveloped. Although they needed the assistance of the League because of the war against Japan, they did not necessarily want to be assisted by 'generous Western powers' and to be civilised according to Western models (Amrith and Sluga 2008: 264).

Rajchman was strongly sympathetic to such opinions, with the result that he was highly regarded by the Chinese. In preparation for the special sub-committee of the League of Nations' Health Committee, he worked with them to prepare a new scheme that would transfer control of the co-operation, especially financial, almost entirely to the people on the spot. This scheme also envisaged the breakup of the three units of experts and placing the technical personnel under the direct disposal of the Chinese government (TNA 1938b).

When the scheme was not accepted by the special sub-committee, Rajchman prepared a new plan. According to Neville Goodman of the British Ministry of Health, who participated in the sub-committee, this was 'an extremely ingenious document' insofar as it used words and phrases derived from already accepted documents to give a large role and greater responsibility to the Epidemic Commission in China (TNA 1938b, 1939a).[7]

However, all financial questions that fell under the authority of the Assembly had to be submitted to its Fourth Committee, which was in charge of the budget and financial questions, as well as the financial Supervisory Commission which consisted of independent advisers on the Secretary-General's estimates of the budget. When the Supervisory Commission met in Paris on 14 and 15 November 1938, it accepted the conclusions of the sub-committee, except as regards the grants-in-aid. It also made it clear that the Secretary-General would retain the power to effect transfers within the framework of the budget, and it was understood that the entry into force of the scheme was subject to the payment in full of China's contribution to the League for 1938 (OJ 1939b). The League could not hand over the financial control of the co-operation to the local authorities because it was funded by contributions from the member states. Also, the timing of Rajchman's initiative was not good because the

[7] The document can be seen in OJ 1939a.

League was preoccupied with thinking about its own retrenchment after Italy had given notice of its withdrawal in December 1937.

The Chinese did not welcome the final scheme adopted by the Supervisory Commission. It took nearly three months for it to pay its contribution to the League, making co-operation possible in 1939. Meanwhile, the Japanese military had occupied Guangzhou and Hankou in October 1938 and the areas of anti-epidemic work retreated southwestwards to Yunnan. In 1939, Robertson also came to work in Yunnan as the chief technical expert for the League, making him the only one of the three heads of the units of experts to continue to work with China on technical co-operation. The contracts of some others, including Lasne and Hawes, were not renewed.

Due to the war, it was expected that the Yunnan-Burma Road would have to be widened which would lead to an increase in the flow of traffic and commodities between the populations at its two ends. Therefore, Robertson proposed a special epidemiological survey in the region, to which the League and China agreed (TNA 1939a). The first survey was from June to August 1939, which Robertson conducted with three Chinese members of the epidemiological survey unit of the League of Nations. Not limiting his survey to the Chinese side of the border, he found out that bubonic plague at Namhkam in British Burma was an urgent problem to be controlled. A rough map that he drew shows that the plague existed in the south of Namhkam, and near Bhamo along the road between the two towns, leading Robertson to appeal to the authorities of British Burma to inoculate the entire population in Namhkam and eradicate rats and prevent the possibility for the disease to be carried over into China by the newly expanded Burma Road and the increased movement of people (TNA 1939b).

Another urgent problem noticed by Robertson was malaria. The existence of various diseases in the south-western part of China had been known since the days of San Guo Zhi [*The Records of Three Kingdoms*], which was written in China towards the end of the third century CE and has been popular and read widely in Eastern Asia. *Zhangqi* was one of those diseases, and in 1935–1936, only a few years earlier than Robertson's survey, it had been confirmed that this was indeed malaria (Ling et al. 1936: 1826). Based on his epidemiological survey, Robertson thus prepared a plan to control malaria in Yunnan, to be submitted to the Chinese authorities. One point he suggested was that co-operation between the authorities of British Burma and China would be necessary (TNA 1939c).

In September 1939, shortly after World War II broke out in Europe, Robertson was informed by Geneva that the Chinese government would not require his services in the next year. It turned out that it had requested the Public Health Service of the United States to send experts instead. The British Foreign Office considered this development to be a result of the League's retrenchment policy. Robertson suspected it was part of a Chinese plan to keep the British out of Yunnan.

Although Chang Li's extensive study of China and the League suggests that there were more personal reasons (Chang 1999: 118), Robertson seems to have made a significant point for understanding the growing impact of nationalism in China. It should be recalled that the co-operation that took place in 1939 was carried out in a part of China where the question of empires was even more complicated than in the coastal region. Yunnan bordered on the British and French Empires, while the government of the Republic of China had inherited the imperial character of the Qing Empire's rule there and considered it to be a 'backward' region. Although China needed the League's assistance to fight against Japan, it did not necessarily want outsiders to know about and report on the real situation in the borderland. Furthermore, Robertson's survey was not limited to Chinese territory, proposing a degree of cross-border co-operation with British Burma. As he continued to send his reports not only to the League but also to the British Foreign Office, it could be said that the British Empire seems to have been at least as dominant in his mind as the international organisation.

It should also be recalled that, from the beginning, not all Chinese welcomed international co-operation wholeheartedly. Individuals like T. V. Soong certainly enjoyed good relations with Rajchman and were keen on working with the League, but such westernised figures were a small minority in their vast country. For others, the difference between co-operation with the League and a form of foreign intervention that infringed on Chinese sovereignty sometimes became unclear. Although China was a beneficiary of technical co-operation, they saw the paramount goal of politics since the establishment of the Republic in 1912 as achieving freedom from subjugation to the imperial powers. Controlled as it was by the imperial powers, the League could never be fully trusted.

International Co-operation Versus Nationalism

It has been argued above that the record of Japan and China in the League provides ample evidence for an exploration of the tensions between using technical projects to build international co-operation and nationalist politics. Of course, the distinct experiences of the two states reflect their different levels of development, domestic politics and relative international power.

The impact of nationalism on Japan's relationship with the League is most evident in its aggression in Manchuria and its departure from the organisation when its deeds were not recognised as legitimate by the other members. Despite this, however, internationalists on both sides had a degree of success in allowing Japanese personnel to continue to attend technical committees and commissions. That this partial co-operation continued until the end of October 1938, ten months before the outbreak of World War II in Europe, is a testament to the value that the country attributed to having a role in the League, not only to develop its technical work but also as a way to maintain some degree of honour and prestige in international society. Ultimately, the influence wielded by internationalist individuals such as Yokoyama, the French-educated Japanese diplomat at Geneva, was eroded after the decision to withdraw, despite the support they managed to win inside the League of Nations itself. It should still be noted that Japan continued to play a *de facto* role in the League by engaging in its technical projects for several years after what is considered to be its *de jure* withdrawal in 1935.

Nationalism was also increasingly influential in the very different domestic context of China between the world wars. The Nationalist government only managed to exert its control over much of the former Qing Empire as late as 1928, following years of division in the wake of the 1911 republican revolution. Although some members of the political elite were keen on working with the League, and China was the clear beneficiary of such co-operation, they were far from united in this view. High among their concerns was the fear that the League's technical work might infringe upon their sovereignty. The League was thus suspected to be another way to maintain international control over the country at worst and maintain its inferior status at best. Co-operation was thus only tolerated insofar as it kept the League on China's side in its developing war with Japan. As soon as more appropriate support was forthcoming from the United States, it was not so welcome.

Despite the very different trajectories taken by Japan and China, there was one common factor that shaped their relationship with the League. Those who were interested in international co-operation constituted a small minority in both countries, even among the elite. Therefore, they had to deal with widespread scepticism towards an organisation whose mainstays were Britain and France, the traditional imperial powers in Eastern Asia. Moreover, most ordinary people did not even know of the existence of the League. Having said this, China's greater success in using the League might partly be attributed to the fact that more of the members of its political elite who were interested in international co-operation were also in positions of power and influence than in Japan. By better utilising the talent of those who were educated in the West, in pursuit of clearer goals, it was the Chinese who were better able to reconcile the tensions between domestic nationalism and international co-operation in ways that would ultimately raise their country's status in the world, rather than diminishing it.

Abbreviations

FRUS	Foreign Relations of the United States
JACAR	Japan Center for Asian Historical Records, National Archives of Japan
NGB	Nihon Gaikō Bunsho [Documents on Japanese Foreign Policy]
NGB-MJ	Nihon Gaikō Bunsho, Manshū Jihen [Manchurian Incident] dai 3 kan [Volume 3]
OJ	League of Nations Official Journal
TNA	The National Archives, Kew

References

Akami, Tomoko. 2017. Imperial Polities, Intercolonialism, and the Shaping of Global Governing Norms, *Journal of Global History* (12/1), 4–25.

Amrith, S. and G. Sluga. 2008. New Histories of the United Nations, *Journal of World History* (19/3), 251–274.

Chang, Li. 1999. *Guoji hezuo zai Zhongguo: lianmeng jiaose de kaocha 1919–1946* [International Co-operation in China: An Examination of the Role of the League of Nations]. Taibei: Zhongyang Yanjiuyuan Jindaishi Yanjiusuo [Academia Sinica].

FRUS. 1934a. Vol. III: p. 119. Grew to Hull, 20 Apr.

FRUS. 1934b. Vol III: p. 123. Grew to Hull, 21 Apr.

Goto-Shibata, Harumi. 1995. *Japan and Britain in Shanghai, 1925–31.* Basingstoke: Macmillan.

Goto-Shibata, Harumi. 2017. Adachi Mineichirō to Kokusai Renmei no hanji senkyo [Adachi Mineichirō and the election of the PCIJ judges at the League of Nations]. In *Adachi Mineichirō*, eds. Yanagihara Masaharu and Shinohara Hatsue, 193–214. Tokyo: Tokyo Daigaku Shuppankai.

Goto-Shibata, Harumi. 2020. *The League of Nations and the East Asian Imperial Order, 1920–1946*. Singapore: Palgrave Macmillan.

Ishijima, Noriyuki and Kubo, Tōru eds. 2004. *Jūkei Kokumin Seifu shi no kenkyū* [History of the Chongqing National Government]. Tokyo: Tokyo Daigaku Shuppankai.

JACAR. 1930. Shidehara to the representative in Geneva, 26 September. Ref. B04014039100 image 55.

JACAR. 1935, Kokusai Renmei fujin jidō mondai ikken [On the League of Nations, the issue of traffic in women and children] (B-9-10-0), Yokoyama to Hirota, 25 June. Ref. B04122142400 images 56 to 58.

Kamiyama, Akiyoshi. 2000. Mayaku Seizō Seigen Jōyaku hijyun mondai - Kokusai Renmei dattai no ichimen [Progress in the Ratification by Japan of the Convention for Limiting the Manufacture and Regulating the Distribution of Narcotic Drugs: One Aspect of the Japanese Withdrawal from the League of Nations]. *Gaikō Shiryōkan Pō* [Journal of Diplomatic Archives], 14: 51–56.

Katō, Yōko. 2007. *Manshū Jihen kara Nicchū Sensō he* [From the Manchurian Incident to the Sino-Japanese War]. Tokyo: Iwanami Shoten, shinsho.

League of Nations. 1939. *The Development of International Co-operation in Economic and Social Affairs, Report of the Special Committee.* Geneva. A.23.1939.

Ling, L. C., K. B. Liu and Y. T. Yao. 1936. Studies on the So-called Changch'i, Part II. Changch'i in Yunnan. *Chinese Medical Journal* (50/12): 1815–1828.

MacMillan, Margaret. 2013. *The War that Ended Peace*. London: Profile Books.

Makino, Masahiko. 2020. *Fusen Jōyaku* [The Pact of Paris]. Tokyo: Tokyo Daigaku Shuppankai.

Makino, Nobuaki. 1990. *Makino Nobuaki nikki* [Diary of Nobuaki Makino]. Itō Takashi et al. eds. Tokyo: Chūō Kōronsha.

Manderson, Lenore. 1995. Wireless Wars in the Eastern Arena: Epidemiological Surveillance, Disease Prevention and the Work of the Eastern Bureau of the League of Nations Health Organisation, 1925–1942. In *International Health Organisations and Movements 1918–1939*, ed. Paul Weindling, 109–133. Cambridge: Cambridge University Press.

Mitrany, David. 1975. *The Functional Theory of International Relations*. New York: St Martin's Press.
NGB. 1933a, 172. Showa ki 2, dai 2 bu, dai 2 kan [Showa era 2, part 2, vol. 2], 172. Satō to Uchida, 1 Apr.
NGB. 1933b, 182. Uchida to Itō, 19 Aug.
NGB. 1933c, 203. Yokoyama to Hirota, 20 Nov.
NGB. 1933d, 210. Yokoyama to Hirota, 26 Dec.
NGB. 1934. Showa ki 2, dai 2 bu, dai 3 kan [Showa era 2, part 2, vol. 3]: 16, Yokoyama to Hirota, 24 Jan.
NGB. 1935. Showa ki 2, dai 2 bu, dai 4 kan [Showa era 2, part 2, vol. 4]: 34, Yokoyama to Hirota, 24 May.
NGB-MJ. 1933a, 319. Uchida to representatives to the League of Nations in Geneva, 20 Feb. Betsu-den ('Kakugi kettei [Cabinet decision]')
NGB-MJ. 1933b, 320. Uchida to representatives, 21 Feb.
NGB-MJ. 1933c, 351. Uchida to Sawada, 28 Feb.
NGB-MJ. 1933d, 371. Sawada to Uchida. Arrived on 17 Mar.
NGB-MJ. 1933e, 373. Uchida to Sawada. 18 Mar.
Nish, Ian. 1993. *Japan's Struggle with Internationalism: Japan, China and the League of Nations, 1931–1933*. London and New York: Kegan Paul International.
Nishimura, Shigeo, Ishijima, Noriyuki and Tajima, Nobuo (eds). 2011. *Nicchū Sensō no kokusai kyōdō kenkyū 4 kokusai kankei no naka no Nicchū Sensō* [International Cooperative Study on the Sino-Japanese War Vol. 4 The Sino-Japanese War in International Relations]. Tokyo: Keiō Daigaku Shuppannkai.
OJ. May 1934, p. 428. Cancellation by the Mexican Government of its note of December 3rd, 1932, notifying its intention to withdraw from the League of Nations.
OJ. Dec. 1937, annex 1685, C/China/23. Letter from the Chinese government to the Secretary-General.
OJ. Jan. 1939a. pp. 40–42, Appendix. Report of the Sub-Committee which met on Oct. 14th and 15th, 1938.
OJ. Jan. 1939b. pp. 39–40, C.468.M.311.1938.X, 21 Nov. 1938. Technical Collaboration between the LN and China, Scheme of Anti-epidemic Action, Report of the Supervisory Commission.
Pedersen, Susan. 2015. *The Guardians*. New York: Oxford University Press.
Satō, Naotake. 1963. *Kaiko 80 nen* [Looking Back at My Eighty Years]. Tokyo: Jiji Tsūshinsha.
Saya, Makito. 2015. *Minzoku gaku, Taiwan, Kokusai Renmei* [Folklore, Taiwan, the League of Nations: Yanagida Kunio and Nitobe Inazō]. Tokyo: Kōdansha.
Shinohara, Hatsue. 2012. *US International Lawyers in the Interwar Years: A Forgotten Crusade*. Cambridge: Cambridge University Press.
TNA. 1933. FO371/17079, F2186/33/10, LN, no. A (extra) 42. VII, annex.

TNA. 1934a. Strang Minute. 5 Nov. FO371/18193, F6385/2203/23.
TNA.1934b. Strang (UK Delegation, Geneva). 12 April. FO371/18193, F2203/2203/23
TNA. 1934c. Malkin minute, 26 Apr; Outfile to. C.E.S. Dodd, Tokyo. 14 May. FO371/18193, F2203/2203/23
TNA. 1934d. From UK Delegation (Geneva). 16 October. FO371/18193, F6215/2203/23
TNA. 1935a. Orde minute, 15 March; To the Japanese Ambassador, 13 March. FO371/19367, F1255/134/87
TNA. 1935b. FO371/19370, F3298/299/87. LN, No. C.224/1935/XI (86th session of the Council. Extract from final minutes of the 2nd meeting held on 22 May, Geneva); FO371/19370, F4923/299/87, Coles to Makins, unnumbered, 26 Jul.
TNA. 1938a. From Robertson to Cadogan. 21 June. FO371/22113, F6694/120/10
TNA. 1938b. Report from Goodman. 10 November. FO371/22114, F12061/120/10
TNA. 1939a. Robertson to A. L. Scott. 2 March. FO371/23443, F2633/52/10
TNA. 1939b. From Clark Kerr, enclosure (British consulate-general, Yunnanfu, to Chungking, 22 Aug). 16 September. FO371/23443, F11538/52/10
TNA. 1939c. From Shanghai chancery to Far Eastern Department, enclosure (A scheme for malaria control on the China-Burma Route, by Robertson, 20 Sept.). 18 October. FO371/23443, F12778/52/10
Tohmatsu, Haruo. 2011. *Nihon Teikoku to Inin Tōchi: Nanyō guntō wo meguru kokusai seiji 1914–1947* [The Japanese Empire and Mandates: International Politics on the former German Islands North of the Equator 1914–1947]. Nagoya: Nagoya Daigaku Shuppankai.
Tomizuka, Kazuhiko. 2003. 'Renmei dattai no konpon gi' to Nihon gaikō ni okeru 'Tōa' gainen no keisei [The Meaning of the 'Withdrawal from the League' and the Making of the Concept of 'East Asia' in Japanese Diplomacy]. *Kokugakuin Daigaku Nihon Bunka Kenkyūjo Kiyō* [Bulletin of the Institute of Japanese Culture, Kokugakuin University] (92), 147–172.
Usui, Katsumi. 1995. *Manshūkoku to Kokusai Renmei* [Manchukuo and the League of Nations]. Tokyo: Yoshikawa Kōbunkan, 1995.
Walters, F.P. 1952. *A History of the League of Nations*. London: Oxford University Press.
Yasuda, Kayo. 2014. *Kokusai seiji no naka no kokusai hoken jigyō* [International Health Work in International Politics: From the League of Nation's Health Organization to the WHO and UNICEF]. Kyoto: Minerva Shobō.

Global Networks Between Civilisations

The Far-Eastern Bureau of the League of Nations: Linking the Regional and International Orders Through Health Work

Kayo Takuma

Introduction

Shortly after its inception, the League of Nations was criticized for focusing too much on Western Europe. By the late 1920s, however, it was proactively expanding its activities in the Asia-Pacific region, prioritizing health projects where the management of infectious diseases such as cholera and typhus had been a major issue since before World War I. The Far-Eastern Bureau of the League of Nations Health Organization (LNHO) was thus established in 1925 to supervise cooperative efforts in the field of health. This chapter assesses the organization's role in Asia and its legacy by tracing the chronology of its 26 years of operation, through the change of its name to the Singapore Epidemiological Intelligence Station in 1947 down to its closure in 1951.

K. Takuma (✉)
Tokyo Metropolitan University, Tokyo, Japan

C. R. Hughes and H. Shinohara (eds.), *East Asians in the League of Nations*, New Directions in East Asian History,
https://doi.org/10.1007/978-981-19-7067-2_4

The Bureau's status as the regional office in Asia for overseeing cooperation in the collection and dissemination of infectious disease information and other kinds of health work was given a legal foundation by the International Sanitary Convention that was signed in 1926. Even though it had to suspend operations in 1941, due to World War II, an indication of just how vital its work had come to be is that the Allied powers called on it to resume its activities soon after the end of hostilities, due to an increasing demand for information about how infectious diseases had spread among the troops. Although the Bureau would ultimately be replaced when the newly established United Nations (UN) began to be more active in the health field, its legacy can be seen in the significant role it played in shaping the International Sanitary Regulations that were adopted in 1951, under the supervision of the World Health Organization (WHO).

The development of the Bureau's role during the interwar period also had important implications for the broader evolution of global governance by linking the different political orders that had come to co-exist in Asia. While the League had begun to play a leading role at the international level, specialists and government officials on the ground forged their own transnational links. Due to the fact that infectious diseases know no borders, the work of the Bureau inevitably played a special role in creating the institutions, networks and regulatory regime that combined these different levels into one relatively well-functioning system.

There is nothing particularly novel about a perspective that examines international relations at the time through health projects. Harumi Goto-Shibata, for example, has examined the international order in Asia by focusing on technical cooperation among the League of Nations with regard to China (Goto-Shibata 2016). It is clear from her research that activities deemed to be 'technical' and 'apolitical' were closely entangled with politics in practice. While presenting a similar a point of view, this chapter aims to take the analysis further by paying attention to the impact of the Bureau's activities on global health governance today. Section "Introduction" thus begins by examining the features of the League's initiatives and the chronology of its earliest health projects; Section "Establishment of the League of Nations Health Organization (LNHO)" describes how its health projects in Asia influenced the regional order; Section "The LNHO Far-Eastern Bureau" finishes by examining why and how the Bureau continued its activities despite World War II (as the Intelligence Station); Section "Continuing the Bureau's Work During and After World War II" explores how the legacy of its work has endured in postwar Asia down to the present, when the COVID-19 pandemic has given an unprecedented degree of urgency to the discussion of the global management of infectious diseases.

Establishment of the League of Nations Health Organization (LNHO)

World War I and Infectious Diseases

Before World War I, the International Sanitary Convention of 1903 stipulated the obligations of states regarding infectious diseases that crossed national borders. The Office International d'Hygiène Publique (OIHP) had been established to manage this, but the scope of its work was limited to specific diseases such as cholera and plague. The spread of infectious diseases during the war was thus viewed as an opportunity to widen the international community's systems of cooperation on health. Pathogens such as malaria were serious enough, but the outbreak of a new strain of influenza, popularly known as 'Spanish Flu,' took a horrifyingly high toll (Barry 2005: Chapter 1).[1] One calculation estimates that up to 100 million people fell victim to the disease between 1918 and 1923 (Spinney 2017).

The threat of infectious diseases continued to grow after the end of the war, especially because typhus spread with the massive movement of soldiers and displaced people, along with the wave of refugees escaping from the Russian revolution and civil war. When Poland's Department of Health requested assistance from the OIHP, however, it was not able to provide the funds or personnel required (Borowy 2009: 43–45). After Henry Davison, chairman of the War Council of the American Red Cross (ARC), alerted the allied nations' leaders to the threat at the Paris Peace Conference, a fact-finding research group was formed in May 1919 that included high-level health officials from the United States, Britain, France, and Italy. The research group's deployment in Poland revealed that infectious diseases were spreading even more than had been expected in Eastern Europe, leading to a recognition of the pressing need to deal with this by creating new and more extensive international frameworks for managing the situation.

The Epidemic Commission and the Establishment of the LNHO

The League of Nations would play a leading role in the formation of these frameworks. When its Covenant came into effect in January 1920, Article 23 (f) stipulated that the member states 'will endeavour to take steps in matters of international concern for the prevention and control of disease.' Accordingly, the spread of typhus in Eastern Europe became an important matter under the organization's jurisdiction. Eric Drummond, the League's first Secretary General, highlighted the need to establish a bureau that would specialize in health problems with which the existing bureaus were unable to cope. In April 1920, the League hosted an international health conference on Drummond's initiative at which discussions were held on ways to deal with typhus in Poland. It was at this event that the Polish microbiologist, Ludwik Rajchman, proposed dispatching an international commission to support relief efforts in his country. Based on his recommendation, the Epidemic Commission was formed in February 1921 and sent to Poland, where it developed activities that focused on the areas with the most urgent needs and greatest damage. When the situation improved dramatically as a result of these efforts, there was huge support for the creation of a permanent health organization under the supervision of the League. In August 1921, the LNHO Provisional Health Committee was established, and Rajchman was appointed as its Medical Director, having played a central role in the Epidemic Commission (Borowy 2009: 45–51).

The LNHO progressed from being a temporary organization to a permanent one in the autumn of 1923. Although the need for cooperation on global health meant that it would play a particularly important role in the management of information on infectious diseases before World War II, it would go on to take on projects that went beyond this scope, creating a legacy of activities and a new interpretation of 'health' that would be passed on to the WHO after the war (Yasuda 2014).

Although several specialist commissions were established for different purposes under the supervision of the LNHO, the Malaria Commission that was established in 1924 would last the longest. Malaria was extraordinarily powerful during World War I, particularly in the Balkan Peninsula and Turkey and, after the war, it spread to Europe, Africa, and Asia with the flow of returning soldiers and human migration. In 1923, Rajchman called it 'the most important infectious disease issue in Europe' and established the commission in the LNHO the following year, with funding from the Rockefeller Foundation in the United States. Apart from surveying the spread of the disease in every country that it reached, the LNHO also encouraged collaborative research by gathering scientists from around the world and even took on projects to train malaria specialists (Borowy 2009: 239–240). The management and planning of the program were undertaken by well-known researchers from various countries, including Andrew Balfour of the London School of Hygiene and Tropical Medicine and Bernhard Nocht of the Hamburg Institute for Tropical Diseases, creating important links between the new organization and their transnational networks (Borowy 2009: 248–249).

The international standardization of medical materials was another function taken on by the LNHO. This was increasingly important for the methods and units of measurement for chemical substances due to rapid improvements in treatments due to innovations such as serotherapy and vaccines since the nineteenth century. The lack of universal units of measurement posed an obstacle not only to the international distribution of medicines and treatments but also to research in the international community. Aiming to eliminate this hindrance, the LNHO thus established a Standardization Committee. This first endeavored to standardize blood serum and then vitamins (Borowy 2009: 115–116, 154–155) and to collate and develop international statistics and guidelines, paving the way for the global distribution of treatments and pharmaceuticals.

As these 'technical' and 'apolitical' initiatives grew, they began to play a lubricating role in the fractious environment of postwar international relations. This was particularly important for Germany, which had been excluded from the League and treated with suspicion since its defeat. It was illogical to exclude such a country from collaboration on health because its scientists had won 5 Nobel Prizes in Physiology or Medicine between 1901 and 1922. The fact that Germany's Hamburg Research Institute for Tropical Medicine was deeply involved in the activities of the Malaria Commission shows how the organization played a crucial role in improving relations and building trust, not just in the health field but also between Germany and the League's member states (Borowy 2009: 81–83, 116, 453).

The LNHO Far-Eastern Bureau

Aside from developing these projects, the LNHO also took on the task of managing infectious disease information services. The Epidemiological

Intelligence Service was established in Geneva to perform this function, providing data around the world including to Washington or Alexandria. In 1925, in response to appeals from Asia, the LNHO Far-Eastern Bureau was set up in the British Straits Settlement of Singapore. Although a degree of health cooperation had already developed in the region between neighboring states that tackled similar health issues, this would only expand to the truly international level between the world wars. The Far-Eastern Bureau played a crucial part in this movement by collecting radiograms with information on infectious diseases from various places. It distributed these in the form of a Weekly Bulletin from 12 radiogram stations in Singapore, Bandung (Java), Saigon (present-day Ho Chi Minh City), Shanghai, Tokyo, Karachi, and Geneva (WHOAa 1946). Japan's colonial health authorities, starting with the Taiwan Government General, also communicated directly with the Far-Eastern Bureau. The information that the Bureau transmitted on infectious diseases was also used by states that were not members of the League (Yasuda 2014: 42–43).

The expanding role of the Bureau also had legal implications. This is because the International Sanitary Convention, that had been signed in 1903, had to undergo piecemeal revisions in response to changes in the international environment. When alterations were made in 1926 with regard to the increase of sea traffic after the war, Article 7 clearly stipulated that the Bureau was to be the Asian regional office and would be tasked with carrying out appropriate coordination between the agencies tasked with collecting information on infectious diseases—including the OIHP.

The Bureau thus came to play an essential role in the management of the International Sanitary Convention in addition to its functions as a branch of the League in Asia (WHOAa 1946). In 1925, it was communicating with 47 different locations. By the following year, this number had almost doubled and would further rise to around 180 locations by 1938, stretching from Eastern Asia to the Mediterranean. Aside from this, the Bureau was engaged in research on topics such as the Black Plague and pneumonia that brought together specialists from many countries. As the LNHO carried out development programs in Asia, the Bureau also assisted the LNHO in conducting the programs.

The Far-Eastern Bureau and Regional Order in Asia

The establishment of the Far-Eastern Bureau allowed associated countries in Eastern Asia to get access to information on infectious diseases and, consequently, to reduce the number of patients with those diseases, as well as posting other positive improvements. The development of a global health project in Eastern Asia also signified that the League—which had previously developed activities that were mainly focused on Europe—was expanding the geographical scope of its activities. Moreover, projects undertaken by the Bureau allowed Asian countries such as Japan, India, and China to maintain a local connection with the League rather than meeting in Geneva, which still took one month to reach by ship. Countries such as Britain or France that had colonies in Asia also saw the Bureau as an important hub for health administration in the territories under their control.

The Bureau held a particularly important position in Japanese diplomacy. Initially, each member country dispatched one representative to the advisory committee, which was its decision-making body. Japan, however, acquired the right to also send representatives from its colonies, including Korea and Taiwan. For the purpose of maintaining a diplomatic profile with the League, it was seen as important that Japan should receive what it considered to be proper treatment and make contributions that were appropriate as a permanent member of the League Council. Even after withdrawing from the League, Japan continued to pay its contribution to the Bureau until the late 1930s and held a deputy directorship there until shortly before World War II (Yasuda 2014: Chapter 2).

The extension of the Bureau's influence beyond health administration and into the broader international relations of the time was not limited to high diplomacy between states. Because health work in the interwar period tended to develop at the regional rather than the international level, professional networks had formed in the associated countries in Asia (Sealey 2011: 435). By focusing on organizations such as the Far-Eastern Association of Tropical Medicine (FEATM), the Bureau played a role in bringing this cooperation into the framework of the League's activities in the region (Akami 2016). Even for Japan, health administration could be integrated into international or regional health cooperation through the participation of its colonial representatives in the Bureau. It is in these ways that the Bureau connected the multiple cooperative frameworks at the imperial, international and regional levels in the interwar period.

Continuing the Bureau's Work During and After World War II

The Bureau was able to continue with its activities until January 1942, after which it relocated to Canberra at the invitation of the Australian government to escape from Japan's invasion of Singapore. By November of that year, its work had been suspended (LONa 1945). However, the health environment deteriorated in Asia during the war, and infectious diseases were widespread. For example, although the number of Black Plague infections had been decreasing in Asia before the war, it began to go up during the 1930s in China and Burma along with the outbreak of the Second Sino-Japanese War, when the Burma Road was closed to prevent aid from reaching China. The number of cholera infections had also been increasing since 1940, even spreading to countries that had never been infected by it before, such as Siam (WHOAb 1947). Under such circumstances, responding to the quick resumption of infectious disease information services was seen as an urgent problem.

It is during the last year of the war that the newly established UN organizations began to take a leading role in managing international issues that impacted on healthy policy. In November 1944, in response to an appeal from the Chinese government (LONb 1944), the United Nations Relief and Rehabilitation Administration (UNRRA) established information offices in Chongqing, China, and Sydney, Australia (LONa 1945). It also established a health division during the war and developed centers for information on infectious diseases in Washington and London (WHOAb 1947). That same year, as air traffic expanded, the International Sanitary Convention was revised and the job of managing them, which had previously been performed by the OIHP, was taken over by the UNRRA (LONc 1946). In this regard, during the war in Asia the UNRRA followed the precedent set of activities of the Far-Eastern Bureau in providing substantial services for the provision of information on infectious diseases.

On August 15, 1945, when Singapore was liberated from the Japanese occupation, LNHO personnel quickly tried to reopen the Far-Eastern Bureau. With what was left of the League continuing to operate until it was finally disbanded in April 1946, it was believed that reopening an information office under its auspices would show the world that the LNHO was still a force to reckon with in the field of global health (LONd 1944). The League's supervisory board (formerly its General Assembly) thus decided to reopen the Bureau and approved covering the costs from the budget for the 1946 fiscal year (LONd 1944). In January 1946, the League decided to once again cooperate with the UNRRA to provide infectious disease information services through a regional office, based on the 1944 International Sanitary Convention, just as it had done before the war with the Far-Eastern Bureau (WHOAa 1946). The more the preparations progressed toward reopening the Bureau, however, the less support the League received from associated countries in Asia, including India. This was because international trust in the organization had decreased considerably. At a time when the formal establishment of the UN had been agreed upon, many countries were resistant to resuming the activities of its surviving bureaus, despite the fact that the Far-Eastern Bureau had been so helpful before the war (LONe 1945).

Many actors also recognized that there was no diminishment of the need to resume infectious disease information services in Asia as soon as possible, however. During the postwar period, infections continued to spread throughout the region due to an increase in the volume of traffic and movement of people. This included a rise in cholera in several Asian countries in 1946, including Cambodia, Indonesia, Laos, and China (WHOAb 1947). In January that year, the allied nations under the South East Asia Command thus requested the UNRRA to establish the Epidemiological Intelligence Station in Singapore and resume infectious disease information services in Southeast Asia (LONf 1946). However, the UNRRA refused to take on the requested infectious disease work on a permanent basis, because it was only supposed to be a temporary organization (WHOAa 1946).

Faced by this situation, the Supreme Allied Commander in South East Asia, Lord Louis Mountbatten, established a Port Health Section in Singapore and instructed the high commanders of all forces stationed in Southeast Asia to gather information on infectious diseases in their divisions, in accordance with the 1944 International Sanitary Convention. In May 1946, when the health divisions of the high commands were closed, their infectious disease information services were taken over by the Special Commissioner in Southeast Asia, Lord Killearn, who employed staff from the pre-war Far-Eastern Bureau to continue in their established lines of work. On June 27, 1946, the Bureau thus resumed using radiograms and the postal service to transmit information on infectious diseases for harbors as well as for the health authorities of associated countries (WHOAb 1947).

From Allied Command to the WHO

However, with the Special Commissioner managing the intelligence station, problems began to gradually surface as various countries began to express dissatisfaction with his reluctance to transmit and collect information (WHOAc 1946). Despite his position, Killearn unintentionally revealed that he wanted the UN organization to take over the work as soon as possible, because the capacity and facilities required to do the work permanently were excessive and the management costs were also high (WHOAd 1946).

When the establishment of the WHO was agreed in June 1946, the British representative thus proposed that it should establish an Epidemiological Intelligence Station in Singapore, in line with the pre-war Far-Eastern Bureau. Based on this proposal, in April 1947, the WHO Interim Commission took over the infectious disease information services that had been managed by the Special Commissioner, including the Far-Eastern Bureau's pre-war facilities and the 12 radiogram stations that had been used by its branches (WHOAe 1947). It was simultaneously decided that the Bureau would be renamed the Singapore Epidemiological Intelligence Station (WHOAf 1947) and that it would gather, then transmit, information on infectious diseases in Eastern Asia and manage International Sanitary Conventions in the relevant regions (WHOAb 1947).

The UNRRA, which had managed the International Sanitary Convention in 1944, was dissolved at the end of 1946. The OIHP, which had played a central role in its management before the war, suspended its infectious disease information services after January 1, 1947 (WHOAg 1946). Accordingly, the management of the International Sanitary Conventions was unified under the supervision of the WHO Interim Commission. However, until a new director was appointed for the Commission, Dr. Lucius Nicholls, a leading British bacteriologist and nutritionist, acted as interim director of the Special Commission. On 30 December, the WHO Interim Commission appointed Major PM Kaul from India as director of the Intelligence Station (WHOAb 1947). Many of the key political and diplomatic actors in Eastern Asia thus recognized the usefulness of the infectious disease information services that had been initiated by the League in the region, and they were eventually handed over to new organizations after the war, despite the existence of differing opinions on the way forward.

The Continuation and Expansion of the Bureau's Pre-war Activities

Under the supervision of the Singapore Epidemiological Intelligence Station, the pre-war activities of the Far-Eastern Bureau continued and infectious disease information services improved, becoming more efficient in targeting a wider area. This required better infrastructure to meet demands for information about infectious diseases, which continued to grow due to the rise in air traffic. In addition to the 12 pre-war radiogram stations, new ones were established in Indonesia, Taiwan, and China. Whereas before the war the Bureau had been communicating with 247 ports at most, by March 1948 the Intelligence Station was exchanging information with 283 ports and health authorities (WHOAh 1948). Almost all connected actors were able to obtain data on infectious diseases within 24 hours of it being received by the Station, with ships at sea also being able to obtain it from every port (WHOAb 1947). In this way, all were able to respond to situations as they followed the same lines as the Bureau's pre-war activities, only working more quickly and with more flexibility.

The content of the material that was transmitted also expanded compared to before the war, when communications had been limited to cholera, plague, and smallpox. However, after the war, the Station began to take the initiative regarding information on other infectious diseases, such as Japanese encephalitis and polio. Moreover, after 1948, under the supervision of the Intelligence Station, the statistical analysis services that had been conducted by the Bureau before the war were resumed, highlighting the number of infections and fatalities from illnesses in every Asian country. Aside from this, surveys were periodically carried out on the vaccination and infectious disease regulations of every country as part of the management of the International Sanitary Conventions, which also allowed the Station to play a more effective role in coordinating responses to requests for information on infectious diseases (WHOAh 1948). The Weekly Bulletin that had been published every week by the Bureau also continued to be issued under the supervision of the Station. Although the format was altered in accordance with the WHO periodicals, some of its issues continued to adopt the conventions of its pre-war form. The number of copies printed had exceeded 500 per week by 1948, which rose to 750 by the middle of that year (WHOAi 1948).

As described above, Japan had continued to correspond with the Bureau until shortly before the war. Once the war was over, it resumed this activity with the Station. This was requested so that surrounding countries such as India could obtain information on infectious diseases in Japan. At that time, Japan only permitted passengers to enter the country if they had received vaccinations for cholera within the previous four months or vaccinations for typhus within the previous 60 days, even if they arrived from regions where cholera and typhus had not spread. This was considered to be an overly strict requirement by existing international standards and attracted complaints from the governments of neighboring countries such as India. The Intelligence Station thus requested the Supreme Commander for the Allied Powers (SCAP) in Japan to make changes to the entry regulations, which was immediately accepted (WHOAj 1949). As the increasing volume of traffic and movement fueled fears of large-scale spread of infectious diseases, therefore, the Station continued to play the key role in coordinating actors, preventing disorder, and constructing a foundation for building regional cooperation in the field of health that had previously been conducted by the Bureau.

The Changing Status of the Intelligence Station

When the WHO established regional offices in the immediate postwar years, it planned to open one in Southeast Asia on January 1, 1949, even before it opened one for the Eastern Mediterranean on 1 July. Until then, the Intelligence Station had been the main center for gathering and distributing information on infectious diseases in the Asian region. Although it did not hold the position of the WHO's Asian regional office—which handled a wide range of health issues in Asia—there soon came an opportunity to re-examine its position. In February 1949, WHO Director-General, Brock Chisholm, suggested that it should be maintained even if the countries located in Asia and Africa were divided up between the regional offices. A report on the organization's usefulness, which was planned to submit to the second World Health Assembly (WHA) in June 1949 indicated that the usefulness of the pre-war Bureau and the Intelligence Station had been recognized by WHO executives, including Chisholm, who wanted to eventually raise it to the status of the WHO's Asian regional office (WHOAk 1949).

The third meeting of the WHO Executive Board, which was held from February to March 1949, also included discussions regarding the position of the Intelligence Station. At that time, it was decided that a WHO regional office would be established and have jurisdiction over the West

Pacific, including Australia, China, Indochina, Indonesia, Japan, Korea, New Zealand, the Philippines, and the Malay Archipelago. Director Kaul suggested that the Station should be maintained regardless of the establishment of such a regional office and opposed the establishment of a new one in Asia with the aim of providing infectious disease information services and quarantine services (WHOAl 1949).

However, the Intelligence Station was unable to adequately assume the duties of a WHO Asian regional office. Kaul himself stated that it was extremely small in scope, highlighting the importance of somehow improving it in order to respond to the various issues that it confronted, along handling the massive amount of statistics and information for an area as vast as the West Pacific (WHOAl 1949). Kaul's worries must have eventually resonated within the WHO because it did not decide to promote the Intelligence Station to the position of regional office in the end. Instead, when a working group that was set up to establish a regional office in the West Pacific held a meeting in 1950, it decided to name the organization the WHO Western Pacific Regional Office (WPRO) and temporarily locate its headquarters in Hong Kong. At the first WPRO meeting, held in May 1951, it was decided that the headquarters would be moved to Manila, which took place in August.[2]

Establishment of the International Sanitary Regulations (1951)

The Intelligence Station was not, therefore, promoted to the status of a WHO regional office and its life finally came to an end when the new International Sanitary Regulations were adopted in 1951. However, the activities and experiences of the 26 years through which the Station and the Bureau had worked were reflected strongly in the development of the international health administration that followed. This is largely because the new sanitary regulations had to take account of the conventions that had existed before the war in a somewhat chaotic way, which were not overruled by the new ones, which left the signatory states obliged to observe and implement all of them.

When the WHO Charter came into effect in 1948, it aimed to resolve this issue by giving the WHO the authority to adopt regulations necessary for international communicable disease control. Those that were adopted would automatically be enforced by all member states, unless one indicated that it could not accept them, effectively unifying the management of the postwar international regulatory regime for communicable diseases under the supervision of the WHO. At the fourth World Health Assembly (WHA), held on May 25, 1951, the new International Sanitary Regulations replaced 12 pre-existing international sanitary conventions and related agreements that had existed before the war, in light of consideration of changes in the international environment (WHO 1952: 1–2; Fidler 2005: 333).

Although the establishment of the International Sanitary Regulations marked the end of the Intelligence Station in Singapore, its legacy lived on insofar as the new rules made use of its experiences and those of its predecessor, the Bureau. This can be seen in Article 3, which follows the communication methods practiced by the Bureau and the Station by obliging all nations to announce any outbreak of cholera, typhus, smallpox, or yellow fever to the WHO by telegram within 24 hours. This particular formula was chosen because, when drafting the regulations, the American representative had suggested that the Far-Eastern Bureau's communication methods should be expanded worldwide because they had been extremely helpful (WHO 1952: 43). Moreover, Article 9 adds the obligation of states to inform the WHO quickly, not only if there is an outbreak of specific infectious diseases but also when an outbreak is no longer observed. This, too, was a customary practice under the supervision of the Bureau and the Station, which had maintained its freedom and capacity to quickly communicate when the risk of infection no longer existed (WHO 1952: 304).

The Legacy of the Far-Eastern Bureau

By providing infectious disease information services in Asia, the Far-Eastern Bureau contributed to large-scale improvement of public health in the region after World War I. In addition to this, it expanded the activities of the League of Nations itself into Asia, which had previously been biased toward Europe, and played a useful role in enhancing its overall presence as an international organization. Moreover, the framework of regional health cooperation that it developed helped the LNHO to play a leading role in the building of a global health system.

Although the Bureau was recognized by many actors for its beneficial work at all levels, its activities and functions were taken over after World War II, albeit after many unexpected events, including changing of its name under the supervision of the WHO to the Singapore Epidemiological Intelligence Station. Despite the fact that it did not survive and was never promoted to become the WHO Asian regional office, the enduring significance of its decades of working experience on subsequent global health governance can clearly be seen in the formulation of the International Sanitary Regulations of 1951, which became a cornerstone of infectious disease information services. Renamed the International Health Regulations (IHR) in 1969, they have been further revised in response to changes in the international environment. In 1981, for example, it was decided to remove smallpox from the list of targeted diseases due to its successful eradication. In 2005, the list of targets was expanded to include 'public health emergencies of international concern' in order to respond to newly emerging threats, such as biological terrorism. Moreover, the 2005 revisions also changed the text regarding communications media following the spread of the Internet. This has made it possible for the WHO to take into account reports from sources other than notifications or consultations by member states.

Despite such revisions, however, there have been absolutely no changes since the era of the League of Nations to the method whereby signatories to the regulations must, within a specified period, let the supervisor (the WHO) know about the infectious disease situation in their own countries. The way of disseminating the information that is collected and transmitted by the WHO has thus been customary practice for more than a century. It is in this way that what was originally the comparatively simple work of the League in Asia has come to seamlessly link governance at the regional and international levels and should be remembered for helping to build a strong foundation for global health governance today. In this sense, the activities of the Far-Eastern Bureau and the Intelligence Station in Asia are one part of the valuable legacy that the League bequeathed to the postwar international community.

It has become particularly important to recognize and further explore both the achievements and the failures of this history since the COVID-19 pandemic has rudely reminded humanity of the trans-border nature of diseases and the terrible costs that can be incurred in the absence of effective international cooperation. The need for more cooperation at the regional level is also attracting attention as part of the discussion of the defects in the system of global health governance. As political divides in international society grow in tandem with growing United States-China confrontation and Russia's invasion of Ukraine, the system of cooperation that had been formed under the WHO is in danger of fragmentation and needs an overhaul. There are already signs of revitalization at the regional level and among like-minded countries. Since the COVID-19 pandemic, revisions to the IHR 2005 have been discussed, with the United States proposing amendments in January 2022 that would strengthen the authority of a regional office to evaluate the degree of emergency in any situation by stipulating that, 'A Regional Director may determine that an event constitutes a Public Health Emergency of Regional Concern and provide related guidance to States Parties in the region either before or after notification of an event that may constitute a public health emergency of international concern is made to the Director-General, who shall inform all States Parties' (WHO 2022: 6).

Concrete steps are already being taken to further build health cooperation within each region. The European Union, which had previously been reluctant about integration in the field of health, has moved forward to establish the European Health Union. This will allow member countries to share health or medical information and cooperate in other aspects of their health work, with the aim of strengthening preparedness and effective responses for any future pandemic in the region (European Commission). Similarly, in September 2021, the Latin American countries announced the establishment of a Regional Platform to Advance the Manufacturing of COVID-19 Vaccines and Other Health Technologies in the Americas. Due largely to the failure or late action of the WHO and the COVAX facility, the African Union has also strengthened its regional health cooperation systems and established the African Vaccine Acquisition Trust [AVAT] as part of its COVID-19 Vaccine Development and Access Strategy, with the goal of vaccinating at least 60% of the continent's population. African countries have also moved to strengthen their regional cooperative framework through initiatives such as signing the African Medicines Agency Treaty, which came into effect in 2022.

In Asia, however, cooperation during the COVID-19 pandemic has been fragmentary, especially in comparison with Europe and Africa. Japan, China, and South Korea had already begun to convene an annual health ministers' meeting in 2007. In response to COVID-19, they held a Tripartite Health Ministers' Meeting in 2021, which issued a joint statement regarding strengthening mutual cooperation. However, due to the diplomatic tension that has been growing among these countries over a range of political and security issues, it is unclear to what extent this will be upheld. More positive, perhaps, is that Japan announced a plan to establish the ASEAN Center for Public Health Emergencies and Emerging Diseases (ACPHEED) in 2020, which is expected to strengthen cooperation between Japan and Southeast Asia on health security in what is now called the 'Indo-Pacific' region, along with the United States and India. Just as the Far-Eastern Bureau was needed to connect the multiple cooperative frameworks that emerged between the two world wars, building a new center for pandemic preparedness and response may be necessary for present-day Asia. Looking at the world shortly after the global financial crisis of 2008, at least one leading historian of World War I and the Paris Peace Conference has felt it apt to refer to the quote attributed to Mark Twain that 'History does not repeat itself, but it rhymes' (Macmillan 2013). If this is indeed the case, analysis of the role of the League and its legacy of international health cooperation between the wars shows that it is not a wholly tragic epic.

Notes

1. It should be noted that despite the common practice of using the name 'Spanish Flu,' the pandemic did not actually originate in Spain. Epidemiologists are still unclear about where it first emerged. See the discussion in Spinney (2017).
2. For a view of the present-day activities of the office see: http://www.wpro.who.int/about/in_brief/history/en/ (accessed 11 June 2022).

References

Akami, Tomoko. 2016. A Quest to be Global: The League of Nations Health Organization and Inter-Colonial Regional Governing Agendas of the Far Eastern Association of Tropical Medicine 1910–25. *International History Review* 38 (1): 1–23.

Barry, John M. 2005. *The Great Influenza: The Story of the Deadliest Pandemic in History*. New York: Penguin Books.

Borowy, Iris. 2009. *Coming to Terms with World Health: The League of Nations Health Organisation 1921–1946*. Frankfurt, Berlin, Bruxelles, New York and Oxford: Peter Lang.

European Commission. European Health Union: Protecting the Health of Europeans and collectively responding to cross-border health crises. https://ec.europa.eu/info/strategy/priorities-2019-2024/promoting-our-european-way-life/european-health-union_en.Accessed 30 June 2022.

Fidler, David P. 2005. From International Sanitary Conventions to Global Health Security: The New International Health Regulations. *Chinese Journal of International Law* 4 (2): 325–392.

Goto-Shibata, Harumi. 2016. *Kokusaishugi to no Kokutou: Nihon, Kokusai Renmei, Igirisu Teikoku* (Grappling with Internationalism: Japan, the League of Nations, and the British Empire). Tokyo: Chūō Kōron Shinsha.

LONa. 1945. Memorandum by Gautier, 7 November. R6199/8D/43351-341.

LONb. 1944. Stowman to Gautier, 29 November. R6151/8A/42474-42474.

LONc. 1946. Biraud to Sawyer, 5 January. R6199/8D/43351/341.

LONd. 1944. Memorandum by Gautier, 15 August. R6150/8A/42169-41755.

LONe. 1945. Gautier to Boudreau, 30 November. R6150/8A/41755-41755.

LONf. 1946. Clarke to Lehman, 21 January. R6199/8D/43351-341.

Macmillan, Margaret. 2013. *The Rhyme of History: Lessons of the Great War*. The Brookings Institution. http://csweb.brookings.edu/content/research/essays/2013/rhyme-of-history.html. Accessed 20 June 2022.

Sealey, Anne. 2011. Globalizing the 1926 International Sanitary Convention. *Journal of Global History* 6 (3): 431–455. https://doi.org/10.1017/S1740022811000404.

Spinney, Laura. 2017. *Pale Rider: The Spanish Flu of 1918 and How It Changed the World*. London: Vintage.

WHO. 1952. International Sanitary Regulations: Proceedings of the special committee and of the 4th World Health Assembly on WHO Regulations No. 2. Geneva: 1–2.

WHO. 2022. US Proposal for Amendments to the International Health Regulations. https://healthpolicy-watch.news/wp-content/uploads/2022/02/C.L.2.2022-IHR-amendments-English.pdf. Accessed 11 June 2022.

WHOAa. 1946. Memorandum by Biraud, 29 January. 452-6-1.

WHOAb. 1947. Epidemiological Intelligence Station, Annual Report for the year 1947. 452-6-13.

WHOAc. 1946. Statement by Dr. Mani at the 1st meeting of WHO, 24 July. 452-6-1.

WHOAd. 1946. Officer at Health Intelligence Section, H.M. Special Commissioner's Office, South East Asia, to Gautier. 30 October. 452-6-1.

WHOAe. 1947. UN Press Release No.66, 16 April. 2-2-14.

WHOAf. 1947. Chisholm to Nicholls, 26 April. 452-6-2.

WHOAg. 1946. Biraud to Health Intelligence Section, H.B.M. Special Commissioner for South East Asia, 10 December. 452-6-1.

WHOAh. 1948. Report for the quarter ending 31 December 1948. 452-6-13.

WHOAi. 1948. Kaul to Biraud, 7 October. 452-6-13.

WHOAj. 1949. Report of the Singapore Epidemiological Intelligence Station for the month of July 1949. 452-6-13.

WHOAk. 1949. Siegel to Biraud, 4 February. 452-6-14.

WHOAl. 1949. Biraud to Kaul, 11 March. 452-6-3.

Yasuda, Kayo. 2014. *Kokusai Seiji no Naka no Koksai Hoken Jigyou: Kokusai Renmei Hoken Kikan kara Sekai Hoken Kikan, Yunisefu E* (International Health Work in International Politics: From the League of Nations Health Organization to the WHO and UNICEF). Tokyo: Minerva Shobo.

Japanese International Lawyers and the Codification of International Law in the League of Nations

Rikiya Takahashi

Introduction

Recent studies of international history have done much to cast light on the various activities of the League of Nations in all their complexity, debunking the traditional, simplistic view that the organization was a complete failure. What has yet to be adequately investigated, however, is the League's project for advancing the rule of law in the international arena through codifying international law.[1] This chapter elucidates this topic by exploring Japan's active involvement in the codification efforts of the League during the 1920s, as evidenced by the draft code of international law submitted to the organization by the Japanese Society of International Law (JSIL).

The codification of international law is generally defined as the process of reducing customary international law, the bulk of which has historically been unwritten, to a written code (Jennings and Watts 1992: 97). International society first embarked in earnest on this task at The Hague

R. Takahashi (✉)
Yokohama City University, Yokohama, Japan

C. R. Hughes and H. Shinohara (eds.), *East Asians in the League of Nations*, New Directions in East Asian History,
https://doi.org/10.1007/978-981-19-7067-2_5

peace conferences of 1899 and 1907. Particularly dramatic progress was made after the formation of the League, as there was a proliferation of the number of multilateral conventions that were concluded, compared to the pre-World War I years (Rosenne 1992: 635). Such was the strength of this international trend of codification in the early years that it was described as the 'order of the day' (Scott 1931: 10).

The codification project is particularly significant for achieving a more complete understanding of Japan's relationship with the League, which has been described in studies as one of reluctance to engage in the development of international law. This is because previous work has tended to focus on its attitude toward the regulation or outlawry of war, such as the 1924 Geneva Protocol and the 1928 Paris Peace Pact (Ikō 2002; Shinohara 2012). This overlooks the country's broader role in the advancement of international law as a whole, including the codification of the laws of peace.

As the League began preparation for the project of codification in 1925, Japanese international lawyers swiftly launched a scheme for their cooperation. In 1926, the JSIL identified nine topics which might reasonably be considered as and submitted a draft convention on each. This contribution was widely acclaimed by the international community. In 1928, the Assembly of the League even passed a resolution which singled out Japan for gratitude due to the valuable assistance provided by the JSIL. This project, carried out with the de facto support of the Ministry of Foreign Affairs, ended up forming a cornerstone of Japan's relationship with the League.

This chapter explains the process of Japan's contribution to the project by first providing a brief background survey of how the codification of international law came to be on the League of Nations' agenda. It then discusses in detail the draft code submitted by the JSIL. Lastly, it provides some tentative speculation on why certain individuals at the JSIL and the foreign ministry became such zealous proponents of codification.

Background to the League's Efforts to Codify International Law

The Covenant and International Law

Before understanding how the codification of international law came to be undertaken by the League, it is important to recognize that the framers of the Covenant at the Paris Peace Conference expected little of international law when designing the postwar international order. United States President Woodrow Wilson, the moving spirit of the new organization, was even downright hostile to it, as we shall see. This is not surprising given the way that international law had been ruthlessly trampled underfoot on the battlefields of World War I, and that the modest achievements of The Hague peace conferences were nowhere to be seen. The framers were understandably wary of seeking hope once more in the power of such a discredited instrument of international relations.

Wilson's almost obsessive 'anti-legal prejudice' is widely known among historians (Wertheim 2011: 829–830). In fact, his antipathy was so deep-seated that he allowed the State Department's lawyers no part in drafting the League Covenant (Patterson 1976: 293–294). He also opposed the jurists' cherished dream of a world court. The Covenant in its final form, though it retained provisions on an international court and the judicial settlement of disputes, thus gave short shrift to international law. The preamble merely contained an abstract statement committing the contracting parties to 'the firm establishment of the understandings of international law as the actual rule of conduct among Governments'; the articles themselves made no mention of how to work toward that goal, let alone any specific procedures for achieving it.

It was only with the establishment of the Permanent Court of International Justice (PCIJ) that the League turned to the task of codifying international law. This work began in February 1920, when the Council of the League set up the Advisory Committee of Jurists made up of legal experts from various countries including all the great powers to draft its statute. From Japan, Mineichirō Adachi, a diplomat and experienced international lawyer, was appointed. The committee drew up a draft statute over the course of about a month, beginning in June 1920, which it then submitted to the League with three resolutions. The first of these recommended that the League regularly convene a conference to carry on the work of the two Hague peace conferences by adopting general treaties (LNACJ 1920: 747–749).

This resolution was spearheaded by the American member of the committee, Elihu Root, who saw the establishment of a permanent international court and the codification of international as the twin pillars of the international legal order. As Root himself later wrote, if a system of dispute resolution revolving around an international court was to prevail, it was necessary to clarify what law actually prescribes. Were the PCIJ to be established while international law still consisted in the main of customary law with its ill-defined norms, governments would refuse to sign up to its statute due to fear of being the target of arbitrary decisions. Root thus believed that the highest priority was to push ahead with codifying international law and define its provisions, making judicial decisions more predictable for national governments (Root 1925).

The Debate in the Assembly

When the codification of international law came up for discussion at the historic first Assembly of the League, on November 15, 1920, it immediately encountered a serious obstacle in the form of Britain's adamant opposition. The resolution of the Advisory Committee of Jurists that recommended codification was referred to the Third Committee, which was responsible for the establishment of the PCIJ, on the grounds that it was simply an adjunct to the draft PCIJ statute. The rapporteur and the Belgian member of the committee, Henri La Fontaine, continued to promote the project by proposing that steps be taken to convoke an international codification conference in accordance with the Advisory Committee's resolution, which secured the support of smaller states. Britain and the self-governing dominions of Canada and New Zealand, however, dissented mainly on the grounds that international law was not amenable to codification, and that it was premature for the League to undertake such a task. In the end, the Portuguese representative and acting chair, Affonso Costa, virtually rammed through the report in the face of its opponents. This was at the price of a considerable watering down of the proposal, so that it merely 'invite[d] the Council…to consider what would be the best methods of co-operative work to adopt for the more precise definition and more complete co-ordination of the rules of international law which are to be applied in the mutual relations of States' (LND 1920b Reel 38: 326–328, 588–589). Given such extremely circumspect language, even holding the codification conference was not taken as a given.

When the Third Committee's report was presented to the Plenary of the Assembly, even this modest proposal met with opposition. Lord Robert Cecil, attending as the South African delegate—and speaking, presumably, for the British Empire—expressed opposition on the grounds that international relations had undergone such significant changes since World War I that it would be perilous to embark on codification while the situation was still so unsettled. The attempts of the president of the Assembly to win him over fell on deaf ears. The resolution accordingly failed to pass and had to be abandoned (LND 1920a Reel 37: 744–747). Subsequently, as the League's activities gradually got off the ground, the issue of codification remained in limbo.

Circumstances changed, however, in 1924, when, at the fifth Assembly, Sweden proposed that the issue of codification be taken up again. Following further discussions in a subcommittee, the First Committee passed a draft resolution by the Assembly requesting that the Council convene a committee of jurists to prepare a list of the subjects of international law. These were to be identified as ripe for regulation by international agreement and having the support of the opinions of the member states (OJ 1924a: 25–28). After some minor changes in wording, the resolution was adopted by the Assembly with no significant opposition (OJ 1924b: 121–125). On December 11, the Council established the Committee of Experts for the Progressive Codification of International Law (CPDI), made up of seventeen jurists representing 'the main forms of civilization and the principal legal systems of the world' (two of whom were to be appointed later) (LN Doc. C.812.(1).1924.V). Michikazu Matsuda, the director of the Japanese mission to the League of Nations in Paris, was accordingly chosen as a member.

Preparations for a Codification Conference

The CPDI convened four times in Geneva between 1925 and 1928. At its second session, it decided to send out questionnaires seeking each government's views on seven subjects, all of which belong to the field of the laws of peace: (1) nationality, (2) territorial waters, (3) diplomatic privileges and immunities, (4) responsibility of states in respect of injury caused in their territory to the person or property of foreigners, (5) procedure of international conferences and procedure for the conclusion and drafting of treaties, (6) piracy, and (7) exploitation of the products of the sea (LN Doc. C.L.25.1926.V). Then, at its third session, after examining replies to questionnaires it had sent out, it finally adopted the seven subjects as lending themselves to codification (LN Doc. C.196.M.70.1927.V; C.197.M.71.1927.V).

In June 1927, upon receiving the CPDI's report, the Council decided to recommend three of the seven subjects to the Assembly for codification: (1), (2), and (4) (LN Doc. A.18.1927.V). In September, the Assembly formally adopted these three subjects and decided to hold an international codification conference in The Hague (LN Doc. A.133.1927.V). The League of Nations Codification Conference in The Hague (referred to below as 'the Hague Conference') began in March 1930 and lasted a month. It was attended by forty-seven countries, including the United States, a non-member of the League. The first codification conference under League auspices was thus finally convened almost a decade after the 1920 submission of the recommendation of the Advisory Committee of Jurists to commence the work.

The Codification Project and Japan

This section examines Japan's role in the codification project, as evidenced by the international law code drafted by the JSIL. It should first be noted that this was not a priority for the Japanese government's dealings with the League. When a preparatory committee was convened to discuss the stance to be adopted by the Japanese delegation to the first League Assembly, the codification issue was not even mentioned. The government was primarily interested in how to prevent the grant of compulsory jurisdiction to the PCIJ (DAMOFAJ 1920).

Despite this low priority, Japan was favorably disposed toward codification. Its cooperative attitude is evident in the actions of senior government officials. Adachi, Japan's representative during the first Assembly, for example, displayed considerable adroitness when he attended the sessions of the Third Committee. In the absence of explicit instructions from Tokyo, he tacitly supported the advocates of codification from the sidelines. When New Zealand tried to block the proposal from La Fontaine, ostensibly because of concerns about the additional financial burden involved, Adachi countered that such fears were groundless (LND 1920b: 327). The Japanese government's endorsement of the codification project is most apparent, however, in the JSIL's formulation of an international law code and the foreign ministry's official blessing for its experts to become an active voice in the international community.

How the JSIL Came to Submit a Draft Code

The first stage in the codification process was, as we have seen, the CPDI's selection of subjects to codify. During the selection process, the CPDI sought the views of several renowned academic organizations, including the Institut de Droit International, the International Law Association (ILA), and the American Society of International Law, on which subjects were amenable to codification. CPDI chairman Hjalmar Hammarskjöld was instrumental in deciding which academic organizations to turn to, and the choice fell mainly on the organizations that the Advisory Committee of Jurists, mentioned above, had invited to assist in the task of codification (LON 1925).

Although Japan was not consulted, it was not completely deprived of a voice. The ILA, one of the bodies solicited by the CPDI, was an international academic association based in London with branches in other countries, including one in Tokyo. Before replying to the CPDI, ILA headquarters solicited the views of its branches. This request reached the Japanese branch at the end of March 1925 (DAMOFAJ 1925a). At around the same time, CPDI member Matsuda, having attended its first session, suggested that the JSIL take this opportunity to study the question of codifying international law and submit an opinion (TCB 1926: 1).

The opportunity was seized by Tadao Yamakawa, who was then on the JSIL board and had long served as the Navy Ministry's legal adviser. The JSIL and the Japanese branch of the ILA, though formally separate organizations, were in effect virtually identical, and Yamakawa also served on the board of the latter. On being contacted by ILA headquarters, Yamakawa, 'hoping that the members of our Society will join this difficult undertaking', consulted with Saburō Yamada and Sakutarō Tachi, both of whom had been key figures at the JSIL in its early years (Yamada 1957: 59). It was subsequently decided that the JSIL should lend a hand to the League's codification program, and a study group consisting of fifteen experts was set up (TCB 1926: 99–100).

The study group, which met a total of forty-one times over a period of roughly a year beginning in June, finished drafting a code on nine subjects, which included those on the agenda of the Hague Conference, namely nationality, territorial waters, and the responsibilities of states. The JSIL's draft code was sent to ILA headquarters in June 1926 (DAMOFAJ 1926a).

The Significance of the Japanese Draft Code

The code submitted by the JSIL exceeded the expectations of the League and by extension of the international community, in two regards. First, the League had never expected to receive any input from a Japanese academic organization. The JSIL ensured it would be noticed, however, by sending the document not only to ILA headquarters but also directly to Hammarskjöld via CPDI member Matsuda (DAMOFAJ 1926b). Although the JSIL and the Japanese branch of the ILA were effectively one and the same, officially it was the latter from which the CPDI had sought assistance. If a draft code was to be submitted to the League, the natural procedure to follow would have been to send it from the Japanese branch of the ILA to ILA headquarters and then from the ILA to the CPDI.

But the JSIL was determined to make the draft code an explicit and exclusive contribution from Japan. When Yamakawa, Yamada, Tachi, and their colleagues met on May 1, 1925, to discuss how to respond to ILA headquarters' request for views, they thus promptly decided to send a draft code 'in the name of the JSIL directly to the League secretariat in Geneva, apart from the reply to the headquarters of the ILA', despite the fact that 'the JSIL has not been consulted in any way by the League of Nations' (DAMOFAJ 1925b). This was before it had even been decided to establish the study group tasked with drawing up a code, let alone what that code was to contain. It was of paramount importance for the Japanese jurists to present the global community with a draft code prepared by a Japanese international law society, as opposed to a mere branch of the ILA.

In addition to this, even if the JSIL was going to lend a hand to the CPDI, there had been no request for the latter to draft a code. Its main task was supposed to be to identify subjects to codify in the form of international conventions, not to draft the actual conventions. Yet the JSIL, not content simply to prepare a list of subjects, assumed the task of drafting an entire code in the form of a set of international conventions on each subject. The Secretariat of the League, which was assisting the CPDI with its work, was left quite bewildered.

When, in August 1926, Matsuda presented the draft code to Hugh McKinnon Wood of the Secretariat's Legal Section and asked him to pass it on to Hammarskjöld, he was at a loss for an answer. The draft code could only serve a purpose at the international codification conference that was to be convened after the subjects to be codified had been determined by the CPDI. This meant the document was worse than useless to the CPDI at that point in time. On the other hand, refusing to accept it was not really an option because it would put Matsuda, who was in effect acting on the instructions of his government, in an awkward position. After much vacillation, McKinnon Wood, on Hammarskjöld's advice, made the best of the situation by circulating the JSIL code within the CPDI for reference only (LON 1926).

It is true that the almost excessive zeal of the Japanese for codifying international law was not confined to a single academic organization but shared by the government itself to no small degree. Indeed, the draft code was prepared with considerable involvement from the Ministry of Foreign Affairs. Yamakawa, who led the JSIL's effort to formulate the draft code, was the Director-General of the Treaties and Conventions Bureau of the Ministry at the time. He submitted the draft text to the study group to ensure that it reflected the Ministry's views. The study group held its meetings in Yamakawa's office in the Ministry, and three junior diplomats were assigned to it as secretaries (TCB 1926: 3). Once the JSIL had completed the draft code, moreover, the Ministry actively promoted it, instructing diplomatic missions abroad to distribute it to prominent individuals overseas (DAMOFAJ 1926c). Although it was ostensibly nothing but an unofficial recommendation by an academic body, its compilation by the JSIL and submission to the CPDI means it can be regarded as a semi-official project of the Japanese government.

The Reaction of the International Community

The submission of the draft code to the League 'became the talk of the international law community abroad', wrote Yamakawa when recounting this period in his memoirs (Yamakawa 1962: 114). This is not an exaggeration. In 1928, the JSIL received the greatest boost to its international reputation when a resolution by the Assembly of the League included a statement of appreciation for its 'valuable assistance, for the study of the questions to be dealt with by the [Hague] Conference, which is already being afforded...by the study groups which have been formed, more particularly in the United States of America and in Japan' (OJ 1928: 9).

The members of the JSIL were naturally delighted that Japan's contribution had been recognized by the Assembly. On receiving a copy of the Assembly's resolution from the League Secretariat, the JSIL decided to 'repay the favor' by publishing a piece on the League's codification project, written by Yamada, in its journal, Kokusaihō gaikō zasshi [Journal of International Law and Diplomacy] (Yamada 1929a; 1929b: 92–93).

Earlier, in July 1926, before the Assembly's resolution, Sanford D. Cole of the ILA had sent a letter to Yamakawa concerning the following month's ILA conference in Vienna. This stated that although the committee report had already been printed for the conference, in view of the importance of the JSIL's draft code, extra copies had been produced and distributed to the membership with the code appended, prior to the event (DAMOFAJ 1926d). Cole also brought up the JSIL's draft code in his report to the conference, explaining that a Japanese academic association had spent an entire year laboring over it (ILA 1927: 397). In addition, the JSIL donated a copy of the draft code at the request of the Peace Palace Library in The Hague. It also decided to donate a copy of each issue of Kokusaihō gaikō zasshi to the library, starting with the first issue that had been published in 1927 (DAMOFAJ 1927).

The JSIL's activities thus aroused interest in many quarters. In May 1929, evidently encouraged by this favorable reaction abroad, the JSIL re-constituted its codification study group with a few changes in membership. This met more than ten times, and by mid-January 1930 had finished working on a draft code concerning six subjects that were not ultimately included on the agenda of The Hague Conference, including piracy, consular status, and judicial cooperation in criminal matters (JSIL 1930: 1–12).

A 'National' Code—Yet Not Entirely So

What then did the JSIL's draft code, which attracted such interest abroad, actually contain? Owing to limitations of space, rather than presenting a detailed discussion of what the code said, it is more pertinent to stress that it has a very national character, insofar as it expresses a Japanese viewpoint, yet it does not represent Japan's formal government policy. Given that the project was conducted with the involvement of the foreign ministry and the proclivities of international law experts in those days (Akashi 2013: 122–143), it had to reflect Japan's national interests to some degree; yet it was not seriously conceived as a means of achieving any specific policy objectives.

This point is well illustrated by the JSIL's convention on 'Principles concerning the Acquisition and Loss of Nationality' in its draft code. Article 6 of this reads, 'A State shall not make any discrimination between individuals on the ground of race, nationality or religion, in the matter of naturalization or other mode of the acquisition of nationality'. This shows the clear influence of the issue of racial equality that had been a major concern of the Japanese since the Paris Peace Conference. Coincidentally, this question had flared up again in Japan in 1924, when the United States prohibited any 'alien ineligible to citizenship' from entering the country under Section 13c of its amended Immigration Act. Immigration from Japan into the United States had effectively been banned.

Yamada, the author of the original version of the draft convention, had been outraged at the 'Hainichi Imin Hō' [Japanese Exclusion Act], as the legislation was known, and vociferously protested to the United States (Hatano and Terasawa 1983: 11). Describing the intent of Article 6, he accepted that governments should in principle be free to set their own terms of naturalization, this being one aspect of their exercise of sovereignty. However, he added that prohibiting discrimination on the grounds of race or nationality in the matter of naturalization 'must be characterised as an inherently justified restriction in maintaining world peace'. He thus adumbrated his concern about the strained state of Japan-US relations without mentioning the US by name (Yamada 1926: 33–34).

The Japanese government, however, had little appetite for asserting demands for racial equality on the international stage. As has been pointed out elsewhere, since the failure of its proposal for racial equality at the Paris Peace Conference, it had decided to avoid broaching the subject of racial equality for the time being, on the grounds that it would impede the resolution of other important issues with Britain, the United States, and the other Western powers (Banjō 2017: 62–64). Indeed, the draft version of the instructions on the nationality question that was to be given to the Japanese delegation to the Hague Conference contained a direction—probably at the initiative of Yamada, who appeared to be involved in drawing up those instructions—to propose a ban on discrimination based on race in the matter of acquisition or loss of nationality (MOFAJ 1992: 617–618). But Harukazu Nagaoka, the Japanese plenipotentiary to the Conference, urged Tokyo to rethink that idea for pragmatic reasons: not only did the proposal have no chance of passing, he wrote in a memorandum, but 'if it is submitted and ignominiously defeated, other issues of a similar nature are liable to be adversely affected as well' (MOFAJ 1992:

628). As a result, the direction to propose a ban on racial discrimination was deleted from the delegation's instructions.

Although the convention drafted by Yamada contained some elements with specific relevance to Japan, therefore, its potential impact on other areas of policy meant that it could not be adopted as the official government position. The JSIL itself appears to have recognized that the provisions in the code that it had drafted itself were only a partial statement of what was ideal for its own country (TCB. 1926: 292–295).

The Idea of Codification Behind the Draft Code

The provisions in the JSIL's draft code were, therefore, not necessarily something that the Japanese government could espouse as its formal policy at an international conference. Yet it was more than just a collection of the pet ideas of a body with no official status. If it was the effective outcome of a government project that involved the foreign ministry, its progress depended on the ambitions of certain individuals both there and in the JSIL. Yamakawa, Yamada, Tachi, and the other international lawyers involved in drafting the code have little to say about why they were so enthusiastic, and no documentary evidence giving a clear answer has been found. A passage in a December 1924 newspaper article about the CPDI may, however, provide a clue when it notes that Viscount Kikujirō Ishii, the Japanese representative on the League Council, 'is interested' in the codification project. It then goes on to explain:

> Viscount Ishii is devoting himself to the codification of international law because, he argues, while Article 15, Paragraph 8, of the League of Nations Covenant, a provision unfavorable to Japan, provides matters which by international law are solely within the domestic jurisdiction of a country and so on, 'international law' is still a highly amorphous body, possessing no definite form, and no one knows where the borderline between domestic and international law lies; it is therefore necessary to make international law more complete and to systematise it; hence Japan should seek to mitigate the disadvantages of the provision, through the development of international law. (OAS 1924: 1)

Although the grammatical subject is 'Ishii', this may be taken to mean that it was the government of Japan, rather than him personally, that was interested in codification. That Ishii himself, despite uncertainty about what international law said, was skeptical about the need for codification was made clear when he once remarked, 'We have not been so inconvenienced, have we?' (Ishii 1930: 277).

If this article is overall an accurate description of what Yamakawa and the other individuals at the JSIL and the foreign ministry intended, the following seems to be clear. What the Japanese were concerned about was the clarification of the scope of Paragraph 8 of Article 15 of the Covenant. This states that if one of the parties to a dispute claimed that that dispute arose 'out of a matter which by international law is solely within the domestic jurisdiction of that party', and the League Council found that to be the case, the Council would not intervene. Yamakawa and his colleagues lavished so much effort on the codification project because they reckoned that defining exactly what constituted matters that could be considered to be solely within the domestic jurisdiction of a state would make it possible to limit the scope for arbitrary assertions by any party to be used by the Council to intervene in its internal affairs.

Such thinking resembles the reasoning that led Root to see an increased resort to the international court and the codification of international law as two sides of the same coin, as described above. Although the Japanese jurists were discussing the Council and Root was more focused on the international court, both were motivated by the belief that promoting the peaceful resolution of disputes required enhancing the predictability of decisions made by those institutions, which in turn meant defining the rules of international law. It is true that the two sides disagreed during the deliberations of the Advisory Committee of Jurists, insofar as Root was in favor of granting the court compulsory jurisdiction while Adachi, on behalf of Japan, was opposed to this. However, Japan's position on compulsory jurisdiction softened until the real gap between the two sides appears to have become negligible (Yanagihara 2014).

It is fair to say that the Japanese international lawyers by and large recognized the need for codification in accordance with Root's reasoning. Tachi, for instance, had argued as far back as 1914 that 'the future development of international legislation, it must be said, is closely related to the project of gradual codification in international fora' (Tachi 1914: 834–837). This was because he realized that if an international court like the PCIJ was ever to come into being, a code with clearly defined provisions would plainly be of greater use than customary international law for the purposes of interpretation and application. This emphasis on the importance of codification as a means of developing international law continues to be evident in the papers that Tachi occasionally published on the topic in later years (Tachi 1922, 1930, 1931).

It may seem only natural that scholars of international law would, by the nature of their profession, see codification as desirable. To understand the significance of the work of the Japanese advocates, it is thus important to stress that objections to the idea were raised by academics outside Japan. Even in the American legal community, which, like its Japanese counterpart, enthusiastically supported codification, there was a vigorous debate between proponents and skeptics. A minority argued that codification would impede the natural evolution of customary international law (Hale 1930), or that it was enough to wait for a body of court precedents to build up at the international or domestic level (Reeves 1921). In Britain, too, such prominent intellectuals of the day as Philip J. Noel-Baker and James Leslie Brierly did not see codification favorably (Baker 1924; Brierly 1931).

In Japanese academic circles, by contrast, no doubts were expressed about the advisability of codification. Despite the views expressed by individuals such as Ishii, cited above, there is no evidence that the question ever provoked scholarly debate. Advocates of the idea at the JSIL and the foreign ministry were united in this conviction and did not easily waver. In the absence of closer and precise analysis based on the discovery of additional evidence, it may be concluded that this belief was what spurred Yamakawa and his colleagues to draw up their distinctly Japanese version of the code and submit it to the League.

The Significance of Sub-state Actors

It has been frequently observed that the pre-war Japanese academic discourse on international law is tinged with nationalism (Ōnuma 1986; Zachmann 2010). This is clearly the case for scholars like Tachi and Yamada, who were close to the government. However, the effort made by Japanese lawyers to promote the codification of international law provides new insights into the complex thinking that arose between nationalism and the commitment to some kind of internationalism.

When The Hague Conference was held in 1930, it undoubtedly failed to live up to the expectations of the Japanese advocates. It adopted only one convention and agreed on just three protocols, all on the single issue of nationality. Yet they continued to press their case in the years that followed. While the JSIL remained sanguine about future prospects, Tachi learned from the setbacks of the Conference that it was best to advocate a fresh attempt by focusing on the codification of the laws of war, rather than peace. Noting that pessimists about the codification project at the League believed that the next conference should be put off for a decade, he argued that such a change of focus was an expedient measure that was necessary to maintain sufficient interest and enthusiasm to keep the project alive (Tachi 1931: 6–7). Kazuo Matsubara, who was involved in drawing up the JSIL code with Tachi, also made an impassioned call for a more incremental approach, stating:

> [The codification project] is not the kind of thing that should be cut short after being attempted just this once...though whether it will take fifty years for the project to succeed or longer cannot be foreseen. Indeed, this type of project should be permanent and ongoing; it should not be cut short after fifty years either...Call it 'gradual codification.' At any rate, the project must move ahead, even by degrees. (Matsubara 1931: 10–11)

Leaving aside the question of whether such as stance can reasonably be described as 'legal internationalism', it seems safe to say that the lawyers who bent their efforts to presenting their own draft code of international law to the League did share a belief in preserving the international order through the development of international law.[2] Their enthusiasm suggests that advocates of codification, such as Tachi, Matsubara, Yamakawa, and others at the JSIL and the foreign ministry, assumed that if international relations were to be regulated by the systematization of international law, then Japan itself should be subjected to this.

It is fair to say that the drafting of the JSIL code was itself motivated by a kind of nationalism, insofar as its advocates wanted to make a distinctly 'Japanese' contribution to the work of the League. Yet the project to put codification into practice also reveals how this could be conditioned by attempts to reconcile such pride with the belief that law should be an instrument for regulating international relations. Going beyond the state as actor to look at the work of individuals and organizations below the state is thus a good way to gain deeper insights into the true complexity of the nexus between international and domestic politics in the inter-war period.

Notes

1. Aside from a 1972 general historical survey on the codification project by the renowned Israeli jurist, Shabtai Rosenne, which has not been followed up by further studies (Rosenne 1972).
2. The term 'legal internationalism' is used by Akira Iriye to stress 'legal agreements and institutions for the sustenance of an international community' (Iriye 1997: 25).

References

Akashi, Kinji. 2013. Sakutaro Tachi: A Blend of Scholarship and Practitionership, and Its Fate in Japan. *Japanese Yearbook of International Law* 56: 122–143.

Baker, P.J. 1924. The Codification of International Law. *British Yearbook of International Law* 5: 38–65.

Banjō, Kenji. 2017. Takokukan kankei no naka no imin mondai to nihon gaikō: Gaikokujin rōdōsha taigū mondai heno kanyo to 'Adachi shūsei' [Japanese Diplomacy and the Multilateral Discussions on Immigration Problems: Japanese Commitment to Equal Treatment of Foreigners and Japanese Amendment of Geneva Protocol in 1924]. *Amerika Taiheiyō Kenkyū* 17: 59–75.

Brierly, J.L. 1931. The Future of Codification. *British Yearbook of International Law* 12: 1–12.

DAMOFAJ. 1920. Kokusai renmei sōkai junbi kyougi iinkai gijiroku [Minutes of the Consultative Committee for the Preparation of the Assembly of the League of Nations]. August 2–September 17. 2.4.2.0.20-1-1.

DAMOFAJ. 1925a. Letter from the Secretary of the Codification Committee of the ILA to the Director of the Japanese Branch of the ILA, March 26. B.10.2.0.8, Vol. 1.

DAMOFAJ. 1925b. Memorandum, May 1. Kokusai renmei no kokusai hōten hensan jigyō ni kansuru eikoku kokusaihō kyōkai honbu yorino shōkai no ken ni taisuru uchiawasekai kettei jikō gairyaku [Summary of the Decisions in the Meeting on the Inquiry from the ILA Headquarters in Britain]. B.10.2.0.8, Vol. 1.

DAMOFAJ. 1926a. Letter from the Director of the Japanese Branch of the ILA to the Secretary of the Codification Committee of the ILA, June 7. B.10.2.0.8, Vol. 1.

DAMOFAJ. 1926b. Official correspondence from Tokyo to The Hague. June 10. No. 16. Nihon kokusaihō gakkai yori teishutsu no kokusai hōten-an sōfu no ken [On Dispatch of the Draft Code Submitted by JSIL]. B.10.2.0.8, Vol. 1.

DAMOFAJ. 1926c. Unofficial correspondence from the Director-General of the Treaties and Conventions Bureau to the Heads of Overseas Diplomatic Establishments, June 12. Kokusaihō gakkai oyobi kokusaihō kyōkai nihon shibu kokusai hōten-an sōfu no ken [On Dispatch of the Draft Code Presented by JSIL and the Japanese Branch of the ILA]. B.10.2.0.8, Vol. 1.

DAMOFAJ. 1926d. Letter from the Honorary Secretary of the Codification Committee of the ILA to the Director of the Japanese Branch of the ILA. July 20. B.9.2.0.2-4, Vol. 2.

DAMOFAJ. 1927. Official correspondence from Tokyo to The Hague. No. 5, February 28. Nihon kokusaihō gakkai no shuppan-butsu kizō kata ni kansuru ken [On the Gift Periodical from JSIL]. B.10.2.0.8, Vol. 2.

Hale, Richard W. 1930. Territorial Waters as a Test of Codification. *American Journal of International Law* 24 (1): 65–68.

Hatano, Ribō and Terasawa, Hajime. 1983. Yokota Kisaburō sensei ni kiku (daiikkai) [An Interview with Professor Yokota Kisaburō (First session)]. *Hōgaku kyōshitsu* 28: 6–17.

Ikō, Toshiya. 2002. *Kindai nihon to sensō ihōka taisei: Daiichiji sekai taisen kara nitchū sensō he* [Modern Japan and Outlawry of War: From the First World War to the Sino-Japanese War]. Tokyo: Yoshikawa kōbunkan.

ILA. 1927. *Report of the Codification Committee. Report of the Thirty-Fourth Conference Held at the Imperial Palace and at the Chamber of Commerce, Vienna*, August 5th to August 11th, 1926. London: Sweet & Maxwell, Ltd.

Iriye, Akira. 1997. *Cultural Internationalism and World Order*. Baltimore and London: Johns Hopkins University Press.

Ishii, Kikujirō. 1930. *Gaikō yoroku* [Diplomatic Commentaries]. Tokyo: Iwanami shoten.

Jennings, Robert and Watts, Arthur. 1992. *Oppenheim's International Law*, 9th edition, vol. 1. Burnt Mill: Longman.

JSIL. 1930. Furoku: Nihon kokusaihō gakkai ketsugi kokusai hōten-an (dai-ni) [Appendix: The Second Draft Code Adopted by the Resolution of the JSIL]. *Kokusaihō gaikō zasshi* 29 (3): 1–12.

LON. 1925. Letter from J. A. van Hamel to George W. Wickersham. February 6. Box R1275, 19/42143/10950.

LON. 1926. Letter from Hugh McKinnon Wood to Hjalmar Hammarskjöld. August 16. Box R1275, 19/42821/10950.

LNACJ. 1920. Procès-verbaux of the Proceedings of the Committee, June 16th-July 24th, 1920: with Annexes. The Hague: Van Langenhuysen Brothers.

LND. 1920a. Reel 37. The Records of the First Assembly. League of Nations Documents, 1919–1946 (microform). Research Publications, 1973–1975. Vol. 3. Records of the Assembly.

LND. 1920b. Reel 38. Minutes of the Third Committee. League of Nations Documents, 1919–1946 (microform). Research Publications, 1973–1975. Vol. 3. Records of the Assembly.

Matsubara, Kazuo. 1931. Kokusai hōten hensan kaigi wo kaerimite [The Hague Codification Conference]. *Kokusai chishiki* 11 (3): 7–15.

MOFAJ. 1992: *Gaimu-shō, ed. Nihon Gaikō Bunsho* (Shōwa-ki dai-ni-bu dai-ni-kan [Documents on Japanese Foreign Policy (Shōwa Era, Series I, Part 2, Vol. 2)]. Tokyo: Gaimu-shō.

OAS. 1924. Kokusai hōten hensan [The Codification of International Law]. December 10: 1.

OJ. 1924a. Minutes of the First Committee, Records of the Fifth Assembly 24.

OJ. 1924b. Text of the Debates, Records of the Fifth Assembly 23.

OJ. 1928. Resolutions and Recommendations Adopted by the Assembly during Its Ninth Ordinary Session 63.

Ōnuma, Yasuaki. 1986. 'Japanese International Law' in the Prewar Period: Perspectives on the Teaching and Research of International Law in Prewar Japan. *Japanese Annual of International Law* 29: 23–47.

Patterson, David S. 1976. The United States and the Origins of the World Court. *Political Science Quarterly* 91 (2): 279–295.

Reeves, Jesse S. 1921. International Society and International Law. *American Journal of International Law* 15 (3): 361–374.

Root, Elih. 1925. The Codification of International Law. *American Journal of International Law* 19 (4): 675–684.

Rosenne, Shabtai. 1972. Introduction. In *League of Nations Committee of Experts for the Progressive Codification of International Law (1925–1928)*, ed. Rosenne ed., Vol. 1, pp. xxix–cxxiv. New York: Oceana Publications, Inc.

Rosenne, Shabtai. 1992. Codification of International Law. In *Encyclopedia of Public International Law*, vol. 1, ed. Rudolf Bernhardt, 632–640. Amsterdam: North-Holland Pub. Co.

Scott, James Brown. 1931. The Progress of International Law during the Last Twenty-Five Years. *Proceedings of the American Society of International Law* 25: 2–34.

Shinohara, Hatsue. 2012. *US International Lawyers in the Interwar Years: A Forgotten Crusade*. Cambridge: Cambridge University Press.

Tachi, Sakutarō. 1914. Kokusai hōten hensan [Codification of International Law]. *Kokusaihō gaikō zasshi* 12 (10): 829–837.

Tachi, Sakutarō. 1922. Heiji kokusai hōki ni kansuru kokusai-teki rippō jigyō no hitsuyō [The Necessity for the Project of Codification in the Field of Laws of Peace]. *Gaikō jihō* 428: 583–590.

Tachi, Sakutarō. 1930. Kokusai renmei no kito suru kokusaihō no kaishin-teki hōten hensan [The Progressive Codification of International Law Proposed by the League of Nations]. *Hōritsu jihō* 2 (3): 27–30.

Tachi, Sakutarō. 1931. Senji hōki hensan no hitsuyō [The Need of the Codification of Laws of War]. *Gaikō jihō* 627: 1–7.
TCB. 1926. Gaimu-shō jōyaku-kyoku [Treaties and Conventions Bureau of the Ministry of Foreign Affairs of Japan]. In *Nihon kokusaihō gakkai oyobi kokusaihō kyōkai nihon shibu kokusai hōten hensan jigyō* [The Codification Project by the JSIL and the Japanese Branch of the ILA]. Tokyo: Gaimu-shō.
Wertheim, Stephen. 2011. The League That Wasn't: American Designs for a Legalist-Sanctionist League of Nations and the Intellectual Origins of International Organization, 1914–1920. *Diplomatic History* 35 (5): 797–836.
Yamada, Saburō. 1926. Kokusaihō-jō kokuseki no tokusō ni kansuru gensoku (ni) [Principles concerning the Acquisition and Loss of Nationality (2)]. *Kokusaihō gaikō zasshi* 25 (6): 18–38.
Yamada, Saburō. 1929a. Kokusai renmei to kokusai hōten hensan [League of Nations and the Codification of International Law]. *Kokusaihō gaikō zasshi* 28 (2): 1–31.
Yamada, Saburō. 1929b. Waga kokusaihō gakkai ni taisuru renmei sōkai no sanji [Acknowledgement from the Assembly of the League of Nations to Our Society of International Law]. *Kokusaihō gaikō zasshi* 28 (2): 92–93.
Yamada, Saburō. 1957. *Kaiko-roku* [The Memoir]. Tokyo: Yamada Saburō sensei beiju shukuga-kai.
Yamakawa, Tadao. 1962. *Watashi no ashiato* [My Footprints]. Self-published book. Available in Tadao Yamakawa Papers (Private Collection), Modern Japanese Political History Materials Room, National Diet Library, Tokyo.
Yanagihara, Masaharu. 2014. Kindai nihon to kokusai saiban: 'Saiban girai' wa shinwa nanoka? [International Adjudication and Modern Japan: Is the Reluctant Litigant a Myth?]. *Kokusaihō gaikō zasshi* 113 (3): 1–24.
Zachmann, Urs Matthias. 2010. War and International Order in Japan's International Legal Discourse: Attitudes among Japanese International Lawyers during the 1920s. *Review of Asian Pacific Studies* 35: 103–120.

Intellectual Entanglements Between the League of Nations and Eastern Asia: Modernism or Anti-modernism?

Takashi Saikawa

Introduction

In July 1942, a round table discussion took place in the Japanese magazine *Bungakukai* in the atmosphere of excitement triggered by the attack on Pearl Harbor. Titled '*Kindai no Chōkoku*' (Overcoming Modernity), the symposium is notorious as a wartime episode in which intellectuals enthusiastically glamorized Japanese military expansion while setting the guiding principles for the dubious idea of the Greater East Asia Co-prosperity Sphere.[1] As a number of studies have shown, the symposium itself, in which participants with various academic and political backgrounds promoted their own theories, resulted in an 'uncannily ideological emptiness', failing to define the essential question of what overcoming modernity meant (Takeuchi 1979: 275).[2] What is not so well known is that this symposium named itself *Chiteki Kyōryoku Kaigi*

T. Saikawa (✉)
Takasaki City University of Economics, Takasaki, Japan

C. R. Hughes and H. Shinohara (eds.), *East Asians in the League of Nations*, New Directions in East Asian History,
https://doi.org/10.1007/978-981-19-7067-2_6

(Commission for Intellectual Co-operation) and it had a historical precedent for the intellectual endeavour. Tetsutarō Kawakami, the president of the symposium, mentioned this in his closing remarks, as follows:

> Symposia of a similar format were held about ten years ago at the League of Nations by the Committee for Intellectual Co-operation, with several chaired by Paul Valéry. There one could see the mobilization of intellectuals as a stopgap measure of preserving the Treaty of Versailles, whose contradictions had already begun to be exposed. Toward this end, it was skillfully contrived that the topic for discussion be 'How Are Europeans Possible?' First-rate intellectuals thus exhausted their minds in trying to strip the body from the intellect. The attempt to ban political statements from the proceedings succeeded remarkably in the end in strengthening the political effects of their discourse as a whole. Although versed in intellectual etiquette, the participants' chorus sounded empty amid the emasculated if apparently rich and gorgeous harmony. Their forlorn hopes are revealed today by the state of European Politics. (Calichman 2008: 149–150)

As Kawakami stated, Paul Valéry, who served as one of the leading members of the sub-committee of arts and letters in the International Committee on Intellectual Co-operation of the League of Nations, hosted several conferences on a wide range of topics in the 1930s.[3] However, it is difficult to find an ideological linkage between Valéry's projects under the auspices of the League of Nations and the argument of 'Overcoming Modernity' in Japan. The former, regarded as a product of liberal internationalism represented by the League, stands in stark contrast to the latter as part of Japanese fascist ideology.[4] This chapter explores this missing link by examining how the idea of intellectual co-operation was embraced in Japan and China.

Since its beginning in 1922, the International Committee on Intellectual Co-operation (ICIC) of the League had been conscious of the conceptual ambiguity of intellectual co-operation and had made continuous efforts to define it. This ideological indeterminacy left room for each country to interpret the concept from its own point of view. Among others, Japan and China as non-Western members had respectively developed an original view on intellectual co-operation differing from the ICIC. At the same time, there was a deep cleavage in the meaning of intellectual co-operation between Japan and China in line with their different domestic and international contexts (Saikawa 2014). Focusing on different understandings of intellectual co-operation between the ICIC, Japan and China, this chapter demonstrates the multiple forms of intellectual co-operation that the ICIC had put into practice not only in Europe but also in the non-Western world. In this respect, this chapter also attempts to argue against recent studies that mainly draw the transnational characteristic of the ICIC's enterprise from the limited perspective of Europe (Laqua 2011, for example).

Japan's Version of Intellectual Co-operation: *Gakugei Kyōryoku*

Although the Japanese National Committee on Intellectual Co-operation was established in 1926, the concept of intellectual co-operation had not been well defined even in the ICIC. Therefore, the process of creating the national committee reflects how intellectual co-operation was understood, interpreted and accepted in Japan. This can immediately be seen in the way that the Japanese translation of 'intellectual co-operation' as '*gakugei kyōryoku*' carries a significance that contrasts to some degree with the original one set by the ICIC.

Firstly, this is because it implies that intellectual co-operation was expected to be undertaken by the government. In practice, this can be seen from the way that Japan's National Committee on Intellectual Co-operation (NCIC) was established at the initiative of the Japanese foreign ministry (Saikawa 2014: 75–87). The strong influence of the government is also apparent in its organizational structure. Article 1 of the proposal to establish the organization goes so far as to prescribe that 'this committee on international cultural exchange should act to cooperate with the work of intellectual co-operation by the League of Nations as a Japanese national committee under the direction of the Foreign Minister' (DAMOFAJ, n.d.a). In addition, Article 3 stipulates that 'the chairman and members should be appointed among high officers of related ministries and persons with learning and experience by the Cabinet upon the request of the Foreign Minister' (DAMOFAJ, n.d.a). It is thus clear that the Japanese NCIC was controlled by the foreign ministry and deprived of the autonomous power to decide its own composition, even in the planning stages.

The same holds true for the NCIC's financial resources. These were initially provided from the budget of the foreign ministry that was allocated to implementing the Versailles Peace Treaty (DAMOFAJ, n.d.b). Although, in 1927, the NCIC was transferred to the League of Nations

Association of Japan and financed by its budget, the financial sponsorship and oversight by the foreign ministry still continued. This is because, when the NCIC was transferred, the governmental subsidy to the Association was also increased from 50,000 to 70,000 yen (DAMOFAJ, n.d.c). Furthermore, in its official letter to the Association, the foreign ministry instructed that the increased amount should be used specifically for the work of intellectual co-operation (DAMOFAJ 1927).

The foreign ministry thus continued to maintain indirect but effective control over the NCIC even after it was transferred to the private League of Nations Association of Japan. Moreover, even the latter organization cannot be considered to have been a purely private organization. Subsidized by the Japanese government, one of its main purposes was to support Japanese foreign policy and promote the national interest under an arrangement generally called 'national diplomacy' (***kokumin gaikō***). It should also be pointed out, however, this close relationship with the government was not unique to the League of Nations Association of Japan but can also be seen in its counterparts in other countries, such as Britain and France (MacCarthy 2011; Guieu 2008; Birebent 2007).

The continuing influence of the government over the NCIC that was facilitated by this arrangement led to its being known as an 'illegitimate child of the foreign ministry' (DAMOFAJ, n.d.b). However, avoiding integrating it into the government structure did allow it a degree of camouflage as a private organization based on domestic academic associations. This is evident from the fact that Saburo Yamada, who was a scholar of private international law rather than a governmental officer, was invited to chair the NCIC, which was then swiftly transferred to the League of Nations Association of Japan.[5] The foreign ministry might have chosen this arrangement because it paid close attention to the need to present the ICIC as an organization that put more emphasis on the participation of intellectuals than governments. Yet it is also possible that the ministry understood that the work of intellectual co-operation could be implemented more successfully by individuals and private associations.

Secondly, the Japanese NCIC was initially designed to be an organization for international cultural exchange that would involve co-operation between the government and the private sector. Initially referred to as either the National Committee on International Cultural Co-operation (***Kokusai Bunka Kyōryoku Kokunai Iinkai***) or the Committee on International Cultural Exchange (***Kokusai Bunka Kōkan Iinkai***), it was intended to become a large-scale organization for international cultural exchange headed by the foreign minister. The original plan thus listed a wide range of names as possible members of the committee that ranged from the Foreign Minister and other high officials of related ministries to academics of public and private universities (DAMOFAJ, n.d.a). Moreover, the budget of 53,885 yen that was allocated to the committee exceeded the amount of governmental subsidy provided for the League of Nations Association of Japan (DAMOFAJ, n.d.a).

The influence of the state can also be seen in the way that the guiding principle of the NCIC was based on the idea of Harmony between Eastern and Western Civilizations (*Tōzai Bunmei no Chōwa*). This is explicit in the proposed plan, which explained that the project 'must be in accord with our long-standing policy that we establish this national committee in the hope of letting people know the true state of affairs in our country, which has often been misunderstood, and further that the committee will contribute to the cultural fusion of the East and the West' (DAMOFAJ, n.d.a). Despite this alignment with government policy, this vision of a large-scale organization for international cultural exchange with the lofty ambition to build harmony between civilizations was doomed to fail before it had got off the ground, when the NCIC was reduced to a mere six members and its budget was drastically cut to just one-third of the planned amount.[6]

A third feature of the Japanese NCIC was its primary purpose to introduce the nation's culture to Western countries. Originally, the ICIC had expected each national committee to serve as a liaison organization with a view to their function to execute the investigations and decisions of the ICIC in their respective countries (Committee on Intellectual Cooperation 1924: 24–35). In Japan, however, the national committee was regarded as a useful channel to broadcast Japan's opinions to the world or, more precisely, as an organ to introduce Japanese culture and provide a 'true understanding' of Japan for Western people. A brochure published by the Japanese NCIC clearly articulates that this task was the top priority, when it states:

> The primary purpose of our committee is to introduce Japanese culture. In terms of international co-operation, it must be an urgent task to show the true nature of Oriental culture to Western people who often know very little about it. (NCIC 1928: 18–19)

Saburo Yamada shared this perception of the ultimate goal of the NCIC, stating that 'the main purpose of our committee is not merely to assist the investigations at the request of the ICIC or its Institute but also to introduce our culture to Western countries' (Yamada 1929: 61). This proactive attitude to the introduction of Japanese culture to the West paradoxically intimates a sense of inferiority towards the Western nations. While Japan was in both name and reality one of the world powers occupying a seat in the Council of the League, there remained a strong sense that it was not yet properly appreciated and respected in Europe and America. In this regard, Japan's intellectual co-operation was also motivated by a strong sense of frustration towards the West.

Nevertheless, the aim of introducing Japanese culture was not necessarily the product of a one-sided argument by the Japanese NCIC alone. The ICIC itself also expected the Japanese committee to showcase various aspects of Japanese culture. For example, it requested that Japan donate materials on its fine arts, and encouraged it to exhibit the cultures of Korea, Taiwan and Manchuria, which were then under the rule of the Japanese Empire (DAMOFAJ 1929). In this way, considering the overlapping interest of the ICIC's requests for introducing Japanese culture with its own, the mission of the Japanese NCIC was not necessarily shaped by its political dogma alone.

Nonetheless, the crucial issue lies in how the Japanese NCIC conceptualized the purpose and dynamics of this mutual understanding. From the perspective of its members, introducing their own rather one-sided, 'correct' and 'true' version of Japanese culture was a way to further mutual understanding between Japan and Western countries. The assumption that the Japanese people inherently had the most accurate comprehension of their home country and were therefore in a good position to enlighten Western people about the essence of their culture naturally precluded the need for any degree of reciprocity. It was a way of thinking that only further problematized Western misapprehensions while failing to advance Japanese comprehension of Western civilization. This myopic view is reflected in the way that the NCIC proceeded to devote most of its efforts to exporting Japanese culture through the ICIC to Western countries, while it supported hardly any projects that were aimed at domestically implementing ICIC policies or promoting a better understanding of foreign cultures in Japan.

The process of establishing Japan's NCIC thus makes it clear that the Japanese government had become aware of the significance of cultural diplomacy as one of the new dimensions of foreign policy after World War I. This meant, on the one hand, that already existing diverse but disorganized international cultural exchange activities could be systematized and expanded. On the other hand, it meant that the government would be a central player in this domain. In this regard, the foundation of the organization signifies the beginning of the Japanese government's active involvement in the field of international cultural exchange.[7] The NCIC presented a new channel for promoting national interests and the government sought to make the most of the opportunity in pursuit of its own broader policy purposes (DAMOFAJ, n.d.a).

When assessing the Japanese NCIC's noble intentions to facilitate cultural harmony between the East and the West, however, it would be wrong to see it as a fully-fledged organ of the state. The guidelines for its establishment even make clear that the foreign ministry recognized its autonomy to a certain degree (DAMOFAJ, n.d.a). Nevertheless, this was to change in connection with the growing adversarial relationship between Japan and the League after the Manchurian Incident in 1931. After that, the government not only came to disregard the autonomy of the NCIC but also planned to create a new organization for international cultural exchange, which came to fruition with the establishment of the Society for International Cultural Relations (*Kokusai Bunka Shinkōkai*) in 1934. Although this was still based on the model provided by the NCIC, it is fair to conclude that the original organization is best understood to have been 'merely a temporary institution as well as a preparatory committee for the future' (Yamada 1926: 11).

China's Version of Intellectual Co-operation: *Shijie Wenhua Hezuo*

In the early 1930s, the cooperative relationship between the ICIC and China rapidly intensified. In particular, the League's Mission of Educational Experts to China in 1931 served as the catalyst for forging a firm relationship between the two. The Chinese government initially proposed the project with a view to fully utilizing the ICIC and the League in general for its own national reconstruction. Yet the ICIC was also actively involved in defining the mission's purposes and the selection of its members. In fact, it is through the implementation of this project that the ICIC came to establish a new identity for itself as a centre of intellectual and cultural exchanges between the East and the West. At the same time, the mission became the first experiment for the ICIC to directly assist a particular government.[8]

The Chinese government was initially spurred by the League's educational mission to create its own NCIC after Henri Bonnet, Director of the International Institute of Intellectual Co-operation, met with Chinese intellectuals and members of the Chinese Ministry of Education to discuss how to improve contacts between China and his organization (LNA, n.d.a: 13–14). From the point of view of the government, the collaboration with the ICIC was understood as a way to promote its own efforts towards national reconstruction. It therefore stressed the need to establish a centre that would both serve as a mediator of exchanges between Chinese and Western cultures and work to integrate the different cultural organizations that existed inside China (LON, n.d.a: 14–15). With this view in mind, the foundation of a Chinese NCIC was agreed upon in principle by Bonnet and the Ministry of Education. The two sides also drafted a plan which stipulated that the NCIC should devote the greater part of its activities to educational issues, particularly exchanges of teachers and students, while also dealing with questions of science as well as arts and letters (LON, n.d.b: 1–5).

However, it was not until 1933 that the idea of establishing a Chinese NCIC was realized. Li Yuying, who is better known outside China as Li Shizeng, would play a leading role in the course of its creation. A scholar and politician who had participated as an anarchist in the revolutionary movement of Chinese activists in Paris, he held prominent positions in the national educational administration, including being a member of the Commission of Education, the president of National Peiping University, a founder of the National Palace Museum and the president of the National Academy at Peiping (Beijing). Although the famous linguist and philosopher, Wu Zhihui served as the Chinese member of the ICIC and acted as the president of its national committee, Li became the driving force with his constant initiatives for building co-operation between the national organization and the League. This was made possible by both Li's intimate friendship with Wu and his considerable knowledge of the West, and particularly French culture.

Li began the full preparations for the creation of the Chinese national committee after his return from a trip to Europe in 1932, where he had exchanged views on this matter with key figures of the ICIC (UNESCO 1932). It was agreed between Li and the ICIC that the Chinese NCIC should be regarded as a 'coordinating body among Chinese organizations with characteristics of intelligence, education, arts and science' (LON 1933a). Based on this plan, the organizing committee for the Chinese NCIC, which consisted of twenty-five members appointed by the Ministry of Education, was held in Shanghai in June 1933 (LON 1933b). As almost all members of the organizing committee had some relationship with the Ministry of Education, it is obvious that the Chinese NCIC was formed under the strong influence of the government. Moreover, in parallel with the establishment of its NCIC, the Chinese government set up its permanent mission of delegates to the ICIC in Geneva. Though this was formally presided over by Wu Shihui, Li Yuying assumed his post as the first permanent delegate (UNESCO 1934).[9]

From its inception, the very name given to the Chinese NCIC reveals both the broad expectations and the particular goals of the Chinese government's interest in intellectual co-operation. The term 'intellectual co-operation' translated into Chinese as '*shijie wenhua hezuo*' literally means 'world cultural co-operation'. At this point, the Chinese NCIC already had a general understanding of what intellectual co-operation was. Presenting a comprehensive vision of international intellectual co-operation, it classified this as three forms: (1) intellectual co-operation directly implemented by the League of Nations, (2) intellectual co-operation implemented in collaboration between the League and each national cultural organization, and (3) intellectual co-operation implemented by each national cultural organization (Chen 1933: 49).

Among these, the Chinese NCIC laid special emphasis on the third form, recognizing the urgent need to act as a centre for integrating the various domestic cultural organizations that existed inside China. This is a corollary of the overarching goal to achieve national reconstruction under the initiative of the Chinese government. On the other hand, this does not mean that the scope of intellectual co-operation envisioned by the Chinese was confined to governmental activities. In fact, Li Yuying explicitly argued that the NCIC should deal not only with intergovernmental relations but also with the relationship between societies, including peoples and social institutions (Li 1970a: 371). Intellectual co-operation was thus conceptualized from the start as a joint initiative between the public and private sectors in China. At the ICIC in 1937, Li, acting on behalf of Wu Zhihui, raised the question of intellectual co-operation from the point of view of its social aspects:

> The Intellectual Co-operation Organisation should work not only, as it were, 'horizontally' with the idea of co-operation between the different countries, but also in a vertical sense, with a view of establishing good understanding between the different classes of society. That was... the purpose which M. Wu Shi Fee [Wu Zhihui] had in view in founding the various settlements in China. That was the angle from which he viewed the standardisation of methods of training. (LON, n.d.c: 30)

In addition to international understanding among nations, the leading Chinese members of the ICIC thus emphasized the development of mutual understanding within a society or a nation to be one of the two major functions that the ICIC should serve. This argument resulted partly from Li's sympathies towards socialism, a legacy from his earlier days as an anarchist. Primarily, however, it was derived from the critical situation of the ongoing civil war between the Nationalist Government and the Communists in China at the time, in which social integration and national unity were most needed. In this regard, the socialistic tinge of Li's understanding of intellectual co-operation was something of a reinterpretation of the ICIC's fundamental principles that reflected the pressing needs of China's domestic politics.

At the same time, the Chinese understanding of intellectual co-operation was underpinned by the perception of an ideological dichotomy between China and the West, which was tantamount in meaning to a distinction between China and the 'international'. For example, while stressing the importance of studying the issues regarding cultural exchanges between the East and the West, Li Yuying focused more attention on China itself vis-à-vis the West (Li 1970b: 245). Particularly in discussing China's intellectual co-operation with the ICIC, he often deployed the term '*zhongguo guoji*', which can best be translated into English as 'Sino-international'. In his view, international culture, which had long been dominated by Western cultures, would never be complete unless it incorporated Chinese culture (Li 1970c: 271–272). In this regard, China was strongly motivated by a sense of mission for the diffusion of Chinese culture particularly in the West, asserting its historical and cultural uniqueness in the world (Li 1970c: 275–275; 1970d: 280). From this point of view, in addition to the work of intellectual co-operation as a way to contribute to its national reconstruction, the Chinese NCIC also became engaged in a propaganda campaign to introduce Chinese culture to the Western people.

The deteriorating relationship with Japan was another reason why the Chinese intellectuals and government were so keen on establishing the NCIC to promote cultural co-operation in the 1930s, building on the information about the ICIC that had already been introduced to China during the 1920s (You 1925; He 1926; Zhang 1927). As explained above, after the Manchurian Crisis, the Japanese government had launched an increasingly aggressive cultural diplomacy towards Western countries around the same time, establishing its Society for Promotion of International Cultural Relations in 1934, in place of its own NCIC. This move induced a sense of vigilance among Chinese intellectuals, who detected in it Japan's intention to promote the cultural invasion of China and the justification of the establishment of its puppet state of Manchukuo (Liu 1935: 141). In total opposition to Japanese cultural imperialism, and in view of the fact that other major governments like Britain, France and Germany were also engaged in organizing cultural diplomacy for the sake of their own national interests, Chinese intellectuals argued that such a national organization for cultural exchange should also be created in China (Liu 1935: 155–157). The Chinese NCIC was thus expected to undertake the mission to engage in the propaganda war among governments as well as to implement its other projects of building China's domestic cultural infrastructure and promoting Chinese civilization as a part of the League's mission of using intellectual dialogues to establish international peace.

Conclusion

It has been argued above that the ICIC's idea of intellectual co-operation was understood and interpreted in ways that differed according to the varied domestic circumstances in Japan and China. A general conclusion can be drawn that the practice of *gakugei kyōryoku* in Japan was confined to the international level as a way to serve the policy of introducing Japanese culture to the West. There is little evidence that the Japanese NCIC gave much thought at all to its work inside Japan itself. For China, on the other hand, the idea of *shijie wenhua hezuo* focused not only on allowing people in the West to better understand the significance of Chinese culture but also as a way to strengthen its own cultural unity through the reorganization of the educational system at the domestic level.

As Li Yuying put it, the Chinese NCIC considered and implemented vertical intellectual co-operation as well as horizontal. In contrast, the Japanese preoccupation with horizontal intellectual co-operation meant that it was to be conducted outside the country, especially in the Western states. Given the fact that even the ICIC was not sufficiently aware of the need to implement vertical intellectual co-operation in each country, China's multi-layered model was to have a greater impact in the long term. Indeed, the historical significance of the ICIC's elitist attitude has been noted by individuals who worked in the ICIC. James Shotwell, an American member, even saw the scant attention that it paid to issues such as elementary school teaching as contributing to the failure of the League to prevent the outbreak of World War II (Shotwell 1944). Gilbert Murray, who long served as chairman of the ICIC, also attributed the emergence of Hitler to the ICIC's lack of effort to improve national education in Europe (Murray 1948: 82–83).

The second conclusion is that there was a substantial difference in the attitudes of Japan and China towards Western civilization. In accord with Japan's model of intellectual co-operation, it was commonly regarded as completely different in nature from its own national culture, while the cultural status of the West itself was ambiguous. China's model, on the other hand, readily adopted and harnessed Western civilization for the cause of its national reconstruction and unification. At the same time, it endeavoured to highlight the uniqueness and originality of Chinese traditional culture when engaging in intellectual co-operation at the international level.

It needs to be recognized that differentiating one's own culture from Western civilization is a dilemma that inevitably confronts all extra-European states in the process of modernization. Japan and China were no exceptions to this, even though it might be said that Japan had more successfully dealt with the problem since the Meiji period. However, the ideological confusion caused by the antinomy between Western civilization and Japanese culture would return with a vengeance in the form of the anti-modernist or anti-Western enthusiasm that broke out after the outbreak of Japan's war with the US, which is well represented in the argument on 'Overcoming Modernity' at the 1942 symposium with which this chapter began. From this perspective, the idea of 'Overcoming Modernity' was not just a by-product of Japanese fascism but one possible outcome of long-standing attempts to address the theoretical challenges of defining one's own culture and identity that were faced by actors across the non-Western world.

Finally, some responsibility for the way in which intellectual co-operation evolved under the auspices of the League should be attributed to actors in the West who harboured their own tendency to 'overcome modernity'. In the aftermath of World War I, having witnessed the destruction caused by modern technology, a number of intellectuals argued that the West was in decline itself. This motivated European intellectuals like Valéry to seek to overcome serious crises such as war, social contradictions and *la crise de l'esprit* in the Western world through the resurgence of European traditional culture, particularly based on a 'European spirit'. In this light, it is possible to say that the different versions of international co-operation that appeared in locations as varied as the Japan of Tetsutaro Kawakami, the president of the 1942 symposium on 'Overcoming Modernity', and among intellectual elites in China and Europe, had common origins in the cultural crisis of modernity that swept the world in the inter-war period.

Notes

1. The symposium appeared in the October and November 1942 issues of Bungakukai (Kawakami and Takeuchi 1979; Calichman 2008).
2. This is despite the fact that the question of overcoming modernity is often framed in terms of ideological antinomy, such as tradition/modernity and east/west, when modernity is historically reconsidered during the transition from modernism to postmodernism in Japan. See Harootunian 2001.
3. Starting with the centennial anniversary of Goethe's death in 1932, a series of conferences were held every year at the initiative of Valéry on such themes as 'the future of culture' (1933), 'the future of the European spirit' (1933), 'art and reality, art and the state' (1934), 'the formation of modern man' (1935), 'towards a new humanism' (1936), 'Europe, Latin-America' (1936) and 'the future fate of letters' (1937).
4. For this reason, the expansion and development of fascism in Japan is described as a defeat of the Japanese internationalists as well as the supporters of the League of Nations. For example, see Nish 1993.
5. Saburo Yamada spent most of his life in academia and held various positions such as Professor of Law at Tokyo Imperial University, President of Keijo Imperial University during the period of Japanese colonial rule over the Korean Peninsula, and President of the Japan Academy after World War Two. He chaired the Japanese National Committee on Intellectual Co-operation until 1936 when the committee was incorporated into the newly established Kokusai Bunka Shinkokai (Society for International Cultural Relations).
6. The committee members included Saburo Yamada (Chairman, Professor of Law at Tokyo Imperial University), Masaharu Anesaki (Professor of Religion at Tokyo Imperial University), Mikinosuke Miyajima (Director of the Kitasato Institute), Kinichi Komura (Member of the House of

Peers), Harukazu Nagaoka (Director of the Foreign Ministry), Ken Kuriya (Director of the Ministry of Education). In 1927, two influential members, Inazo Nitobe and Aikitsu Tanakadate, joined the committee. As for its finance, the national committee's actual 1927 budget amounted to about 13,000 yen. Even in 1930, four years after its establishment, only about 15,000 yen was allocated to the committee (DAMOFAJ nd. d).

7. In terms of governmental involvement in international cultural exchange, the Japanese government embarked on two different projects in the 1920s: Gakugei Kyōryoku (Intellectual Co-operation with the League of Nations) and Taishi Bunka Jigyō (Cultural Programs Toward China). As mentioned above, Japan's intellectual co-operation started with the establishment of its national committee in 1926. By contrast, cultural programs toward China, which were financed with reparations from the Qing Dynasty following the Boxer Rebellion in 1900 and were based on the Special Account Act for Cultural Programs toward China in 1923, were initially implemented as a joint project between Japan and the Republic of China. The programs included establishing research institutes in China, such as the Peking Humanities Institute, promoting student exchanges through subsidies to Tōa Dōbun Kai (East Asia Common Culture Association), and so forth. However, with the escalation of tensions between the two countries, these programs eventually became part of Japan's cultural imperialism in China (Teow 1999).
8. For details on the League of Nations' Educational Mission to China in 1931, see Chang 2012: 44–55; Saikawa 2014: 179–207.
9. Hu Tianshu served as Secretary-General.

References

Birebent, Christian. 2007. *Militants de la Paix et la SDN: Les mouvements de soutien à la Société des Nations en France et au Royaume-Uni, 1918–1925*. Paris: l'Harmattan.

Calichman, Richard F. 2008. *Overcoming Modernity: Cultural Identity in Wartime Japan*. New York: Columbia University Press.

Chang, Li. 2012. *Guoji hezuo zai Zhongguo* [International Co-operation in China]. Taipei: Institute of Modern History, Academia Sinica.

Chen, Hexi ed. 1933. *Shijie Wenhua Hezuo: canjia guolian shijie wenhua hezuohui di shi ci huiyi zhi baogao* [International Intellectual Co-operation: Report on the Participation in the Fourteenth Session of the ICIC]. Shanghai: Shijie bianyiguan.

Committee on Intellectual Co-operation. 1924. Minutes of the Third Session. League of Nations.

DAMOFAJ. n.d.a. Kokusai bunka kokan kokunai iinkai secchi ni kansuru ken [On the Establishment of the National Committee on International Cultural Exchange]. *Gakugei kyōryoku kokunai iinkai kankei.*

DAMOFAJ. n.d.b. Gakugei kyōryoku iinkai seiritsu jijo" [Conditions of Establishing the National Committee on Intellectual Co-operation]. *Kokusai renmei gakugei kyōryoku iinkai oyobi kokusai gakuin kankei ikken*, vol. 7.

DAMOFAJ. n.d.c. Kokusai renmei kyōkai showa ninendo jigyō keikaku narabini sono yosansho [Business Plan and Budget of the League of Nations Association of Japan in 1927]. *Kokusai renmei kyōkai ikken*, vol. 3.

DAMOFAJ. n.d.d. Kokusai Renmei kyōkai showa yonendo jigyō keikaku narabini sono yosansho [Business Plan and Budget of the League of Nations Association of Japan in 1930]. *Kokusai renmei kyokai ikken*, vol. 3.

DAMOFAJ. 1927. Meireisho kokusai renmei kyōkai [Order to the League of Nations Association of Japan]. 25 April. Kokusai renmei kyōkai ikken, vol. 3.

DAMOFAJ. 1929. From Michikazu Matsuda to Kijuro Shidehara. 8 December. *Gakugei kyōryoku kokunai iinkai kankei.*

Guieu, Jean-Michel. 2008. *Le rameau et le glaive: Les militants français pour la Société des Nations*. Paris: Presses de Sciences Po.

Harootunian, Harry. 2001. *Overcome by Modernity: History, Culture and Community in Interwar Japan*. Princeton: Princeton University Press.

He, Zuolin. 1926. Guoji zhishijie de hezuo yundong [Movement of International Intellectual Co-operation]. *Dongfang Zazhi* 23 (19): 35–42.

Kawakami, Tetsutaro and Yoshimi Takeuchi (eds.). 1979. *Kindai no chōkoku* [Overcoming Modernity]. Tokyo: Fuzanbo.

Laqua, Daniel. 2011. Transnational Intellectual Co-operation, the League of Nations, and the Problem of Order. *Journal of Global History* 6 (2): 223–247.

Li, Yuying. 1970a. Shijie wenhua hezuo zhongguo daibiaotuan zuzhi dagang chenbao dahui beian Tongqi [The Organizational Outline of the Chinese Delegation to the ICIC Reporting on the Preparatory Notice for the Conference]. In *Li Shizeng Xiansheng Wenji* [Collected Works of Li Shizeng], vol. 2, pp. 370–373. Taipei: Zhongguo Guomindang Zhongyang Weiyuanhui Dangshi Weiyuanhui. Originally published 1943.

Li, Yuying. 1970b. Zai di er ci quan guo jiaoyu huiyi jiangyanci [Lecture at the Second National Education Conference]. In *Li Shizeng Xiansheng Wenji* [Collected Works of Li Shizeng], vol. 2, pp. 242–249. Originally published 1930.

Li, Yuying. 1970c. Zhongguo guoji xueshu wenti [International Scientific Issues in China]. In *Li Shizeng Xiansheng Wenji* [Collected Works of Li Shizeng], vol. 2, pp. 270–276. Originally published 1953.

Li, Yuying. 1970d. Shijie wenhua [World Culture]. *Li Shizeng Xiansheng Wenji* [Collected Works of Li Shizeng], vol. 2, pp. 277–281. Originally published 1954.

Liu, Deming. 1935. Guoji wenhua shiye shi shenme? [What Is International Cultural Exchange?]. *Waijiao Yuebao* 6 (6): 141–157.

LON. n.d.a. Ci-joint rapport préliminaire du directeur de l'Institut international de coopération intellectuelle sur la mission d'éducateurs envoyés par la Société des Nations en Chine. R2256.

LON. n.d.b. Note au sujet de la constitution d'une Commission chinoise de coopération intellectuelle. Annexed to LNA nd. a.
LON. n.d.c. International Committee on Intellectual Co-operation, "Nineteenth Session, Minutes: Third Meeting held in Paris on July 13th, 1937, at 10 a.m." R4003.
LON. 1933a. From IIIC to Cheng Yinfun. 21 January R3995.
LON. 1933b. From Tchen Hoshien to J.D. de Montenach. 7 July R3974.
MacCarthy, Helen. 2011. *The British People and the League of Nations: Democracy, Citizenship and Internationalism, c.1918–45*. Manchester: Manchester University Press.
Murray, Gilbert. 1948. *A League of Nations: The First Experiment (1939). From the League to U.N.*, 65–83. London: Oxford University Press.
NCIC (National Committee on Intellectual Co-operation). 1928. *Gakugei no Kokusai Kyōryoku* [International Intellectual Co-operation]. Tokyo: Kokusai Renmei Kyokai.
Nish, Ian. 1993. *Japan's Struggle with Internationalism: Japan, China, and the League of Nations 1931–1933*. London: Routledge.
Saikawa, Takashi. 2014. *From Intellectual Co-operation to International Cultural Exchange: Japan and China in the International Committee on Intellectual Co-operation of the League of Nations, 1922–1939*. Ph.D. Thesis. University of Heidelberg.
Shotwell, James. 1944. Preface in Kandel, I.L. *Intellectual Co-operation: National and International*. New York: Columbia University Bureau of Publications.
Takeuchi, Yoshimi. 1979. Kindai no Chōkoku [Overcoming Modernity]. In *Kindai no chōkoku*, ed. Tetsutaro Kawakami and Yoshimi Takeuchi, 273–341. Tokyo: Fuzanbo.
Teow, See Heng. 1999. *Japanese Cultural Policy Toward China: A Comparative Perspective*. Cambridge, MA: Harvard University Press.
UNESCO. 1932. From Henri Bonnet to Gilbert Murray, 11 December. A.I.16.
UNESCO. 1934. Délégation chinoise auprès des Organisation international de Coopération intellectuelle, Bureaux à Genève et à Shanghai. 11 June. A.I.135.
Yamada, Saburo. 1926. Kokusai renmei to gakugei kyōryoku [League of Nations and Intellectual Co-operation]. *Kokusai Chishiki* 6 (6): 2–11.
Yamada, Saburo. 1929. Gakugei kyōryoku kokunai iinkai daihyōsha kaigi no gaikyō [Overview of the General Conference of Nations Committees on Intellectual Co-operation]. *Kokusai Chishiki* 9 (11): 54–65.
You, Xiong. 1925. Guoji lianmeng yu xuewen yishu zhi guojihua [League of Nations and the Internationalization of Arts and Sciences]. *Dongfang Zazhi* 22 (19): 44–54.
Zhang, Fuliang. 1927. *Guoji Zhishi Hezuo Yundongshi* [History of the International Intellectual Co-operation Movement]. Shanghai: Shangwuyin shuguan.

Picture of Prince Charoon, Siam's Representative to the League (*Source* United Nations Archives at Geneva)

Picture of Mineichiro Adachi, Japan's Representative to the League (*Source* United Nations Archives at Geneva)

Member States

Siam's Attempt at Neutrality: Coping with the League of Nations' Multilateralism

Teewin Suputtikun

Introduction

This chapter analyses how Siam attempted to use membership of the League of Nations to consolidate its independent sovereign status while not allowing multilateralism to generate bilateral frictions with the colonial powers and put the goal of revising the unequal treaties with them at risk. When the organisation was in the process of being established, members of the country's ruling elite doubted whether the victors of World War I would really regard their country as civilised enough to become a part of international society, even if they did steadfastly adopt Western standards and had abandoned neutrality to join the war on their side. This was partly because they had been struggling to retain monarchical rule in the face of demands for broadening political participation that was compatible with the Enlightenment trend that was sweeping across continents.[1] As Foreign Minister, Prince Devawongse, put it before the Paris Peace Conference, 'unless and until Siam had a representative government, she would not be admitted to the League of Nations' (TNA

T. Suputtikun (✉)
Chulalongkorn University, Bangkok, Thailand

C. R. Hughes and H. Shinohara (eds.), *East Asians in the League of Nations*, New Directions in East Asian History,
https://doi.org/10.1007/978-981-19-7067-2_7

1918a). Devawongse also knew, however, that exclusion 'would have an extremely adverse effect on our prestige and might make us lose our freedom later on' (TNA 1918b: 2). Unconcerned about the attitude of the United States, he cautioned against the prospect of being left out if, surreptitiously, 'Britain and France had settled between themselves the division and the destruction of Siam for their own respective benefit' (TNA 1918a).

Siam was thus faced with the daunting task of consolidating its status by catching up with what were considered to be the international standards of modernity and using the status of League membership as leverage for abolishing the unequal treaties to which their country had been submitted by the colonial powers.[2] This posed unprecedented challenges for Siam's diplomats, because the League required its members to constantly voice their opinions, decide the stance to take on difficult questions and to take action accordingly, even if only through voting. Devawongse was also aware that membership would be expensive, due to financial contributions to the League's coffers, the costs of stationing diplomats in Geneva and the need to facilitate and manage long-distance communications (TNA 1920a: 15). Most difficult was that Siam would have to 'globalise her foreign affairs' and make decisions concerning matters outside a traditional realm of interest that had barely stretched beyond its own borders (Suntarawanit 1990: 25). Any mistakes might derail the strategy of 'omnidirectional friendship' with various powers that had long been used by Siam to balance one imperial power against another.

At first glance, this appears to have encouraged a very limited role in the League (Hell 2010: 41). To better understand how Siam's policymakers weighed their options, however, it is necessary to examine three broad themes: How they perceived the purpose of the League, with regard to both the country's own foreign relations and the nature of the organisation itself; what constituted their primary concerns and preferences when engaging with the League's agendas; and what perceptions and motivations shaped their pattern of decision-making and behaviour. This chapter will show how Siam's elite shared the hopes of other small nations that the principles the League brought to the international relations would restrict the arbitrary actions of big states. Yet they were also very cautious about the practicality of using the international body to serve Siam's highest national interest because they saw the organisation largely as an arena for competition between the great powers.

The result was a kind of selective enthusiasm to engage with relatively uncontroversial socio-economic agendas that might help both to further the domestic modernisation process and to demonstrate a willingness to support global governance. When the League addressed high political disputes between the big powers, Siam thus abstained or maintained neutrality. Wait-and-see tactics and voting with the majority were used when matters were not directly relevant to its own interests. Even when issues did have a direct impact, it was seen as better to avoid being seen as a hindrance by occasionally adjusting Siam's own interests flexibly enough to not have to challenge the will of the majority and abstaining rather than making objections to reflect its position. Due to its relative smallness or just being an amateur in the multilateral arena, more often than not Siam just expected that problems would be solved somewhere else, without requiring it to make a judgement, or hoped that the League's decisions would not pressure the country to act against its own interests.

Although this attitude has been described as driven by a kind of 'realism' (Hell 2010: 46), it is important to note that Siam's policy elite gave much thought to how their country was viewed by others. By using an analytical framework that has more in common with constructivist and foreign policy analysis approaches to international politics and taking into account domestic ideational factors, it is possible to shed more light on how the attempt to maintain neutrality ultimately led the country to face a grave dilemma when it had to deal with the rupture between China and Japan over Manchuria. Aware of the need to be seen by international audiences to take a stance, Siam's policy elite was subjected to pressures from a variety of opinions and expectations about whether to define the nation by prioritising its identity as a sovereign state, a responsible member of international society, a small state, or an Asian state. Maintaining a low profile by adopting a position of neutrality did not always work, but it may have been the optimal strategy for Siam, even as the world entered the tumultuous 1930s.

To support the above proposition, it is necessary to first present a brief survey of Siam's situation at the end of World War I. This will be followed by an examination of Siam's actions in the League in two periods: the League's early years of forming and amending its rules, and the Manchurian Incident in its second decade. These cases, taken together, capture how Siam viewed and reacted to the pressure brought by the League. Moreover, whereas the former illustrates Siam's expectations for the League and how its role was developed accordingly, the latter shows how this affected the decision-making process in the face of a major crisis.

Siam's Manoeuvrings Towards the End of World War I

Siamese policymakers formed their perspective on the League and their strategy towards it before and during the 1919 Paris Peace Conference. Over time these views were consolidated through interactions in the multilateral setting and by learning from what other states said, expected and did. At that time the elite at the helm of foreign policy, as in other areas of government, consisted mainly of royalty and nobles whose authority derived from the tradition of absolute monarchy. From the start of the 1910s to the first five years of the League, Siam was under the reign of HM King Vajiravudh, Rama VI of the Chakri Dynasty. Awareness that his regime had been under increasing pressure made the country's performance in the diplomatic field one of the key tools for retaining the King's legitimacy (Sattayanurak 2012: 11–20; Numnonda 1981: 11–20).

Not long after the beginning of his reign, Rama VI had met the major international challenge of the outbreak of World War I in Europe by declaring neutrality. This was to avert domestic divisions over which side Siam should take. There was a strongly positive attitude towards Germany among some sectors of the elite, partly because many German personnel had been employed by various domestic agencies (Suntarawanit 1990: 18; Vella 1978: 108–109). It was also due to the need to maintain the omnidirectional friendship with many powers that had been central to Siam's traditional strategy for surviving in the predatory world of colonialism. This, of course, was also helpful when it came to acquiring material assistance from abroad.

Britain and France had long posed the major threats to Siam. Both frequently demanded territorial concessions in exchange for revision of the unequal treaties they had forced on the country, which provided their personnel with extraterritoriality and kept trade tariffs low (Duke 1999: 170–173). Siam had sought to remove such disadvantages since the reign of Rama V (1868–1910) and, in the process, incrementally exchanged bits of her territory in return for concessions granting greater autonomy (Numnonda 1981: 86–90). The employment of American advisors as negotiators in this process was characteristic of a willingness to borrow from Western expertise when it was necessary to keep the different powers at bay (Numnonda 1981: 81–105; Oblas 1972). This balancing of the British and French practice of imposing their own advisors across wide-ranging areas of policy is a good example of omnidirectional diplomacy at work, prior to the existence of the League (Nuchpiam 2016: 63–64).

Despite this suspicion towards Britain and France, however, the King and his foreign policy hands, like Prince Devawongse, could still have a positive attitude when it came to the Entente.[3] As Germany indulged in actions such as unlimited submarine warfare, it became easier to argue to domestic audiences that the Central Powers fought war unscrupulously and with no regard for the fate of small nations (Suntarawanit 1990: 22).

Staying neutral, moreover, had made Siam a haven for German propaganda, espionage and sabotage activities that threatened the Entente's position in Asia. Collective efforts to persuade the government to change course were thus initiated by the Russian minister in Bangkok and supported by the French, both aspiring to bring a faster end to the war by winning over as many neutral states as they could. Concerned that Siam might be isolated in the emerging international order as more nations abandoned neutrality, and aware that the country was obliged to uphold the peace as a signatory of the 1899 Hague Convention on the Laws and Customs of War (Suntarawanit 1990: 33, 37), the King decided in late 1917 to join the conflict 'on the side of Right and Justice' (*Bangkok Times* 1920). It was also hoped that, apart from securing a place in the coming new order, this provided an opportunity to provide assistance to France and Britain, which, no matter how trivial, could help to persuade both to treat Siam as an equal.

Devawongse made this clear when he wrote in his instruction to the country's delegates to the Paris Peace Conference that 'the object of Siam in going into the war...was to safeguard her existence as an independent sovereign state. She hopes to be able, with the assistance of her Allies, to safeguard that existence, and naturally also to be allowed to exercise freely all the rights and attributes that appertain thereto, such as the right of jurisdiction, the rights of control over revenue and national resources' (TNA 1918/1919a: 17). With the decision to join the League framed by this desire to revise the treaties that imposed extraterritoriality and tariff restrictions, Siam frequently complained to the organisation that these unequal treaties were obstructing it from acquiring sufficient resources to fulfil its duties as a League member (Nuchpiam 2016: 85). Despite such appeals, however, Siamese elites continued to prioritise the use of bilateral channels and American negotiators outside the League's framework when addressing these issues, motivated as they were by scepticism towards the organisation's practicality, especially when it came to protecting the interests of small states.

The Presumption of Neutrality in the League's First Decade

Uncertainty during the prelude to the Peace Conference and past experience in dealing with the imperial powers thus heavily coloured the observations of Siam's policymakers during the League's first decade. Their ability to live up to its ideals was further limited as this scepticism was reinforced by interactions with the organisation and observations of the great powers' politics. The complexity of multilateral diplomacy concerns over what kind of conduct would be appropriate for developing Siam's identity, and the fear that entanglement in the conflicts of others might aggravate bilateral ties with the colonial powers, all led them to presume that neutrality and indecision was the preferred tactic for navigating unfamiliar waters.

This uncertainty and lack of confidence was exacerbated by widespread self-doubt about Siam's eligibility to be part of the founding process. A good example is Prince Chakrapong Phuvanart, Rama VI's younger brother, who had advocated Siam's joining the war as a way to achieve treaty revision (Suntarawanit 1990: 34, 36). He told Devawongse that the only reason Siam might be excluded from the League had less to do with its 'mode of government' than whether it was a country 'of European culture'. Convincing the Europeans to stop imposing extraterritorial jurisdiction would thus make it more eligible by showing that the country measured up to Western standards (TNAu 1918: 13). This much-ado-about-nothing reflects not just a painful self-awareness of the country's inferior status but also how internal infighting between adherents to the *status quo* regime and advocates of new political thinking had found its way into foreign policy deliberation by juxtaposing Siam's existing political structure against the 'modern' form of government (Petchlertanan 2012: 3).

As far as Devawongse was concerned, joining the war already served as Siam's entrance ticket. Before coming to this conjecture, he had consulted Siam's ministers in Europe as to whether having a representative government was required for League membership. Prince Charoonsak Kridakorn (Charoon), the minister in Paris, who went on to hold the position of first permanent representative to the body until 1928, reassured him that this appeared to be just a myth circulating at home. He could not have been clearer when he wrote, 'from here, I do not have any feeling that they will exclude Siam from the meeting since they regard Siam as an ally'. However, he also mentioned caution in France about the League's feasibility, saying, 'it will not succeed because it is difficult and the French people do not trust Germany and abhor to see her join this same body with France until she verifiably shows that she is trustworthy' (TNA 1918c: 24).

Arguments over how to understand the nature of the League and its impact on the world formed another set of questions that members of the ruling elite had to argue over. Exchanges between Siam's delegates and the Foreign Minister kept in the National Archives of Thailand illustrate that the tendency to view the organisation as a venue for great power politics was always tempered by hopes that multilateralism and rule of law would somehow benefit small states. Devawongse's twelve-point Instruction to the Royal Siamese Delegates to the Peace Conference, issued in late 1918, elaborates the view that Siam should be enthusiastic towards an international effort that presented the opportunity 'to secure for herself what she deems it her right to have, that is a full acknowledgment of her position of equality with the free and progressive nations of the world and an opportunity to work things out for herself in her own way and without the restrictions...' (TNA 1918/1919a 1918d: 17). He goes on to argue that the establishment of a permanent peace and the elimination of the causes of future wars was of 'the greatest interest to Siam'. He is also optimistic that President Woodrow Wilson's Fourteen Points will be built into the governance of the League and that they are compatible with 'the interest of Siam and the human world' (TNA 1918/1919a 1918d: 17).

Perhaps most interesting is how Devawongse is able to link Siam's *raison d'etat* with *raison de système*,[4] as illustrated in the following passage from his Instruction:

> It is apparent that the League of Nations would be false to the purpose of its formation if any nation could dominate it by physical superiority. It is not meant that the nations forming the League are to be equal in every respect, for just as social equality is a myth so one nation like an individual will always possess superiority in many ways; but just as the safety of society demands laws shielding the weak individual from aggression of

> the strong, so the League will upon like principle guard the safety of the smaller nation against the greater. This is the reign of law sustained by the highest organized opinion of mankind. (TNA 1918/1919a 1918d: 17)

This grand vision informs Devawongse's specific instructions for using multilateral diplomacy to '...secure recognition from the Great Powers of Siam as a fully autonomous state, entitled to full recognition as a member of the family of Nations to have a modern treaty, one which will give the model for all future treaties of commerce'. He is also careful to warn, however, that this main aim is to be achieved by taking care 'not to arouse antagonisms which may interfere with the successful accomplishment of the object sought'. Moreover, he instructs the Delegates '...to follow the lead of Great Britain, France, and the United States, in matters as to which there is agreement among these Powers. Should there be disagreement among them, the Delegates are instructed either to abstain from voting or to apply for special instructions' (TNA 1918/1919a: 17). From this early stage, fathoming the attitude of the major powers and being attentive to their political games thus provided the focus through which Siam's Foreign Ministry perceived the operation of international politics.

Managing Politics Among the Powers

The perception that the new international order would be dominated by the interests of most powerful states was soon reinforced by reports from the delegates in Paris. Charoon, for example, wrote, 'It seems that the constitution of the League of Nations will be decided upon without asking the opinion of smaller nations and that when finished and decided upon by the great powers it will be laid before the full conference where adoption will be forced without discussion or objection, with none daring to refuse to accept and be excluded' (TNA 1919b: 23). True to the strategy of avoidance, Charoon held that 'it would be good policy for us to keep quiet make no fuss, which will do more harm than good for our aim' (TNA 1919b: 23). Devawongse's response reaffirmed the Ministry's limited expectations and realistic outlook, stating, 'It is only natural that the Great Powers should decide upon the matter. They are able to dominate the whole world if they like but they are humane enough to choose as much as they can to do justice to the rest of the Powers' (TNAv 1919: 56).

This perception of a hierarchically ordered world explains why Siam took a passive stance and remained quite inactive throughout the League's existence (Hell 2010: 198). It should not be overlooked, however, that a simultaneous change was occurring in the way that the country saw its own identity. Deciding what aims and actions were appropriate for a small state in the emerging international setting had to accommodate the desire for recognition and lack of certainty about the country's status. Apart from considering Siam a friend of the great powers, it was also one of many small states trying to meet the qualifications of being a modern, sovereign country. The remark, 'Siam as a small state', was thus frequently repeated in the discourse to rationalise policy options. For instance, when Charoon assessed the League's emerging rules, he reported that Articles 10, 24 and 25 of the Covenant seemed 'most advantageous to small states such as ourselves' (TNA 1919b: 66). Those articles dealt respectively with the mutual guarantee of territorial integrity and the promotion of governance in various low political fields, both topics that would help small states to resist domination and achieve modernisation. He went on to express his appreciation by stating, 'I do not think there is the slightest objection to any of the terms, they are much better than I expected' (TNA 1919b: 66).

The importance of self-image can again be seen when the decision had to be taken to appoint an assistant to advise Siam's delegates in Paris. The Siamese authorities, being accustomed to having foreigners advise them in wide-ranging domestic reforms, initially considered a French national (TNA 1918c: 24). Charoon argued that an American would be better (TNA 1918c: 245). Despite this, he was appalled when he found out that Devawongse planned to send an American with the status of 'Assistant Delegate', which he took to imply that the individual would sit alongside Siam's representatives in the venue. He thus strongly protested on the grounds that appointing a foreigner as a government representative would lead other nations to think that '...Siam has not developed enough to take care of her own affairs and has to have a Westerner appointed to represent her' (TNA 1918c: 24). While appreciating the practical need to borrow Western expertise, Siamese policymakers thus remained sensitive about how this would affect the perception of their country as a sovereign state abroad (TNA 1918c: 66).

Interestingly, apart from this concern for Siam's image, Charoon also explained his objection by resorting to an analysis of the politics of the powers that seems to have permeated the perception of the Siamese elites. He warned, 'We should not think that because he is an American whose country has been on the Allied side, Britain and France should not feel suspicious about our decision. In fact, paranoia always reigns in all nations' minds. Even when the Allied soldiers say they are close friends and love one another, the reality may be the opposite' (TNA 1918c: 24). Charoon also voiced his concern about a clause to be put in Article 21 of the Covenant that gave approval for the principle of the Monroe Doctrine, ensuring that the United States retained its sphere of influence, which '...will weaken the Covenant and lead other Great Powers to reserve certain rights or general principles also' (TNA 1918c: 69–74). This concern about efforts to maintain spheres of influence at the expense of the League's principles was deepened for Siam by the prospect that Japan might claim its own Monroe Doctrine in East Asia and the Pacific (TNA 1918c: 78).

Siam and the Racial Equality Clause

Japan raised another issue for Siam's identity politics when it strove to consolidate its position as the lone Asian great power by pressing for the so-called racial equality clause to be included in the preamble of the Covenant. This was a complex challenge because it had sensitive implications both for Siam's security and its identity. Charoon warned of the awkward position that would arise if Siam's delegates had to vote for a motion on which the major powers could not agree. The dilemma was thus cast in sharp relief, between supporting Devawongse's order to approve decisions of the Western powers for the greater cause of treaty revision (Hell 2010: 45), or following the strong feelings of Siam's delegates that Japan's proposal should be supported for reasons of what International Relations theorists now call 'ontological security' by regarding it as a fellow Asian nation with Japan (Mitzen 2006). The latter position could also be considered a matter of vital principle, insofar as the concept of racial equality could help strengthen the League's ideal of universality. The need to placate Japan was yet another factor.

A distinct note of irony can be detected in Charoon's comment on the process used to ensure the failure of the initiative. Noting that the majority voted in favour, he comments that 'the minority reserved to themselves the right to contest the vote, so the proposal was not adopted, a strange result of the voting system' (TNA 1918c: 69–74). This bewildering result was in fact made possible when President Wilson, who chaired the Commission, invoked the unanimity principle in order to placate Britain, on whom the United States relied to make the League operational. Charoon attributed it to Britain's aversion to seeing India and her dominions as equals when they became League members. Worried that the Japanese were considering whether to bring up the question, he explained '...it will be awkward for us because as a principle for our self-respect we are bound to vote for it but it may not be politic to do so in view of our aim' (TNA 1918c: 69–74). To his relief, Japan dropped the proposal after it had been rejected twice by some of the major powers (Hell 2010: 45). Explaining that this was a great relief for everyone, he warned that it was quite possible that the setback for Japan might make it work 'for the creation of the Doctrine of Monroe for the Continent of Asia', a venture which he hoped would fail (TNA 1918c: 77–79). There is no indication that the Siamese delegates prepared a way to react if they were to be faced by such a dilemma.

The Dispute Over Article 10

Canada's move to abolish Article 10 of the Covenant is another case during the early postwar years that demonstrates Siam's small faith both in the League's ability to put its noble principles into practice and its impact on the nation's identity (Hudson 1925: 929; TNAw 1921: 178). This came as the League's Council set up a commission to collect and study the amendment proposals from member states wishing to modify the rules of the League from late 1920. Article 10 which obliged members to cooperate with the League against any aggression towards the territorial integrity and political independence of states was considered to be the core principle of the Covenant. Canada felt it necessary to propose abolishing the article due to concerns about US aversion to making such a commitment. For Siam, however, this would have an adverse impact on the 'mutual guarantee' principle that Devawongse saw as important for small states. The delegates explained this dilemma in a report to Devawongse as follows:

> [Canada's delegation] hoped by this means to bring the US into the League, and argued that the practical value of the article was nil, so that its deletion would not in reality entail any serious consequence. The greatest opposition came from the small states, who regard this article as the charter of their liberty and independence. They well knew that in practice it would

> not mean much, but to them it has a certain moral significance which spells security and freedom from attack. (TNA 1923a: 48–56)

Emphasising Siam's shared identity with the small states, they concluded that, 'our interest in this matter bound up with that of the small states, and so, like them, we voted for the postponement of the consideration for any amendments of the article' (TNA 1923a: 48–56).

Devawongse concurred, adding that no matter how the article was revised, it would not persuade the United States to change its mind (TNA 1923b: 57). By the time the League called for members to submit their views on the issue, in mid-1923, Devawongse had been replaced as Foreign Minister by his son, Prince Traidos Prabandh, who was also advised to oppose the Canadian motion by his American advisor, Eldon James. As James explained, 'President Wilson used to say that (Article 10) was the heart of the Covenant, and I am not sure but that he was right. However, weak the guarantee may be, it is, nevertheless, a guarantee of territorial integrity and I think that it should stand until experience has demonstrated the existence of a necessity for a change' (TNA 1923c: 74).

In the end, Siam joined with other members to block Canada's proposal, which failed to gain enough support due to abstentions (Hudson 1925: 929–930). This role can be described as attentive at best, constrained as it was by the priority of maintaining a generally passive and low-profile stance. Without asserting their own proposal for amendment of the Covenant, Siam's delegates kept watchful eyes on how member states, especially small ones, expressed themselves. Under Devawongse's order to 'give support to a successful end to any issue deemed beneficiary to His Majesty's government' (TNA 1920b: 21), they reflected how passivity had become an important characteristic of foreign policy.

This passivity even reflects a willingness to adjust the understanding of the national interest according to the evolution of the multilateral consensus, while limiting any opposition to abstention from voting. For instance, when Siam was displeased with a revision of the rule determining financial contributions, which resulted in the raising of Siam's shared from three units to ten, it did not publicly voice dissatisfaction, unlike states such as Persia, Cuba, Lithuania and Luxembourg. Charoon merely reported 'we did not think it would be in our interest to vote for it. Our units of the contribution this year are exactly the same as those under the scale submitted last year viz ten units instead of three under the Postal Union Scale and in conformity with our previous conduct we abstained from voting in the matter' (TNA 1923d: 48–56). Dewavongse's response reflects a combination of frustration that other states had to pay an equal or lesser share than Siam, even though they were richer, but also his resignation to the situation when he concludes, 'But it is clear from your message that we cannot do anything to alter that because it has been agreed upon' (TNA 1923b: 57).

Neutrality in the Manchurian Crisis

Siam's stance of passive neutrality was to face its most severe test with the Manchurian Crisis, which resulted in the unilateral establishment and recognition of the state of Manchukuo by Japan in 1932. It should be borne in mind that this took place in the broader context of the radical shifts of power that occurred all over the world during the Great Depression of the 1930s. In Siam, dissatisfaction with royal absolutism had reached boiling point in June 1932 when the progressive group, Khana Ratsadon, staged a revolution and replaced the absolutist rule of Rama VII (1925–1935) with a constitutional monarchy (Petchlertanan 2012).

The details of the Manchurian Crisis are covered more extensively in other chapters of this book. Suffice it to point out here that the Siamese diplomats noted China's immediate appeal to the League to put pressure on Japan to halt her hostility, or at least to lend China the legitimacy and moral support it needed to tackle the situation (TNA 1932a: 80–83). With the principle of 'collective security' under strain, Siam found itself at the centre of attention, posing a severe test for its neutrality when it became the only state to abstain from a vote by the Council to repudiate Japan's justification of its invasion, in line with the recommendations of the report by Lord Lytton on behalf of the League. The only other exception was Japan itself, even though its vote against the findings was not counted because it was a party to the dispute (*Bangkok Daily Mail* 1933). Siam's extreme caution was thus widely interpreted as support for Japan, much to its dismay.

Siam's immediate response to the emerging rupture between Japan and China had, in fact, been to maintain good relations with both. The former was an increasingly important trading partner while the latter was deemed a long-time friend that the government did not want to antagonise (Nuchpiam 2016: 175–176). This approach was consistent with the well-established strategy of cultivating friendship with multiple powers and seeking help for its flagging economy. On the other hand, upholding the authority of the League was a matter that could not be ignored, especially when small European states were demanding strong measures (TNA 1932b: 336–375). Being an Asian nation, however, made Siam's deliberations somewhat more complicated.

Indecision thus remained the most tempting expedient for bypassing the dilemma. Sticking with the course of 'complete neutrality' meant not even supporting the authority of the League to decide who had violated the Covenant and activate Article 16, which obliged members to impose economic sanctions. The cables between the Foreign Ministry and Prince Pridi Debyabongs Devakula, Siam's temporary envoy to the special session of the Assembly on the Sino-Japanese dispute (TNA 1932c: 7), reveal that the government's first concern was that the imposition of an economic boycott 'would create difficulty in our trade relations' (TNA 1932d: 13). Foreign Minister Traidos thus ordered Pridi to find out whether Article 16 would automatically take effect if the Assembly were to rule on who had violated the Covenant (TNA 1932c: 18).

When Pridi asked for an opinion from a German official, the reply was that if the Assembly determined that a party had violated the Covenant, then Article 16 would be immediately invoked without the need for a separate agreement (TNA 1932e: 78–79). Pridi preferred to concur with an Irish delegate, who believed that the special Assembly would most likely appoint a committee to report on the case and ask the conflicting parties to enter into a conciliation process without touching Article 16 (TNA 1932f: 28; 1932g: 84–87; 1932h: 28). This reinforced the willingness to put pragmatism before principle when looking at the League, especially when it came to dealing with inter-state conflicts. But this did not rule out recognising the legitimacy and authority of the League as the main venue for conflicting parties to make appeals and justify their causes. Siam's anxiety about the impact of having to impose binding measures also reflects how it felt compelled to respect and comply with any multilateral resolutions coming from the League. Yet Pridi's report shows how Siam's belief in the efficacy of such measures was limited by an underlying scepticism, pointing out that even the Chinese delegation was aware that the use of Article 16 would not be effective in practice (TNA 1932h: 28). Knowing that many states would not seriously observe such action, they knew that China had to fight to defend itself and would not ask others to provide military assistance, and wanted and expected only moral support (TNA 1932a: 80–83). Pridi was also aware, however, that China saw the threat to invoke Article 16 as a useful way to pressure Japan to go to conciliation, rather than face a special Assembly (TNA 1932h: 28).

Bearing in mind such considerations, Traidos was able to inform the Office of the King's Secretary that the Assembly was unlikely to invoke Article 16 and argue that keeping to the stance of neutrality and avoiding severing commercial ties with any of the concerned countries was in Siam's interest (TNA 1932i: 36). He, therefore, instructed Pridi to support any resolution intended to facilitate negotiations, not believing that the Assembly could pass a resolution preventing Japan from using force in the future. The government's stance thus became opposition to invoking Article 16 or attributing final responsibility until all the essential facts of the crisis had been determined. Under the prevailing economic conditions, it was particularly reluctant to place an embargo on commerce with Japan and wanted to avoid involvement in any decision that might be considered to be either anti-Japanese or anti-Chinese (TNA 1932j: 40).

Pridi had adopted this cautious approach by carefully avoiding any mention of the Sino-Japanese dispute when approached by the Chinese Minister to Berlin. When requested for support, he had taken 'extreme caution not to make opinions that could be interpreted that we were supporting one side' (1932a: 80–83). Siam was thus relieved when the Assembly took steps short of invoking Article 16, with most of the big powers preferring to search for a compromise through negotiations in Shanghai between China and Japan, along with the other interested powers (TNA 1932k: 51–52). Seeing as this was compatible with Siam's aim to refrain from making judgements against any state, Pridi just sat silently throughout the meeting at which this was decided (TNA 1932l: 128). The agreement of the Assembly to set up the Committee of Nineteen to study the Lytton Report also helped to avoid the need for Siam to take a clear position, allowing Pridi to play a game of wait-and-see as he hoped that 'the wind would blow her way' (TNA 1932m: 134–137, 140).

Despite these favourable circumstances, Siam's identity crisis is evident in Pridi's report on how the small European states repeatedly urged the League to take more decisive actions.[5] Among the opinions collected in Siam's Foreign Ministry is that of the Norwegian delegate, who saw the crisis as posing 'a major test for the League's practicality', with any steps having 'incalculable consequences' for the principle of the mutual guarantee of security (TNA 1932b: 138–172). Pridi noted how such states were prepared to deny the major powers by calling for an 'energetic effort to safeguard the authority of the League' (TNA 1932k: 51–52). Rather than shake the resolve to avoid strong measures or work in solidarity with small states, however, Pridi told the government:

> If we focus only on the fact that Siam is also a small country, when a fellow state is under attack, we should then sympathize and concur with the opinions expressed by the representatives of other small states. But those representatives who dare say so are not countries that have an interest in East Asia. Siam is different because our national interest is at stake. . . [As instructed] I shall strictly maintain our neutral stance and vote in favor of a conciliatory measure, rather than a strong one. (TNA 1932b: 152)

It is thus that Siam's identity as an Asian state actually provided its diplomats with an excuse to avoid acting in unity with other small states to preserve the League's principles and authority, as a major international crisis developed in its own neighbourhood.

The Unintended Consequences of Abstention

In late 1932, when the Lytton Report was ready for deliberation in the Special Assembly, the conditions that had allowed Siam to remain indecisive began to evaporate. However, Siam remained ambivalent partly due to developments at home. In June 1932, a revolution had replaced the King's absolute rule with a constitutional monarchy.[6] As a consequence, the figures who had steered the country through increasingly troubling international scenes were replaced. The new Foreign Minister, Phraya Srivisar Vacha, had to decide on what stance to take when the Committee of Nineteen submitted its recommendations on implementing the Lytton Report to the Assembly in February 1933. The Report rejected Japan's claims and sympathised with China's position and urged League members not to recognise the newly formed state of Manchukuo, which was deemed to be nothing more than Japan's puppet (*Bangkok Times* 1933a).

The secretary of the Legation in London, Luang Bhadravadi, was assigned to attend the crucial meeting by Siam's representative to the League, Prince Damras Damrong Devakula (TNA 1933b: 298). Having been in Geneva to assist Pridi when the special meetings on the crisis were convened, Bhadravadi was fully aware of the long-standing neutrality policy. Despite the dramatic shift in the domestic form of government, therefore, the senior officials in the Foreign Ministry avoided substantial change (Hell 2010: 198). This was confirmed when the Japanese consul in Bangkok used his farewell visit as a pretext to lobby for Siam's support, to which the Permanent Secretary of the Foreign Ministry, Phraya Apibarn Rajamaitri, responded 'We have taken a neutral stance and do not want to alienate both of our friends', showing an ambivalence reminiscent of the response Pridi had given to the request of the Chinese in Geneva (TNA 1933c: 8). According to Apibarn's report, although the Japanese guest acknowledged the chance of winning the vote was slim, he had anticipated that a considerable number of states would abstain and hoped that Siam would join them (TNA 1933c: 8). The determination to adhere to the policy of avoiding entanglement in others' conflicts proved to be stronger for Siam.

Perception and Misperception of the Alignment with Japan

The temptation to interpret Siam's abstention as the start of a process of alignment with Japan has been made stronger by the fact that it did eventually become Japan's ally in the Pacific War and estranged from China (Hell 2010: 206). This could be further reinforced by the way in which Japan interpreted the abstention as being in its favour. As one member of its Lower House declared, 'at a time when Japan is faced by unfriendly nations in the West it is doubly welcome to find a fellow-Asiatic friend and the Government ought to pay special attention to this when drawing up her future Far Eastern policy' (*Bangkok Times* 1933b).

However, archival evidence does not support this as an accurate representation of Siam's intentions or that there was a link between the two periods. What happened as a result of the abstention was actually more of an unintended consequence, leading to a misperception that took some effort to rectify. Rather than any movement away from neutrality, the rationale presented to the international audience and circulating among Siam's officials in 1933 clearly restates that the intention 'to strictly remain neutral as much as possible' had not changed. The instruction for Bhadravadi to abstain, sent by Srivisar to Siam's legation in London, states in the most unassuming and simple way that the government 'does not want to take a side' (TNA 1933d: 10).

That this was received without any fuss might reflect how the uncertainty in Siam's internal politics made it difficult to reconsider a stance that had already been decided (Hell 2010: 204). It also suggests a sheer lack of awareness that Siam's action might be misunderstood, let alone that it would become the only member of the Assembly to abstain. One retrospective analysis that appeared in the newspaper, *Thaimai*, even pointed out that had more states in the meeting abstained, Siam would have been able to pass the test without being noticed (*Thaimai* 1933). If the Foreign Ministry had believed that this view was true, however, its job was made harder by profuse displays of gratitude from Japan. There have been different interpretations of whether this expression of gratitude was sincere or orchestrated to serve as propaganda to compensate for Japan's loss of face (Hell 2010: 208). The documents collected by Siam's Foreign Ministry, however, show the extent to which the unassuming abstention was seen as sensational by many sectors in Japanese society (TNA 1933e 1933: 84–99). The cautious tone prevalent in the exchanges between the Ministry and its overseas officials on how to handle this and clarify Siam's true intention reveals intense frustration over the way in which the attempt to maintain neutrality was wrongly and unjustly understood (TNA 1933f: 106).

Further evidence can be found in the emphasis that Bhadravadi put on Siam's neutrality when asked by Japan's representative and a news correspondent about its motives after the vote on 24 February and the walkout by the Japanese delegation (TNA 1933f: 106). Apibarn, at the Foreign Ministry, gave the same answer emphasising Siam's neutral stance when questioned by a correspondent from the *Osaka Mainichi* (TNA 1933g: 15). The Ministry was also appalled to learn from Damras Damrong that a warning by the chief of the Japanese delegation, Yōsuke Matsuoka, that 'if Europeans try to crush Siam, we will not let them; if necessary, we would fight for her', was widely disseminated by the European press (TNA 1933h: 20).

Damras also became concerned about press rumours in Geneva that armaments delivered to Siam by Britain, including 20 tanks, would end up supplying Japan (TNA 1933h: 20). This prompted the Foreign Ministry to issue a communique on 2 March 1933, clearly denying the story and explaining that the government's policy to remain neutral in the dispute between China and Japan was the reason for abstaining in the vote over Manchuria, explicitly stating:

> It is the policy of His Majesty's Government to be neutral in the controversy between China and Japan regarding Manchuria. For this reason, its

> representative at Geneva abstained from voting . . . Rumours appearing in the foreign press that His Majesty's Government is acting as an agent for Japan in the purchase of arms or in any way aiding Japan are entirely without foundation. (TNA 1933i: 24)

Srivisar, the Foreign Minister, explained to Siam's representative in Geneva that, 'Our abstention has clearly made other people think that we side with Japan. To dispel that misunderstanding, the government has issued a communique to explain our policy to the public' (TNA 1933j: 50).

As well as the news clippings and reports that the Ministry kept receiving from abroad, particularly disturbing, was a plethora of letters expressing gratitude from various bodies and individuals in Japan (TNA 1933k: 84–99). This strong and seemingly sincere display of gratitude caused much awkwardness because Siam's authorities did not want to reject such courtesy. This is reflected by Srivisar's reply to a report from the Legation in Washington about the Japanese ambassador's thankful attitude, in which he points to the danger that the letters and congratulations from Japan would lead people to think that Siam had abstained out of sympathy, '...while, in fact, we only tried to be as neutral as possible' (TNA 1933f: 106). He goes on to explain that, 'if in the future any Japanese should call or write to express his thanks for our attitude at Geneva, it would be well not to reply; otherwise it may give rise to a misunderstanding' (TNA 1933l: 108–109). This order was also sent to Siam's Ministers in Tokyo and Paris, who had reported similar incidents (TNA 1933m: 111; 1933n: 113).

The Foreign Ministry's collection of clippings from Thai newspapers also shows its concern over media opinion at home, which was interestingly divided. One view that echoed among various newspapers was to criticise the abstention as inappropriate. Considering that other states were treating the Assembly like a court and making clear judgements, to abstain was to be like a judge who did not fulfil his task. If the government had decided not to get involved then it might just as well have instructed its delegate not to attend at all, which would at least have had the advantage of preventing misunderstandings (*Thaimai* 1933: 19–20). When asked by a journalist why Siam had not pondered such a choice, Apibarn replied that the delegate was already there and that his presence was emblematic of Siam's attempt to comply with the League's formalities, as well as its belief that neutrality was a proper option (*Prachachart* 1933: 28).

Hedging and the Dilemma of Small Powers

This insistence on maintaining a stance of pragmatic neutrality throughout the life of the League makes it quite different from the other Eastern Asian members of the organisation, China and Japan. It has been argued above that this was shaped by its relatively small size and the determination not to jeopardise the strategy of maintaining good relations with the imperial powers that had allowed it to avoid becoming the victim of colonisation. Siam's policymakers were also cautious from the start about actively using the League to pursue national interests and their scepticism steadily increased as the organisation came to be seen as more of an arena for competition between the great powers in the inter-war years.

It is wrong, however, to overlook how the country's ruling elite did regard the League as significant for the principles that it brought to international relations. Despite initial concerns that membership might force domestic political change, they shared the hope of other small nations that the new world body would impose some meaningful restrictions on the arbitrary acts of the big states and make multilateralism the source of a new kind of legitimacy in international politics. More specifically for Siam, this meant using membership to pursue the goal of having Siam's sovereignty more fully recognised, especially by encouraging revision of the unequal treaties. This would, in turn, earn the prestige important for consolidating its status as a modern and capable state.

The fact that the neutrality policy became highly problematic with the development of the Manchurian Crisis does not indicate that there was paralysis, incompetence, or complete failure on the part of Siam. Seeking to enjoy the opportunities presented to small states by multilateral international organisations while avoiding being dragged into conflicts always presents a dilemma for small states. It is called 'hedging' in post-Cold War developments of the international politics of Southeast Asia, where actors seek to maintain good relations with the United States and China while building international organisations such as the Association of Southeast Asian States (ASEAN) and supporting the UN system (Haacke 2019).

In this respect, Siam was somewhat ahead of its time because a similar attitude informed its rather minimal and passive roles in the League, especially when it came to confronting the high political issues concerning international security. It is true that the preferred option of neutrality did backfire to some degree during the Manchurian Crisis, by inadvertently feeding perceptions that the country was taking Japan's side. This, however, reveals not so much deficiencies on the part of Siam's diplomats as the faults and limitations of the League's project to change the anarchical nature of international society in the early twentieth century. It remains to be seen whether the present-day states of Southeast Asia will fare any better as they struggle to build international organisations and seek security while maintaining good relations with the increasingly antagonistic big powers.

Notes

1. See, for example, Greene (1999) and Numnonda (1981: 11–24).
2. See, for example, Duke (1999), Oblas (1971) and Hell (2010: 11–19).
3. For the debates on the King's attitude see Suntarawanit (1990: 110).
4. For the concepts, *raison d'etat* and *raison de système* see Adam Watson (1992: 14).
5. This kind of attitude was prevalent in statements made by representatives from various small nations. Their opinions were found in the Official Reports on the Extraordinary Sessions of Assembly of the League of Nations that were sent to Siam's Foreign Ministry (TNA. KT 96.1.6.2/3).
6. For more on the background events see Batsan (1984).

References

Bangkok Daily Mail. 1933. Japan Quits League Following Adoption of Committee Report. 25 February. TNA, KT 96.1.6.2/9: 4.

Batsan, Benjamin A. 1984. *The End of the Absolute Monarchy in Siam*. Melbourne: Oxford University Press.

Duke, Pensri. 1999. *Kan tangprathet kap ekkarat lae athippatai khong thai: tangtae samai ratchakan thi 4 thueng sin samai chomphon p. phibunsongkhram* [Thailand's Foreign Affairs and Her Independence and Sovereignty: From King Rama IV to the End of the Phibunsongkhram Administration]. Bangkok: Text and Journal Publication.

Greene, Stephen Lyon Wakeman. 1999. *Absolute Dreams: Thai Government Under Rama VI, 1910–1925*. Bangkok: White Lotus Co. Ltd.

Haacke, Jürgen. 2019. The Concept of Hedging and Its Application to Southeast Asia. *International Relations of the Asia Pacific* 19 (3): 375–417. https://doi.org/10.1093/irap/lcz010. Accessed 16 July 2022.

Hell, Stefan. 2010. *Siam and the League of Nations: Modernisation, Sovereignty and Multilateral Diplomacy, 1920–1940*. Bangkok: River Books Co., Ltd.

Hudson, Manley O. 1925. Amendment of the Covenant of the League of Nations. *The Harvard Law Review Association* 38 (7): 903–953.

Mitzen, Jennifer. 2006. Ontological Security in World Politics: State Identity and the Security Dilemma. *European Journal of International Relations* 12 (3): 341–370.

Nuchpiam, Theera. 2016. *Tua ton mai khong sayam nai loka: kan tangprathet nai samai ratchakan thi VII* [Siam's New Identity in the World: Its Foreign Affairs during King Rama VII]. Bangkok: Prajadhipok-Rambhai Barni Foundation.

Numnonda, Thamsook. (1981). *Kanmueang lae kan tangprathet nai prawattisat Thai* [Politics and Foreign Affairs in Thai History]. Bangkok: Thai Watana Panich Press Co., Ltd.

Oblas, Peter B. 1971. A Very Small Part of World Affairs' Siam's Policy on Treaty Revision and the Paris Peace Conference. *Journal of the Siam Society* 59 (2): 52–74.

Oblas, Peter B. 1972. Treaty Revision and the Role of the American Foreign Affairs Adviser 1909–1925. *Journal of the Siam Society* 60 (1): 171–186.

Petchlertanan, Thamrongsak. 2012. *Patiwat 2475 lai ratthathammanun* [1932 Revolution in Siam and Constitutions]. Bangkok: The Foundation for the Promotion of Social Science and Humanities Textbooks Projects.

Prachachart. 1933. Rao mi sitthi khrai cha rusuek yangrai mai tong wan [We Have Our Right, Do not Fear for Others' Feelings]. (In Thai). 3 March 3. TNA, KT 96.1.6.2/9: 28.

Sattayanurak, Attachak. 2012. *Kan plianplaeng lokkathat khong chonchan phunam thai tangtae ratchakan thi IV- phoso 2475* [Changes in Perception of Thai Elite Class From King Rama IV to 1932], 3rd ed. Bangkok: Chulalongkorn University Press.

Suntarawanit, Chalong. 1990. *Prathet Thai kap kanmueang lok: kan khaosu songkhramlok khrang thi nuen* [Thailand and World Politics: Entry into the World War]. In *Nayobai tangprathet Thai bon thang phraeng* [Thailand's Foreign Policy in Dilemma], ed. Chanthima Ongsurak. Bangkok: Thammasat University Press.

Thaimai (New Thai). 1933. Opinion. 27 February 27. TNA, KT 96.1.6.2/9: 19–20.

The Bangkok Times. 1920. The Problems of To-day. Translation of His Majesty's Reply to the Members of the Royal Family and Public Officials. 5 January.

The Bangkok Times. 1933a. Report and Recommendation of The Committee of Nineteen. 20 February. 20. TNA, KT 96.1.6.2/9: 3.

The Bangkok Times. 1933b. A Fellow Asiatic Friend. 1 March. TNA, KT 96.1.6.2/9: 21.

TNAu 1918 Prince Chakrapong to Prince Devawongse. KT 96.1/1.

TNAv. 1919. Prince Devawongse to Prince Charoon. KT 96.1/1.

TNAw. 1921. Canada's Proposal to Omit Article 10. KT 96.1.2/4: 178.

TNA. 1918a. Prince Devawongse to Prince Charoon. 21 November 21. KT 96.1/1.

TNA. 1918b. Prince Devawongse to Phraya Buri Navarasth. KT 96.1/1.

TNA. 1918c. Prince Charoon to Prince Devawongse. 5 December. KT 96.1/1.

TNA. 1918/1919a(1918d). Instruction to the Royal Siamese Delegates to the Peace Conference. KT 96.1/.

TNA 1919b. Prince Charoon to Prince Devawongse. 4 February. KT 96.1/1.

TNA. 1920a. Prince Devawongse to Phraya Buri Navarasth (August 18, 1920a), TNA, KT 96.1/14, p. 15.

TNA. 1920b. Prince Dewavongse to Prince Charoon . 21 September. KT 96.1.2/4.

TNA. 1923a: Prince Charoon and Phraya Ratchawangsan to Prince Devawongse. 23 January 23. KT 96.1.2/7.

TNA. 1923b: Prince Devawongse to Prince Charoon and Phraya Ratchawangsan. 3 March 3. KT 96.1.2/7.

TNA 1923c. Eldon James's Opinion to Siam's government. KT 96.1.2/7.

TNA. 1923d. Prince Charoon and Phraya Ratchawangsan to Prince Devawongse. 23 January. KT 96.1.2/7.

TNA. 1932a. Record of Conversations between Prince Pridi and M. Liou Vontao (Chinese Minister in Berlin). 29 February. KT 96.1.6.2/2.

TNA. 1932b. Extraordinary Session of the Assembly—Verbatim Report of the Second and Third Meetings. 5 March. KT 96.1.6.2/3.

TNA. 1932c. Prince Traidos to Prince Pridi, KT 96.1.6.2/2.

TNA. 1932d. Chao Phraya Mahithorn to Prince Traidos, TNA, KT 96.1.6.2/2.

TNA. 1932e. Summary of Conversation between Prince Pridi and Dr. Goppert [An Official in Germany's Foreign Ministry]. 29 February. KT 96.1.6.2/2.

TNA. 1932f. Prince Pridi to Prince Traidos. 13 February. KT 96.1.6.2/2

TNA. 1932g. Record of Conversations by Prince Pridi During the Dinner at the Head of Chinese Delegation's the Residence. KT 96.1.6.2/2: 84–87.

TNA. 1932h. Prince Pridi to Prince Traidos. 29 February. KT 96.1.6.2/2

TNA. 1932i. Urgent Dispatch from the Foreign Ministry to HM Office of Secretary. 3 March. KT 96.1.6.2/2.

TNA. 1932j. Prince Traidos to Prince Pridi. 4 March. KT 96.1.6.2/2

TNA. 1932k. Prince Pridi to Prince Traidos. 5 March. KT 96.1.6.2/2

TNA. 1932l. Foreign Ministry to HM Office of Secretary. 19 March. KT 96.1.6.2/2.

TNA. 1932m. Prince Pridi to Prince Traidos. 7 March. KT 96.1.6.2/2.

TNA. 1933a. Japan Quits League Following Adoption of Committee Report. *Bangkok Daily Mail* (February 25, 1933a), TNA, KT 96.1.6.2/9, p. 4.

TNA. 1933b. Prince Damras to Drummond. KT 96.1.6.2/7.

TNA. 1933c. Memorandum of Discussion between Phraya Apibarn and the Japanese Consul Who was about to Return to Japan. 18 February 18. KT 96.1.6.2/8.

TNA. 1933d. Phraya Srivisar to the Siamese Minister, London. 22 February. KT 96.1.6.2/8.

TNA. 1933e. KT 96.1.6.2/8: 84–99.

TNA. 1933f. Phraya Srivisar to Siam's Minister in Washington, D.C. KT 96.1.6.2/8.

TNA. 1933g. Phraya Apibarn's Memorandum. 26 February 26. KT 96.1.6.2/8.

TNA. 1933h. Prince Damras Damrong to Phraya Srivisar. 27 February. KT 96.1.6.2/8.

TNA. 1933i. Communique issued by The Ministry of Foreign Affairs (March 2, 1933i), TNA, KT 96.1.6.2/8, p. 24.

TNA. 1933j. Phraya Srivisar to Siam's Representative to the League of Nations (Confidential). 14 March 14. KT 96.1.6.2/8.

TNA. 1933k. KT 96.1.6.2/8: 84–99.

TNA. 1933l. Phraya Srivisar to Phraya Subarn Sompati (London). KT 96.1.6.2/8.

TNA. 1933m. Phraya Srivisar to Siam's Minister in Tokyo. 13 April.

TNA. 1933n. Phraya Srivisar to Siam's Minister in Paris. KT 96.1.6.2/8.

Vella, Walter F. 1978. *Chiyo! King Vajiravudh and the Development of Thai Nationalism*. Honolulu: The University Press of Hawaii.

Watson, Adam. 1992. *The Evolution of International Society: A Comparative Historical Analysis*. New York: Routledge.

Japan's Diplomats in the League Council: The Challenge of Managing Power and Ideals in the Pacific Settlement of Disputes

Hatsue Shinohara

Introduction

The League Council is like a body that governs the world.

> I think the brilliant Spaniard, Salvador de Madariaga, was right when he remarked in the League Council during the Manchurian affair that everyone knows who is the aggressor.

The first of the above remarks was made by a Japanese diplomat, Mine-ichirō Adachi, who supported and contributed to the activities of the League as a delegate to its Council (Adachi 2011: 164). Respected by his fellow statesmen for his legal knowledge, patience, and decisive management of meetings, in 1930 he made a speech delivered at the Japanese branch of the League of Nations Union in which he went so far as to describe the Council as qualified to be a governance body for the world

H. Shinohara (✉)
Waseda University, Tokyo, Japan

C. R. Hughes and H. Shinohara (eds.), *East Asians in the League of Nations*, New Directions in East Asian History,
https://doi.org/10.1007/978-981-19-7067-2_8

(Adachi 2011: 164).[1] The second remark, by a contemporary scholar, signifies that when the Manchurian affair was discussed, member states at the Council had a clear idea of which country was the aggressor (Berdahl 1937: 97). While Adachi could thus speak highly of the Council before a Japanese audience in 1930, just one year later it had become evident that it was the aggression of the country that he represented that was in breach of the fundamental principles of the organization to which he was so committed.

Adachi thus personifies the tension between the ideal of making the use of force illegitimate for the settlement of international disputes and the ways in which national governments pursue what they consider to be their vital interests in the absence of world government. From the perspective of International Relations theory, this gulf between ideals and reality is what underpinned the 'first great debate' between advocates of international governance and the 'realists' who dismissed them as 'utopians.'[2] Japan's invasion of Manchuria and the League's inadequate response is undoubtedly a key event in the realist narrative. It has been extensively discussed by scholars who have tended to focus on the policies of the major powers, the League's discussions and attempts to find a resolution to the crisis, and Japan's withdrawal (Thorne 1972; Nish 1993; Ogata 1964). Most important is the widespread perception that it was the failure to implement the commitment to collective security that led to the League's demise (Eloranda 2011).

This chapter seeks to provide a different perspective by looking at the proceedings of the Council to illustrate how it developed foundational and procedural mechanisms for promoting the pacific settlement of conflicts. By focusing on the actors involved in these debates, it is possible to begin to explore the links between the two themes that run through this book, namely the relative success of the functional work of the League and the failure of its high diplomacy when it came to preventing conflict between states. This shows how the attempts of the diplomats to strengthen the remit and capacity of the Council were motivated by a faith in the organization that was not altogether destroyed by its failure over Manchuria.

Section one sets the context for this analysis by looking at the discussions on the institutional development of the Council in the 1920s. The achievements in developing the rapporteur and commission of enquiry systems involved a lively debate over how to make the growing competence of the body comply with its remit as stipulated in the Covenant.

Section two then explores how the commitment of Japan's diplomats in Geneva became increasingly frustrated as the Council attempted to strengthen its role in the pacific settlement of disputes. Section three then examines how the discursive process evolved as the diplomats had to try to live up to the expectations of the League and the conflicting demands of their government in Tokyo after Japan commenced its military actions in Manchuria. Although they had to take the side of the latter, the chapter concludes with a brief discussion of the ways in which their idealism was not completely erased but remained a factor when it came to rebuilding international order in the wake of World War Two.

The Institutional Development of the Council in the 1920s

By the time the Council convened its last session, on 14 December 1939, the League had sat for a total of one hundred and seven sessions. Established by the Covenant as one of the three main bodies of the League, along with the Assembly and the Secretariat, there is a surprising lack of scholarship on its history and how it functioned from the perspective of academic work on the nature of international organizations.[3] This is all the more remarkable in light of the wide authority given to the body, which Article 4 of the Covenant stipulates as being 'to deal at its meetings with any matter within the sphere of action of the League or affecting the peace of the world.'

This remit reflects the high expectations that many held for the League in its initial years, and the wide range of problems that remained unsettled in the aftermath of World War One. The main function of the Council was to give the great powers a leading role in the settlement of international disputes. Article 4 of the Covenant thus gives permanent representation to the 'Principle Allied and Associated Powers', namely Britain, France, Italy and Japan, with four other seats allocated to other members who were selected by the Assembly for limited terms—later expanded to nine in September 1926. As a permanent member, therefore, Japan enjoyed a special status as one of the three Eastern Asian members of the Council. China, for its part, even though being considered too internally divided and late in paying its contributions won the support of the Assembly to take a seat as a non-permanent member from January 1921 to January 1923, and from September 1926 to September 1928. Fortunately for Japan, however, Sino-Japan issues did not become an agenda item of the

League before China was re-elected to the Council in September 1931. Its diplomats in Geneva thus had had plenty of time to establish Japan's status as *primus inter pares* and to learn how member states could make efforts to enhance the role of the Council in resolving conflicts before the outbreak of the Manchurian crisis.

From its establishment to the late 1920s, the League gradually solidified the institutional procedure and mechanism to settle conflicts in a peaceful manner. This entailed two broad approaches: one was legal development, such as the discussion of the Protocol for the Pacific Settlement of International Disputes—better known as the Geneva Protocol—which will be discussed in section two below with a focus on the role played by Japan; the other was more pragmatic, insofar as it concerned developing ways to make the daily management of the Council more effective. This included practices such as the creation of the 'rapporteur' system, the mission of enquiry, the nomination of a special committee, and the publication of a committee report.

The Rapporteur and Commission of Enquiry Systems

The genesis of the pragmatic approach can be found on 17 May 1920, when the Council met in Rome for its fifth session and agreed upon the Rules of Procedure of the Council of the League of Nations. Article 2 of this document gave the Council (or its president) the power to appoint rapporteurs to take the leading role in resolving issues by conducting investigations, providing mediation, and presenting suggestions, with the assistance of the Secretariat if necessary (*OJ* 1920: 272).[4] Table 1 shows the nationalities of the rapporteurs that were announced at the first public meeting of the Council and the issues that they were responsible for. Table 2 shows how more middle and lesser powers were given the role of rapporteur toward the end of the 1920s, as more issues were added to the Council's agenda.

Japan was initially given responsibility for reporting on the implementation of the 1919 treaty to protect minorities in the newly recognized state of Poland, a remit that was later broadened to the protection of minorities in general. As will be discussed below, this allocated to Japan one of the League's most difficult problems, presenting its diplomats with an opportunity to demonstrate how they could rise to the challenges of their country's leadership role.

Table 1 Nationality of rapporteurs in 1920

Issues	*Rapporteur (1920)*
Switzerland's entry into the League	Britain
Order of procedure for the Council	Italy
Saar Basin	Greece
Danzig	Belgium
Permanent Court of International Justice	France
Transit	Spain
Health	Brazil
Polish Minority Treaty	Japan

Compiled by the author, data from *Official Journal of the League of Nations* (1920: 30–31)

Table 2 Nationality of rapporteurs 1928–1930

Issues	*Reporter (1928–1929)*	*Reporter (1929–1930)*
Finance	Cuba	Canada
Economics	Germany	Germany
Transportation	Poland	Poland
Public Health	Spain	Cuba
International Law	Italy	Italy
Finance of the League	Persia	Cuba
International Bureau	Venezuela	Venezuela
Mandate	Finland	Finland
Minorities	Japan	Japan
Disarmament	Rumania	Spain
Saar	Italy	Italy
Danzig	Chile	Britain
International Cooperation	France	France
Opium	Canada	Yugoslavia
Trafficking of Women and Children	Britain	Persia
Humanitarian issues	Venezuela	Peru
Welfare of Children	Canada	Yugoslavia
Refugees		Venezuela

Data from *Official Journal of the League of Nations* (1928: 1652; 1929: 1669)

Another result of the Council's activities was the normalization of the dispatch of enquiry commissions. This practice began when the proposal was made to send a commission to Russia at the third session of the Council meeting, in March 1920. Lord Balfour, who presented the proposal, explained that the idea had originally come from the International Labor Organization, which had argued that examining labor conditions in Russia would help to clarify the general political situation in the country (*OJ* 1920: 61–62). The Council again dispatched a commission in 1920 in response to a claim by the Swedish-speaking population of Finland's Aaland islands to the right to become unified with Sweden. After agreeing that the body would be composed of members from third-party countries, a Belgian, a Swiss, and an American were sent to examine the situation. Nitobe Inazō, an internationally renowned writer and educator who had assumed the position of deputy Secretary-General, in charge of the League of Nations Secretariat Information Section, played a key role in formulating the solution, which was to leave the islands under Finnish control, while demilitarizing them and granting autonomy (Nish 1993: 10).[5] The practice of sending commissions was further embedded in Council practice in 1924, when a Belgian and a Hungarian, with a Swede as president, were sent to look into the dispute between Turkey and Britain over possession of the former Ottoman territory of Mosul.

It thus became standard practice for the Council to send a commission to the site of any dispute (Secretariat 1930: 29, 38–39). A mechanism to select the representatives of third-party countries to go to areas of conflict and collect useful information was gradually developed and in the mid-1920s the approach was successfully used to settle a number of conflicts. Most notable is the dispute that developed when Greece sent its military into Bulgarian territory in October 1925 and Bulgaria immediately appealed to the League. In what Francis Walters regards as 'a classic example of the application of the Covenant,' (Walters 1986: 314) the Council responded by demanding that all military actions should be suspended and dispatched military attachés from France, Britain and Italy to the scene. When these military personnel told the two armies to halt their actions, the Greek troops duly evacuated from the frontier, leaving the attachés *in situ* to confirm that Bulgaria was able to reoccupy the territory.[6] After the danger of hostilities was ended, an enquiry commission composed of civilian officials was sent to the region to produce a report, which the Council used to conclude that Greece should pay reparations.

The Council had thus sent two different missions: one composed of military personnel who had been active during the conflict, and the other comprised of civilian representatives to investigate its causes and propose a solution.

Examination of Article 11 of the Covenant

The successful management of the conflict between Greece and Bulgaria provided the Council with an opportunity to discuss what kind of preventive measures it might be able to take for resolving future conflicts. During the ensuing debate, members from France, Finland, and Poland proposed studying whether it could provide a swifter response to emerging crises. The Council then nominated a Special Committee, which produced a report entitled 'Questions relating to the Application of Articles 11 and 16 of the Covenant' (*OJ* 1927: 218–228). The interpretation of these articles was important for clarifying the Council's remit, because Article 11 was phrased in the broadest terms to oblige the Secretary-General to bring to the Council 'Any war or threat of war, whether immediately affecting any of the Members of the League or not', and for the League to 'take any action that may be deemed wise and effectual to safeguard the peace of nations.' Article 16 gave the Council considerable powers to carry out this responsibility, permitting it to call on members to contribute effective military, naval, or air forces. These powers, however, were in danger of being rendered ineffective by the lack of any obligation for member states to enforce Council decisions and by the absence of a system of compulsory arbitration.[7]

On 8 December 1926, the rapporteur, Eduard Beneš of Czechoslovakia, who was the chief architect behind the Geneva Protocol, thus explained that the report highlighted the need to further study the possibilities for employing Article 11 and the means to facilitate communication between the Secretariat and states when the danger of war was imminent. High hopes for the Council's ability to extend its functions were expressed by A. van Karnebeek, for the Netherlands, who remarked that 'the Covenant was a marvelous instrument containing infinite riches.' Vittorio Scialoja of Italy also endorsed the positive aspects of the Covenant, comparing it to an 'unexplored treasure mine' where 'unexpected riches were discovered.' However, as a legal specialist and one of the drafters of the Covenant, he also injected a note of caution, suggesting that it was necessary to investigate the relationship of Articles

11 and 16 to Article 15, which obliges the Council to refer a dispute to the Assembly at the request of any of the involved parties. In contrast, Nicolas Titulescu from Romania supported a more progressive interpretation of Article 11, saying that it was 'not only the pivot of all the preventive action of the Council, which was of much greater importance.' The British statesman, Sir Austen Chamberlain, also emphasized pragmatism when assessing the report, noting that 'theory came from practice much more than practice from theory.' (*OJ* 1927: 133–134).

A resolution to further study the issue was adopted on 8 December 1926 (*OJ* 1927: 137–138). On 15 March the following year the committee, headed by Louis de Brouckère[8] of Belgium, duly published a report under the title, 'Methods or Regulation which would enable the Council to take such Decisions as may be necessary to enforce the Obligations of the Covenant as expeditiously as possible.' This made suggestions concerning what the Council could do, based on the Application of Article 11 to previous incidents. By distinguishing cases where there was no threat of war from those where it was imminent, it clearly emphasized investigation and negotiation rather than the use of force, stating that 'the very general nature of Article 11 allows any action that does not imply recourse to war against the recalcitrant State.'[9]

When the Council continued the discussion on 15 June, Beneš referred back to the original debate in December, agreeing with Karenbeck, Tituesco, and Chamberlain that the document contained 'to a certain extent a new departure' in the interpretation and application of Article 11. Karnebeek noted that 'emphasis had been laid on Article 16; that emphasis remained unchanged. Article 11, however, had been left us in the shade.' When Beneš suggested that the Council adopt the report, Scialoja emphasized the importance of the proposal, which, he pointed out, had arisen 'due to experience.' Beneš responded by stressing that because the report was legal in nature, it was right that it should be thoroughly discussed. Finally, it was suggested that a resolution be adopted to allow the Council to adopt measures and methods that 'may be necessary to enforce the obligations of the Covenant as expeditiously as possible' and that the contents of the report should be communicated by the Secretary-General to the member states (*OJ* 1927: 764–766). On 8 December 1927, the Council finally adopted the proposal that had originally been presented in March and passed a resolution stating that it should be given 'the methods or regulation' that would enable it 'to take such decisions as may be necessary to enforce the obligations of the Covenant as expeditiously as possible' (*OJ* 1928: 125).

The determination of the Council to continue exploring the possibility of taking preventive measures based on Article 11 is quite remarkable, given that it was in the context of growing opposition to the ratification of the Geneva Protocol. The March 1927 report thus came to be known as the Brouckere Report and attracted considerable attention from contemporary scholars (Eagleton 1933: 243; Berdhal 1937: 96–97). If nothing else, the discussion reveals not only how the Council was developing as a multilateral forum where member states could express and exchange their views and opinions but also how it had come to be regarded as the guardian of the Covenant.

One can safely assume that toward the end of the 1920s, what was known as the 'Geneva Spirit' was more than just a symbol or slogan to those involved in the League. Most member states, too, had come to believe that the League was making a deliberate effort to fulfill its mission to observe and promote the principle of the pacific settlement of disputes and thereby establish a stable and pacific international order. Importantly, the League's handling of disputes and certain of its practices were not based solely upon the Covenant but were also evolving gradually as the Council attempted to resolve the gaps and inconsistencies in the system that had been put in place in 1919. Furthermore, as shown by the extensive debate over the interpretation of Article 11, the open discussion and exchange of opinions in the Council helped to encourage discourse and nurture the perception that a conciliatory spirit was indispensable for further consolidating the good functioning of the League.

Japan and the Pacific Settlement of Conflicts in the 1920s

Japanese Diplomats in the League

Even though Japan was not well prepared for the Paris Peace Conference, the country was honored to gain the status of a permanent member of the Council and proceeded to actively participate in several fields of the League's activities. As other chapters in this book show, this included work in such fields as technical cooperation, programs from the International Committee for Intellectual Cooperation, and the codification project. Due to the lessons that had been learned at the Paris Peace

Conference, Tokyo made sure to send first-class diplomats with extensive language capabilities and legal expertise to the League's headquarters in Geneva, such as Inazō Nitobe.

Francis Walters recollects how such diplomats worked diligently, mentioning the names of Mineichirō Adachi, Kikurijō Ishii, and Naotake Satō in particular. They did their best to support proceedings and patiently listened to all speakers through what were often long and tedious discussions and were particularly persistent in trying to resolve the German-Polish minority issues. Walters vividly illustrates Adachi's role in the matter, remarking: 'Adachi's learning was profound, and, unlike most Japanese, his brain and temper functioned with more than Latin rapidity' (Walters 1986: 496, 407). David Hunter Miller, who drafted the Covenant, emphasized that this was a new departure for the country when he stated, 'Japan taking an active part in European affairs is following the example of Italy when the latter became a Great power by participating in matters which had no direct concern to herself' (Matsushita 1929: 113–114).

Despite the novelty of their role, the Japanese diplomats were familiar enough with the atmosphere of the League at Geneva to understand that other countries were anxious to gain permanent seats on the Council. Spain and Brazil, for example, had explored the possibility but had still not been able to join. Noting that Japan was assigned to 'the position that makes other countries jealous', Satō emphasized that if it was unable to fulfill its mission, 'the position of our country will be unrespectful' and could end up making Japan look like a merely nominal member. The League, for its part, asked Japan to be in charge of minority issues because the country, in the opinion of Secretary-General Eric Drummond, could maintain a neutral position precisely because it was not European. When the Japanese delegates agreed to assume the role of rapporteur on the issue, they knew that such problems in postwar Europe were of vital importance for international stability and of a highly complex nature. As Satō put it: 'we have to dive into the turbulent wave of European politics' (Satō 1963: 236, 208).

By the late 1920s, therefore, the Japanese diplomats were heavily involved in the thorny issue of the status of the German minority in Upper Silesia, which had been incorporated into Poland after the war. This was becoming politically complex partly because Germany saw it as an opportunity to regain the territory.[10] From 1928 to 1929, the Council meetings were thus heavily focused on the case. Adachi, who had assumed the role of rapporteur since September 1928, helped settle the issue by repeatedly arguing at Council meetings that the involved parties should reach a compromise. By showing a conciliatory spirit, he remarked, they would demonstrate that the Council was functioning well.

On 15 December 1928, the Council held a meeting in the Swiss city of Lugano, which included the discussion of eight petitions that had been presented by Germans living in Upper Silesia. Adachi detailed each of the issues raised, such as the education available to Germans in Silesia and the transfer of property rights. In addition to addressing such specific problems, Raoul Dandurand proposed that the minority protection regime itself should be re-examined and revised. Influenced by the experience of his own country, Canada, where different minorities lived together in relative stability, he claimed that the current system was unequal because not all states were obliged to protect minorities. The division between Poland and Germany was deep, however. In substance, the existing system favored the former, so the Polish representative, Auguste Zaleski, supported it. The German representative, Gustav Stresemann, expressed his country's frustration, asking, 'Is it M. Zaleski's purpose to wage a war of words against Germany?' At the end of the session, the president of the Council, Aristide Briand, thanked Adachi for 'a meticulous investigation of the questions' and closed the session by saying that the Council would not be indifferent to the 'sacred cause' and 'sacred right' of minorities (*OJ* 1929: 57–58, 68–70, 70–71).

When the Council discussed Dandurand's proposal on 6 March, 1929, Stresemann was in favor, saying that the minority system should be reconsidered because the League had already been established for ten years. He stressed that it was only natural for people to speak their mother tongue, remarking, 'it may be said that history endeavors to prove the truth of the saying of Goethe, who puts men, State, and nation on their guard against the inconstancy of fortune.' However, Austen Chamberlain, who had been highly involved in resolving minority issues, put his support behind the existing system. After some further exchange of views, the Finnish representative proposed breaking the impasse by nominating Adachi as rapporteur to examine Dandurand's proposal (*OJ* 1929: 518–522, 523–526). At the end of the session, Adachi declared:

> This morning, I entered the Council Chamber with a certain degree of apprehension...Nevertheless, at the end of this discussion, I feel greatly strengthened, for all our colleagues...have shown the greatest goodwill in

> seeking to achieve a harmonious co-operation of the peoples...The Council is to sit tomorrow morning, and I hope that I shall be in a position to provide a text which will give complete satisfaction and which will attain the great object of the League, whose sacred duties to minorities were defined at Lugano by the former President of the Council; those minorities, it should be remembered, exist side by side with majorities in the different countries. (*OJ* 1929: 532)

In addition to Adachi's skillful and eloquent handling of the Council meetings, the Japanese delegates offered their mediation services by inviting Germany and Poland to communicate directly. This was successful in allowing the two parties to reach a temporary settlement, which came as something of a surprise to Drummond. Satō was thus able to describe a meeting of the Council in Madrid, in 1929, as having proceeded smoothly, writing that 'Ambassador Adachi read the report convincingly and decisively, and Germany and Poland supported the resolutions. When the issue came to the Council meeting, everything looked fine' (Satō 1963: 211, 231–215). Even though the Japanese diplomats' efforts did not entirely solve the German minority issues in Upper Silesia on this occasion, their contributions were acknowledged and appreciated. In this regard, it could be said that they had risen to the challenge and fulfilled the mission of a permanent member of the Council.

Upon his return to Japan, Adachi was thus upbeat about the prospects for the League. In an address to the Tokyo branch of the League of Nations Union, titled 'Has the League Developed Well?' he remarked that its evolution had been timely and that international relations had become more organized in the wake of World War One (Adachi 1930). However, when the active participation of the Japanese diplomats in European affairs did not receive strong backing from the Japanese Government, Satō deplored its indifference. After arriving home, he had been told by the head of the Information Section of the Foreign Ministry, Toshio Shiratori, who would later become an advocate for the Axis Alliance, that Japan did not need to be involved in League affairs that were not immediately related to national interests. Satō saw through this false dichotomy, believing with a somewhat greater degree of prescience that 'Sooner or later, Sino-Japan issues will be discussed at the League. Unless Japan has not accomplished important tasks at the League, no member will take a sympathetic position toward Japan' (Satō 1972: 453–454).

Tokyo's Passivity Toward Reinforcing the Pacific Settlement of Disputes

It was in the discussions over the Geneva Protocol that the gap became increasingly visible between the determination of the Japanese diplomats in Geneva to fulfill the responsibilities of a permanent member of the Council and the lack of support in Tokyo for initiatives to strengthen the means of facilitating the pacific settlement of conflicts.

The Japanese government found the original draft for adoption by the General Assembly to be problematic because it proposed naming a party that started a war due to conflicts stemming from domestic issues as the aggressor if it failed to exhaust all other measures according to the League's procedure. Afraid that this might leave Japan condemned as such if it went to war with the US over the issue of immigration, officials in Tokyo instructed Adachi to propose a revision (JHACR 1924a, November). On 28 September 1924, at the last stage of the discussion, he thus introduced a resolution which suggested that the Covenant itself should be revised if the draft protocol was not changed. Other members were surprised by this, because Adachi's proposal would have the effect of strengthening the Council's regulation over war, even though Japan had previously opposed such a trend. Such was the confusion that this came to be called the 'Japan Incident' (Unno 1972: 54). In practice, however, Adachi's proposal was similar to a filibuster strategy insofar as it was intended to just prolong the discussion. Although he would later recall that it was driven by his view that Article 11 of the Covenant and the Protocol article were inconsistent, the tone of his writing appears to be more apologetic than this would suggest (Adachi 2019). Even Adachi, who had played a significant role in the Council, could do nothing but follow Tokyo's instructions on the matter.

After the Protocol was approved unanimously by the General Assembly, Tokyo scrutinized the issue in preparation for further discussion at the December 1924 Council meeting. As part of this preparatory work, Dr. Sachi Takutarō, a legal advisor to the Foreign Ministry, wrote a report on 'Domestic and International Issues', while other officials contributed by translating and studying an article on the topic by Edwin O. Borchad, a scholar of international law at Yale Law School (JCAHR 1924b, November 18). Both authorities were known to have a traditional view of international law that was critical of the League's efforts to regulate war (Shinohara 2012: 37–63). The view that the Tokyo officials were looking for a loophole to avoid supporting the Protocol is supported by the discussion that took place in a top-secret meeting on the Japanese position on 8 November, during which the head of the treaty section remarked that 'ratifying the Protocol in its original form was a too hasty decision, and we should never support this position.' The main fear was that opening the door to the League's intervention in domestic issues might hamper Japan's policy toward China. The minutes of the meeting recorded one participant as complaining that 'The Protocol went too far to regulate war' (JCAHR 1924c, November 18). The historian Yoshiro Unno goes a step further by arguing that it was naturally difficult for Japan to support the protocol because it did not even like the Covenant itself (Unno 1972: 55).

Japan was not alone in harboring concerns over the direction being taken by the drafting of the protocol, however, which became clear when it appeared as an item on the agenda of the Council's meeting of 12 March 1925.[11] The president, Aristide Briand, gave a long speech that commended it, describing it as an important measure because 'The League of Nations must retain and increase its strength.' However, there had been a change of government in Britain and the new MacDonald administration was less favorable toward the protocol than its predecessor. Although it was defended by Hymans on behalf of Belgium and Guani for Uruguay, Ishii on behalf of Japan stated very diplomatically that, 'The Japanese government has not yet completed the study and examination of this all-important question of the pacific resolution of international conflicts. Therefore, it is not yet in a position to define its attitude one way or another.' Beneš, the rapporteur for the issue, mounted a defense by saying, 'We want peace and security and, I have already said, I think we shall get them sooner or later through some system applying the leading ideas of in one form or another the Protocol' (*OJ* 1925: 451–453, 456–457, 460). In the end, however, only Czechoslovakia ratified the Protocol.

Tokyo's deep concerns over the broader implications of any attempt to regulate war appeared when it was unwilling to support attempts to harmonize the Covenant with the attempt at the 'outlawry' of war in the 1928 Pact of Paris.[12] Also known as the Kellogg-Briand Pact, this was not a product of the League, but aimed to make it illegal to use war as an instrument of national policy. It thus went further than the Geneva Protocol, which at least left room for the conduct of certain types of war. When the League appointed a committee to study the issue, Japan was afraid that any further attempt to regulate the use of force might ultimately impinge on its right to self-defense (Shinohara 2012: 93–95). Despite these reservations, however, Japan did follow suit when fourteen other nations formed the first wave to sign the treaty.

The Japanese diplomats in Geneva, including Adachi and Satō, thus faced a dilemma. While they dutifully carried out the task given to their country as a permanent member of the Council, they had to prioritize Tokyo's instructions regarding how to stop the League's efforts to encourage the pacific settlement of disputes from going too far. Realizing that the League's ideals in this respect were not compatible with Japan's foreign policy, especially in possible future actions in China, they worked with great diligence to find fault with proposals such as the Geneva Protocol, designed to close loopholes in the Covenant that might be used to justify the use of force against aggressor states under certain circumstances. The limits of this balancing act would be tested by the Manchurian Crisis.

The Manchurian Crisis and Discussions at the Council

By the time Japan started its invasion of Manchuria on 18 September 1931, the Council had been transformed from what it had been when it was originally established in 1920. Even though member states had failed to ratify the Geneva Protocol, it continued to discuss how to promote the League's principles and improve its own functioning. Moreover, US support for the Kellogg-Briand Pact contributed to the context within which China, having just won a seat on the Council, immediately appealed to the body against Japan under Article 11 of the Covenant.

Even though back-room negotiations among the great powers took place and the Secretary-General attempted to mediate between the two disputants, it can be argued that the procedure specified in the Covenant was carried out faithfully. This involved holding discussions that show a total and sincere commitment to carrying out the obligations of the League and an exhaustive attempt to meet the most difficult diplomatic challenge of following due process to achieve the pacific settlement of a territorial dispute in the middle of a military crisis. This view is supported by the numerous talks that took place, dispatches from the commission of enquiry into the situation, and published reports.

Despite criticism that the weakness of the concept of collective security was revealed by the lack of will on the part of member states to implement the recommendations that were made, Japan was at least condemned as the aggressor.[13] In this regard, it can be said that the Council had achieved the institutional and procedural legitimacy that it had sought for itself, and that it succeeded in rendering Japan's actions unjustifiable in the view of member states. The more specific measures that were taken by the League and the content of the Lytton Report into the crisis have attracted wide scholarly attention and are covered in some detail in other chapters of this book. Therefore, this analysis will focus on understanding the significance of the discursive process in the Council meetings, showing how the formulation of shared thoughts and ideas is indispensable not just for building the foundation for collective action but also for constructing the intersubjective and ideational nature of international legitimacy.

The start of this process can be seen with the reaction of the Council to the air strike that Japan launched against the city of Jinzhou, some distance from the site of the original attack at Mukden. This occurred on 8 October, just as the Japanese government announced that it would withdraw its forces. Such was the shock of the League members that they recalled Aristide Briand to act as chair of the Council. Despite suffering ill health, this long-time supporter of the organization had played an essential role in concluding the Pact of Paris and was well placed to bring his rich experience to managing the Council meetings that took place in October, November, and December (Walters 1986: 481).

During the first phase of the discussions, Japan's position became more difficult when the topic was raised of inviting a US delegate to attend. Seeing this as unfavorable to his country, the Japanese representative on the Council, Kenkichi Yoshizawa, argued that a committee of experts should be nominated to discuss the issue because it was a matter that impinged on the League's constitution. Lord Reading, a delegate from Britain, countered that it would be 'unfortunate if the very important question which at present divided the Japanese and the Chinese Governments were to be in any way put on the side or its solution postponed because an accessory constitutional question had been raised.' He was supported by the Spanish delegate, Madariaga, who remarked that he was a little 'surprised' that the discussion had been derailed by such 'a subtle legal point' and instead asserted that 'consideration should be given to the infinitesimal extent to which the Council might be departing from the spirit of the Covenant.' Two votes were then held. The first, the Japanese proposal to create a committee of experts to investigate the issue, was rejected by twelve to two, with only Germany throwing its support behind

Japan. In the second, on whether to invite a US representative to attend, thirteen 'yeas' overruled Japan's solitary 'nay' (*OJ* 1931: 2326–2329).

The next day, 16 October, Yoshizawa repeated his opposition to US participation, appealing to an opinion of the International Court of Justice that the Council should reach unanimity on such a question. Lord Reading candidly responded by regretting that he was unable to agree with the Japanese representative and noting that the League would be unable to deal with the Manchurian Crisis if it got deeply involved in debating such a constitutional question. Instead, he insisted, 'our real purpose, our important purpose, our solemn purpose', was to 'determine one of the most important questions that have ever come before the Council of the League of Nations.' Madariaga shared this sense of gravity when he said, 'We are probably faced with the most serious problem which the Council of the League has ever had to solve.' Reflecting a degree of idealism, he added that 'the League of Nations must have the support of all the moral force it can obtain to ensure peace.' This sense of mission was further reinforced when Briand ended the session by reminding the participants that all members had 'pledged themselves to maintain peace' (*OJ* 1931: 2331–2335).

The next meeting, held on October 23, was attended by Lord Robert Cecil, who, sensing the gravity of the crisis that the League was facing, stated that the British government found it 'extremely difficult' to see how incidents such as the bombing of Jinzhou could 'be justified by any known principle of international law.' Pointing to the contradictory actions taken by the Japanese government, he pressed on Yoshizawa the importance of clarifying 'what the Japanese government has in mind.' Briand also asked Yoshizawa what the Japanese government intended as a solution (*OJ* 1931: 2348–2350).

When the Council reconvened the next day, on 24 October, the most notable figures of Briand, Cecil, Madariaga, and Scialoja all showed their frustration with Japan. Madariaga, for instance, made a lengthy statement in which he insisted, 'I would very respectfully point out to the Japanese that the present case is an extremely dangerous one. The League of Nations is based on respect for the territorial integrity and political independence of its members.' He then went on to complain that the very fact that the Japanese troops had gone outside the zone around their section of the Manchurian railway 'has tended to increase rather than decrease insecurity.' He then pointed out the contradiction in Yoshizawa's position by citing a statement he had made on 13 October. Cecil expressed a similar sense of urgency when he urged, 'Evacuation must take place first. Discussion of the treaties may follow' (*OJ* 1931: 2353–2354). It is in this context that, in accordance with League procedure, on December 12 the chairman of the Council proposed and adopted the resolution to dispatch the commission of enquiry to Japan, China, and Manchuria under the leadership of Lord Lytton.

When the Council met in January 1932, the military situation had worsened further with Japan's attack on Shanghai. At the Council meetings that month and in February, both Japanese and Chinese delegates presented detailed information to support their positions. On January 30, the Chinese delegate then proposed the application of Article 15, which was opposed by Satō on behalf of Japan. The Council, he argued, had already discussed the issue based on Article 11. If China's appeal was to now fall under Article 15, then the whole basis of the discussion would be changed. In response, the president of the Council and the Secretary-General stated that there was no legal reason to rule out an appeal to Article 15.

In subsequent Council meetings, even though Satō defended Japan's position by submitting additional information, it was evident that Japan was on the defensive. Other delegates became increasingly forthright in expressing their frustration. Lord Cecil reminded Satō that he himself had previously remarked that, 'the Japanese Government has no territorial ambitions in China, whether in Manchuria or elsewhere.' He further argued that after the commission of enquiry had examined the conditions in China, its report would be 'a very important element' in any decisions, and reminded Satō that the resolution of 10 December committed the two contesting parties 'to adopt all measures necessary to avoid any further aggravation of the situation.' Madariaga, for his part, remarked that, since 18 September, the situation had changed for the worse. Noting the Japanese delegate's plea for flexibility, he added, 'I am sure that he himself will agree that the Council has endeavored to show the greatest understanding and patience' (*OJ* 1932: 346–370). On 19 February 1932, the president of the Council proposed a resolution to the effect that the General Assembly would discuss the case under the application of Article 15 of the Covenant.

The discussions held at the Council meetings from October 1931 to February 1932, even before the Lytton Commission had revealed its verdict, thus show the difficult situation that the Japanese delegates faced when having to defend their country's actions, and how their statements were the subject of increasingly harsh rebukes from other members. The contents of the Lytton Report and the process of Japan's withdrawal will not be discussed here, because they are covered in detail in other chapters. What is important to note is how the discussions in the Council show the tension that had come to exist between the earlier attempt of Japan's diplomats at the League to use the organization to boost their country's international legitimacy and status as a great power and the emergence of a foreign policy driven by the growing forces of nationalism and militarism at home.

Between Power and Ideals: The Long Shadow of the League

There can be no doubt that the Manchurian crisis painfully reveals the dilemma of Japan's diplomats in Geneva, who had to choose between staying true to their faith in the League and their will to support their country's position. However, it would be wrong to say that it destroyed their belief in the importance of building international organizations altogether. Adachi, who left the League to assume a position as a judge at the Permanent Court of International Justice, is said to have been plagued both physically and mentally by Japan's aggression and the League's response. When he passed away in the Netherlands, in 1934, appreciation of his contribution to the PCIJ was marked by a state funeral in that country and an obituary in the *New York Times* (NYT 1934). He was torn between his desire to support the League and his inherent loyalty to his nation. After all, the Japanese diplomats in the League were 'nation-centered internationalists' who supported and adhered to the League's cause only so far as it served Japan's priority—the pursuit of its interests in China and the persistence to maintain the leeway to use force as deemed necessary.[14]

One had to wait for the end of World War Two for Japan to finally realize that its ambivalent policy toward the League had ended up being so costly for the country, its people, its neighbors, and the rest of the world. The ideals that they had helped to foster in the League did have a longer-term impact, however, as is shown more clearly by Satō's life story. Having survived the war, including serving as ambassador to the Soviet Union from 1942 to 1945, he became the first delegate to the United Nations when Japan finally joined the organization in 1956. In an article he published in 1947, he clearly stated his belief that the failure to stop Japan's aggression and prevent it from leaving the League was not solely due to the organization itself. Comparing the commitment and support of the members of any international organization to the coal used to power a locomotive, he concludes: 'Whether the UN functions or dysfunctions depends upon the determination of member states' (Satō 1947: 1–5). This sounds all the more credible in light of Satō's failed attempt to defend his country's position at the Council during the Manchuria affair, knowing all along that Tokyo's policy and the actions of the Japanese military were in clear defiance of the League's cause and principles.

The failure to find a solution to the Manchurian crisis should not, therefore, be allowed to completely obscure the long-term impact of the wider range of activities of the Council, such as the discussions related to Article 11 of the Covenant, its work on minority issues, and the practices of investigation and analysis that it developed. Taken together with the extensive technical work of the League that is discussed in other chapters of this book, this helped to establish the foundations for much of the work carried out under the auspices of the UN today. That a key diplomat such as Satō could emerge from World War Two still committed to the building of the successor to the League shows that the policies and judgements hammered out in its Council were at least consistent and persuasive enough to sustain the norms that support the pacific settlement of disputes, such as the notion of 'collective legitimacy.'[15]

It can be concluded, therefore, that while technical cooperation can provide public goods in fields such as health and development, engaging in conflict resolution is what helps to turn collective expectations into international norms. Members of the Council understood this when they insisted on following due process at the time of the Manchurian crisis, even though they knew that there was no need to wait for the adoption of the final report presented by the Lytton Commission to determine that Japan was the offending party. One British official even wrote that the League's policies had made it clear that Japan's departure from the organization should have been expected, telling Foreign Secretary Sir John Simon, 'I do not doubt that they would prefer to quit that body rather than renounce the line which they have taken up' (FO 1932). By maintaining procedure, however, the Council could be used to reveal Japan's attitude as insincere and inexcusable and to provide the other members with a platform to express their frustration.

Some scholars go so far as to argue that Japan supported the League eagerly and enthusiastically (Dickinson 2013: 60–83, 2018: 587–599). This needs to be tempered to a large degree, however. As is shown by the attempts of the Japanese delegates to defend their country's position by making various minor and legally spurious points, the efforts of diplomats who are dedicated to working through international organizations are doomed to failure when their own governments are set on a different course. Yet the practice of bringing together representatives to meet in person, discuss the items on the agenda, and reach tangible results in the form of resolutions and agreements on a broad range of issues can establish the foundation of the discursive sphere that is essential for collective expectations and understandings to emerge and develop. This is the kind of activity that Inis Claude Jr. draws attention to with respect to the UN when he insists that it is not derogatory to describe an international organization as a 'debating society', given that discussion and debate are necessary to fulfill 'the function of collective legitimization' which is one of the essential features of all such bodies (Claude 1966: 373; Lenz and Viola 2017; Franck 1988; Zaum 2016).

From this perspective, the Council played an important role in the long-term institutionalization of a collective and multilateral forum to facilitate the development and solidification of ideas that support the pacific settlement of disputes. Although that principle had been fixed and promulgated by the Covenant, its creative interpretation and implementation were left to the Council. Its failure to do this effectively over Manchuria was one of the major steps leading to the ultimate failure of the League. However, the need to have an arena for the exploration and testing of ideas of international order has continued down to the present day in the form of the UN Security Council. That the practice of allowing the five Permanent Members to exercise veto power over its decisions has become a matter of serious contention, especially since Russia's invasion of Ukraine in February 2022, shows how the reconciliation of international governance with the freedom of powerful states continues to be a central question of international relations today (Thompson et al., 1922). The above chapter shows that by looking at the role of Japan's diplomats in the League on one hand and the institutional and normative developments that took place at the League on the other, it is possible to show that the ways in which actors have to deal with specific problems in international organizations not only illustrate but also show how it is possible to transcend the realist-utopian dichotomy. In line with the constructivist turn that has become influential in International Relations theory since the end of the Cold War, what is required to understand this kind of process is a framework for analysis that can account for the complex interplay between the material power of states and the ideational factors shaping cooperation.

Notes

1. Although the Foreign Ministry took the lead in establishing the League of Nations Union in Japan, it was still able to carry out some of its own activities when it came to publications and hosting lectures. For more on the Union see Birn (1981) and McCarthy (2009).
2. The most renowned and eloquent of the 'Realist' texts is of course Carr's 1939 polemic (Carr 1981). See Akami's chapter in this volume for a critical discussion of Carr's Realism.
3. Notable exceptions to the lack of work on the Council are Müller (2020) and Lipscy (2017: 200–245).
4. For recent works on the Secretariat see Gram-Skjoldager Ikonomou (2019) and Dykmann (2015). Ranshofen-Wertheimer (1945) is a classic, but helpful for grasping the entire Secretariat.
5. For more on Nitobe and the League see Burkman (2008) and Liang (2017).
6. It is possible to interpret this case as the first peacekeeping mission carried out by an international organization.
7. For a contemporary discussion of the need to strengthen the measures of the Covenant for preventing war, see Williams (1924).
8. For Brouckère see Henri (1970).
9. The full report, Reduction of Armament, is in *OJ* (1927): 832–833.
10. For minority issues and the League see Raitz von Frentz (1999), Fink (2004), and Meijknecht (2012).
11. Originally, the Council planned to discuss the protocol in December, but due to the change of the British government, it was postponed to the March 1925 meeting (*OJ* 1925: 124).
12. For the outlawry of war movement and international lawyers' discussion of the Pact, see Shinohara (2012: 64–91), Hathaway and Shapiro (2017), and Hendrickson (2020).
13. For the outlawry of war movement and international lawyers' discussion of the Pact, see Shinohara (2012: 64–91), Hathaway and Shapiro (2017), and Hendrickson (2020).
14. For 'nation-centered internationalism,' see Liang (2017): 173–174.
15. For the possible implications of this work for International Relations Theory, see Mahoney (2014).

References

Adachi, Mineichirō. 2011. *Adachi Mineichirō: Shokan o chushin ni shie* [Letters of Adachi Mineichirō]. Yamagata: Adachi Mineitiro Hakase Kenshokai.

Adachi, Mineichirō. 2019. Junebu Giteisyo to yo no shusei [The Geneva Protocol and My Proposal]. In *Sekai Bankoku no Heiwa o kishite* [For the Peace of the World], ed. Yanagihara Masaharu, 203–207. Tokyo: University of Tokyo Press.

Adachi, Mineichirō. 1930. Kokusai Renmei no hattatsu wa kenzen nariya [Has the League of Nations Developed Well?]. *Kokusai Chisiki* 10 (6): 7–17.

Berdahl, Clarence A. 1937. The Implications of the Kellogg Pact concerning American Foreign Policy. *New York University Law Quarterly Review* 15: 82–107.

Birn, Donald S. 1981. *The League of Nations Union, 1918–1945*. Oxford: Clarendon Press.

Borchard, Edwin O. 1924. The Distinction between Legal and Political Questions. *Proceedings of the American Society of International Law*: 50–57.

Burkman, Thomas. 2008. *Japan and the League of Nations: Empire and World Orders*. Hawaii: University of Hawaii Press.

Carr, E.H. 1981. *The Twenty Years Crisis 1919–1939: An Introduction to the Study of International Relations*. Basingstoke: Macmillan Press.

Claude, Inis. 1966. Collective Legitimization as a Political Function of the United Nations. *International Organization* 20: 367–379.

Dickinson, Frederick R. 2013. *World War I and the Triumph of a New Japan, 1919–1930*. Cambridge: Cambridge University Press.

Dickinson, Frederick R. 2014. AHR Forum: Toward a Global Perspective of the Great War: Japan and the Foundations of a Twentieth-Century World. *American Historical Review* 119: 1154–1183.

Dickinson, Frederick R. 2018. More than a 'Moment': 'Woodrow Wilson and the foundations of twentieth-century Japan.' *Japanese Journal of Political Science* 18: 587–599.

Dykmann, Klaas. 2015. How International was the Secretariat of the League of Nations? *The International History Review* 37: 721–744.

Eagleton, Clyde. 1933. The Attempt to Define War. *International Conciliation* 15: 237–287.

Eloranda, Jari. 2011. Why did the League of Nations fail? *Cliometrica* 5: 27–52.

Fink, Carole. 2004. *Defending the Rights of Others: The Great Powers, the Jews and International Minority Protection, 1878–1938*. Cambridge: Cambridge University Press.

FO (UK Foreign Office). 1932. Lindley to Sir John Simon, 25 November. National Archive FO 262/1802.

Franck, Thomas. 1988. Legitimacy in the International System. *American Journal of International Law* (82/4): 705–759.

Gram-Skjoldager, Karen, and Haakon A. Ikonomou. 2019. The Construction of the League of Nations Secretariat. Formative Practices of Autonomy and Legitimacy in International Organizations. *International History Review* 41: 257–279.

Hathaway, Oona, and Scott Shapiro. 2017. *The Internationalists: How a Radical Plan to Outlaw War Remade the World*. New York: Simon & Schuster.

Hendrickson, David. 2020. How Many Cheers for the Peace Pact? *American Political Thought* 9: 144–169.

Henri, Rolin. 1970. Louis de Brouckère et l'action pour la paix. *Bulletin de la Classe des lettres et des sciences morales et politiques* 56: 578–590.

JCAHR [Japan Center for Asian Historical Records]. 1924a. Heiwa giteisyo ni taisuru Nihon shusei-an [Japan's revision of the Protocol], November. B04122433300bb0129.b-1142.

JCAHR. 1924b. Kokunai mondai oyobi Kokusaimondai ni tuite [Domestic and International Issues]; Horitsu mondai to Seijimondai tono sai [Differences between Legal and Political problems], November 18. B04122433300bb0129.b-1142. This is the full translation of Borchard (1924b).

JCAHR. 1924c. Kokusai Renmei Heiwa Gitei-sho Kenkyu Iinkai dai 3 kai Gijiroku [The proceedings of the third study meeting on the League's Protocol], November 18. B04122322600bb0129b.

The League of Nations. 1920, 1925, 1927, 1928, 1929, 1931, and 1932. *Official Journal*.

Lenz, Tobias, and Lora Anne Viola. 2017. Legitimacy and Institutional Change in International Organizations: A Cognitive Approach. *Review of International Studies* 43: 939–961.

Liang, Pan. 2017. National Internationalism in Japan and China. In *Internationalisms: A Twentieth-Century History*, ed. Glenda Sluga, 170–177. Cambridge: Cambridge University Press.

Lipscy, Phillip Y. 2017. *Renegotiating the World Order: Institutional Change in International Relations*. Cambridge: Cambridge University Press.

Mahoney, Joseph O. 2014. Rule Tensions and the Dynamics of Institutional Change: From 'to the Victor Go the spoils' to the Stimson Doctrine. *European Journal of International Relations* 20: 834–857.

Matsushita, Masatoshi. 1929. *Japan in the League of Nations*. New York: Columbia University Press.

McCarthy, Helen. 2009. Leading from the Center: The League of Nations Union, Foreign Policy and 'Political Agreement' in the 1930s. *Contemporary British History* 23 (4): 527–542.

Meijknecht, Anna. 2012. The Minority Protection System between World War I and World War II. *The Max Planck Encyclopedia of Public International Law*, Vol. VII, ed. Rudiger Wolfrum, 275–276. Oxford: Oxford University Press.

Müller, Thomas. 2020. Institutional Reforms and the Politics of Inequality Reproduction: The Case of the League of Nations' Council Crisis in 1926. *Global Society* 34: 304–317.

New York Times. 1934. Judge Adachi, 65, Dies in Amsterdam. 28 December.

Nish, Ian. 1993. *Japan's Struggle with Internationalism: Japan, China, and the League of Nations, 1931–1933*. London: Kegan Paul International.

Ogata, Sadako. 1964. *Defiance in Manchuria*. Berkeley: University of California Press.

Raitz von Frentz, Christian. 1999. *A Lesson Forgotten: Minority Protection under the League of Nations: The Case of the German Minority in Poland*. New York: St. Martin's Press.

Ranshofen-Wertheimer, Egon F. 1945. *International Secretariat: A Great Experiment in International Administration*. Washington, DC: Carnegie Endowment for International Peace.

Satō, Naotake. 1947. Kokusai Renmei no Keiken to Kokusai Rengo [The experience of the League of Nations and the United Nations] *Hitotsubashi Ronso* (18): 1–5.

Satō, Naotake. 1963. Kaiko 80 nen [The Eighty Years in Retrospect]. Tokyo: Chuokoron.

Satō, Naotake (ed.). 1972. Nihon Gaikoushi, Vol. 14, 453–454. Tokyo: Kashima Kenkyujyo Shuppankai.

Secretariat of the League of Nations. 1930. *Ten Years of World Co-operation*. London: Hazel, Watson and Viney.

Shinohara, Hatsue. 2012. *US International Lawyers in the Interwar Years: A Forgotten Crusade*. Cambridge: Cambridge University Press.

Thompson, Shamala Kandiah, Landgren, Karin, and Romita, Paul. 1922. The United Nations in Hindsight: Challenging the Power of the Security Council Veto. *Just Security*, 28 April. https://www.justsecurity.org/81294/the-united-nations-in-hindsight-challenging-the-power-of-the-security-council-veto/ Accessed 22 June 2022.

Thorne, Christopher. 1972. *The Limits of Foreign Policy: The West, the League and the Far Eastern Crisis of 1931–1933*. London: Hamish Hamilton.

Unno, Yoshirō. 1972. *Kokusai Renmei to Nihon* [The League of Nations and Japan]. Tokyo: Hara shobo.

Walters, Francis P. 1986. *A History of the League of Nations*. Reprint version, Connecticut MA: Greenwood Press.

Williams, John F. 1924. The Geneva Protocol of 1924 for the Pacific Settlement of International Disputes. *Journal of the British Institute of International Affairs* (3/6): 288–304.

Zaum, Dominik. 2016. Legitimacy. *The Oxford Handbook of International Organizations*, ed. Jacob Katz Cogan et al., 1107–1125. Oxford: Oxford University Press.

China's Response to the Ethiopian Crisis (1935–1938)

Chang Li

Introduction

The 1935–1937 war between Italy and Ethiopia, which culminated in the colonization of the latter, has been much studied by historians. Very little has been said, however, about its implications for Eastern Asian actors in the League of Nations. This chapter starts to fill the gap by looking at how China managed the opportunities and risks that the crisis presented. Central to its response was the need to navigate the tension that arose between the League's commitment to the pacific settlement of disputes and the territorial integrity of states on the one hand, and the pursuit of the narrower interests of the great powers on the other. The outcome was of great importance because China had been grappling with the same problem in the League since Japan's invasion of Manchuria in 1931, which is covered in the following section of this book.

With Ethiopia being so geographically distant from Eastern Asia there was more potential for China to maintain a good relationship with Italy than with Japan, despite Mussolini's expansionist foreign policy. Yet

C. Li (✉)
Institute of Modern History, Academia Sinica, Taipei, Taiwan

C. R. Hughes and H. Shinohara (eds.), *East Asians in the League of Nations*, New Directions in East Asian History,
https://doi.org/10.1007/978-981-19-7067-2_9

China's government and diplomats had to balance this priority against the need to maintain the credible commitment of the members of the League to the principles of the Covenant. This was complicated by a context in which public opinion was having a growing impact on foreign policy and the great powers were pre-occupied with avoiding another war in Europe. Although the diplomats ultimately failed to win all that they hoped for, their activities shed new light on how Eastern Asians used the League to shape international norms in ways that outlasted the life of the organization itself.

The Impact of the Ethiopian Crisis on China's Relationship with Italy

Maintaining a good relationship with Italy was important for China because it was one of the permanent members of the League Council, until its withdrawal from the organization on 11 December 1937. Moreover, the two countries had maintained relatively strong ties in the first half of the twentieth century. When they upgraded their legations to embassies in June 1934, Italy became the first Western country to establish an embassy in China. The military dimension to the relationship was increasingly important as China's government faced the challenges of fighting both Japan and the growing communist insurgency. This included an Air Mission sent by Prime Minister Benito Mussolini (1921–1943) to help the Nationalist government modernize its air force. Six naval officers from China's Ministry of the Navy were trained at l'Academie Navale de Livourne during 1935–1939, and nine more officers from the Guangdong local navy were dispatched to study at Regia Mario Italiana, in 1937. In early September 1935, Generalissimo Chiang Kai-shek (1887–1975) instructed H. H. Kung (1880–1967), his Minister of Finance, to purchase two to eight high-speed torpedo-boats, and demanded that they be secretly transported to the city of Hukou along the Yangzi River in Jiangxi province by the following February. Chiang also wanted to purchase 30 aerial torpedoes and 100 mines, which the Chinese ambassador to Italy, Liu Wendao (1893–1967), was entrusted to acquire within two months (CHCKS 2014: 682–683).

Such factors had to be taken into consideration when the Chinese government formulated its reaction to the request made to the League by Emperor Haile Selassie (1892–1975) for arbitration between his country and Italy, in early January 1935. The crisis had begun with the Walwal

Incident of December 1934, when skirmishes took place on the Ethiopian border between a detachment of the emperor's army and Somali troops in the service of Italy. Although the League tried hard to encourage arbitration and negotiation, it had little to show for its efforts after the first year. By July 1936, it had backtracked on its initial resolve to impose sanctions on Italy due to recognition that such an approach had little prospect of changing what had become the de facto occupation of Ethiopia.

A fuller analysis of the conflict and the actions of the League can be found elsewhere.[1] It is remarkable, however, that little attention has been paid to China's response or the links between the crises in Ethiopia and Manchuria. This could be due to an assumption that China lacked the power or motivation to play a significant role in a conflict from which it was geographically so far removed. Its diplomats did, however, keep close track of developments and frequently reported back to their Ministry of Foreign Affairs (MOFA). What their observations show is an awareness of how the immediate responses of other states to the crisis were driven not by a strong commitment to the League's principles of collective security and territorial integrity but by the strategic interests of the major powers.

The implications of the crisis for Japan were naturally highest in the minds of diplomats. This can be seen in a report submitted by Yang Jie (1889–1949), the Chinese ambassador to the Soviet Union, to the Nationalist government leader Chiang Kai-shek, which had been prepared by a Chinese Military Attaché, dated 22 March 1935. Noting that Japanese officers trained and commanded the Ethiopian army and provided it with weapons, he proposed that its interests in the country would be impaired by Italy's occupation. It was for this reason, he proposed, that Japan had twice lodged protests against Italy. On the other hand, the Japanese government had also suggested that if Italy would stop providing weapons to China, Tokyo would be more willing to negotiate with Rome on the Ethiopian question. From Yang's viewpoint, the Italian government would have to assess its interests in Africa before taking Japan's suggestion into consideration (CKSA 1935a).

The diplomatic correspondence also indicates the dilemma posed by China's need to maintain good relations with Italy. When the Italian ambassador to China, Vincenzo Lojacono, visited Chinese foreign minister, Wang Zhaoming, on 30 August, 1935, he made his government's case by stating that while it was determined to occupy Ethiopia it still hoped to contain the situation as a limited colonial war. If the League Council authorized Britain to take military sanctions against Italy when it met the following month, he warned, it would risk expanding the conflict into a European war. As such, Lojacono expected the Chinese representatives to the League to support Italy, or at least not to oppose it. Considering the possible consequences, Wang claimed that China would not give approval to the aggression made by Italy, but also stated that mutual amity between two countries should be promoted. He thus requested the Chinese representatives to the League, Yan Huiqing (1877–1950) and Quo Tai-chi (1890–1952), to 'remain silent' on the Ethiopia question. If the discussion reached the stage when voting was needed, the representatives were supposed to ask for further instructions from the MOFA (CKSA 1935b). Chiang Kai-shek approved what Wang suggested (CKSA 1935b).

China's position on the sanctions issue was also influenced to a large degree by a reluctance to alienate the other great powers on the Council. The embassy in London was aware that the British government was trying to find ways to stop the Ethiopia question from undermining its own relationship with Italy and driving it into a closer alignment with Germany. It thus reported to Chiang Kai-shek in June 1935 that Anthony Eden (1897–1977), minister for the League of Nations and soon to be British foreign secretary, had met Mussolini in Rome and told him that his government was prepared to give its colonized territory near Ethiopia to Italy so as to reduce the tensions. Mussolini had refused to accept the offer, however (CKSA 1935c).

Chiang Kai-shek's personal documents of September to October 1936 reveal a high degree of concern over the prospects for war. Sometimes, he was uncertain whether it would break out, while at other times he was optimistic that France might help to calm the turbulence. Some indication of how he had to balance the priorities of maintaining a good relationship with Italy and maintaining the League's principles can be seen from an entry dated 26 September, where he turns his attention to China's procurement of six Italian heavy-bombers, which should have been transported three months earlier (CHCKS Vol. 4: 691). He writes, 'It is not good timing to request the Italian government for the follow-up of the procurement at this critical stage. But in contrast to the Italo-Abyssinian [Ethiopian] crisis, the situation in East Asia has a ten-fold impact on our country. In view of this fact, I have to push it' (SLGB 2008: 467–468).

Chiang did not completely discount the possibility that China could play a positive role. In a diary entry for 2 October, he records that H. H. Kung had suggested that he should use his personal friendship with

Mussolini to persuade him to settle the dispute peacefully. Although he did not think this would work, he thought it would be a good idea if Liu Wendao could at least try to catch Mussolini's intention (CKSD 02-10-35). Chiang's preference for a peaceful resolution was no doubt influenced by the need to maintain diplomatic pressure against Japan's use of force in Manchuria, but his diaries also show that it was coloured by a personal sense of morality. In response to the launching of an attack by Italy on Ethiopia on 3 October, 1935, for example, he borrowed from Confucius to write, 'The person [Italy] who initiated evil actions would probably have no posterity'. Despite this, and his expectations for an early ceasefire, Chiang could still compliment Mussolini by writing, 'His adventurous spirit really makes him a powerful and strong man' (CKSD 1935a).

The conflict deepened, however, when Italian troops crossed the Ethiopian border. On 7 October an investigative committee established by the League Council submitted a report which found Italy to be in breach of Article 12 of the Covenant, making it appropriate to take action under Article 16. On 10 October, the Assembly voted to constitute a Committee of Coordination, tasked with applying a range of sanctions. Shortly before the vote, Wang Zhaoming pointed out to Chiang that China had to support economic sanctions, but that this would not harm Sino-Italian relations because both the League and Italy knew what the voting would bring, to which Chiang agreed. Liu Wendao also suggested to the MOFA that China should cast its vote in support of the measures. By the following year, their view was borne out as the League proceeded to discuss revocation of the sanctions it had tried to impose.

The turning point had come when Italy presented the League with a *fait accompli* by proclaiming its sovereignty over Ethiopia and installing King Vittorio Emmanuele III (1869–1947) as the Emperor of Ethiopia on 9 May, 1936. When the Council recognized this de facto situation and called for the Assembly to vote on whether to maintain the sanctions issue, Lojacono asked China's MOFA to instruct its representative to vote in favour of revocation. China's Executive Yuan (cabinet) accordingly resolved that: 'The Ministry of Foreign Affairs instruct the Chinese representatives to vote for revoking sanctions on Italy' (NGA 1936). China thus became one of 44 countries to vote in support of the motion to revoke when the Assembly met on 5 July, and the sanctions were lifted ten days later. This did not stop Italy from forging a closer relationship with Germany, however, which had just violated the 1925 Pact of Locarno by sending its troops into the Rhineland in March, putting the two countries on course to eventually become allies outside the League.

Managing Public Opinion: A Controversial Documentary

The Chinese government also had to learn how to balance the concerns of high diplomacy with the increasing importance of public opinion in foreign policy. A good example of this is an incident that arose when a Russian documentary film, *Abyssinia*, was shown at the Isis Cinema in Shanghai shortly after the Italian invasion, leading to a serious disturbance that created several months of friction between China, Italy, and Russia. Produced by the Soyuzkino Production Company and directed by Vladimir Yeshuria and Boris Zeitlin, this documentary consisted of two parts. The first introduced the environmental features and social aspects that characterize Ethiopia, including its natural resources of gold, silver and coals mines, oil fields, military terrain, and the hardship of the peasants. The second part was a newsreel about the war in 1934.

As far as Italy was concerned, it was appropriate for its embassy to protest about the showing of any films deemed to be offensive to the nation and its people, including some American-made films which tended to criticize the Fascist regime or poke fun at Italian stereotypes. Before such movies were released in China, especially in Shanghai, the Italian Embassy would request censorship and China's MOFA would refer the cases to the National Motion Picture Censorship Committee (NMPCC) for further discussion. Sometimes the country of the production company would request its embassy to help in solving any related problems.

On 21 January, 1937, Ferrajolo, a secretary at the Italian Embassy in China, reported to the Chinese MOFA that the showing of an anti-Fascist film like *Abyssinia* might trigger unpleasant reactions because a number of Italian seamen had disembarked at the port. In view of this, the MOFA suggested that Mayor Wu Guozhen (1903–1984) of the Shanghai Municipal government should temporarily suspend the showing. At 3 pm on 22 January, some armed policemen, led by a police inspector, went to the Isis to try to order the staff to not show the film and refund the tickets. Some members of the audience protested that this was completely unjustifiable because a permit had been granted to show the film on 15 January (AH 1937a: 95).

The Italian Embassy was satisfied with the Shanghai Municipal government's quick response and expected the film to be banned from any further showing in Shanghai or elsewhere in China because 'it is inadmissible that a third Country may do propaganda hostile to a nation friendly to China within the territory of the Republic' (AH 1937b: 92–94). Since the movie was a Russian production, two Russian employees working in the Isis passed this information on to their embassy, which soon lodged a strong protest to the MOFA in a memorandum of 3 February (AH 1937c: 105m).

The NMPCC thus decided to re-examine the film and on 8 February, Hsu Mo and Chen Jie, vice-ministers of the MOFA, and Fang Zhi, Director of the Central Propaganda Department, were invited for a discussion. It was then decided that the following contents should be removed: (1) Chinese subtitles concerning the Italian invasion of the colony; (2) the voice-over of the Italian aerial attack on Ethiopia; (3) narratives about Ethiopia made by a Russian News photographer; (4) clips of Italian aeroplanes being shot down and seven people getting injured; (5) the footage of Italians using poison gas; (6) the footage of a bombing of the Red Cross; (7) the voice-over of the Italian occupation of the capital of Ethiopia. After the offending elements were removed as requested, the Isis received a two-day permit to screen the film, but only three times a day. Despite these compromises, however, the Italian Embassy was still not satisfied and again warned about an upcoming disturbance (AH 1937d: 17).

The incident duly occurred when *Abyssinia* was shown on 20 February. According to a report produced by the Isis, during the afternoon screening of the film about 30 to 40 seamen from Italian warship Lepanto had been seated in the hall with about 100 people in plain clothes. At about 3:45 pm the mariners started to smash up the facilities and some broke into the projector room to damage the projector and several films. The Russian manager, David I. Abromovich, and a Russian member of staff, Dimitri Kirichenko, were injured. Four Chinese policemen on the scene merely stood and watched, when an investigation by the Shanghai police confirmed the contents of the cinema's report, it concluded that the riot had been directed by staff in the Italian consulate (AH 1937e: 33).

Immediately after the incident, the Shanghai Municipal government addressed a protest to the Italian consulate general (AH 1937f: 31). On the morning of 22 February, the Italian chargé d'affaires, Desandre, went to see Minister Wang at the MOFA where he complained that *Abyssinia* was nothing more than communist propaganda aimed at defaming Fascism, Italy, and the Italian army. According to him, it was howls of mocking laughter from the Chinese audience that had upset and irritated the disciplined Italian seamen, leading to their relatively aggressive response. Minister Wang expressed his disappointment that a diplomat could take sides like this to cover up an act of deviance that had been committed by his countrymen (AH 1937g: 48, 50). An official letter of protest from the MOFA to the Italian Embassy held that the riot was intentionally planned and that the Italian Embassy had not taken any steps to prevent it beforehand. It urged the embassy to have the perpetrators punished, to ensure that the film was returned to the cinema, and to see that compensation was paid for the losses incurred (AH 1937h: 126). The Russian consulate expressed similar expectations and decided to wait for the results (AH 1937i: 69).

In order to close the case as early as possible, the MOFA instructed Liu Wendao to negotiate with the Italian foreign ministry. However, the negotiations did not go as anticipated because Italy refused to deal with the aftermath of the riot and the ministry continued to insist that *Abyssinia* was an anti-Italian film. In response to the specific requests of the Chinese MOFA, it claimed that the film had been damaged beyond repair in the riot, that despite its concern for the injured no substantial compensation could be offered, and that the perpetrators had evaded capture (AH 1937j: 840). In fact, the Italian Foreign Ministry had no intention to negotiate with the Chinese ambassador and instructed its diplomats in Nanjing to respond to the Chinese MOFA instead. It made clear to its embassy that the acceptance of the following prerequisites was essential for any resolution: provision of evidence of the violence caused by the perpetrators; that the return of the already damaged film was out of the question; and that the compensation of 92,791 Chinese yuan requested by the Isis was completely unacceptable, although 20,000 yuan could be provided as compensation to the injured staff. Despite three months of discussion the negotiations remained deadlocked. When Rome got to know that the two injured staff were Russians it refused to pay any compensation at all (AH 1937k: 177).

The Exchange of Recognition Between Italy and Japan

That the Ethiopian crisis and Japan's invasion of Manchuria both posed a test of the principles embedded in the Covenant posed a particularly thorny question for the Chinese government. As discussed in the following section of this book, the failure of the League to punish Japan after the Lytton Commission had decided that it was the aggressor in Manchuria had become a burning issue in the Chinese press. The pressure on the government to take a stance on the issue only grew further, however, when Italy's request for recognition of its annexation of Ethiopia gave it a common cause with Japan's search for support for recognition of its puppet-state of Manchukuo.

China's MOFA first heard about the possibility of a mutual recognition agreement between Italy and Japan in mid-November 1936. It ordered its embassy to Rome to clarify the situation and ambassador Liu Wendao duly reported back that the Italian foreign minister had confirmed that the Japanese Embassy had proposed mutual recognition two months earlier, but that Italy had not responded (AH 1936a: 1).

Even so, deeply concerned about the recognition exchange proposal, the MOFA ordered its embassy to Tokyo to follow how the relationship between the two countries was developing. Its subsequent report, dated 17 November, includes an analysis of the situation written by an influential Japanese critic which points out that if Italy did recognize Manchukuo, it would incur the dissatisfaction of the Chinese and that Italy would have to sacrifice the benefits it gained from its trade with the country. It also emphasized that since Manchukuo was economically blocked from access to international trade, there was no need for Italy to grant it recognition (AH 1936b: 4).

However, the Chinese Embassy to Rome also found that its Japanese counterpart had taken substantive actions to promote the exchange of recognition. The Italian foreign office admitted that it was negotiating with the Japanese ambassador and there was a possibility that the Italian consulate at the city of Harbin, in Manchukuo, would be moved to Fengtian, that would leave it no longer subordinate to either Italy's Embassy in either Japan or China, but directly to the foreign ministry in Italy (AH 1936c: 21). Victor Hoo Chi-tsai (1894–1972), a Chinese delegate to the League, read from the press that Italy would soon recognize Manchukuo and was eager to learn more about the attitude of the Chinese government to such a development. He suggested that if China decided to make a formal complaint against Italy's recognition of Manchukuo, it should also lodge a protest with the League and distribute copies of the text to all its members (AH 1936d: 22).

The Italian ambassador to China, Vincenzo Lojacono, called on foreign minister, Chang Chun (1889–1990), on 30 November 1936, to try to explain the situation. He stressed that Italy had indeed been informed by Japan that the Manchukuo government had agreed to have the Italian consulate general set up in the city of Shenyang, but that this was only an oral agreement with no official record. He then added that Italy also wanted to set up an observation post on the Eastern Soviet border to conduct business transactions with China and guard against the spread of communism. As a result, it was Italy's intention to continue cooperation with China. When Chang repeated his question about Italy's intentions regarding recognition of Manchukuo, Lojacono emphasized that the consulate general did not have official diplomatic status and that it was not located in Manchukuo's capital of Xinjing (Changchun), which indicated an attitude of non-recognition. In response, Chang said that China would make an immediate announcement that Italy had no intention to recognize Manchukuo. Upon hearing this, Lojacono appeared to be reluctant and said that he had to confirm with Rome (AH 1936e: 25). The MOFA, however, was concerned that such assurances that Italy would not recognize Manchukuo at the legal level were belied by its intention to set up the consulate general in Shenyang. Lojacono then expressed his personal views regarding the issue, pointing out that Italy was not going to join the Anti-Comintern Pact with Germany and Japan. Although it shared Germany's anti-communist stance, there was no intention to take any concrete actions to sign a pact with Japan like that which had been made between Germany and Japan (AH 1936f: 25).

After this meeting, the MOFA immediately assigned Liu Wendao to visit the Italian Foreign Minister, Galeazzo Ciano, to confirm details regarding the move of the Italian consulate general. Liu wanted had to make sure whether the Italian government had recognized Manchukuo or was preparing to do so (AH 1936c). As soon as he received the instruction, he paid a visit to Ciano on 30 November, who explained that locating the consulate general in Manchukuo was only following the steps taken by other countries. Explaining that Italy had no intention to recognize Manchukuo, he emphasized that developing its relations with Japan would not be at the cost of its friendship with China. As for the conflicts between China and Japan, he said that Italy would like to negotiate in China's favour given that Italy and Japan enjoyed good diplomatic relations (AH 1936g: 27). The next day, Liu reported to the MOFA about his visit to Ciano and suggested making public Ciano's statements that 'Italy had no intention to recognize Manchukuo' and 'Italy's friendship with China would not be at the cost of its relations with Japan' and that the import of his words should be emphasized in the press. With Ciano's statements announced to the public, the Italian government would find it harder to explain itself to the international community if it contradicted the assurances it had given to China (AH 1936h: 27).

After this, relatively, positive news was received from Ciano, however, the MOFA obtained information from the General Staff Headquarters that the Japanese ambassador to Italy, Sugimura Yōtarō, together with his secretary, Watanabe, and military Attaché, Numuta, had already had secret contacts with the Italian Ministry of Foreign Affairs' Division of Eastern Affairs, and Department of Military and Political Affairs. The topics for negotiation had included Japan's recognition of Italy's annexation of Ethiopia in exchange for Italy's recognition of Manchukuo, and a commitment by Japan, Germany and Italy to cooperate in fighting against Communism and the Soviet Union, with Japan serving as the military police force of the East. It had then been decided that Japan would go ahead and recognize Italian sovereignty over Ethiopia, that an agreement to set up the Italian consulate in Shenyang would be announced imminently, and that the two states would join with Germany in a tripartite cooperation to oppose communism and the Soviet Union. To help take this plan forward, the deputy dean of the Istituto Italiano per il Medio ed Estremo Oriente in Italy, Jucee, would be assigned to visit Japan under the pretext of delivering lectures (AH 1936i: 38). When Jucee had left Rome on 23 October and taken a tour by ship to arrive in Japan on 2 November, ambassador Sugimura had gone to the station in Rome to see him off. The intelligence also indicated that Jucee was accompanied by staff from the Japanese Embassy. Moreover, on 11 November, Numuta had taken the ship, Sengen Muru, back to Japan (AH 1936i: 38).

Considering this information to be 'vital to the future of our country', the General Staff Headquarters called it to the special attention of the MOFA. But the ministry only responded by instructing the Chinese Embassy to Japan to keep close track of what Jucee was doing (AH 1936j: 38–41). The ensuing report to the MOFA indicated that he had made contacts with scholars in Tokyo and delivered several academic speeches, but it was unclear whether he was engaged in any political activities (AH 1936k: 42–43).

Then came the information in a news report of 28 November that the spokesman of the Japanese foreign ministry had confirmed to foreign correspondents in Tokyo that Japan would sign an important agreement with Italy. The MOFA was greatly concerned about the contents of any such agreement, especially anything related to an exchange of recognition (AH 1936l: 26). Two days later, it was reported by a news agency that Rome had announced that Italy and Japan had in fact signed an agreement confirming mutual recognition of Manchukuo and the annexation of Ethiopia. The MOFA was very confused by these conflicting pieces information (AH 1936m: 27). Ciano, after all, had explained to Liu that setting up a consulate in Manchukuo was just following the example set by other countries and did not mean that Italy would recognize Manchukuo. He had also stressed that Italy had informed Japan many times that his country would never sacrifice its friendship with China for the purpose of improving its amicable relationship with Japan (AH 1936n: 40).

China was not alone in being worried about these developments. Reports in the press in March 1937 that the Italian government would consent to the establishment of a Manchukuo consulate office in Italy triggered serious concern on the part of France. On March 11, the French ambassador to China, Paul Naggiar, thus met with foreign minister Wang Chonghui to express their mutual concerns regarding the recognition issue. Naggiar pointed out that two French consulates had been stationed in Shenyang and Harbin, respectively, before the founding of Manchukuo and that the two consuls stationed there had been appointed for 12 years. The appointment of new consuls or the issuing of consul exequaturs by Japan to recognize their legal status would mean that Manchukuo had gained de facto recognition from France. Due to these considerations, Naggiar explained, the French government would not appoint new consuls. Wang expressed his affirmation of the decision made by the French government and emphasized that, based on the resolutions of the League of Nations, member nations should grant neither de jure nor de facto recognition to Manchukuo. He maintained that consuls located in Manchuria were only supposed to interact with local government officials on general affairs that were not relevant to political relations. He also speculated that Italy had probably only consented to the establishment of its Manchukuo consulate because Japan had agreed to downgrade its embassy in the Ethiopian capital of Addis Ababa to a consulate, indicating its stance on the Italian invasion of that country (AH 1937a: 66–68).

When Naggiar met Wang for a further discussion, on 26 March, however, he announced that the exequatur that the Italian consul in Shenyang had received was issued in the name of Aisin Gioro Puyi, Japan's puppet emperor, which meant that Italy had formally recognized Manchukuo. Under such a circumstance, France could in fact follow Italy and grant recognition to Manchukuo, regardless of the League's resolution to the contrary. Naggiar also claimed that he found it quite incomprehensible that a former Italian minister of finance had been invited to be an advisor to the Chinese government. Vice-minister Xu responded by explaining that his government would try to maintain relations with Italy, but not sacrifice China's interests for the sake of keeping that friendly relationship (AH 1937b: 63–64).

When Italy and Japan finally signed their joint recognition agreement on 1 June, the Italian foreign ministry claimed that it was limited to economic affairs and unrelated to politics. In July, however, Japan launched its all-out invasion of China, and on 29 November, Italy announced its recognition of Manchukuo and the establishment of an embassy in its capital, Xinjing (Changchun). China's MOFA responded by lodging a protest with Ciano (AH 1937c: 48).

These developments came as no surprise to Wellington Koo, China's ambassador to Paris.[2] Drawing on experience of the League that went back as far as the Paris Peace Conference and through working with the Lytton Commission on Manchuria, his view was that Italy's recognition of Manchukuo was not beyond prediction. He further pointed out how 'the Italian government showed its support for the non-recognition principle in the League Assembly but then took an opposite stance', which left the MOFA no choice but to send a memorandum of protest to Rome, the full text of which was also delivered to the members of the League. On 3 December, the Italian consulting Team in the National Aviation Committee was dismissed by the Chinese government and ambassador Liu was recalled from Italy by Chiang Kai-shek in January 1938. A breach of diplomatic relations between China and Italy was imminent (AH 1937d: 56).

Britain's Note on Recognizing Italy's Annexation

China's dilemma had thus become acute. Its appeal to the League against the invasion of Manchuria in 1931 and the establishment of the puppet-state of Manchukuo the following year had been successful insofar as it had led the organization to reaffirm the non-recognition principle, even though it was disappointed by the failure to impose sanctions on Japan. When the League had dealt with the invasion of Ethiopia in 1935, China had hoped to strengthen its own position by supporting the Assembly's resolutions on non-recognition and imposing sanctions against the aggressor, albeit knowing that the measures would prove to be so ineffective that no substantial harm would be done to its relationship with Italy. The developments in the relationship between Italy and Japan that followed soon proved to be at China's cost, however.

Equally concerning was that the manoeuvring of the great powers outside the League over the status of Ethiopia threatened to further undermine the credibility of the non-recognition principle. Most important was a change of attitude by the British government, which signalled a move towards recognition of Italy's control over Ethiopia. This was part of the broader policy of appeasement, designed to prevent the strengthening of Italy's alignment with Hitler's Germany and avoid another war in Europe. It began to become apparent in April 1938, when, after signing an agreement with Germany, Britain requested the discussion of Ethiopia be put on the Council agenda for the 9 May. Faced with a possible challenge to the resolutions that had earlier been made by the Assembly, China was torn between standing firmly in support of the non-recognition position on the one hand and maintaining its alliance with Britain on the other (AH 1938a: 5).

Mired in indecision, China consulted other states. When its ambassador to the United States, C.T. Wang, sought a meeting with Cordell Hull, however, he was told that the secretary of state was away on holiday. His under-secretary merely conveyed the message that he 'regrets u[i]nability to advise on question on political nature pertaining to Chinese government but adds China should know what is best to protect her own interest' (AH 1938b: 31).

The responses from members of the League were obviously determined by their own various interests. Sweden was undecided as to whether to vote for recognition as proposed by Britain but said that it would follow the majority opinion rather than acting alone in such a case (AH 1938c:

17). Iran said it would act in concert with other small states if they had a unanimous stance when it came to a vote. If the small states were divided and the bigger ones reached an agreement on Britain's proposal, then it would go with their decision. In other words, Iran would only make its final decision when the Council met in Geneva (AH 1938d: 24).

Maxim Litvinov, the People's Commissar of Foreign affairs for the Soviet Union, responded that his government had no objection to the British note but added that Ethiopia was entitled to claim the right to a seat at the Council session. He pointed out that France had agreed to the British proposal and that Britain might not even put it to a vote. He explained that this procedure would have serious implications for dealing with the Manchurian question, so China might find it necessary to make a statement in order not to compromise herself on a matter of principle. The Soviet government, he maintained, would not oppose if it did this (AH 1938e: 20–21). Support for a vote was more forthcoming for the Northern European states. Brazil, however, merely circumvented all procedural niceties by recognizing the King of Italy as the Emperor of Ethiopia on 24 April (AH 1938f: 29).

When the Chinese ambassador to London, Quo Tai-chi, made further inquiries about the contents of the British note, he soon came to learn that it proposed giving every state the freedom to make its own decision as to whether to recognize the Italian annexation. In this regard, while Quo knew that Anglo-Chinese relations were important, he also felt that gaining US sympathy was equally important and the that the opinions of public advocates of world peace should also be seriously considered, being concerned that the fate of the non-recognition principle would play a vital role pertaining to the future of Manchuria as well as other Japanese occupied territories in China. In view of these facts, he felt that China should stick to her principled stance (AH 1938g: 18–19). He gained support for this stance from Sun Fo (1981–1973), the son of Sun Yat-sen and the President of China's Legislative Yuan (parliament), who was visiting Europe at that time (AH 1938h: 23).

When Quo met the deputy Under-Secretary of the British foreign ministry, Alexander Cadogan, on the evening of 27 April, he let him know that the note was a big blow to the prestige of the League. As far as the Sino-Japanese conflict was concerned, Quo suggested that one way to appease criticism and maintain the mutual interests of Britain and his own country would be for the Assembly and the Council to propose a resolution to grant a loan to China. If France would not get involved in a discussion of the loan, it would look even better for Britain to promote such a proposal (AH 1938i: 32–33). Anthony Eden, the British foreign secretary, expressed his agreement | (AH 1938j: 41–42).

What concerned China most at this stage, however, was whether it was possible to discuss the Sino-Japanese question before the Ethiopian question was raised. Victor Hoo Chi-tsai was thus told to keep his attention on the situation at the League (AH 1938k: 48). At noon on 9 May, 1938, Anthony Eden and Wellington Koo had a discussion in Geneva in which Koo insisted that China's proposal should be discussed early in the discussion to ensure that a concrete plan would be agreed for its requested loan and that an offer of financial for its military resistance against Japan would be forthcoming (AH 1938l: 53–54).

When the Council met for a closed-door meeting on 9 May, it was agreed that the Ethiopian representative could be invited to speak to the body (AH 1938l: 55). The following day Lord Halifax presented a statement to the Council which explained that the motive for Britain's agreement with Italy was to reduce tension between the two states and establish the conditions for stability from the Mediterranean to the Indian Ocean, which was received enthusiastically by the other members. The only exception was Litvinov, who welcomed the agreement but added that dealing with bilateral pacts also had to take into consideration relations between the two parties concerned and the rest of the world. He then made a clear allusion to the on-going Sino-Japanese war, stating, 'We have to take into consideration the effect which such agreements may have on those problems which are still before the League of Nations and still remain to be dealt with' (*OJ* 1938, May–June: 306).

This was followed by a long appeal from Wellington Koo, who proceeded to spell out how the Council had failed to address the issues that China had raised concerning Japan's aggression in its previous meetings. Noting that 'a wave of so-called realism is sweeping over the West', he argued that the facts deserved attention and a call for action 'not alone in China's interest, but also for the cause of international law and order and the well-being of humanity' (*OJ* 1938, May–June: 306–308). The following morning Koo made another speech and in the afternoon proposed that a discussion of the Sino-Japanese question should be held the next day. When the British and Soviet representatives said that they were not ready for such a discussion, however, the chairman decided to leave the final discussion of the British note until 13 May.

At the Council meeting on 12 May, at which Emperor Haile Selassie was present in person, Lord Halifax opened with a statement that revealed some of the serious implications that arose from the decision to recognize Italy's sovereignty over his Ethiopia. Britain's decision, he explained, reflected his government's opinion that the steps already taken by the League in the course of the Ethiopian dispute could not be held to constitute any binding obligation on the member states to withhold recognition until a unanimous decision had been made. Given the freedom of action that this allowed, it was reasonable to recognize that the Italian government had obtained control over virtually all of the former territory of Ethiopia, and that '...there is no organized native authority and no central native administration with the slightest prospect of reconquering the country'. Looking at the broader ramifications of this decision for international order, he accepted that it would have implications for the dispute over Manchuria, but explained that '...when, as here, two ideals are in conflict – on the one hand, the ideal of devotion, unflinching but unpractical, to some high purpose; on the other, the ideal of practical victory for peace – I cannot doubt that the stronger claim is that of peace' (*OJ* 1938, May–June: 334–335).

The following day, the Council members again expressed their support for the British position, with the Polish representative, M. Komarnicki, going so far as to explicitly state that, 'if the League continues to confine itself to rigid procedure, serving only to perpetuate sources of conflict – as was the case, for instance, in the "Manchukuo" affair – it is to be feared that its role as an organ of international cooperation will inevitably be diminished' (*OJ* 1938, May–June: 343).

This was challenged by Wellington Koo when it came to his turn to speak. Appealing to the delegates to not so readily put the facts on the ground above the principles of the Covenant, he explained that his government attached the greatest importance to those principles. Focusing on the non-recognition principle, he explained that this was '...not only because of recent and current developments in the Far East and of its desire to see peace and security re-established in that region on the basis of law, treaty and justice, but also because of the general interests of peace and the welfare of the whole world'. The Chinese government, he concluded, would not be able to subscribe to the British position (*OJ* 1938, May–June: 344–345).

On that day, nine of the 15 members of the Council spoke in favour of allowing individual states the freedom to decide whether or not to recognize Italy's sovereignty over Ethiopia. Only China and New Zealand supported the representative of Haile Selassie in speaking against the British position (*OJ* 1938, May–June: 346). The president then declared that the discussion was closed with a clear majority in favour of the principle that each country should be free to determine its own attitude in the light of their own situation and obligations. In a somewhat confused attempt to square this with the core principles of the Covenant, he added that the decision should not be interpreted as amounting to a pronouncement on questions of principle or the retraction of past judgements, or any line of future conduct that should be binding on members. When the decision was submitted to the Assembly China joined with the small minority of just the Soviet Union, New Zealand and Bolivia to insist on non-recognition of the Italian annexation.

Conclusion

The above analysis reveals much about the distinctive role that China played as one of the three Eastern Asian states in the League. Like Siam, it had good reasons to try to adopt a passive stance that would minimize the dangers of entanglement in disputes between the big powers. During the ten years of the Nanjing Decade (1928–1937), the priority of the government was to make great efforts in national reconstruction. This required emphasizing good relations with the European countries and the United States. Italy was important as a permanent member of the League Council and a source of substantial assistance for the nation-building project.

The possibilities for pursuing this strategy were always limited by the struggle with Japan over Manchuria, however. Because Italy's attack on Ethiopia had serious implications for how the League dealt with that problem, China's room for manoeuvre was increasingly constrained. At the heart of its dilemma was the need to uphold the commitment of the League to its stated principle of inviolable state sovereignty when this impinged on the foreign policies of the most powerful states. Whereas China's relationship with Japan had deteriorated to the point where it had little to lose by lodging an appeal for arbitration in the case of Manchuria, it enjoyed good relations with Italy when it launched its attack on Ethiopia. Maintaining this situation was made more complicated as public opinion began to have a greater impact on foreign policy, as shown by the embarrassment over the showing of the film, *Abyssinia*.

Comparisons with Japan's role in the League are, of course, even more limited because the two states played the very different roles of victim and aggressor. By going below the level of the state, however, Shinohara's chapter raises some interesting questions about how even Japan's international-minded diplomats attempted to play a positive role in promoting the ideals of the League, although they were doomed to failure by the rise of militarism in their own government and society. China's sub-state actors might have been more successful in this respect. Chiang Kai-shek, for example, was a military figure whose attachment to the Confucian values of justice and righteousness was compatible with the League's commitment to the pacific resolution of international disputes. Moreover, even though China was a relatively weak state that lacked sufficiently well-trained soldiers and the advanced equipment needed to resist invasion, the League did provide a platform for diplomats like Wellington Koo to join with the representatives of other victims of aggression, such as Ethiopia, to try to articulate and consolidate the League's core values.

Given this limited power, China's refusal to support Britain's proposal on recognizing the Italian annexation of Ethiopia should be recognized as significant for several reasons. In the short term, its diplomats could use the dispute to help build the case for humanitarian aid and economic and moral support from the League in their country's war against Japan. In the longer-term, their direct experience of the shortcomings of the League put them in a good position to help to shape a better understanding of the tensions between international governance and the imperative for states to pursue their own interests. It is no accident that some, like their Japanese counterparts, would bring this to bear on the work of rebuilding international organisations after World War Two. Quo Tai-chi, for example, served as China's representative on the UN Security Council for a brief period in 1947. Victor Hoo Chi-tsai was appointed assistant Secretary General in 1946 and served in various positions before the Republic of China gave up its seat to the People's Republic of China in 1971.

Best known is Wellington Koo, who was a founding delegate to the UN, served as ambassador the United States and became a judge at the International Court of Justice in 1956, serving for three years as its vice president. The understanding of the Chinese actors that collective security could not depend on idealism alone but could only be implemented with the support and determination of the most powerful states is summed up well by a speech that he delivered at the Academy of Diplomacy in Paris in December, 1937, in which he asserted his belief that:

> A most effective triangle in defence of liberty and peace would be that of Great Britain, the United States and France. United by a community of ideals and blessed with unlimited resources of military and economic power at their disposal...they will prove to be an anchor-sheet in the present stormy world. (Koo 1937)

Koo and his colleagues were all too aware at that time that the most powerful states had failed to play this role when it came to applying the principles of the League to the cases of Ethiopia and Manchuria. The jury is still out on whether they are more willing and able to do so in the twenty-first century.

Notes

1. For a concise but detailed account of the actions of the Council and Assembly see Spencer (1937). For a survey of great power diplomacy towards the Abyssinian question see Baer (1976).
2. For more on Wellington Koo and his background see the chapter by Hughes in this volume.

References

AH. 1937a. The Isis Cinema to Shanghai Police Station, January 21. Yidali zhuhua shilingguan qingqudi ruyi yingpian [Italian Embassy and Legation ask for ban on films offensive to Italy]. 020-070500-0009.

AH. 1937b. Shanghai Municipal Government to MOFA, 3 February. Yidali zhuhua shilingguan qingqudi ruyi yingpian [Italian Embassy and Legation ask for ban on films offensive to Italy]. 020-070500-0009.

AH. 1937c. Russian Embassy memorandum to MOFA, 3 February. Yidali zhuhua shilingguan qingqudi ruyi yingpian [Italian Embassy and Legation ask for ban on films offensive to Italy]. 020-070500-0009020-070500-0009.

AH. 1937d. MOFA to the Shanghai Municipal Government, 19 February. Yishiguan qingqudi ruyi yingpian fangying [Italian Embassy and Legation ask for ban on films offensive to Italy]. Vol. 1. 020-042005-0006.

AH. 1937e.Shanghai Municipal Government to MOFA, 20 February 20. Yishiguan qingqudi ruyi yingpian fangying [Italian Embassy and Legation ask for ban on films offensive to Italy]. Vol. 1. 020-042005-0006.

AH. 1937f. Shanghai Municipal Government to MOFA. Attachment, 20 February. Yishiguan qingqudi ruyi yingpian fangying [Italian Embassy and Legation ask for ban on films offensive to Italy]. Vol. 1. 020-042005-006, p. 31.
AH. 1937g. The record of Minister Wang's meeting with Desandre, 22 February. Yishiguan qingqudi ruyi yingpian fangying [Italian Embassy and Legation ask for ban on films offensive to Italy]. Vol. 1. 020-042005-0006.
AH. 1937h. The report of the police station to the Shanghai Municipal Government. Yishiguan qingqudi ruyi yingpian fangying [Italian Embassy and Legation ask for ban on films offensive to Italy]. Vol. 1. 020-042005-0006.
AH. 1937i. The memorandum of Russian Consulate, 25 February. Yishiguan qingqudi ruyi yingpian fangying [Italian Embassy and Legation ask for ban on films offensive to Italy]. Vol. 1. 020-042005-0006.
AH. 1937j. Liu Wendao to MOFA, 25 February. Yishiguan qingqudi ruyi yingpian fangying [Italian Embassy and Legation ask for ban on films offensive to Italy]. Vol. 1. 020-042005-0006.
AH. 1937k. Liu Wendao to MOFA, 2 July. 020-042005-0007.
AH. 1936a. Liu Wendao to MOFA, 14 November. Riyi jiaohuan chengren Abixiniya yu Manzhouguo' [Exchange Recognition of Abyssinia and Manchukuo]. 020-010102-0163.
AH. 1936b. Chinese Embassy to Japan to MOFA, 17 November. Riyi jiaohuan chengren Abixiniya yu Manzhouguo' [Exchange Recognition of Abyssinia and Manchukuo]. 020-010102-0163.
AH. 1936c. Liu Wendao to MOFA, 24 November. Riyi jiaohuan chengren Abixiniya yu Manzhouguo' [Exchange Recognition of Abyssinia and Manchukuo]. 020-010102-0163.
AH. 1936d. Victor Hoo Chi-Tsai to MOFA, 26 November. Riyi jiaohuan chengren Abixiniya yu Manzhouguo' [Exchange Recognition of Abyssinia and Manchukuo]. 020-010102-0163.
AH. 1936e. MOFA to Chinese embassy Rome, 30 November. Riyi jiaohuan chengren Abixiniya yu Manzhouguo' [Exchange Recognition of Abyssinia and Manchukuo]. 020-010102-0163.
AH. 1936f. MOFA to Chinese embassy Rome, 30 November. Riyi jiaohuan chengren Abixiniya yu Manzhouguo' [Exchange Recognition of Abyssinia and Manchukuo]. 020-010102-0163.
AH. 1936g. Liu Wendao to MOFA, 30 November. Riyi jiaohuan chengren Abixiniya yu Manzhouguo' [Exchange Recognition of Abyssinia and Manchukuo]. 020-010102-0163.
AH. 1936h. Liu Wendao to the MOFA, 1 December. Riyi jiaohuan chengren Abixiniya yu Manzhouguo [Exchange Recognition of Abyssinia and Manchukuo]. 020-010102-0163.

AH. 1936i. The General Staff Headquarter to the MOFA, 7 December. Riyi jiaohuan chengren Abixiniya yu Manzhouguo [Exchange Recognition of Abyssinia and Manchukuo]. 020-010102-0163.
AH. 1936j. MOFA to Chinese Embassy to Japan, 9 December 9. Riyi jiaohuan chengren Abixiniya yu Manzhouguo [Exchange Recognition of Abyssinia and Manchukuo]. 020-010102-0163.
AH. 1936k. Hsu Shih-ying to MOFA, 6 January. Riyi jiaohuan chengren Abixiniya yu Manzhouguo [Exchange Recognition of Abyssinia and Manchukuo]. 020-010102-0163.
AH. 1936l. The MOFA to Chinese embassy Rome, 28 November. Riyi jiaohuan chengren Abixiniya yu Manzhouguo [Exchange Recognition of Abyssinia and Manchukuo]. 020-042002-0013.
AH. 1936m. The MOFA to Chinese embassy Rome, 30 November. Riyi jiaohuan chengren Abixiniya yu Manzhouguo [Exchange Recognition of Abyssinia and Manchukuo]. 020-042002-0013.
AH. 1936n. Liu Wendao to MOFA, 30 November. Riyi jiaohuan chengren Abixiniya yu Manzhouguo [Exchange Recognition of Abyssinia and Manchukuo]. 020-042002-0013.
AH. 1937a. The meeting record of Wang Chonghui and Naggiar, 11 March. Riyi jiaohuan chengren Abixiniya yu Manzhouguo [Exchange Recognition of Abyssinia and Manchukuo]. 020-042002-0013.
AH. 1937b. The meeting record of Xu Mo and Naggiar, 26 March. Riyi jiaohuan chengren Abixiniya yu Manzhouguo [Exchange Recognition of Abyssinia and Manchukuo]. 020-042002-0013.
AH. 1937c. Liu Wendao to MOFA, 29 November. Riyi jiaohuan chengren Abixiniya yu Manzhouguo [Exchange Recognition of Abyssinia and Manchukuo]. 020-010102-0163.
AJ. 1937d. Wong Kwong Yue to S. Scaroni, 3 December. Riyi jiaohuan chengren Abixiniya yu Manzhouguo [Exchange Recognition of Abyssinia and Manchukuo]. 020-010102-0163.
AH. 1938a. An abstract of Recognition of Italian Annexation. Guanyu chengren Yi bin Abyssinia [About recognizing Italian annexation of Abyssinia]. Taipei, Academia Historica, 020-042002-0028.
AH. 1938b. C. T. Wang to MOFA, 28 April. Guanyu chengren Yi bin Abyssinia [About recognizing Italian annexation of Abyssinia].020-042002-0028.
AH. 1938c. Wang Jingqi (Stockholm) to MOFA, 19 April. Guanyu chengren Yi bin Abyssinia [About recognizing Italian annexation of Abyssinia]. 020-042002-0028.
AH. 1938d. Yu Ming (Moscow) to MOFA, 25 April. Guanyu chengren Yi bin Abyssinia [About recognizing Italian annexation of Abyssinia]. 020-042002-0028.
AH. 1938e. Yu Ming (Moscow) to MOFA, 19 April. Guanyu chengren Yi bin Abyssinia [About recognizing Italian annexation of Abyssinia]. 020-042002-0028.

AH. 1938f. Chinese Legion (Rio de Janeiro) to MOFA, 26 April. Guanyu chengren Yi bin Abyssinia [About recognizing Italian annexation of Abyssinia]. 020-042002-0028.
AH. 1938g. Quo Tai-chi to MOFA, 19 April. Guanyu chengren Yi bin Abyssinia [About recognizing Italian annexation of Abyssinia]. 020-042002-0028.
AH. 1938h. Sun Foo to MOFA, 26 April. Guanyu chengren Yi bin Abyssinia [About recognizing Italian annexation of Abyssinia]. 020-042002-0028.
AH. 1938i. Quo Tai-chi to MOFA, 27 April. Guanyu chengren Yi bin Abyssinia [About recognizing Italian annexation of Abyssinia]. 020-042002-0028.
AH. 1938j. Alexander Cadogan to Quo Tai-chi, 19 April. Guanyu chengren Yi bin Abyssinia [About recognizing Italian annexation of Abyssinia]. 020-042002-0028.
AH. 1938k. Quo Tai-chi to MOFA, 19 April. Guanyu chengren Yi bin Abyssinia [About recognizing Italian annexation of Abyssinia]. 020-042002-0028.
AH. 1938l. Wellington Koo to MOFA, 9 May 9. Guanyu chengren Yi bin Abyssinia [About recognizing Italian annexation of Abyssinia]. 020-042002-0028.
Baer, George W. 1976. *The Coming of the Italian-Ethiopian War*, 1976. Stanford Calif.: Hoover Institution Press.
CHCKS. 2014. *Jiang Zhongzheng xiansheng nianpu changbian* [Chronological history of Mr. Chiang Kai-shek], Vol. 4. Taipei: Academia Historica.
CKSA. 1935a. Yang Jie to Chiang Kai-shek March 22. Yiban ziliao [General Materials)]. 002-080200-00216-025.
CKSA. 1935b. Wang Zhaoming to Chiang Kai-shek, 30 August. 002-080200-00248-030
CKSA. 1935c. British attitude toward Italo-Abyssinian Dispute—Report to Chiang Kai-shek by the Chinese Embassy in London. 002-080200-00249-067.
CKSD. 1935a. The first week introspection record.
Koo, Wellington. 1937. The Problem of the Pacific and Collective Security. An address by Dr. V.K. Wellington Koo, Chinese ambassador at Paris, at a meeting of the Academy of Diplomacy, 17 December. In *Japanese Aggression and the League of Nations.* 1938. Vol. 3, Geneva: Press Bureau of the Chinese Delegation, 1937–1940: 48.
NGA. 1936a. Chiang Kai-shek to the Nationalist Government. Guolian zhicai Yidali shishi banfa (Implementation measures on sanctioning Italy by the League of Nations), July 14. 001063000001155.
SLGB. 2008. *Jiang Zhongzheng zongtong dang'an: Shilue gaoben* [The Chiang Kai-shek collections: The Chronological Events] (33), Vol. 13, Sep.–Oct. 1935.
Spencer, John H. 1937. The Italian-Ethiopian Dispute and the League of Nations. *American Journal of International Law* (31/4): 614–641.

Picture of the Lytton Commission, the Earl of Lytton (front row left), and Wellington Koo (right) (*Source* United Nations Archives at Geneva)

Manchuria

Aborted Ideas of an Internationally Administered Manchuria: The Background to the Lytton Report

Haruo Tohmatsu

The Manchurian Incident broke out on 18 September 1931 and represents the first of the major setbacks in the history of the League. Also known as the 'Mukden Incident' because it began with the detonation of explosives on the railway line owned by Japan's South Manchuria Railway near the city of Mukden, it would be called a 'false flag' action today. Carried out by the Kwantung Army, the military force Japan had based in Manchuria to protect its nationals and property, it was blamed on Chinese activists and used to justify what would become the full occupation of the northeastern provinces of the Republic of China (ROC) and the unilateral establishment of the puppet state of Manchukuo by Japan on 1 March 1932. The League's response to such aggression by one of its founding great powers culminated in the dispatch of an investigation commission under the leadership of Britain's former governor of Bengal, Lord Lytton, in the first half of 1932. The following three chapters in this section of the book will look at the process that led up to the report and the League's

H. Tohmatsu (✉)
National Defense Academy of Japan, Yokosuka, Japan
e-mail: elgar2nd@nda.ac.jp

C. R. Hughes and H. Shinohara (eds.), *East Asians in the League of Nations*, New Directions in East Asian History,
https://doi.org/10.1007/978-981-19-7067-2_10

consequent response, providing insights into how Eastern Asian actors contributed to thinking about the fundamental principles and practices of international politics between the wars.

This chapter will start the discussion by focusing on how the League tried to apply the methods for the international administration of disputed territories that it was already using in Europe and the Middle East, as well as views on regional autonomy that were circulating in China. It will then look at how such thinking influenced the Lytton Report, before drawing some general conclusions about the longer-term implications of the crisis for the League's role in shaping international order.

The League and International Administration Theory in the Early 1930s

Rumors that the Lytton Commission was devising a plan for placing Manchuria under some form of international administration began spreading in the spring of 1932, as it toured Japan, the ROC, and 'Manchukuo,' some six months after the outbreak of the Manchurian Incident. At the end of May 1932, major Japanese newspapers reported that the Commission had contacted Zhang Xueliang, the military strongman who had exercised de facto control over the region on behalf of the ROC, through Miles W. Lampson, the British Minister in Peiping (Beijing). This was to sound Zhang out about the possibility of putting him at the head of a mandatory government that would be established in Manchuria after the conclusion of peace between Japan and China. Zhang, it was said, had expressed great interest in returning to Manchuria.[1]

Although the truth of this story is unclear, it indicates how the idea of looking to solve the problem through some form of international administration was attracting attention. This was quite natural given that a return to the pre-18 September status quo was not acceptable to Japan and that the annexation of Manchuria was out of the question for China. Moreover, although a Northeastern Administrative Council of influential local figures who championed Manchurian independence had emerged, this lacked credibility due its untested ability and the pro-Japanese sympathies of its members.

Within the League's own experience, the most obvious place to look for solutions was the mandate system it had established to govern colonized territories in the wake of World War I. The idea and challenges of placing Manchuria under a League of Nations mandate were thus frequently discussed, with East Asian experts such as Hikomatsu Kamikawa (1889–1988), professor of political science and international relations at Tōkyō Imperial University, taking a leading role.[2]

The mandate system itself was the outcome of a compromise between the British, French, and Japanese desire to annex the overseas possessions of Germany and the Ottoman Empire occupied by Allied forces in World War I, on the one hand, and the principles of non-annexation and self-determination championed by US President Woodrow Wilson on the other. Under Article 22 of the Covenant, mandatories agreed terms for each mandate with the League Council and administered the relevant territory with a degree of League supervision. The mandated territories were, depending on their geographical situation and their population's stage of development, classified into three types: Class A (non-Turkish regions of the former Ottoman Empire), Class B (Germany's former possessions in Central Africa), and Class C (Germany's former possessions in Southwest Africa and the Pacific).

Defined as a form of tutelage for 'peoples not yet able to stand by themselves,' the system presupposed that the mandated territories would one day achieve autonomy. In reality, however, only Class A territories were deemed to have 'reached a stage of development where their existence as independent nations [could] be provisionally recognized.' The Class B and C territories in Africa and the Pacific were in fact rendered as little different from colonies of the mandatory states. Nonetheless, the mandatories were subject to various obligations under the League's supervision and forbidden from annexing the mandated territory.

The Iraq Model

One reason why the mandate question attracted a lot of interest at the time of the Manchurian Incident was the timing and outcome of the case of Iraq. Classified as a Class A British mandate, the country gained independence and joined the League in October 1932, the same month that the Lytton Report was published. The significance of this was seized on by Kamikawa, who argued for the implementation of such a Class A mandate or the equivalent in Manchuria, viewing the relationship between Japan and Manchuria as analogous to that between Britain and Iraq.[3]

Kamikawa's suggestion that Manchuria should be put under the trust of Japan as the equivalent of a Class A League of Nations mandate raised a number of problems, however. First, Article 22 of the Covenant made it clear that the mandate system had originally been designed to apply to the overseas possessions of Germany and the non-Turkish territories of the Ottoman Empire, both of which had been defeated in World War I. If, therefore, the system was to be extended to other regions, the Covenant would need to be amended.

Several attempts were made to do just that during the interwar period. In the late 1920s and early 1930s, for instance, the British Foreign Office, among others, discussed plans for mandating the West African state of Liberia, then bankrupt and chronically unstable, to one of the smaller European countries (FO 1933). The idea was never implemented. If it had been, it would have served as a model for the temporary administration of failed states that was only adopted by the United Nations (UN) in the 1990s and after. A debate also took place in the late 1930s, when Britain and France attempted to appease Germany's demands for the return of its colonies. This revolved around the possibility of placing all the colonies of the great powers under a mandate and equitably allocating their resources.[4]

Even if it had been possible to expand the mandate system, however, this still raised the question of where the source of sovereignty over the mandated territory would lie. Neither Article 22 of the Covenant nor the terms of individual mandates made this explicit, allowing many different theories to be developed by experts on international law. The prevalent view, however, was that sovereignty lay with the population of the mandated territory, at least in the case of a Class A mandate (leaving aside Class B and C mandates, which applied to territories not expected to achieve independence in the near future). Under a Class A mandate, then, it was assumed that the mandated territory would become independent in the near future.[5]

The clear implication was that applying a Class A mandate to Manchuria meant that its sovereignty lay not with the central government of the ROC but in the population of the region. Once Manchurian society was ready to stand alone, it would have been granted independence, following consultations between Japan as the mandatory and the League of Nations as supervisor of the mandate. An independent state would have been created with the blessing of the League of Nations, within the international co-operative framework of which the organization was a cornerstone. Much as Britain had legally nurtured the Kingdom of Iraq during its League of Nations mandate and brought it into its de facto sphere of influence, Japan would have established the state of Manchukuo with the international community's blessing and made it an ally.

The final question over applying the model of the Class A mandate was that Iraq's existing legal status was wholly different from that of Manchuria's. Like the other non-Turkish regions of the Middle East, it had been detached from the Ottoman Empire by World War I, and this had been formalized by the 1920 Treaty of Sèvres. When Kemal Atatürk's Republic of Turkey replaced the Ottoman Empire and sought to build a Turkish nation-state, it had officially renounced sovereignty over these non-Turkish regions in the 1923 Treaty of Lausanne.[6] Although the Ottoman and Qing dynasties were both multi-ethnic empires that were not based on the principle of the nation-state, the similarity ended there. The ROC had replaced the Qing Dynasty in the 1911 Revolution and had not been defeated in World War I. Although Sun Yat-sen is said to have considered at one point, much like Kemal Atatürk, incorporating only the area south of the Great Wall into the territory of the new republic and detaching Manchuria from China, the ROC never explicitly renounced its claims to non-Han areas, such as Mongolia, Tibet, Xinjiang, and Manchuria.[7] Applying the mandate system to Manchuria would thus not have been acceptable to the ROC. It could instead reinforce the legitimacy of its claim by citing the recognition that Manchuria was an integral part of China that was included in the Nine-Power Treaty signed at the 1922 Washington Conference. This would have made it impossible for the League to accept the application of the mandate system to the region without breaching its own commitment to the paramount importance of treaties.

The Saarland and Danzig Models

Aside from the mandate system, another example of the international administration of territory was provided by the cases of the Saarland and the Free City of Danzig. We can assume that these cases would have been considered by members of the Lytton Commission, given that most of its members were West Europeans who would have been well acquainted with them. This study will briefly describe both and consider the problems that would have arisen had either model been applied to Manchuria.

The Saarland and Danzig models were both forms of international administration set up after World War I, when the League had faced the challenge of finding a solution that could accommodate both Germany, which had lost the war, and its neighbors, France and Poland. The Saarland was a coal-producing region with an area of 1,912 square kilometers and more than 90% of its population of 828,000 (in 1933) was of ethnic German descent. France sought to annex the territory, but it was detached from Germany under Articles 45–50 of the Treaty of Versailles instead and placed under the control of a Governing Commission overseen by the League.[8] This body was appointed by the League and consisted of five members, one a citizen of France, one an inhabitant of the Saarland who was not a citizen of France, and three individuals from League members other than Germany or France. It functioned as a council and took decisions by majority vote. It was also stipulated that the final status of the region would be decided in a plebiscite held fifteen years after the commission took over, in 1920. With the overwhelming majority of its inhabitants being German, it reverted to Germany in March 1935 as a result of that plebiscite.

Danzig (present-day Gdańsk in Poland) was a seaport on the Baltic Sea that was also part of Germany until the end of World War I, and 96% of its population of 400,000 was German. Poland, having regained independence after the war, claimed it as an outlet to the Baltic. Instead of accepting this claim, Articles 100–108 of the Treaty of Versailles established it as the Free City of Danzig.[9] It was governed under a High Commissioner appointed by the League of Nations and its German residents had to renounce their German nationality and became nationals of the city instead. The Polish government was empowered to conduct its foreign relations, though the League of Nations was able to impose certain restrictions on Warsaw's actions.

The special features of the Saarland and Danzig models had important implications for the understanding of the sovereignty, future status, and internal security of other contested territories. Regarding sovereignty, neither the Treaty of Versailles nor its annex clearly defined where this lay for the Saarland. It is reasonable to assume, though, that it was with the local population, given that the region's final status was to be determined by plebiscite. In that regard the Saarland closely resembled territories under a Class A League of Nations mandate, where sovereignty was likewise generally thought to lie with the population, even though there was no explicit provision on the matter.

As for security, it was prescribed that the region would be policed and defended by a local gendarmerie. The stationing of foreign forces was not permitted. When France kept its forces in the Saarland after the Treaty of Versailles came into force, it was internationally criticized. After its actions were repeatedly denounced as illegal at the Council of the League of Nations in Geneva, French forces in the region were drawn down after 1927 at the insistence of the Governing Commission. Meanwhile, the forces stationed in the Saarland were joined by British and Belgian units, which only assumed the character of a local gendarmerie when their duties were restricted to guarding the railway (Miyazaki 1964: 36). France's plans to annex the territory by degrees by keeping forces there indefinitely and mobilizing pro-French, anti-German elements of the local population thus proved abortive. In that sense, the international administration overseen by the League succeeded in keeping the ambitions of the powers in check.

Sovereignty over Danzig, on the other hand, lay with Poland, at least insofar as the conduct of foreign relations was concerned, albeit under the aegis of an international administration overseen by the League. This was despite the fact that Poles were only a minority of the population, and that Poland was the historical underdog in relation to the German behemoth. Authority to govern Danzig, on the other hand, lay with the Free City government under the High Commissioner appointed by the League. Moreover, there was no explicit provision concerning the determination of Danzig's future status, unlike in the case of the Saarland. The international administration of Danzig thus had a semi-permanent nature (Miyazaki 1964: 42). Considering that 96% of its population was of German origin, that state of affairs was most unnatural and the failure to address the locus of its sovereignty made it a potential source of conflict.[10] World War II thus started in September 1939 as a conflict between Nazi Germany and the Republic of Poland over Danzig and the Polish Corridor.

Chinese Ideas on Regional Autonomy

To provide a more complete survey of the ideas on international administration that were being discussed in international circles at the time of the Manchurian Crisis, it is important to also look at Chinese notions of regional autonomy. Although Manchukuo was unquestionably an artificial puppet state, its establishment was made possible by the existence of certain elements sympathetic to Japanese schemes to carve out a separate state.[11] When the Lytton Commission toured Manchukuo in the spring of 1932, it conducted formal and informal interviews with individuals from all walks of life and received numerous letters that led it to feel that although most of the population were antagonistic to the puppet state of Manchukuo, they also preferred a high degree of autonomy to strong control by the ROC central government. In that sense, there was an undercurrent of local opinion that agreed with the Lytton Report's position that Manchuria should be seen as an autonomous political entity separate from China south of the Great Wall, without necessarily denying the central government's sovereignty.

There were basically three currents of thinking on local autonomy in China at the time. These focused on the concept of 'provincial autonomy' (*liansheng zizhi*); the Manchurian and Mongolian separatist movements; and the theory of local autonomy in the Three Principles of the People (the ideological orthodoxy of the ruling Guomindang Nationalist Party (GMD) that was attributed to its deceased founder, Dr. Sun Yat-sen).

The proponents of the first of these tendencies argued that China's different regions should retain the autonomy that they had enjoyed since the disintegration of the Qing Empire, while gradually working toward building a unitary state (Chen 1979). This could be described as a kind of federalism. In reality, however, it served as a self-justifying rationale for the perpetuation of the military regimes that had ruled different parts of the country during the period of constant fighting among warlords between the 1911 Revolution and the Northern Expedition of 1925–1927. In fact, the Manchurian-based Mukden clique of Zhang Zuolin had long refused to unite with political forces south of the Great Wall, advocating instead a policy of 'securing the borders to make the people safe' according to the principle of 'provincial autonomy.' His son and successor, Zhang Xueliang, pledged allegiance to the Nationalist government in 1928 only because of his antagonism toward Japan's Kwantung Army and his realization that militarily he was no match for the forces under the control of the GMD government. Despite this, it should not be assumed that the idea of provincial autonomy could never have evolved into a form of federalism.

As for the Manchurian and Mongolian separatist movements, it cannot be denied that these were influenced by the global trend toward Wilsonian self-determination following World War I. Their extent was sometimes blown out of proportion, however, as a pretext to justify Japanese attempts to detach the two regions from China. Manchuria and neighboring Inner Mongolia were, to be sure, historically the cradle of peoples with distinctive ethnic characteristics. Since the Russo-Japanese War of 1904–1905, however, they had become minorities owing to the rapid increase in ethnic Han immigration from south of the Great Wall. Indeed, owing to increasing intermarriage, opinion was divided on whether there existed Manchurian or Mongolian peoples who were sufficiently distinct to be able to claim and exercise national self-determination (Tochigi and Banno 1997: 340–346).

Sun Yat-sen's Three Principles of the People likewise envisaged a form of local autonomy Sun 1929: 118). This would not, of course, go so far as to permit the existence the kind of regionally based military regimes as in the provincial autonomy model, which would pose a challenge to the authority of the GMD. Instead, autonomous local units were supposed to facilitate regional development after the unification of the ROC nation-state. It is important to note this body of thought, however, because it would turn out to be particularly useful when the ROC government decided to accept the main principles of the Lytton recommendations and had to win over GMD hardliners who were opposed to the proposal to make Manchuria an autonomous region under international administration. The Lytton Commission was not, therefore, operating in a complete ideational vacuum as it sought solutions but was exposed to a remarkably creative and fertile discussion of novel ideas at both the international and domestic levels of politics.

The Lytton Report

Formulation of the Recommendations for International Administration

The Lytton Commission spent six months between February and August 1932 touring China, Japan, and 'Manchukuo.' Having considered various cases of international territorial administration, Chinese ideas on regional autonomy, and Japanese arguments for establishing a mandate, the discussion began to focus on the possibility of placing Manchuria under some form of international administration in which the League would play a certain role. The Commission brought up this idea as early as the beginning of March 1932, in a series of discussions with Japanese government leaders.

In a meeting with Foreign Minister Kenkichi Yoshizawa in Tōkyō, on March 7, the commissioners explained that there were three options for resolving the dispute: the annexation of Manchuria by Japan; international administration; or self-government. Considering the first to be out of the question, they asked whether the Japanese government might be willing to accept the second. Yoshizawa replied that this, which would involve countries other than Japan and China, was impractical for reasons of popular sentiment that arose from the fact that Japan's interests in Manchuria had been won as a result of the Sino-Japanese and Russo-Japanese Wars (Usui 1995: 49). Discussion of the question of international administration progressed no further that day, but Lytton must have gained the impression that the Japanese government had a strong antipathy to the idea.

The Commission left Japan on 11 March and arrived in Nanjing, the capital of the ROC, on 27 March, traveling via Shanghai, where military hostilities had just ceased. A round-table conference took place with senior members of the Chinese government on 29–30 March. These were top policymakers, including Wang Jingwei, President of the Executive Yuan; Chiang Kai-shek, Chairman of the Military Council; Luo Wengan, Minister for Foreign Affairs; T. V. Soong (Song Ziwen), Minister of Finance; and Wellington Koo (Gu Weijun), the Chinese assessor to the Lytton Commission.

Lytton sounded out Wang about the possibility of an international administration with extensive League involvement, who replied that a special gendarmerie consisting of Chinese personnel, organized separately from the Chinese army, would be sent to maintain order after the withdrawal of Japanese forces. He added that a committee to lay the groundwork for civilian administration in Manchuria had already been established within the Chinese government, in the fall of 1931, under Wellington Koo's chairmanship (Koo Papers 1932a: 12). It is possible that the essential outlines of what would eventually become the Lytton recommendations were conceived at Chinese prompting on this occasion. If so, Wang had strengthened his case in the eyes of the League by stating that if the Japanese were skeptical about China's ability to maintain the administrative organs and special gendarmerie, his government would be willing to implement any corrective measures recommended by the League of Nations in order to put those doubts to rest (Koo Papers 1932b: 7).

The Commission, having completed its tour of Manchukuo, spent June 1932 in Peiping. There the question of placing Manchuria under international administration was again discussed at a meeting with Chinese government leaders held on 19 June. The Chinese attendees were mostly the same as those who were at the Nanjing conference in March. Although Chiang Kai-shek was away at the front boosting morale, he was the de facto head of the Chinese government, and the meeting must have taken place with his consent. On this occasion Lytton, picking up where the March conference had left off, suggested that China 'set up ... an entirely new administration ... of a more or less autonomous character' in Manchuria, along with 'a special gendarmerie for the purpose of maintaining order.' In response, Wang Jingwei, while basically agreeing with Lytton, stated that he wished to make clear that 'self-government is something quite different from independence' (Koo Papers 1932c: 2).

When weighing these arguments, the Commission had to take into account the views expressed in more than 1,500 letters it had received, officially and unofficially, from local inhabitants during its visit to Manchuria. As mentioned above, while very few of these expressed support for the Japanese puppet state of Manchukuo or restoration of the Zhang Xueliang regime, they also revealed that the local population did not wish to be under the close control of the ROC central government. Lytton, therefore, argued that, out of respect for the local population's wishes, the region should be granted the maximum degree of autonomy that China's territorial integrity would allow. He thus asserted on the one hand that Manchuria might remain autonomous for a long time, even semi-permanently, by stating that 'in the future settlement, Manchuria should be left as a self-contained, largely autonomous body...there [should] be...as large [a] measure of autonomy as possible...' (Koo Papers 1932c: 7). On the other hand, he was careful to add the rider that 'the nature of the autonomy must be consistent with any federal system...for the whole of China' (Koo Papers 1932c: 7–8).

These considerations are reflected in the basic recommendations that the Commission made when it had completed its six-month fact-finding mission. The key points were that the ROC should retain sovereignty over Manchuria, but that the region should be placed under an international administration overseen by the League. This would oversee the establishment of an autonomous government, while internal order was to be maintained by a special gendarmerie. In the meantime, regional security was to be guaranteed through the conclusion of a treaty of non-aggression between Japan, China, and the Soviet Union. The bulk of the report was written in Peiping in July and August, and during the drafting process certain points were discussed that did not make it into the final version (LONa 1932: 5).

The structure of the special gendarmerie was one of the issues that remained unresolved. One proposal was that the Chinese government should organize the force within two years. Another was that half the foreign advisers advising on the force's organization should be Japanese and half should be individuals of other nationalities appointed by the Chinese government (whether that included Chinese nationals is unclear). The final report, however, made no mention of exactly how long it was supposed to take to set up the gendarmerie, nor did it specify the percentage of foreign advisers who were to be Japanese.

The discussion also compared the proposal for a demilitarized, neutral territory of Manchuria with the post-war situation in the Rhineland. The 1925 Locarno Pact that committed Britain, France, Belgium, Italy, and Germany to the guarantee of security in Europe was also frequently invoked as an analogy to the proposed treaty of non-aggression between Japan, China, and the Soviet Union. The possibility was considered, too, of setting up a Sino-Japanese conciliation commission modeled on the Franco-German conciliation commission provided for by Locarno (LONb 1932). Even more intriguing is that the essential character of the autonomous government of Manchuria was likened to the cantons of the Swiss Confederation (LONc 1932). The League of Nations was, needless to say, headquartered in Geneva, so it is not very surprising that Swiss elements permeated the Commission's thinking.

Reactions to the Lytton Recommendations

The above discussions give some important insights into the implications of the final version of the Lytton Report, which was made public on 2 October 1932. It consisted of ten chapters; the proposal on placing Manchuria under international administration as a means of resolving the Sino-Japanese conflict was contained in Chapter 9, 'Principles and Conditions of Settlement' and Chapter 10, 'Considerations and Suggestions to the Council.' The recommendations contained in these two chapters may be summarized as follows (Usui 1995: 103; Tohmatsu 2016: 95).

1. An autonomous government possessing extensive powers should be established in Manchuria, while the ROC retained sovereignty.
2. The autonomous government should be advised in different fields by foreign advisers under the supervision of the League of Nations.
3. Internal order within the region should be maintained by an international special gendarmerie force trained by foreign advisers, and all Chinese and Japanese forces should withdraw from the region, turning it into a demilitarized area.
4. The ROC should conclude a treaty of non-aggression with Japan and the Soviet Union, thus securing Manchuria against external threats.

Japan was in no mood to accept such suggestions. It had already pre-empted the report's release by setting up the new 'state' of Manchukuo and had made this a *fait accompli* by formally recognizing it with the conclusion of the Japan-Manchukuo Protocol on 15 September 1932. On 21 November, the government submitted a position paper to the League that decried the recommendations as mere fantasy, being completely at odds with the reality on the ground in Manchuria. It argued that implementing the plan for the international administration of Manchuria would only exacerbate the situation (Usui 1995: 99).[12]

The Chinese government, by contrast, carefully studied the feasibility of implementing the recommendations. Its basic stance is indicated by an undated memorandum apparently drawn up by Wellington Koo soon after the report was made public (Koo Papers 1932d). Its main points may be summed up as follows:

1. The form of autonomous government to be established in Manchuria would not contravene existing treaties, including the Covenant of the League of Nations, the Kellogg-Briand Pact, and the Nine-Power Treaty.
2. China's territorial integrity would be purely nominal; Manchuria would, at least temporarily, be effectively governed by foreigners.
3. The autonomous government set up in Manchuria under the agreement and declaration made by China and Japan would be permanently neutral.
4. Internal order would be maintained in Manchuria by an international police force or gendarmerie, which, while legally under the

jurisdiction of the ROC government, would in fact be managed and supervised by an international agency.

5. The autonomous government of Manchuria would be an 'international settlement in disguise' and fall under de facto Japanese economic control. To avoid this outcome, the declaration would need to state in advance that the autonomous government was merely provisional, and that China would reassume control in five to fifteen years.
6. Such a form of autonomous government would set a new precedent in international law.

The key point in the Chinese response was that it was essential to secure the safeguard described in (5). Moreover, it implied that unless the Chinese central government possessed the capacity to govern Manchuria effectively, the region would become independent by degrees. In view of these concerns, the government believed that the Lytton recommendations needed to be revised as follows (Koo Papers 1932e).

1. Manchukuo must immediately be dismantled by the League and Japan.
2. The autonomous government should be organized solely by the ROC government, albeit with League assistance.
3. The powers of the foreign advisers to the autonomous government should be of a purely advisory nature; foreign advisers must not be granted actual administrative powers, for doing so would undermine China's administrative unity.
4. While the international police force responsible for maintaining order would be advised by foreign advisers and instructors, its ranks must be staffed solely by Chinese nationals. Making the police force multinational would again give Japan a pretext for intervention.
5. It would be wise to demilitarize Manchuria for the time being, as that would prevent unnecessary tensions with Japanese forces. That would, however, be a purely temporary measure during a transition period.
6. The autonomous Manchurian government's foreign policy must be under the sole jurisdiction of the central government.

The Chinese government had, since the Peiping conference with the Lytton Commission in March and April 1932, consistently shown itself willing to accept, in principle, the idea of establishing an international administration in Manchuria. For China, being no match for Japan either militarily or economically, it could be argued that there was no other way to counter the Japanese while securing the backing of the League and international opinion. The above memorandum on the Lytton Report, however, perhaps suggests a further possibility.

The Manchurian Incident was a clash between a stronger state, Japan, and a weaker one, China. In that regard it resembled the cases of the Saarland and Danzig examined above. Both of those involved forms of international administration imposed for the purpose of resolving a territorial dispute between a stronger and a weaker neighbor—the former between a weakened Germany, the loser in World War I, and the victorious great power France; the latter between newly independent Poland, historically the underdog, and a historically dominant Germany.

In the case of the Saarland, France was granted economic rights in the region, including ownership of its coalmines, but it failed to achieve its original objective of annexing the territory. Instead, it was decided that the Saarland's future status would be determined by a plebiscite held in the fifteenth year after the League of Nations administration commenced in 1920. Even though, during the intervening years, the French government and pro-French residents worked hard to bring about the region's annexation by France, by 1932, when the Lytton Report was being drafted, it was regarded as all but certain that the Saarland would revert to Germany as a result of the plebiscite scheduled to take place in 1935. In the event, the overwhelming majority of the population did vote to rejoin Germany, and that March the Saarland again became part of Germany after a fifteen-year hiatus. During voting the League of Nations sent an international security force consisting of army units from Belgium, Britain, Italy, and Sweden, among others, to maintain order and guarantee that the plebiscite took place (Miyazaki 1964: 48–49).

The Free City of Danzig, on the other hand, enjoyed greater autonomy than the Saarland under a High Commissioner appointed by the League of Nations, and there was no provision for deciding the final status of the region by plebiscite. But the Polish government was empowered to conduct the Free City of Danzig's foreign relations, and German residents of Danzig were required to give up their German nationality. These arrangements kept German influence within Danzig in check. It is quite conceivable, therefore, that in accepting the Lytton Commission's proposal for placing Manchuria under international administration, China's leaders viewed their country's position as analogous to that of Germany in relation to the Saarland and Poland in relation to Danzig.

Of interest in this regard is the career of Wellington Koo (1888–1985), who accompanied the Lytton Commission as its Chinese assessor.[13] An alumnus of Columbia University and an experienced diplomat, he had been China's representative at the League of Nations in the early 1920s and was thus was well acquainted with the details of the international administration of the Saarland and Danzig (*OJ* 1920: 45ff.). In 1920–1921, when reporting to the League Council, he had called for compliance with the provisions governing the international administration of both regions and emphasized the importance of maintaining the neutrality of the gendarmerie that kept order in the Saarland. At the council meeting of June 20, 1921, he condemned as illegal the ongoing French military presence in the region, where the exercise of its power was supposed to be prohibited under the annex to the Versailles Treaty.

Koo was the ROC's de facto diplomatic representative in its negotiations with the Lytton Commission. It is, therefore, quite plausible that the Chinese government considered the possibility of placing Manchuria, for the time being, under an international administration on the Danzig model (an autonomous government possessing broad powers, but with the ROC retaining sovereignty). Then, when international conditions were favorable, this could be replaced with an administration on the Saarland model, giving Manchuria an autonomous government that would exercise power for a limited period, with the region's ultimate status to be decided in a future plebiscite—even if that meant temporarily retreating from the official position of the Nine-Power Treaty that Manchuria was an inseparable part of the ROC. Manchuria's 30 million inhabitants, being more than 90% Han Chinese, could be expected to vote to rejoin China if a plebiscite was held. But there was a prerequisite: the ROC south of the Great Wall would first need to become a politically and economically stable state. These considerations would have been compatible with the GMD government's priority of rooting out the growing power of the insurgent Communist movement and building up the domestic economy, even if this had to entail temporarily shelving the Manchuria issue.

The memorandum was well timed for the convening of the Chinese government's foreign policy committee in Nanjing on October 12 to discuss the Lytton Report. On October 15, the Minister for Foreign

Affairs, Luo Wengan, visited Chiang Kai-shek, Chairman of the Military Council, who was staying in Hankou, to request his instructions. Chiang largely supported the proposed revisions in the memorandum but went further. Besides the demilitarization of Manchuria, he identified the two additional future goals of concluding a multilateral security treaty modeled on the Locarno Pact and establishing a Sino-Japanese conciliation commission to settle minor disputes (Usui 1995: 107). What Chiang and the Chinese government envisaged, therefore, was almost identical to the original version of the Lytton recommendations. Or it might be more accurate to say that the proposal for the international administration of Manchuria contained in the Lytton Report should be understood as the outcome of the joint work of the Lytton Commission and the Chinese committee tasked with laying the groundwork for the civilian administration of Manchuria, chaired by Wellington Koo, which strongly influenced the April 1932 conference in Nanjing.

Conclusions and Analysis

When the Lytton Report was submitted to the League Council in September 1932, it was recognized that Manchuria did not easily fit into the existing framework of sovereign nation states. It was, therefore, widely accepted in one form or another, both in Japan and elsewhere, that the region should be placed under some type of special administration. Even the ROC, despite its condemnation of the founding of the 'state' of Manchukuo, was no exception.

Several factors were influential in shaping the discussion of what form that special administration should take. This included seeking inspiration in previous examples of international territorial administration by the Western powers since the second half of the nineteenth century. It also entailed thinking about the relevance of the League's mandate system and the international administrations it had devised for Danzig and the Saarland. Certain ideas on regional autonomy that were current in China after the 1911 Revolution were also important, such as the concept of 'provincial autonomy.' It is noteworthy, too, that something akin to an embryonic version of today's UN Peacekeeping Forces was contemplated during the drafting of the Lytton Report, which stands as an early example of the recognition that a police force tasked with maintaining order is one of the keys to the success of any international administration.

This idea might have arisen under the influence of discussions on establishing a permanent League of Nations force which occurred at the World Disarmament Conference, which was held in Geneva at the same time as the Manchuria issue was being debated.[14]

While the proposal on the international administration of Manchuria contained in the Lytton Report thus built on precedents, it also took account of the various specific factors behind the Sino-Japanese dispute that had intensified until it became outright conflict in 1931–1932. In view of the volatile state of Sino-Japanese relations, however, the report could do no more than suggest the principles on which such an administration would be based. If the Lytton recommendations had been acted on in some form, the outcome would very likely have resembled the League's administration of Danzig or the Saarland, rather than a condominium or protectorate on the nineteenth-century model or a League of Nations mandate. There are several conceivable scenarios for what might have happened next.

The worst-case scenario is that the international administration of the Manchuria region might have sparked a fresh Sino-Japanese conflict. After all, the international administration of Danzig, far from alleviating German-Polish tensions, ended up igniting World War II. In retrospect, Danzig thus serves as a lesson to teach that establishing an internationally administered territory on a semi-permanent basis between two states that are not necessarily on friendly terms can exacerbate tensions and furnish a pretext for the use of military force.

The best-case scenario is that Manchuria might have peacefully reverted to the ROC upon termination of the international administration, just as the Saarland was restored to Germany in accordance with the results of a lawfully conducted plebiscite. To make this work, it would have been of paramount importance to limit the term of the international administration and make provisions for a plebiscite on deciding the region's final status. The Chinese government appears to have been aware of this in its discussion of the Lytton Report, when it insisted that the existence of the autonomous Manchurian government be limited to a term of five to fifteen years (Koo Papers 1932d).

A third possible scenario is that an international administration, especially one of considerable duration, might have allowed the inhabitants of Manchuria to develop their own distinctive regional and political identity. Then they could have had the choice of establishing a new country in accordance with the Wilsonian principle of national self-determination, that was neither part of the ROC nor the puppet state that Japan had created. In that case, the international administration would have performed a function similar to that of a Class A League of Nations mandate, stipulated in the preamble to Article 22 of the League Covenant to be overseeing the 'tutelage' of 'peoples not yet able to stand by themselves.'

Which scenario would have played out if the proposal for the international administration of Manchuria had been agreed and accepted would have depended not only on its form but also on the state of international politics more broadly? This depends not only on the bilateral relationship between China and Japan but also on the overall condition of Eastern Asia, which would also have to take account of the roles of the Soviet Union, the United States, and Britain. Moreover, unlike Danzig and the Saarland, with their small territories and populations, Manchuria covered an area as large as Western Europe and had a population of 30 million. It was hemmed in by several countries of dissimilar character: the Soviet Union, a socialist state; China, still in turmoil even after the Northern Expedition as the Nationalists and the Communists battled for supremacy; and Japan, which was turning its back on international co-operation and reverting to nineteenth-century-style power politics. For these reasons, establishing an international administration in Manchuria was a quite different kettle of fish from doing so in Europe, with its relatively homogeneous collection of states. Manchuria was indeed 'without an exact parallel in other parts of the world' (Lytton 1932: 126).

A discussion that took place during the early days of the Pacific War casts another interesting sidelight on these possible scenarios. On 17 March 1942, exactly a decade after the establishment of the actual 'state' of Manchukuo, the US Council on Foreign Relations convened a study group in New York to discuss post-war plans based on the assumption of Japan's defeat, which is in itself quite astonishing given that Allied forces all over the Asia–Pacific were fleeing before the Japanese onslaught at that time. One of the items on the agenda was the status of Manchukuo after the war.[15] The meeting was chaired by George Blakeslee, professor of International Relations at Clark University. He had accompanied the American representative on the Lytton Commission, General Frank R. McCoy, and was now an adviser to the State Department. The secretary was Hugh Borton, later professor of Japanese Studies at Columbia University, who was to be involved in shaping post-war American policy toward Japan. Most of those in attendance were influential American politicians, businessmen, and journalists of the older generation.

Alongside the idea of dismantling Manchukuo after the war and immediately restoring the region to the ROC, the participants again debated the possibility of imposing some form of international administration and even leaving the state of Manchukuo intact. The grounds for this were that a regional and political identity distinct from China proper might have emerged in the decade since Manchukuo was created, which would be impossible to dismantle without a total disregard for popular sentiment. It was also pointed out that Manchuria had long been a separate political, economic, and cultural entity from China south of the Great Wall, lying as it did beyond the pale of traditional Chinese civilization. Lingering Russian or Soviet influence in northern Manchuria was also a factor to be considered. It was even argued that the Japanese presence in Manchuria ultimately contributed to the stability of East Asia. The establishment of a 'semi-independent Manchuria under international guarantees' was thus proposed—which was exactly what the Lytton Report had recommended (Blakeslee Papers 1942: 2).

That the American establishment considered that dismantling Manchukuo and restoring the region to the ROC was not the obvious thing to do after the defeat of Japan indicates that it was, even at that point in time, an entity that Hikomatsu Kamikawa had termed an 'international intermediate zone (*kokusai chukan chitai*). Having examined the Manchurian question alongside similar cases in Europe, the Middle East, and Asia, he used this term to describe regions that were disputed by adjacent countries and where theoretical sovereignty and actual politico-economic control diverged.

Of course, the Council on Foreign Relations was a private think tank, and so the views aired at its meetings did not immediately translate into US government policy. In fact, the Cairo Declaration that was issued as a result of the November 1943 conference of the leaders of the United States, Britain, and China, clearly states that 'all the territories Japan has stolen from the Chinese, such as Manchuria, Formosa, and The Pescadores, shall be restored to the Republic of China' (US Dept. of State 1961: 448).

The restoration of Manchuria to the ROC after Japan's defeat subsequently came to be seen among the Allies as a self-evident prerequisite for any post-war settlement. What should be noted here, however, is that in the Japanese translation of the Cairo Declaration, Japan is described as having stolen Manchuria not from the ROC but from the Qing Dynasty.[16] How the debate on the legitimacy of the ROC's assumption of sovereignty over the territories once ruled by the Qing Dynasty unfolded among the Allies in the period leading up to the Cairo Conference is beyond the scope of this chapter, however.[17]

What can be said is that, despite the efforts of the League, confirmation of Manchuria's status as a part of China was ultimately settled by war. Analysis of the interactions that took place between its staff and local actors in Eastern Asia does, however, show how novel attempts were made to articulate some of the most fundamental concepts of international relations, such as sovereignty and the principle of national self-determination. That these efforts failed was due not to a lack of creativity but to the fact that the League lacked the power and means to control the behavior of its members, as they sought to pursue their interests in the context of massive shifts in the global balance of power. The attempt to find a constructive solution to a conflict over territory between the two most powerful of the League's Eastern Asian states thus became the first of a series of failures that would undermine the effectiveness and ultimately the existence of the organization itself.

Notes

1. The Ōsaka Mainichi of May 29, 1932, for example, reported that Lampson and Zhang Xueliang had met in Dalniy (Dalian) and 'drawn up a proposal to place Manchuria under the League's control and entrust it to a new government chaired by Zhang Xueliang and composed of both Japanese and Chinese members.' This article uses the term 'committee rule' (iin tōchi) to distinguish that arrangement from a mandate (inin tōchi) based on Article 22 of the League of Nations Covenant. However, no concrete evidence of such a proposal is found in British Foreign Office documents in the National Archives, London.
2. For Japanese intellectuals' response to the Manchurian Incident in general and to the Lytton Report in particular, see Nish (1993).
3. On Kamikawa's argument on a mandate for Manchuria, see Kamikawa (1932a). On the end of the Iraqi mandate and how Iraq achieved independence, see Evans (1932) and Hudson (1933). For a comparison of the Manchuria and Iraq see Tohmatsu (2015: 225–247).
4. On the question of expanding the mandate system in the context of colonial appeasement policy, see Crozier (1988).
5. On theories on where sovereignty over mandated territories lay, see Taoka (1941: 127–141); Pedersen (2015: 204–232).

6. On the renunciation of claims to non-Turkish regions of the Middle East by the Ottoman Empire and the Republic of Turkey, see Macfie (1998: 194–208).
7. For the theory that Sun Yat-sen considered leasing Manchuria to Japan in return for financial aid, see Fujii (1982). No documentary evidence has been found on the Chinese side to corroborate this theory, however. See Yu (1989: 180–181).
8. The following account of the Saarland's form of government is based on Miyazaki (1964: 29–45) and Wilde (2008: 111–114).
9. The following account of Danzig's form of government is based on Mason (1946: 61–76) and Wilde (2008:114–127).
10. On fundamental causes of conflict inherent in the international administration of Danzig, see Mason (1946: 284–285).
11. A typical example of local reaction to the founding of Manchukuo is the policy of 'securing the borders to make the people safe and not maintaining an army' propounded by the local worthy, Yu Chonghan. See Yamamuro (2006: 54–61). On the social and ideological background of Chinese who took part in setting up the state of Manchukuo, a thought-provoking study is Hamaguchi (1996), especially chapter 2, Manshū jihen to Chūgokujin [The Manchurian Incident and the Chinese].
12. For an unfavorable contemporary assessment of the Lytton recommendations on the international administration of Manchuria, see Kamikawa (1932b).
13. For more information on Wellington Koo's background see the chapter by Hughes in this book.
14. Among the main items on the agenda of the 1932 Geneva Disarmament Conference was a proposal for establishing a permanent League of Nations police force, one of the functions of which would have been to furnish an international gendarmerie to disputed or unstable regions (such as Manchuria or Liberia). See Murray (1933).
15. The following account is based on Borton's summary of the meeting. See Blakeslee Papers. 1942.
16. It is interesting to note that the term 'Chinese' in the American document is translated into Japanese as 'Shinkokujin' (People of the Qing dynasty) by the Japanese Foreign Ministry (MOFAJ 1966: 595).
17. On Allied discussions and negotiations during the Asia–Pacific War about post-war territorial claims and colonial issues, see Lewis (1977).

References

Blakeslee Papers. 1942. Study Group Reports: Do Bases for a Real Peace Exist between the United States and Japan? Fifth Meeting: Concrete Issues in a

Post-War Settlement with Japan, Digest of Discussions. 17 March. File No. 5, Box 3. Clark University Library, Worcester, MA.

Chen, Jerome. 1979. *The Military-Gentry Coalition: China under the Warlords*. Toronto: University of Toronto.

Crozier, Andrew. 1988. *Appeasement and Germany's Last Bid for Colonies*. London: Macmillan.

Evans, Luther H. 1932. The General Principles Governing the Termination of a Mandate. *The American Journal of International Law* 26: 735–758.

FO. 1933. Future administration of Liberia. 20 March, J733/4/24, FO371/17040. National Archives, London.

Fujii, Shōzō, 1982. Son Bun no tainichi taido: Shingai kakumei-ki no 'Manshū' soshaku mondai o chūshin ni [Sun Yat-sen's attitude to Japan, with special reference to the question of leasing 'Manchuria' during the 1911 revolution]. In Ishikawa Tadao kyōju kanreki kinen ronbunshū henshū iinkai, ed., *Ishikawa Tadao kyōju kanreki kinen ronbunshū: Gendai Chūgoku to sekai: Sono seijiteki tenkai* [Essays in honor of the sixtieth birthday of Professor Ishikawa Tadao: Modern China and the world: Its political developments], 127–144. Tōkyō: Keiō tsūshin.

Hamaguchi, Yūko. 1996. *Nihon tōchi to higashi Ajia sekai* [Japanese rule and the East Asian world]. Tōkyō: Keisō shobō.

Hudson, Manley O. 1933. The Admission of Iraq to Membership in the League of Nations. *The American Journal of International Law* 27: 133–138.

Kamikawa, Hikomatsu. 1932a. Manshū inin tōchiron' [On the Manchurian Mandate]. *Gaikō jihō* (650) January.

Kamikawa, Hikomatsu. 1932b. Ritton hōkoku ni okeru kaiketsuan no hihan [Criticism of the proposed settlement in the Lytton Report]. *Kokka gakkai zasshi* [The journal of the association of political and social sciences] (46/11): pp. 1608–1622.

Koo Papers. 1932a. Round Table Conference between Members of the Chinese Government and the Commission of Inquiry. March 29. File 8, Box 5.

Koo Papers. 1932b. Second Round Table Conference between Members of the Chinese Government and the Commission of Inquiry. March 30. File 8, Box 5.

Koo Papers. 1932c. Meeting of Members of the Chinese Government and Commission of Inquiry. 19 June. File 8, Box 5.

Koo Papers. 1932d. A Memorandum on the Findings of the Lytton Commission: III. A Legal Interpretation of the Findings and Recommendations Contained in the Lytton Report. File 23, Box 6.

Koo Papers. 1932e. V. Suggestions for Discussion. File 23, Box 6: 12–16.

Lewis, William Roger. 1977. *Imperialism at Bay: The United States and the Decolonization of the British Empire, 1941–1945*. New York: Oxford University Press.

LONa. 1932. Notes on the Report of the Commission of Enquiry & Bases for Future Sino-Japanese Negotiations. No. 5, Section File S43.

LONb. 1932a. Preparation and Rapport. No. 3, Section File S43.

LONc. 1932b. Notes on the Report of the Commission of Enquiry: VII. Organisation of the Four North-Eastern Provinces. No. 5, Section File S43.

Lytton. 1932. *Report of the Commission of Enquiry (The Lytton Report)*. Geneva: The League of Nations.

Macfie, A.L. 1998. *The End of the Ottoman Empire 1908–1923*. London: Longman.

Mason, John Brown. 1946. *The Danzig Dilemma: A Study in Peacemaking by Compromise*. Stanford: Stanford University Press.

Miyazaki, Shigeki. 1964. *Zaaruranto no hōteki chii* [The Legal Status of the Saarland]. Tōkyō: Miraisha.

MOFAJ (Ministry of Foreign Affairs Japan). 1966. Nihon gaikō nempyō narabini shuyō bunsho [Japanese foreign policy: Chronological tables and major documents]. Vol. 2. Tokyo: Hara shobō.

Murray, Gilbert. 1933. Memorandum on an International Police Force. 20 January. MSS Gilbert Murray. Bodleian Library, University of Oxford. Reel 68, 216, f. 88–97.

Nish, Ian. 1993. *Japan's Struggle with Internationalism: Japan, China, and the League of Nations, 1931–1933*. London: Kegan Paul International.

OJ. 1920. Feb.–June 1920. p. 45ff.

Pedersen, Susan. 2015. *The Guardians: The League of Nations and the Crisis of Empire*. Oxford: Oxford University Press.

Sun, Zhongshan (Sun Yat-sen). 1929. *Sanmin shugi* [The Three Principles of the People], trans. Into Japanese by Kanai Kanzō. Tōkyō: Kaizōsha. English translation (1975) *San Min Chu I: The Three Principles of the People*. Boston: Da Capo Press.

Taoka, Ryōichi, 1941. *Inin tōchi no honshitsu* [Essence of mandate administration]. Tōkyō: Yūhikaku.

Tochigi, Toshio and Banno, Ryōkichi. 1997. *Chūgoku kokumin kakumei: Senkanki higashi Ajia no chikaku hendō* [The Chinese nationalist revolution: Tectonic shifts in interwar East Asia]. Tōkyō: Hōsei University Press

Tohmatsu, Haruo. 2015. Iraq and Manchukuo: state-building in the interwar period. In Kondo Kazuhiko ed., *History in British History: Proceedings of the seventh Anglo-Japanese Conference of Historians*, held at Trinity Hall, University of Cambridge, 11–14 September 2012. Tokyo: [s.n]: 225–247.

Tohmatsu, Haruo. 2016. From the Manchurian Incident to Japan's Withdrawal from the League of Nations. In Tsutsui, Kiyotada ed. *Fifteen Lectures on Showa Japan: Road to the Pacific War in Recent Historiography*. Tokyo: JPIC, 2016): 83–103.

U.S. Department of State. 1961. Foreign Relations of the United States. Diplomatic Papers: The Conferences at Cairo and Teheran 1943. US Government Printing Office: Washington, D.C.

Usui, Katsumi. 1995. *Manshūkoku to kokusai renmei* [Manchukuo and the League of Nations]. Tokyo: Yoshikawa kōbunkan.

Wilde, Ralph. 2008. *International Territorial Administration: How Trusteeship and Civilizing Mission Never Went Away*. Oxford: Oxford University Press.

Yamamuro, Shin'ichi. 2006. *Manchuria under Japanese Dominion*, trans. Joshua A. Fogel. Philadelphia: University of Pennsylvania Press.

Yu, Xintun. 1989. *Son Bun no kakumei undō to Nihon* [Sun Yat-sen's revolutionary movement and Japan]. Tōkyō: Rokkō shuppan.

Public Opinion and the League: Newspaper Coverage of the Lytton Commission in China

Lunhai Mu

Introduction

Even though the Mukden Incident was a dispute between China and Japan in a region far from Europe, it has been described as 'a turning-point in the history of the League and of the world' (Walters 1960: 465). This is because the crisis that ensued became one of the most important tests for the organization's ability to uphold international justice and was the first major step in its ultimate demise. Existing studies have tended to focus on international politics and diplomacy, however, while paying less attention to how it affected public opinion.[1] This is despite the fact that public opinion always played an important role in the life of the League, from the shaping of its foundational ideas to limiting its development when perceptions of its activities turned negative, a downward trend that was only encouraged by the manipulation of the organization at the hands of social elites and political leaders, such as President Woodrow Wilson.

L. Mu (✉)
Wuhan University, Wuhan, China
e-mail: louismu@whu.edu.cn

C. R. Hughes and H. Shinohara (eds.), *East Asians in the League of Nations*, New Directions in East Asian History,
https://doi.org/10.1007/978-981-19-7067-2_11

Nowhere is this attention deficit truer than in the lack of research on the relationship between public opinion and the crisis over Manchuria.[2]

For the purposes of this analysis, public opinion can be defined as 'the voice of the people, a clear and direct utterance from the citizenry' (Peters 1995: 3). In the absence of opinion polls in China during the period concerned, evidence about its development can best be found in the transmission of news and opinion in leading newspapers. This chapter will thus draw mainly on commentaries and editorials in what were known as 'The Four Great Newspapers of the Republic'. These are *The Central Daily News* [*Zhongyang ribao*], the official organ of the ruling Guomingdang [GMD], or Nationalist Party; *The Republic Daily News* [*Minguo ribao*], which was the mouthpiece of the GMD's local branches across the country; and two popular newspapers which tended to have more social influence due to their longer history and pioneering role in the development of modern journalism in China, namely *Shun Pao* [*Shanghai News*] and *Ta Kung Pao*.[3] The survey will also look at *Social Welfare, Tientsin* [*Yi Shi Bao, Tianjin*], established by reformers in 1915 and included by many as one of the Four Great Newspapers, as well as *Kuo Wen Weekly* [*Guowen zhoubao*], a periodical affiliated to *Ta Kung Pao*.[4]

If, as Samuel P. Huntington argues, changes in public attitudes are matched by changes in elite perceptions, these organs can be taken as reasonable indicators of the formation and fluctuation of public opinion (Huntington 2003: 222). Their head offices were in the foreign concessions of the coastal cities of Tianjin and Shanghai, where a relatively liberal environment provided the conditions for free speech and reporting, but their market was nationwide. *Shanghai News* even set up distribution centers in countries such as Japan, the USA, Britain, and Germany. After the Mukden Incident, an upsurge of popular patriotism sharply boosted the circulation of *Shun Pao* and *Ta Kung Pao* to around 200,000 and 100,000 respectively. Although this was only a small proportion of China's population, it was drawn mainly from the elite class of intellectuals, politicians, bureaucrats, and wealthy businessmen.

Looking at the political dynamics of public opinion, social scientists argue that becomes a crucial factor when it threatens to isolate 'deviant individuals and governments' (Noelle-Neumann 1995: 46). By imposing social marginalization or providing popular support for those with a high public standing it creates what Elisabeth Noelle-Neumann calls a 'spiral of silence.' Cases have been studied in which fear of isolation sets this in motion, as, 'Observations made in one context spread to another and encouraged people either to proclaim their views or swallow them and keep quiet until, in a spiraling process, the one view dominated the public scene and the other disappeared from public awareness as its adherents became mute' (Noelle-Neumann 1984: 5,6). This dynamic can be seen at work with regard to the status of the League in China after Mukden, when opinion coalesced around the belief that it would sacrifice the nation's interests in order to reach a compromise with Japan. If it had been seen to be upholding international justice, it could have generated a positive spiral effect of popular support instead. The spiral effect of the widespread perception that it would remain silent toward acts of aggression, thus not only entrapped the League but also served to undermine its standing as it spread from China around the world.

This paper provides insights into how this process unfolded by looking at the fluctuation of Chinese public opinion, with a special focus on perceptions of the Lytton Commission that was sent by the League to investigate the crisis, and the report that it issued. The diplomatic activities of the Commission have already been discussed by Tohmatsu in the previous chapter. Here it is important to stress that such high-level politics took place in the context of high expectations for the among the Chinese public when the crisis began. As it dragged on for nearly one-and-a-half years, this changed to doubt and anxiety and ended with thorough disappointment. Some Chinese scholars have gone so far as to argue that the League's handling of Mukden closely reflects the appeasement policy of the Western great powers toward Japan, which 'enormously encouraged the Japanese fascist's wild ambition of seeking hegemony, aggression, and expansion' (Hu and Luo 1989: 34). This mirrors the history of the League's international image, as it struggled to make hard choices arising from the clash between the principle of upholding international justice and the reality of having to subordinate itself to the demands of the great powers, leading it to ultimately withdraw from the international arena as its lack of the courage and strength needed to criticize its most powerful members became clear.

High Expectations and the Establishment of the Lytton Commission

The Mukden Incident broke out late on the evening on 18 September 1931, when the Japanese army let off an explosion on a Japanese-owned section of the South Manchuria Railway. Although the world was shocked when this incident was used by Japan as the pretext for its full invasion of Manchuria, China lacked the capability for a military response. On 21 September, its representative in Geneva, Dr. Alfred Sze Sao-ke, reported the situation to the League and accused Japan of an act of aggression, requesting '... immediate steps to prevent the further development of a situation endangering the peace of nations' (LON 1932: 5). Three days later, Ta Kung Pao published an editorial which reflected the high expectations in China when it stated that, 'The only reason why the League should exist is to settle international disputes between its members peacefully and prevent wars by the power of international public opinion ... [the Mukden Incident] is the biggest dispute between members since the establishment of the League ... which concerns the future of the world. So the League will have to intervene' (TKP 1931).

The short history of the League up to that time presented good reasons to expect that it would take meaningful action. In 1925, during what became known as 'The Incident at Petrich,' fighting had broken out between Greece and Bulgaria following the shooting of a Greek border guard on the disputed border between the two countries. The League responded by imposing a ceasefire, ordering the withdrawal of Greek troops, and making Bulgaria pay compensation. Given this encouraging example of the organization's capability and will to uphold international justice, one Chinese scholar had felt confident enough to argue that 'the precedent of handling the Greek–Bulgarian crisis is the basis for handling the Sino-Japanese dispute' (Liang 1995: 282).

Although the League accepted China's appeal, however, there was no indication that it would make any kind of intervention that could lead to a settlement of the dispute in Manchuria. Instead, the President of the League Council merely made an 'urgent appeal' to both China and Japan by telegram, asking that they 'refrain from any act which might aggravate the situation or prejudice the peaceful settlement of the problem' (Willoughby 1935: 56). Japan merely responded by objecting strongly to third-party involvement and argued that the incident could be resolved through consultation between the two countries. Even while the Japanese government was attempting to smooth over the events, though, its army was expanding its operations in Manchuria.

Chinese opinion began to turn negative as early as 28 September, when the League expressed its opinion that the incident was just a regional dispute. *Shun Pao* was quick to publish a running commentary entitled, 'Countrymen, Don't Rely on the League,' which demanded to know

'Could the League really help us to uphold international justice? Yesterday the League was satisfied with the government note from Japan ... then, our countrymen felt a deep sense of loss, and thought that the League couldn't help us' (SP(S) 1931a). This blow to public confidence was only made worse when China's request for a neutral inquiry was denied, following an objection from Japan.

It is not true to say that the League was entirely oblivious to Chinese sentiment, however. On 30 September, it did adopt a resolution requesting the withdrawal of Japanese forces to inside the zone around the Manchurian Railway. This, however, appeared to be toothless because it failed to lay out any deadline or punitive measures for failure to comply. Hopes that the dispute could be resolved through bilateral Sino-Japanese negotiations only cast more doubt on the League's willingness to uphold justice in the eyes of the Chinese public. As *Shun Pao* put it in a commentary on 2 October, 'always following the leadership of the Japanese in all respects, we cannot understand how the League can explain this to itself' (SP(S) 1931b).

The situation continued to worsen as the League's evident powerlessness only strengthened Japan's determination to broaden its military operations. After it bombed Tongliao County and the city of Jinzhou on 3 and 8 October, it escalated the challenge to China by changing its strategy from one of 'military withdrawal separated from negotiation' to 'negotiation first, then withdrawal' (Wu 1989: 27). The League's impotence was only thrown into sharper relief when, on 11 October, American Secretary of State Henry L. Stimson roundly condemned the military operations, and was echoed by Britain, France, and other countries. The American statement was praised for showing a 'positive attitude' and providing a 'powerful backup force' that should have encouraged the League and appealed to the Chinese public to cooperate with international society and 'not undertake any deviant behavior' (KW 1931; SP(S) 1931c; TKP 1931). When, on 15 October, America was invited to join the discussion over Manchuria (despite opposition from Japan) and took the opportunity to advocate a firmer attitude, *Ta Kung Pao* was full of praise, describing the development as 'a splendid moment in the history of the League,' which was 'testing true values' and 'verifying real authority.' It insisted that this was 'substantially different from the Tripartite Intervention' of 1895, when Germany, France, and Russia had furthered their own interests by pressuring Japan to return the territory it had taken from

China after defeating the forces of the Qing Empire that year (TKP(T) 1931b).

Despite this more positive tone, however, some doubts remained about the ability of the League to follow through on its statements. *Ta Kung Pao*, for example, urged the Chinese to 'stay alert' until it was clearer to what extent the power of the League could stand the test it was facing. The League appeared to be rising to the challenge when, on 24 October, it passed a resolution mandating the withdrawal of Japanese troops and imposing a deadline of 16 November. Again, however, this was not supported by any action that could have demonstrated the organization's determination to discipline Japan for openly antagonizing its authority. A good indication of the growing awareness of the importance of world public opinion at this time can be seen in a letter sent from George Gilbert Aimé Murray to the Viscount of Chelwood, Robert Cecil, on 9 November 1931, in which he stated that 'the only chance of controlling [Japan], without having to raise the question of absolute coercion, was to show an overwhelming weight of public opinion against her breach of the Covenant and Kellogg Pact' (Thorne 1972: 180).

As the deadline approached, the Chinese public grew more anxious. On 15 November, *Shun Pao* published a running commentary, saying that 'Since the outbreak of the Incident, almost two months have passed, the League always muddles through and puts things off, sitting by and watching the development of Japanese atrocities, truth ravaged by violence, and world peace on the verge of ruin. Each power has a different idea, and the attitude of "watching and waiting" is fairly obvious' (SP(S) 1931d). On 16 November, after Japan refused to withdraw and the League chose not to take substantive action, *Kuo Wen Weekly* published a review under the title 'Where is the Authority of the League?', which questioned its ability to execute the resolutions it had made since the outbreak of the Incident (Teng 1931). *Ta Kung Pao* published an editorial which claimed that Japan's action was 'nothing other than a challenge to international pacifism. If that's tolerable and acceptable, then it will be the end of the world' (TKP(T) 1931c). On 23 November, this was reinforced in another *Ta Kung Pao* editorial, which called the League's acquiescence the 'worst policy' and warned that it would lead to 'the collapse of ostensible world peace' (TKP(T) 1931d).

Although Japan firmly believed that the League would not dare to stop its expansion, it did consider that saving the reputation of the organization would be advantageous for arbitrating an outcome favorable to itself.

This was clearly the intention of the Japanese representative at Geneva and ambassador to Western Europe, when he said, 'Adopting tactics of maintaining the dignity of the League and making use of the League as far as possible was crucially important' (Ogata 2015: 155). On 21 November, he thus proposed that the League should send a commission of inquiry. This successfully changed the focus of discussion toward issues such as the composition of the mission and left the Chinese request for Japan's withdrawal waiting for a definite response. One Chinese scholar, Wu Yin, concludes, 'The birth of the dispatch program of a commission of inquiry is a typical performance of Japan's diplomacy of taking backward as forward and an inevitable by-product of Western Great Powers' appeasement policy toward Japan' (Wu 1989: 32).

Such sentiments were echoed by *Shun Pao* in a running commentary on 23 November, which said, 'We countrymen have to admit that the League's spirit and attitude of safeguarding peace and upholding justice has succumbed to violence' and questioned, '... why the League doesn't have any capability for safeguarding its prestige'(SP(S) 1931e). To make matters worse, the League even threatened to terminate mediation in order to force China to compromise, leading critics at *Shun Pao* to complain that, 'To cover up her own incompetence, the League plans to shift the responsibility of mediation failure to China' (SP(S) 1931f). Infuriated by these repeated compromises with Japan, the paper published a running commentary which asked, 'What on earth is the League? Is it the backup force for truth and peace or the helper of evil? The essence of the League has become more and more obvious since the outbreak of the Mukden Incident' (SP(S) 1931g).

On 10 December, the League finally adopted a resolution to dispatch the Lytton Commission. Although the Chinese public was not satisfied with what it saw as an appeasement policy, this could at least be taken as an indication that Japan had formally accepted the League's authority to mediate and offered some degree of hope that its aggressive behavior would be revealed to the international community. This did not stop *Kuo Wen Weekly* from publishing a review on 14 December, however, which criticized the League's limited resistance to aggression and expressed the belief that the Commission was just the by-product of a 'compromise' with Japan (Yun 1931). This pessimism was given substance when the Japanese army began bombing Jinzhou on 28 December and went on to occupy it on 3 January 1932. When, yet again, this did not trigger any substantive action on the part of the League, *Shun Pao* argued that the organization's reputation was being 'dragged in the dust.' It followed this on 11 January with a call on the people 'to rise up in self-rescue,' and 'to give up meaningless appeals and expectations' (SP(S) 1931h; 1932a). As Walters points out, the resolution was just too late and 'the League had already suffered a severe loss of prestige and of public confidence' (Walters 1960: 482).

In sum, by the time the Lytton Commission was formally established on 21 January 1932, the League's constant concessions to Japan had indicated that it lacked the appetite for confrontation and was only too willing to settle the dispute over Manchuria through peaceful measures instead of using economic or military sanctions. Although America's attitude toward Japan was tougher, even President Hoover had said, 'We will not go along on war or any of the sanctions, either economic or military, for those are the roads to war' (Henig 2010: 144). The Commission seemed to be either too sympathetic to Japan or neutral at the very least, so long as no member of the League showed any sympathy for China (Chen 2021: 177–186). Even the route of the Commission had to be changed under pressure from Japan. With all the signs indicating that the Commission would continue what looked like a policy of appeasement, it is not surprising that *Shun Pao* concluded that 'The Lytton Commission may not achieve anything' (SP(S) 1932b).

The Commission *En Route* to Manchuria and Chinese Opinion

On 3 February 1932, five months after the Mukden Incident, the Commission finally started its journey to Manchuria. It was led by Lord Victor Alexander George Robert Bulwer-Lytton, who had been the British governor of Bengal from 1922 to 1927. Despite the fact that the USA was not a League member, it included the American Major General Frank Ross McCoy, who had gained a positive impression of Japan when he had led a relief mission to Tokyo after the 1923 earthquake. Germany was represented by Dr. Heinrich Schnee, who had a long career as a colonial civil servant and had served as the last Governor of German East Africa. The French member, General Henri Claudel, had served as commander of the French Army of the East, a member of the Advisory Committee on Colonial Defence, commander of the troops in French West Africa, and commander of the French Colonial Corps. He, too, was deemed as having a good feeling toward Japan, especially its military. The Italian, Luigi Aldrovandi Marescotti, was also deemed to be harmless toward Japan.

The group arriving first at Yokohama, on 29 February, and stayed in Japan until 11 March where it talked with individuals from all walks of society. The Chinese public paid close attention to its progress and noticed the grand reception it was given, with *Shun Pao* commenting on how, 'The Commission occupied herself with dinners and banquets from morning till night' (SP(S) 1932c). By contrast, *Social Welfare Tientsin* expressed a popular aversion in China against fawning on the Commission when it published an editorial that appealed to the people to observe 'no extravagance, no over-obsequiousness,' while voicing opposition to Japan's behavior of 'taking every measure to promote propaganda' (SWT 1932a).

The Commission finally arrived at Shanghai on 14 March and stayed in China until 19 April. It undertook extensive field research and had extensive contacts and discussions with people from various sectors of society, including important military and political leaders like Chiang Kai-shek, Wang Jingwei, Zhang Xueliang, T.V Soong, Eugene Chen, and Luo Wengan. The serious way in which it undertook its work gave the Chinese public a glimmer of hope, expressed by *Shun Pao* in a commentary marking its arrival in Shanghai, which said, 'The more we trust and hope the League could love peace, the more severely we blame her. Looking back on what has happened, we must say the League's indecisiveness and turning a blind eye led to an escalation of the situation. But better later than never, we will wait and see what the League will do' (SP(S) 1932d). That same day, *Ta Kung Pao* wrote to the Commission expressing hope that its members 'could fulfill their commitment when they recognize the situation fairly and objectively' (TKP(T) 1932a).

Although the public was quite dissatisfied with the League's powerlessness and inefficiency, therefore, the Commission was still expected to uncover the truth. On 19 March, *Shun Pao* conveyed this message by publishing a running commentary that heaped praise on the way that the League had handled the Greece–Bulgaria crisis, calling it 'sufficient to be an example for any member state' and 'the most brilliant moment in the history of handling disputes by the League.' At the end of the piece, the authors rammed home the message by exclaiming: 'Upholding justice as before, not fearing the threat of power. No matter what the League did before, what matters in the future is to redeem the League's reputation by following the glory of the Greece–Bulgaria crisis' (SP(S) 1932e).

The common concern in China, therefore, was not so much toward the results of the Commission's process but whether the League would have the courage to impartially uphold international justice. As *Ta Kung Pao* put it in an editorial: 'We hope that the Commission members can have the same determination of upholding justice; even if it achieves nothing, you should never curtail the truth by succumbing to might; if this is done, no matter whether you can change the facts or not, you will more than fulfill your commitment' (TKP(T) 1931b).

Mixed signals as to whether the Commission could live up to these expectations soon began to appear. As it was about to enter into the region of Northeast China that the Japanese had recognized as the puppet state of Manchukuo, the Chinese representative, Wellington Koo, was coercively separated from the group. This provocative action by the Japanese was especially sensitive in the eyes of the public because Koo had achieved heroic status for the stance he had taken against Japan's claims at the Paris Peace Conference (see the chapter by Hughes for more on Koo's background). Lytton's response was encouraging insofar as he was tough enough to insist that, 'if there is no Chinese representative, we will not enter into "Manchukuo"'. He also pointed out that Japan had the obligation to protect the Commission because it was able to manipulate Manchukuo at will (Suzushi 1988: 450). Despite Lytton's strong words, however, this obstruction did put a cloud over whether the investigation could be effective. A *Ta Kung Pao* editorial of 25 April thus warned, 'It is not easy to get something valuable, because of the hidden traps all over Northeast China and the omnipresence of fabricated evidence. It's almost impossible to discover anything useful' (TKP(T) 1932c).

Despite the crisis over Koo's participation, the Commission finally assembled in the city of Shenyang to start its investigation of Northeast China on 21 April. Four months had already passed since the resolution to dispatch it had been passed by the League, during which time the whole of Northeast China had fallen into the hands of Japan. This meant that almost all the work was conducted under the strict supervision of its Kwantung Army and the administration of its South Manchuria Railway [Mantetsu]. With its schedule thus controlled and amid widespread fears that any relevant evidence had been destroyed or fabricated during the long period before the Commission began its work, the public began to express serious concerns about any prospect of discovering the truth. The suspicion was only made worse by the way in which information about what the Commission was doing after it entered Northeast China was made strictly off-limits to the Chinese public, resulting in very limited reportage. *Ta Kung Pao* expressed the ensuing sentiment in an editorial that pointed out, 'Since it arrived in Shenyang, contact with the Commission has been almost lost because of strict monitoring by the Japanese army and police, which leaves no room for its free activity' (TKP(T) 1932d).

This frustration and disillusionment continued to grow as the investigation came near to completion. After returning to Peiping on 6 June, then visiting more places to collect additional material, the group finally settled back in the capital on 20 August to concentrate on finalizing its report. With the basic facts already clear before the conclusion was completed, the Chinese public was not optimistic about what the report would recommend. As *Kuo Wen Weekly* explained, on 11 July, 'In the eyes of the Japanese people, China and the League are not worth mentioning. So long as the puppet government [Manchukuo] still exists, even if China wants to concede or the League intends to mediate, it has already become impossible. Now the only method for a resolution is for China and Japan to perish together' (KW 1932a).

Expressions of public pressure grew when, on 23 August, a number of unions representing many industries wrote a joint letter which appealed to the Commission to have the courage to report the truth and consider imposing sanctions on Japan. Ominous for the reputation of the League itself was the way in which the letter went on to state, 'Ever since the Incident, the effect of the resolutions of the League has been almost non-existent...if flagrantly defying international convention like this is so tolerable, then we don't know what in the world the League is. Even though our nation is unfortunately subjugated, from now on all countries may go forward into troubled times' (SP(S) 1932f). Despite this lack of confidence toward the investigation, however, there was still some hope that the Commission would find the truth and publish it. Instead of blindly blaming the League, therefore, public discourse preferred to repeatedly emphasize the significance that the report would have for the reputation of the League itself and for the maintenance of world peace in general.

When the report was finally completed and signed by members of the Commission on 4 September, even though the details of its content had not yet been made public, there was a widespread awareness of its general conclusions. On the same day as the signing, *Shun Pao* thus reported that the Commission's solution for resolving the Sino-Japanese controversy was to apply the Covenant in a way that would recognize the territorial sovereignty of China over the whole Northeast, and that it would be quite disadvantageous to Japan (SP(S) 1932g). The following day, however, the newspaper published a running commentary which showed that this optimism was still heavily tinged by confusion and uneasiness on the part of the public, explaining how, 'On the one hand, our countrymen make arduous efforts and sacrifices, but on the other hand, we still wander and watch-and-wait to see whether the League can uphold justice and righteousness' (SP(S) 1932h).

The seriousness of the test faced by the League was then thrown into sharp relief when the Japanese government learned of the findings of the report before its formal announcement on 15 September and took the pre-emptive action of formally recognizing the puppet government of Manchukuo. When the League did nothing substantive to prevent this, the uneasiness in China intensified. On 26 September, *Shun Pao* made clear what was at risk when it published a running commentary claiming that the fate of the League depended on the measures it would take in response to what was in the report, and that, 'Our countrymen still have illusions to rely on the League...this will lead to the loss of our will to save ourselves' (SP(S) 1932i).

Publication of the Lytton Report

On 2 October, the findings of the Lytton Report were made public simultaneously in Geneva, Nanjing, and Tokyo. Its key findings were confirmation of Chinese sovereignty in Manchuria and verification that this had been violated by Japan, which was also in breach of international convention. It also concluded that the Mukden Incident was an act of Japanese aggression and refused to recognize Manchukuo. Despite this condemnation of Japan, however, the text was carefully worded to avoid provoking the Japanese military. This is evident in its observations that Japanese officers on the spot at the time of Mukden may have thought that they were 'acting in self-defense.' It also noted that the boycott of Japanese goods imposed by the Chinese might have been 'another important factor' (LON 1932: 71, 112). Most sensitive, however, was that instead of ordering the Japanese to withdraw from Manchuria, the report recommended recognition of its special interests in the region. Wunsz King, a counselor of the Chinese Assessor's Office to the Lytton Commission, would later recall that this '...represented a compromise that was designed to meet the wishes of the Japanese more than half way. As a matter of fact, the report appears to have gone much too far in that direction' (King 1965: 45).

The Chinese press was under no illusion that the status of the findings was crucial, because almost all the resolutions of previous disputes handled by the League had been based on such reports. *Ta Kung Pao* thus noted, 'The conclusion of the investigation conducted by the Commission is the final verdict on the responsibility of the Mukden Incident, there is no doubt that its nature and significance is very important' (TKP(T) 1932a). On 3 October, *Shun Pao* published a review which urged readers to 'admire the sharpness of eyes and exactness of attitude' of the investigators, but also condemned the 'lack of recognition' of Japanese invasion in its recommendations and acknowledged that 'when we evaluate the value of the report, we have to sigh with regret.' This was followed by a more negative review the next day, which described how when Chinese people read the document, they would 'unconsciously shiver and tremble with fright.' It warned that 'the country would get nothing if it accepted the findings and that taking it as the basis for economic cooperation with Japan would be tantamount to cooperation between a cat and a mouse.' As far as the newspaper was concerned, the document essentially amounted to nothing more than a sham investigation and mediation that used diplomatic language and took advantage of the complex international situation to conceal the fact that the true aim of the *fait accompli* created by Japan was to deny China's claim to its Northeastern territory (SP(S) 1932j; 1932k).

Similar comments were widespread in other leading newspapers. *Social Welfare Tientsin*, for example, published an editorial on 4 October that condemned the Commission's recommendation to hold an 'Advisory Conference' for being in contradiction to 'the territorial and administrative integrity of China.' The recommendation of a form of co-government and joint management of Manchuria was also slammed as a solution that would only increase contradictions and jealousy between nations and further complicate the issues (SWT 1932b). On 5 October, the *Central Daily News* voiced the view of the GMD in an editorial that refuted the report's defense of Japanese aggression and questioned it for suggesting that the Northeast could belong to both China and Japan CDN (ZYRB 1932a). Most moderate was *Ta Kung Pao*, which mainly focused on how to implement the suggestions, appealing to China's public to 'neither overvalue nor deny it completely' (TKP(T) 1932e).

It is important to note that this public criticism did not go so far as to completely deny the significance of the report but was confined to criticizing the League's tendency to make compromises that would appease Japanese aggression. There was, in fact, some high praise for the way in which the fact-finding mission itself condemned that aggression and recognized China's sovereignty. This was even recognized by *Shun Pao*, which criticized the report most severely. *Ta Kung Pao* also praised how it signified 'the revival of justice' and contained wording 'for maintaining the dignity of the League' (Zhang 1932). Appreciation of these aspects of the report was outweighed, however, by the broad public perception that the substance of the League's response was to satisfy Japanese requests that infringed on China's sovereignty, which resulted in a generally low opinion of the outcome of the fact-finding mission.

The League was anxious to use a process of mediation to ameliorate this negative backlash, which came from Japan as well as China. When this failed to produce any new results, the report was submitted to the League Assembly on 6 December 1932. Two days later, *Shun Pao* published a running commentary which urged member states to break off relations with Japan in order to maintain the League's prestige and called on countries of the world to establish a peacekeeping force, warning that 'the last chance to prove the prestige of the League will be gone forever' (SP(S) 1932l). After the League adopted a resolution on 9 December that referred the report to a Special Committee of Nineteen, with instructions to draw up proposals for a settlement, *Shun Pao* responded with another running commentary which argued that the powerlessness of the League had long been evident to the public, so that 'Our countrymen have exhausted all loyalty...henceforth, there is no other method than to keep fighting on' (SP(S) 1932m).

When Japan refused to accept the report's core idea granting a large measure of autonomy to the Northeastern territory that was consistent with China's sovereignty and administrative integrity, the League had no choice other than to give up the attempt at mediation (Walters 1960: 494). *Shun Pao* responded on 3 February 1933, with a running commentary which claimed that 'It has been confirmed that the League is undependable' and argued that withdrawal would allow China more freedom, and provide 'a new way to seek independence diplomatically' (SP(S) 1933a).

The League's Assembly finally adopted the resolution on the report made by the Committee of Nineteen, in a special meeting convened on

24 February. This final verdict on the Sino-Japanese dispute was much the same as the Lytton Report itself. While it was unsatisfactory to China, however, the fact that it offered no more concessions to Japan allowed *Ta Kung Pao* to be relatively upbeat, carrying an editorial on 25 February which praised the resolution as 'a leaf in the League's glorious history, which restrains a great disturbance of the world,' although it still expressed doubts about how the recommendations would be put into practice (TKP(T) 1933). The next day, *Shun Pao* published a running commentary which appreciated how the League had not caved into Japan's threat to withdraw, and how the Assembly's vote of 42 against one 'at least revealed the true features of Japan to all the countries of the world' (SP(S) 1933b).

Any hopes that Japan would really change its behavior, however, were dashed when the Japanese delegation walked out, which was followed one month later by its formal notice of withdrawal from the organization. Willoughby thus rightly argues, 'If one is to judge by the actual influence exerted by the efforts of the League upon the course of events in the Far East, it must be said that the League failed to secure any substantive results whatever, either by way of conciliation or restraint' (Willoughby 1935: 657).

The reaction of the Chinese press to this train of events reflects the disappointment and confusion of the public toward the League, with the original high expectations of the public dashed. *Kuo Wen Weekly*, for example, posed the rhetorical question, 'What's the result of relying on the League? What's the cost of relying on the League? After the announcement of the Report ... what should we do?' (KW 1932b) *Shun Pao* criticized the 'Waste of months of laborious investigation, with 160 pages of carefully written beautiful words now rendered as wastepaper, while the Sino-Japanese controversy still exists' (SP(S) 1932n). This widespread disappointment and confusion and severe questioning of the fairness of the League's handling of international disputes was the opposite of what it had hoped for. As far as *Ta Kung Pao* was concerned, the suggestions it had agreed on were 'quite the opposite to the principle of impartiality' (TKP(T) 1932f). The sheer amount of time that it had taken to complete the investigation and make the final decision on the report had only further fueled the widespread skepticism, because it had merely given Japan the opportunity to secure its control over Manchuria while leaving the problem unresolved.

Despite this generally negative public opinion, however, key members of the GMD in the Chinese government intended to use the Lytton report as the basis on which to continue diplomatic negotiations with the League and Japan. Chiang Kai-shek himself commented that 'the first eight chapters of the report could be called impartial regarding the responsibility of Japan...so we should accept it based on amendment or reservation, not simply refuse it' (Furuya 1976: 205). Similar remarks were published by leading figures such as the President of the Executive Yuan (Premier), Wang Jingwei, and his predecessor, Sun Fo (Luo 1984: 9419, 9421–9423, 9428–9430). The government thus finally declared that it could accept the report if Japan would do also.

The reasons for this strategy on the part of the Chinese political leadership have been explored by Tohmatsu in the previous chapter. The belief that the League could still be used as a stage for diplomacy with Japan, however, put the Chinese politicians and diplomats at odds with the growing public anger. The intensity of emotions is expressed well by a public telegraph addressed to the League, that appeared under the title, 'Manifestation of China's Public Opinion.' Written by the National Anti-Japanese Military Council in Jehol and the National Salvation Federation in Shanghai. This condemned the Lytton Report as '... nothing but just sophistry and word skills...which sided with Japan and is nothing less than a vast conspiracy of the international community, the essence of which is to transform the status quo of Japan's exclusive control of Manchuria into an international condominium ... This must be firmly opposed by the Chinese people, it is intolerable' (SP(S) 1932o). *Ta Kung Pao* argued that 'Our government and people should prepare our own plans as soon as possible, should never wait and watch as the negotiations proceed in vain' (TKP(T) 1932g). *Social Welfare Tientsin* was even more critical, bluntly making the accusation that, 'Japan seized Manchuria, but none other than the League made it possible' (SWT 1932c). These different attitudes of the Chinese government and the public indicated that the League had lost public support and suffered a fatal blow to its prestige, which also began to pose a challenge to the legitimacy of the ruling GMD. *Kuo Wen Weekly* was under no illusions about the seriousness of the problem when it commented, 'The Lytton Report's defiance of the law is the same as ringing the death knell for herself (the League)' (Ma 1932).

From Internationalism to Nationalism

Analysis of the newspaper coverage of the Manchuria crisis thus reflects how the failure of the League contributed to the movement of Chinese public opinion away from a belief in internationalism and toward a more nationalistic form of politics. In an article in *Ta Kung* Pao, the writer Hu Zushun gives some insights into the broader implications of this setback for the organization, which he attributed to an overly narrow focus on finding the method for resolving the Sino-Japanese controversy, while forgetting that this would represent 'a miniature of the League herself, which shoulders the obligations and responsibilities of the Covenant and other conventions' (Hu 1932). If it had taken an uncompromising stand against aggression instead of trying to achieve a temporary peace at all costs, it might have had some hope of presenting and maintaining the image of an organization dedicated to the firm upholding of justice. According to the American political scientist, Westel W. Willoughby, who acted as an advisor to the Chinese delegation, the League could have taken firm action when Japan threatened to withdraw, by invoking clauses in Paragraph 3 of Article 1 of the Covenant that required a state to meet all its obligations before departing. If Japan had persisted regardless of this, it could have been expelled (Willoughby 1935: 665).

Instead, the League's loss of credibility encouraged newspapers like *Shun Pao* to strongly advocate seeking national salvation through the cultivation of radical anti-Japanese public opinion (Song 1996: 137). Even the relatively moderate *Ta Kung Pao* began to promote 'fighting against external enemies through cross-party unity based on national consciousness.' This was a standpoint that could be summarized in slogans such as 'save the nation from subjugation and ensure its survival' and 'train people how to fight bravely through letting them know shame' (Wu 2002: 9, 144). Newspapers soon began to publish columns containing harsh criticisms of Japan as a way to inspire patriotic enthusiasm, such as *Shun Pao*'s 'Reader' and *Social Welfare Tientsin's* 'Resisting Japanese Opinion.' This moved further and further away from the official foreign policy of the GMD until it sometimes appeared to be in opposition to its strategy of 'ensuring internal safety before resisting external aggression' and placing hope in the League. By August 1932, *Shun Pao*'s criticism of the 'non-resistance policy' had become so radical that Chiang Kai-shek went so far as to order a ban on its delivery by mail.[5] The murder of its owner, Shi Liangcai, was widely held to have been carried out by a GMD special agent (Shen 1983: 178).

This upsurge of nationalistic sentiment in China was not an isolated phenomenon, but a microcosm of the global transformation away from international cooperation and to the revival of nationalism that took place in the early 1930s. As Iriye Akira describes, 'The promising beginnings of cultural internationalism were dealt a crushing blow in the 1930s. The decade was characterized by forces that were the precise opposite of cultural internationalism: exclusionary nationalism, racism, aggression, and mass murder' (Iriye 1997: 91). Within this tide, the change of Chinese public opinion toward the League symbolized an attitudinal shift toward the organization that took place in most countries, until its foundations were eventually shaken.

Walters points out that although there were critics before the Mukden Incident, 'none had as yet chosen to abandon, still less to oppose, the building up of the League as an organic system for the maintenance of peace' (Walters 1960: 466). After the crisis, the League could no longer withstand the severe trials of international politics, so that it lost not only the support of the Chinese public but 'was fast losing its viability as an effective instrument for collective security' (Iriye 1997: 92). In the fallout, Germany and Italy challenged its authority and then withdrew in succession, going on to form an anti-League camp with Japan. While Japan was labeled as an aggressor, the League itself was guilty of setting a bad precedent. Later studies by Chinese scholars point out that the handling of the League 'played an important role for shielding and inciting Japanese imperialism to start wars of destroying world peace and to enlarge aggression against China' (Yi 1981: 332). Simply put, the handling of the Mukden Incident caused the League to lose China and Japan simultaneously and dispelled any concerns on the part of would-be aggressors about interventions by the League.

Some scholars trace this failure to oppose power politics and uphold international justice to the League's lack of any institutional guarantee for the effective implementation of collective security, coupled with the unwillingness of the dominant powers to undertake responsibility for this obligation (Shinohara 2010: 266–267; Willoughby 1935: 662). These problems, however, were in turn due to a lack of public support for a global consensus that only the League could impartially uphold international justice and maintain world peace in perpetuity. Although President Wilson's aims of the pursuit of 'international cooperation' and 'international peace and security' were written into the preamble of the Covenant, this idealism was dead from the start because there was insufficient domestic support in the USA to support joining the organization. As events in China demonstrate, serious international crises like the Mukden Incident only further eroded support by demonstrating how the dominant powers looked after their own security first, so that the institutional guarantees for security contained in the Covenant had almost no function. That the claim to be upholding international justice would degenerate into a tool of power politics was painfully presented to the Chinese public when the Lytton Report effectively recommended satisfying Japan's demands through the 'peaceful means' of sacrificing their own nation's interests in Manchuria.

If the loss of public support contributed to the demise of the League, however, this in turn was a symptom of the deeper issues of identity crisis that were felt particularly acutely in Eastern Asia. The importance of this factor has become mainstream in the discipline of International Relations since the end of the Cold War, with leading constructivists such as Ted Hopf arguing that, 'Identities are necessary, in international politics and domestic society alike ... a world without identities is a world of chaos, a world of pervasive and irremediable uncertainty, a world much more dangerous than anarchy' (Hopf 1988: 174–175). After World War I, publics increasingly began to show what this meant in practice as they lost confidence in the determination and willingness of the League to protect what was valuable to their identity and chose to pursue self-defense instead.

By the time of World War II, it had become commonplace for popular resistance to grow from the roots of a form of domestic politics that expected national governments to preserve the social values of freedom, democracy, and human rights. From this perspective, international relations 'more closely resembles the more ordered and complex world of domestic societies' (Lebow 2008: 570). If the leaders of states had valued the goals of anti-aggression, freedom, democracy, and human rights as much as had growing sections of their domestic societies, the world would have stood behind the mission of the League to uphold international justice. It was the Japanese lawyer and Supreme Court Chief Justice, Kisaburo Yokota, who realized that his own country's aggression in the Mukden Incident amounted to 'an operation against the whole world public opinion' (Yokota 2016: 12). In this respect, the failure of the dominant powers to respond to the high public expectations placed on the League was a key moment in the 'spiral of silence' that ultimately led to the even greater tragedy of World War II.

Notes

1. The most representative study of public opinion toward the Mukden Incident can be found in Bassett (1968), which is limited to Britain. Thorne (1972) also examines public reaction in the West more widely.
2. Correlational studies mainly focus on the opinion of intellectuals toward the League and the Lytton Commission. See Hong Lan (2006), Zheng and Liu (2009).
3. The owner of *Shun Pao*, Shi Liangcai, is honored as 'the King of Journalism' of modern China. See Fang (2005).
4. Sometimes *The Republic Daily News*, *Shun Pao*, *Ta Kung Pao*, and *Social Welfare Tientsin* [Tianjin Yi Shijie] were referred to as The Four Great Newspapers of the Republic.
5. *Shun Pao* was a nationwide newspaper, but it was published in the foreign concessions. Distribution out of the concessions relied on delivery by mail. The ban on mail delivery lasted over a month (Shen 1983: 178).

References

Bassett, R. 1968. *Democracy and foreign policy: A case history: The Sino-Japanese dispute, 1931–33*. London: Cass.

Chen, Haiyi. 2021. Jiuyiba shibian hou guolian diaochatuan daibiao xuanding yanjiu [Study of representatives-election of League investigation commission after the 9.18 Incident]. *Shehuixue Jikan*. 2: 177–186.

Fang, Zhou. 2005. *Yidai baowang Shi Liangcai* [Shi Liangcai: The King of Journalism of an Era]. Beijing: Zhongguo Wenlian Press.

Furuya, Keiji, ed. 1976. *Jiangzongtong milu: Zhong-Ri guanxi bashi nian zhi zhengyan* [Secret records of President Jiang. Authentic account of 80 years of China-Japan relations]. Series 8. (Tr. from Japanese by Central Daily News Press). Taibei: Central Daily News Press.

Henig, Ruth. 2010. *The League of Nations*. London: Haus Histories.

Hong, Lan. 2006. Lidun diaochatuan baogaoshu gongbu qianhou Zhongguo shehui gejie de fanxiang [Social reactions of all strata before and after the publication of report of the Lytton Commission. *Shixue Yuekan* 5: 55–59.

Hopf, Ted. 1988. The promise of constructivism in international relations theory. *International Security* (23/1): 171–200.

Hu, Dekun and Luo, Zhigang, eds. 1989. Di'erci shijie dazhan shigang [Outline history of the Second World War]. Wuhan: Wuhan daxue.

Hu, Zushun. 1932. 'Bushihe yu gongduanren hefa xingshi' de Lytton diaochatuan baogaoshu. [League Report as 'unsuitable arbitrator of legal form'], TKP(T). 25 October.

Huntington, Samuel P. 2003. *The clash of civilizations and the remaking of world order*. New York and London: Simon & Schuster.

Iriye, Akira. 1997. *Internationalism and world order*. Baltimore: Johns Hopkins University Press.

KW. 1931, October 19. (Journalist) Guolian dui Riren zhanling dongbei zhi caipan [The League's judgement of Japan's occupation of the Northeast]. (8/41).

KW. 1932a, July 11. (Dashi Shuping) Guolian yu Bukeshi. [(event review) The League is becoming more and more unreliable]. (9/27).

KW. 1932b, October 10. (Dashi shuping) Laidun baogao gongbu zhi hou [(event review) After the release of the Lytton Report]. (9/40).

King, Wunsz. 1965. *China and the League of Nations: The Sino-Japanese controversy*. New York: St. John's University Press.

Lebow, Richard Ned. 2008. *A cultural theory of international relations*. Cambridge: Cambridge University Press.

Liang, Jingchun. 1995. *'Jiuyiba' shibian shishu: zouxiang lishi yu weilai* [Historical records of the '9.18 incident': Towards history and the future]. Taibei: Shijie shuju.

LON (League of Nations). 1932. Appeal by the Chinese Government: Report of the Commission of Enquiry (signed by the members of the Commission on September 4th, 1932, LON 676809. Peiping [Beijing].

Luo, Jialun ed. 1984. *Geming wenxian* [Documents on the Revolution]. Series 40. Taibei: Zhongyang wenwu gongying she.

Ma, Lian. 1932, October, 17. Laidun baogao shibai [The failure of the Lytton Report]. KW (9/41).

Noelle-Neumann, Elisabeth. 1984. *The spiral of silence: Public opinion, our social skin*. Chicago: University of Chicago Press.

Noelle-Neumann, Elisabeth. 1995. Public opinion and rationality. In *Public opinion and the communication of consent*, eds. Theodore L. Glasser and Charles T. Salmon, 33–54. New York: Guilford Press.

Ogata, Sadako. 2015. *Manzhou shibian: Zhengce de xingcheng guocheng* [The Manchurian Incident: The Process of Policy Formation] (translated from Japanese by Li Tingjiang). Beijing: Shehui kexue wenxian Press.

Peters, John Durham. 1995. Historical tensions in the concept of public opinion. In *Public opinion and the communication of consent*, eds. Theodore L. Glasser and Charles T. Salmon, 3–32. New York: Guilford Press.

Shen, Zui. 1983. *Wo zhe sanshi nian* [Thirty years of my life]. Changsha: Hunan renmin press.

Shinohara, Hatsue. 2010. *Kokusai renmei: Sekai heiwa he no yume to zasetsu* [League of nations: Dream and frustration of world's peace]. Tokyo: Chuo-koron press.
Song, Jun.1996. *Shun Pao de xingshuai* [The rise and fall of Shun Pao]. Shanghai: Shanghai shehui kexue yuan press.
SP(S). 1931a, September, 28. (shiping) Guoren wu tu yilai guolian' [(running commentary) Countrymen don't rely on the League]. No. 21008.
SP(S). 1931b, October 2. Guolian zhi chengji ruci [So little for the achievements of the League]. No. 21012.
SP(S). 1931c, October 13. (Guonei yaodian) Meiguo guli guolian [(Domestic important telegram) America encourages the League]. No. 21022.
SP(S). 1931d, November 15. (Shiping) Cong guoji xingshi tuice shiliu ri yihou zhi guolian yu woguo [(running commentary) Speculation of the relationship between our country and the League from the international situation after the 16th]. No. 21056.
SP(S). 1931e, November 23. (Shiping) Guolian jing jieshou Rifang diaochatuan zhi jianyi ye [(running commentary) The League's Unexpected Acceptance of the Recommendations of the Japanese Investigation Group] No. 21064.
SP(S). 1931f, November 26. (Haiwai dian) Guolian zhunbei tuiwei [(overseas telegram) The League prepares to shirk responsibility].No. 21067.
SP(S). 1931g, December 6. (Shiping) Wuren duiyu guolian zuihou renshi [(running commentary) What our people finally know about the League]. No. 21077.
SP(S). 1931h, December 31. (Haiwai dian) Guolian weixin shaodi. [(overseas telegram) The League with every shred of its prestige swept away]. No. 21102.
SP(S). 1932a, January 11. (Shiping) Yanzhong shiqi guoren yingyou zhi juexing [(running commentary) What awakening our people should have at this grave time]. No. 21108.
SP(S). 1932b, January 11. (Haiwai dian) Guolian diaochatuan weibi youhe chengjiu , [(overseas telegram) The League is unlikely to have any achievement]. No. 21116.
SP(S). 1932c, March 9. (Haiwai dian) Guolian diaocha man an weiyuantuan mangyu yanhui' [(overseas telegram) The League Commission for the Incident busy with banquet]; (Yao wen) Riren zhaodai guolian diaochatuan [(important news) Japan Receives the League Commission]. No. 21166.
SP(S). 1932d, March 14. (Shiping) Jinggao guolian diaochatuan HAN. [(running commentary) A warning letter to the League Commission]. No. 21171.
SP(S). 1932e, March 19. (Shiping) Guolian diaochatuan chenggong zhi xianli HAN. [(running commentary) A letter about the successful precedents of the League Commission]. No. 21176.

SP(S). 1932f, August 23. Benbu News. Geye gonghui dianqing diaochatuan jushi baogao guolian, [(local news) Request telegram from guilds of all walks of life to the Commission: report to the League according to facts]. No. 21329.
SP(S). 1932g, September 4. (Guonei yaodian) Guolian diaochatuan zong baogaoshu zuori qianzi. [(Domestic important telegram) The League Commission's complete report signed yesterday]. No. 21341.
SP(S). 1932h, September 5. (Shiping) Guolian diaocha zhi jieguo ruhe [(running commentary) What is the result of the League's investigation]. No. 21342.
SP(S). 1932i, September 26. (Shiping) Lun guolian yu Riben [(running commentary) Discussion about the League and Japan]. No. 21363.
SP(S). 1932j, October, 3. (Shiping) Guolian diaochatuan baogaoshu zhi jiazhi (shang) [(running commentary) The value of the report of the League Commission (part 1)]. No. 21370.
SP(S). 1932k, October 4. (Shiping) Guolian diaochatuan baogaoshu zhi jiazhi (xia) [(running commentary) The value of the report of the League Commission (part 2)]. No. 21370.
SP(S). 1932l, December 8. (Shiping) Guolian dahui kaimu yihou [(running commentary) After the opening of the League Assembly]. No. 21435.
SP(S). 1932m, December 17. (Shiping) Guolian kaihui zhi jieguo [(running commentary) The outcome of the League meeting]. No. 21444.
SP(S). 1932n, October 6. (Shiping) Lideng baogaoshu fabiao hou [(running commentary) After the release of the Lytton Report)]. No. 31373.
SP(S). 1932o, November 21. (Benbu News) Zhongguo minyi zhi biaoxian [(local news) Manifestation of China's public opinion]. No. 21418.
SP(S). 1933a, February 3. (Shiping) Zhongguo tuichu guolian shuo [(running commentary) Argument for China's withdrawal from the League]. No. 21483.
SP(S). 1993b, February 26. (Shiping) Sishier dui yi [(running commentary) 42 against 1]. No. 21506.
Suzuki, Takashi. 1988. *Riben Diguozhuyi yu Manzhou* [Japanese imperialism and Manchuria]. (tr. from Japanese by Zhou Qiqian). Taibei: Jinhe Press.
SWT. 1932a, March 12. (Editorial) Guanyu jiedai guolian diaochatuan de yijian [Views on the treatment of the League Commission].
SWT. 1932b, October 4. (Editorial) Zai ping diaochatuan baogaoshu jielve [Memorandum of the revaluation about the investigation report].
SWT. 1932c, December 5. (Editorial) Guolian jiejue Zhong-Ri an de shijian xianzhi [The time constraints on the League's solution to the case of China and Japan].
Teng, Xia. 1931, November 16. Guolian weiquan an zai? [Where is the authority of the League?]. *Kuowen Weekly* (8/45).
TKP. 1931, September 24. Guolian fayan hou zhi Liao Ji bei zhan shijian [The Occupation of Liaoning and Jilin after the Speech at the League of Nations].

TKP(T). 1931a, October 13. (Editorial) Jinri zhi guolian huiyi [Today's meeting of the League].
TKP(T). 1931b, October 17. (Editorial) Guolian shishang you shengse zhiyi mu [An impressive scene in the history of the League].
TKP(T). 1931c, November 19. (Editorial) Zhongguo shi jiangtu, guolian shi cunzai [China loses territory, the League loses its existence].
TKP(T). 1931d, November 23. (Editorial) Riben zai guolian zhi yibian zaibian, [Japan's inconstant attitudes in the League].
TKP(T). 1932a, March 14. (Editorial) Jinggao guolian diaochatuan zhujun, [A warning letter to everyone of the League Commission].
TKP(T). 1932b, March 26. (Editorial) Xiang guolian diaochatuan zhiyi yidian [A greeting toward the League Commission].
TKP(T). 1932c, April 16. (Editorial) Guolian diaochatuan chu guan qianqi [The appointed time of the League Commission entering the Northeast delayed].
TKP(T). 1932d, April 25. (Editorial) Guolian congci jiang chongfen renshi Riben [The League will fully know Japan from now on].
TKP(T). 1932e, October 4. [Editorial] Dong sheng shibian zeren queding zhi hou [After the responsibility for the Northeast Incident has been determined].
TKP(T). 1932f, October 14. (Editorial) Du guolian diaocha baogaoshu quanwen [Reading the complete text of the report of the League Commission].
TKP(T). 1932g, October 5. (Editorial) Shifei mingyi, guomin gengxu nuli [Right and wrong is obvious, our people should work harder].
TKP(T). 1932h, December 4. (Editorial) Xu Jiding guolian bimu hou zhi fangzhen [Principles after the closure of the League should be confirmed immediately].
TKP(T). 1933, February 25. (Editorial) Guolian jinhou zhi zeren [The present and future responsibilities of the League].
Thorne, Christopher. 1972. *The limits of foreign policy: The west, the League and the Far Eastern crisis of 1931–1933.* London: Hamilton.
Walters, Francis P. 1960. *A history of the League of Nations.* Oxford: Oxford University Press.
Willoughby, Westel W. 1935. *The Sino-Japanese controversy and the League of Nations.* New York: Greenwood Press.
Wu, Tingjun. 2002. *Xinji <Ta Kung Pao> shigao*, [Historical manuscripts of Xinji Company *Ta-Kung-Pao*]. Wuhan: Wuhan Press: 9, 144.
Wu, Yin. 1989. Qianxi Guolian diaochatuan paiqian an de chulong [Simple analysis of the formation of the League Commission dispatch scheme]. *Waiguo Wenti Yanjiu.* 4: 27–32.
Yi, Xianshi. ed. 1981. *'Jiuyiba' shibian shi* [History of the 9.18 incident]. Liaoning: Liaoning Renmin Press.

Yokota, Kisaburo. 2016. Kokusai minsyu seikatsu no genri [Principles of international democracy-life]. In *Heiwa kokka no identity* [The identity of a peaceful nation], ed. Tetsuya Sakai, 3–20. Tokyo: Iwanami Press.
Yun, Sheng. 1931, December 14. Guolian yijin zuida nuli [The League has done what it could do]. *Kuowen Weekly* (8/49).
Zhang, Diken. 1932, October 18. Dule Guolian diaochatuan baogaoshu zhi hou [After reading the report of the League Commission]. TKP(T).
Zheng, Dahua, and Yan Liu. 2009. Zhongguo zhishijie dui guolian chuli 'jiuyiba' shibian de butong fanying—yi Hu Shi, Luo Longji he Hu Yuzhi weili de kaocha [The various reactions of China's intellectual circles towards the management of the 9.18 Incident by the League of Nations—focusing on Hu Shi, Luo Longji and Hu Yuzhi]. *Kangri Zhanzheng Yanjiu* 1: 123–134.
ZYRB. 1932a, October 5. (Editorial) Guolian diaochatuan baogaoshu pingyi (xia) [Critique of the report of the League Commission (part 2)].

Sovereignty as 'Organised Hypocrisy': China's Diplomats and the Lytton Commission

Christopher R. Hughes

In the previous two chapters of this section, Haruo Tohmatsu looks at the way in which the League of Nations experimented with various models of international administration to manage the dispute over Manchuria , while Lu Munhai analyses the impact of the crisis on Chinese public opinion. This chapter bridges both perspectives by looking in more detail at how the understanding of sovereignty was articulated by China's diplomats as they were sandwiched between the pressures of international and domestic politics. To understand the significance of their strategies, the concept of sovereignty itself will be deconstructed according to the fourfold classification of its meanings by the International Relations theorist, Stephen Krasner (Krasner 1999: 3–42). After a brief survey of how the concept was shaped by China's domestic politics, it will then be possible to show how its various meanings were deployed by diplomats in the debates on Manchuria that took place in the League Council. The chapter

C. R. Hughes (✉)
Department of International Relations, London School of Economics, London, UK
e-mail: c.r.hughes@lse.ac.uk

C. R. Hughes and H. Shinohara (eds.), *East Asians in the League of Nations*, New Directions in East Asian History,
https://doi.org/10.1007/978-981-19-7067-2_12

will then finish with an analysis of the relevant sections of the Lytton Report to gain insights into how the creativity and compromises of the diplomats provides a snapshot of the meaning of Chinese sovereignty between the wars.

Deconstructing Sovereignty

Krasner called his pathbreaking book on sovereignty 'Organised Hypocrisy' because it argues that the meaning of the concept in any specific situation is ultimately decided according to the interests of the most powerful states. To understand what this means in practice, it is necessary to explain that the word can be used in at least four different ways: international legal, Westphalian, domestic and interdependence, each of which is defined in Table 1.

The significance of these different meanings can be shown by looking at the condition of China under the League system. At the 1919 Paris Peace Conference, it had enjoyed international legal sovereignty because its diplomats represented a state that was recognised by other states. Its domestic sovereignty was severely curtailed, however, as illustrated by the fact that the government was involved in an ill-fated peace conference at Shanghai to try to forge consensus between rival factions on who should govern the country, even as its diplomats sat at the negotiating table in Versailles. The weakness of China's claim to Westphalian sovereignty was made clear by the transfer of Germany's concessions in Shandong to Japan and the perpetuation of the unequal treaties that had been forced on

Table 1 Krasner's four dimensions of sovereignty

International legal	Practices associated with mutual recognition, which is usually between territorial entities that have formal judicial independence
Westphalian	The principle that external actors are excluded from the internal political organisation and structures of authority within the territory of the state, which emerged from the 1649 Settlement of Westphalia
Domestic	The formal organisation of political authority within the state itself, and the ability of its public authorities to exercise effective control with the borders of the polity
Interdependence	The ability of public authorities to regulate the flow of information, ideas, goods, people, pollutants or capital across the borders of the state

the country by the major powers since the Opium Wars. Even after the Guomindang (GMD) Nationalists completed their Northern Expedition in 1927 and established a new government in Nanjing, they still had only limited control over the territories of the former Qing Empire and virtually no presence in Manchuria by the time Japan launched its invasion in 1931. As for interdependence sovereignty, despite achieving international recognition the Nanjing government was unable to control foreign actors in its territory, ranging from Soviet agents supporting the Communist insurrection to the foreign businesses that were expanding their grip on the economy under the protection of extra-territorial jurisdiction. Japan's economic domination of Manchuria was just the most extreme example.

Krasner provides a useful theoretical starting point for analysing how China's diplomats could develop strategies to promote their country's sovereignty in such a context. Drawing on the work of James March and Johan Olsen (March and Olsen 1989; 198), he proposes that two types of logic are available to actors in all political and social environments. One is the 'logics of consequences', which 'see political action and outcomes, including institutions, as the product of rational calculating behavior designed to maximise a given set of unexplained preferences'. The other is the 'logics of appropriateness', which 'understand political action as a product of rules, roles, and identities that stipulate appropriate behaviour in given situations' (Krasner 1999: 11–13). In practice, these two types of logic should be understood as archetypes that are combined when addressing specific problems and audiences. According to Krasner, however, it is logics of consequences that dominate the international system in which the roles and identities of actors are more poorly defined than in domestic politics. This was especially true between the two world wars, which saw a remarkable degree of the deconstruction and reconstruction of national identities and state borders, while international lawyers struggled to uphold norms that impinged on the interests of the most powerful states.

Because Krasner is mainly concerned with understanding the ways in which the most powerful states determine sovereignty, however, he pays little attention to how actors in weak states can develop effective diplomatic strategies. The case of China at the time of the Manchurian Crisis shows that this is a significant oversight, given that it had avoided colonisation since the decline of the Qing Dynasty in the mid-nineteenth century. The International Relations theorist, Robert H. Jackson, has coined the term 'quasi-state' (Jackson 1993) for entities that are recognised as states for considerable periods of time, despite having little control over the territories they lay claim to and argues that they endure because the international system abhors a vacuum. This is certainly true of the attitude of the imperial powers towards China, which preferred to recognise the Qing Dynasty than to fight each other over partitioning the country, a view that was formalised when the USA persuaded the European states to renounce spheres of influence by signing up to the Open Door Policy at the turn of the century.

If China's endurance as a quasi-state was a product of great power competition, however, by the time Japan invaded Manchuria sufficient time had passed for a cohort of Chinese diplomats to come to maturity and hone their skills for using the League as a platform on which to consolidate the international dimensions of their country's sovereignty. While Japan tried to legitimise its actions by stressing the weakness of China's domestic and interdependence sovereignty, these diplomats saw the League as an arena to promote its international legal and Westphalian sovereignty by deploying logics of appropriateness and consequences.

China's Diplomats as Performers

China's diplomats were well-equipped to face this challenge. Born in the last quarter of the nineteenth century, they had first-hand experience of the intellectual rupture that was involved in the transition from the universalist Qing Empire to the modern state of the Republic of China through the 1911 revolution and the civil wars that followed. Yet they also viewed this process from a vantage point that was very different from that of the political leaders who had emerged in the domestic sphere. This is because they had been singled out in the last decade of the Qing to be sent to the USA to learn about modernity as part of the ill-fated attempt to reform the tottering imperial system. After that they had posted years of service in Western capitals as diplomats for the string of short-lived governments that followed the revolution.

Most celebrated is the figure of Wellington Koo, who was born in Shanghai in 1888 and graduated with a PhD in international law from Columbia University in 1912. His thesis was the first academic attempt to clarify the origin and extent of the system of extra-territorial jurisdiction that the imperial powers were using to exempt their subjects from Chinese law. This can be seen as a good example of the attempt to use law to untangle the problems that arise when domestic and international notions of sovereignty clash. He was thus well-prepared to take on the task of representing China at Versailles and later as a member of the Lytton Commission.1[1]

Other leading Chinese diplomats at the League during the Manchurian crisis included W.W. Yen (1877–1950), a graduate in political science from Virginia University, and Alfred Sze (1877–1958), who became the first Chinese student to be awarded a master's degree by Cornell after graduating in literature in 1901. Much can be learned about their attitudes from Sze's autobiography (Sze 1962). This narrates how he returned from the USA to China in 1902 to work for the reformist governor of Hubei province, then departed in 1905 as a chaperone for the famous mission of the five ministers sent by the Qing court to Europe and Japan to learn about constitutional government. Returning to China in 1906, he took on posts in railway management and customs supervision, before joining the ministry of foreign affairs in 1910.

The first-hand experience that Sze gained in these formative years included dealing with the complex political and legal issues surrounding railway ownership, the racist treatment of Chinese officials by the British, and knowledge of conditions in Manchuria as the customs superintendent of the city of Harbin. A particularly interesting insight into the role of functional co-operation in the development of the League is that he organised the international medical conference on tackling the plague that swept through Manchuria in 1910. This was significant for the development of the network of individuals who would later become key actors in building the League Health Organisation, which is covered in Takuma's chapter. Sze also saw it as important for forestalling the diplomatic consequences and political pressure that would be applied by Russia and Japan if the Chinese failed to control the disease.[2] Sze was also exposed early on to the embryonic power of nationalism in Eastern Asia when he was tasked with managing the international press coverage of the assassination of the former Japanese prime minister, Itō Hirobumi by the Korean independence activist, An Jung-geun, when he arrived by train for a tour of Manchuria.

The Chinese diplomats were also familiar enough with the policies of the imperial powers to take a sceptical view of the League's idealistic ambitions and they had been sufficiently bruised by political life in China to be adept at managing the relationship between the clashing discourses of sovereignty at the international and domestic levels. This can be seen in the way in which Wellington Koo pursued a logic of consequences during World War I, urging his government to join the Allied powers not out of a commitment to any moral cause but to gain American support for the return of the German concession of Shandong, which had been occupied by Japan. Koo could also use a logic of appropriateness, though. A good example is his appeal to the idealism of President Wilson's Fourteen Points to counter the wishes of his Secretary of State, Robert Lansing, who wanted to recognise Japan's claim to have 'special interests' in Manchuria.

Koo's sophisticated understanding of the multi-faceted nature of sovereignty is revealed, above all, by the speech he delivered to the Council of Ten at Versailles, on 28 January 1919. This appealed to his domestic audience by invoking the politics of national identity, describing Shandong as 'the cradle of Chinese civilization, the birthplace of Confucius and Mencius, and a Holy Land for the Chinese', which drew widespread praise at home. At the same time, Koo appealed to his international audience's post-war faith in the power of international law by proclaiming that the world was entering a 'newly enlightened age' in which there should be respect for the 'fundamental and transcendent rights of China, the rights of political sovereignty and territorial integrity as well as her earnest desire to serve the cause of universal peace' (Craft 2004: 51–52).

Although China failed to secure the return of Shandong at Versailles, the enthusiastic reception of Koo's performance in China showed how public diplomacy in a world of fast, mass communication was making public opinion a significant factor in both foreign policy and the careers of political actors. This was dramatically displayed when the eruption of student-led demonstrations on 4 May 1919 brought down the government for losing Shandong. In the shadow of what was to become the iconic 'May 4 Movement', delegates at the on-going peace conference between the northern and southern governments at Shanghai had felt the need to cable Paris and warn that 'the four hundred million people of China, in the name of justice and righteousness', would never agree to the transfer of territory to Japan. China's diplomats at Versailles deftly dodged the bullet by issuing a press release to explain that they could not sign the Peace Treaty without sacrificing their 'sense of right, justice and patriotic duty', and that they preferred to 'submit their case to the impartial judgement of the world' (King 1965:30; Chu 1981: 29).

Despite having to work for the feeble and ever-changing but internationally recognised government in Beijing, the diplomats scored some important achievements in the years immediately after Versailles, but mainly working outside the League. Most notable was the reining in of the Japanese presence in China at the 1921–1922 Washington Conference, resulting in the inclusion in the Nine-Power Treaty of a commitment to respect the territorial and administrative integrity of China. Japan also renounced the most contentious of the notorious and widely resented Twenty-One Demands that it had imposed in 1915 and promised to withdraw its forces from China and Siberia, surrender the rights it had inherited from Germany in Shandong, and give up certain preferential rights in Manchuria. It remained unclear, however, what such developments might imply for understanding the nature and extent of Chinese sovereignty. The commitment to 'respect the territorial integrity of China', for example, was sufficiently ambiguous for Japan to interpret it as not ruling out the possibility of persuading other states to accept its claim to have 'special interests' in Manchuria. The possibility of success for Japan was indicated by the attitude of the US Secretary of State, Robert Lansing, who believed that the formula had the advantage of making it 'look as if the Conference had accomplished something' (Asada 2007: 101).

The League in Domestic Politics

Koo's performance at Washington was good enough for him to be promoted to Foreign Minister in 1922. Working through the League was more difficult, however. This was not only due to the structural limitations of the organisation, but also because the domestic standing of China's diplomats was diminished by having to work for a string of short-lived, unpopular governments in Beijing. Moreover, the newly emerging forces of the Nationalists and the Communists were highly sceptical towards the League. This went back to World War I for the Nationalists, when their founder and leader, Sun Yat-sen, had insisted that it was foolhardy to trust the western powers and argued that China's interests would be better served by working with Japan as a partner in the world struggle against the white race. Sun's scepticism was equally rooted in domestic politics, as he decried the decision to align with the Allies as no more than a cynical ploy to gain international political and material support for the government of the ruling military clique of General Duan

Qirui (Sun 1928).[3] Sun thus took aim at the diplomats when he dismissed their idea of balancing Japanese power by aligning with the Allies as the mistaken thinking of 'some among the old bureaucrats' who had long harboured a preference for closer ties with the USA. This, for Sun, was symptomatic of a way of thinking going back to the strategies of the Qing Dynasty statesmen, who had been discredited for having conceded territories that would become symbols of China's humiliation, such as the loss of Taiwan after the defeat by Japan in 1895 (Sun 1928).

The scepticism of the Communists also arose from a linkage of support for the League with the politics of domestic legitimacy. On the eve of discovering Marxism-Leninism, the young Mao Zedong had ridiculed Versailles for being dominated by the political magnates and financial tycoons of France, Britain and the USA, and observed how President Wilson was outmanoeuvred by 'thieves' who were only interested in receiving territory and reparations (Mao 1919a: 318; 1919b 321; 1919c 338). In his view, China should not have looked to the League as a source of power but to the new mass movements that were emerging in the wake of the signing of the Peace Treaty in places such as Germany, with their patriotic demonstrations, marches and strikes, and the singing of martial songs and national anthems. Impressed by the Russian revolution, he predicted that future wars would be between classes and that internationalism would not be shaped not by the League but by an alignment of communist states against England and France (Mao 1919d). Believing that the suffering of the vanquished was sowing the seeds of the next war, he predicted with a remarkable degree of prescience that 'in ten or twenty years, you Frenchmen will yet again have a splitting headache' (Mao 1919e: 367).

When Mao produced his seminal analysis of the classes in Chinese society in 1925, he thus called for oppressed nations and classes to rally around the red banner of the Third International and struggle against 'the white banner of counterrevolution, held aloft by the League of Nations' (Mao 1925a: 253). Moreover, because the Communists had been allowed to join forces with the GMD in southern China under the first United Front, he had produced this document in his role as head of the GMD's Nationalist's Propaganda Department. At that time, both parties looked to the Soviet Union for support, having been swayed in 1919 by Moscow's promises to unilaterally renounce the unequal treaties signed by the Czarist regime.[4]

This alignment with the Soviet Union put China's Nationalist and Communist revolutionaries at loggerheads with the diplomats who were serving the internationally recognised governments that came and went in Peiping [Beijing], dominated as they were by the various military leaders who managed to seize sufficient state power. Having emerged from the most modernised sections of the army in north China, Russian expansionism was their primary concern. For Mao, therefore, Koo was nothing more than the head of 'a traitorous group of brokers between the Zhili clique and the British and American imperialists' (Mao 1925b: 242). When the Nationalists marched north, in 1926, they also regarded him as a flunky of the warlord government and he had to seek refuge in the British concession of Weihaiwei.

Koo's return to diplomacy only became possible because the northern military leader, Zhang Zuolin, was allowed to retain control of Manchuria. After Zhang was assassinated in 1928, his son, Zhang Xueliang, employed Koo to develop a strategy to balance Japan's growing presence in Manchuria. This left Koo on the horns of a dilemma as he tried to satisfy Zhang while not antagonising the Nationalist leader, Chiang Kai-shek, who was wary about giving Tokyo any excuse for retaliatory action while he focused on suppressing the Communists. It is in this difficult context that Koo persuaded Chiang to use the League to gain international support and have himself appointed as Foreign Minister in 1930.

Articulating Sovereignty at the League

The linkage between domestic politics and foreign policy was thus already well established when the Chinese government responded to the Mukden Incident by invoking Article 11 in the League Council on 19 September 1931. As the meetings that followed were held in public and widely reported on, the various representatives had to perform in front of multiple audiences. There is no better illustration of the predicament of China's diplomats than the outbreak of student riots after Chiang announced that the question of Manchuria would have to be settled by the League, Koo which drove Koo once again into hiding, this time in the Generalissimo's house.

This was also true for the Japanese delegation as its members insisted that their country was merely taking defensive measures. Japanese commentators had been claiming for several years that no cabinet would be able to withstand public pressure for action when their country's vital interests in Manchuria were threatened (Kawakami 1928: 381). The diplomats thus deployed arguments from their own domestic politics when they claimed to be working in accord with a 'positive policy' framework that had been developed partly in response to public anger at home and opposition criticism of the government for being weak. They attributed such views to the concessions that had been granted to China in the Nine-Power Treaty and attacks on the Japanese consulate and against residents in China during the Northern Expedition.

The 'positive policy' they were referring to was an attempt to clarify Japan's strategy that had been made by the cabinet of the Russophobe general, Tanaka Giichi in 1927. After a meeting with Japan's consuls in China, the decision had been made to present Japan as working with other powers to 'rehabilitate' China, so long as it could establish a strong central government that was formed from moderate factions and would control 'agitators and unruly elements'. Japan would maintain responsibility for peace and order in Manchuria and Mongolia, however, because these territories were deemed to 'have a vital bearing upon Japan's national existence and national defense'. This would be 'not only in view of Japan's position there, but also in the interest of China herself' (Kawakami 1928: 382).

Working within this policy framework, the Japanese delegation had to convince the international audience of the legitimacy of the principle of 'special interests' that they had secured with only partial success at the Washington Conference. At the next meeting of the Council, their representative attempted to do so by explaining how difficult it was for Europeans to appreciate the nature of the relationship between the inhabitants of Manchuria and the large number of Japanese businesses and citizens who had moved there. When the discussion continued the following February, Japan kept the focus on the principle of effective control by claiming that order in Manchuria had broken down to such an extent that it had to take responsibility for protecting Japanese citizens and the large numbers of Korean farmers who had moved to Manchuria from brigands and the large-scale abduction of women.

In the sessions that followed, Naotake Satō continued to develop this line of argument for Japan by placing responsibility for the crisis on China.[5] One element of their case was to insist that the local government of Zhang Xueliang and the central government in Nanjing were organising popular violence and propaganda against Japanese people and property. Only this could explain why the 'fugitive soldiers and bandits' who were attacking the Japanese railway zone were well armed, fed and organised, while irregular forces with names such as the Anti-Japanese Patriotic Legion and Anti-Japanese Blood and Iron Group were often led by army officers (OJ 1932a: 331–332).

The Japanese delegation also began to broaden their appeal to the international audience by shifting attention to the tension that was developing between the Chinese and Japanese residents of Shanghai, where the major powers all had significant interests. Insisting that 'the anti-Japanese organizations imposed their will on Chinese citizens under threat of barbarous punishments which recall the Middle Ages', they warned that the 'anti-foreign' agitation and education would soon be directed at the other powers. Japan was thus not alone as a victim of the 'systematic incitement of the masses' used by the Chinese government to serve its domestic policy, which, 'In its international aspect must be regarded as absolutely contrary to the sprit which governs the relations of modern nations' (OJ 1932a: 331–332).

Alfred Sze responded to this legal challenge by deploying the Westphalian meaning of sovereignty, winning support from the representative, Viscount Robert Cecil, by pointing out that the principle of defensive measures had been rejected by the Council in the case of a claim made by Greece against a police action by Bulgaria in 1925.[6] W.W. Yen then began to push back against the allegations concerning China's domestic politics, rather ingeniously turning Japan's own argument against it by proposing that his country had chosen to bring the issue to the League because, unlike Japan, it was not a 'military nation' (OJ 1932a: 327). He rejected Japan's demand for the Chinese authorities to suppress the 'dangerous thought' of nationalistic feelings by insisting that it was merely a reaction to Japanese aggression. Finally, he appealed to the idealism on which the League was founded by emphasising that the crisis 'puts in gravest jeopardy the entire conception of the settlement of international disputes by pacific means' (OJ 1932a: 328).

This line of reasoning was later reinforced when Yen referred to an opinion that had been voiced by Peru's M. Gonzalez-Prada at meeting of the Council held at Paris on 10 December, that the right of a state to protect the lives and property of its own nationals had to be limited by respect for the sovereignty of the other state. Moreover, providing protection did not authorise the use of military forces to penetrate the territory of another state to carry out police operations. Yen also pointed out that the Nine-Power Treaty guaranteed not only China's territorial integrity, but also its administrative integrity (OJ 1932a: 333). Perhaps Yen's most ingenious strategy, though, was to reinforce his appeal to the powers by appropriating their own colonial logic, which involved a heavy dose of irony. Seizing on a denial made by Satō that Japan had occupied Chinese territory, he quipped that, 'In twenty years Japan has settled only 200,000 of her citizens in Manchuria, while we have settled over 20 millions of our people in Manchuria, proving that our Japanese friends are not very good at colonizing' (OJ 1932a: 333).

The Attack on Shanghai

At the start of 1932, the context of the debate was changed radically when Japan launched an attack on Shanghai. This gave the Chinese some additional leverage for appealing to a logic of consequences rather than the lofty ideals of the League because, unlike in Manchuria, the European powers had to protect their own substantial interests in the city. An indication of how this galvanised the organisation into action is that it is only at this point that the Secretary General urged members to call on their representatives in situ to supply information. China could use this momentum, however, to push for League arbitration, citing the provision in Article 10 of the Covenant that its members 'undertake to respect and preserve as against external aggression the territorial integrity and existing political independence of all Members…'. Moreover, by claiming that the state of hostilities in Shanghai amounted to a 'rupture' in relations with Japan, China invoked Article 15 to call on the Council to investigate and consider the crisis in Manchuria. Aware of the irony of China appealing to the selfish motivations of the powers in China, Satō then attempted to turn Yen's strategy on its head by pointing out that Japan was merely following the precedent of Britain and America, who had bombarded Nanjing in 1927 to protect their interests from Chinese attacks in the city (OJ 1932a: 339–342).

When a committee of international personnel in Shanghai presented a report on the situation in the city, moreover, it provided some ammunition for the Japanese delegates in the Council. It described how a spirit of bitter hostility had been stirred up by the Chinese boycott imposed since the occupation of Manchuria, with students demanding a declaration of war (OJ 1932b). It also noted that the Japanese residents were calling on their government to end their 'intolerable position' through direct action after being the victims of frequent violent incidents and infuriated by derogatory references to their emperor. It added that it was only after the Japanese had sent naval reinforcements that the mayor of Shanghai had begun to meet the demands of the Japanese Consul to control the anti-Japanese movement and to dissolve the anti-Japanese organisations. In response, the British representative, J.H. Thomas, informed the Council that the UK and the USA were dispatching a warship from Hong Kong to Shanghai with a battalion of reinforcements. France, Italy and Germany added that they were also taking necessary steps (OJ 1932a: 352).

This military deployment was welcomed by Satō, who reported that the Japanese consul general had joined with nationals of third-party powers on Shanghai's municipal council to unanimously decide to order the closure of the Chinese Nationalist Party (GMD)newspaper and the headquarters of the Anti-Japanese Association in the city. Claiming that Chiang kai-shek was bringing his army to the neighbourhood, he reported that his foreign minister had requested the governments of the powers to instruct their representatives in Shanghai to induce the Chinese to cease hostilities and withdraw their troops. Satō continued to make these appeals as the fighting escalated, pointing out in a Council meeting on 9 February that boycotts had long been used by China against other nations. This, he proposed, was actively encouraged by the GMD and the Chinese government, as evidenced by 'really extraordinary passages in the school books for young children, which arouse in the pupils strong anti-foreign and anti-Japanese feeling' that could be traced back to before the Manchurian crisis (OJ 1932a: 359). Referring again to the earlier British and American intervention at Nanjing, he pointed out that Japan had also suffered greatly at that time due to 'enormous difficulties with the Chinese government'. There was thus a legitimate obligation for all to ensure the safety of Japanese nationals in the current situation.

Satō's strategy was only partly effective, however. When the Shanghai committee submitted a second report, on 12 February, it concluded that 'a state of open war exists' (OJ 1932c: 379). This led the President of the Council to take the unusual step of appealing to its members, other than China and Japan, to express regret that Japan had not made fit use of the methods of peaceful settlement provided in the Covenant. He specifically invoked the commitment to respect and preserve the territorial integrity and political independence of states in Article 10 and the commitment that Japan had made to respect the territorial and administrative integrity of China under the Nine-Power Treaty. He also reminded Japan of its 'incalculable responsibility before the public opinion of the world to be just and restrained in her relations with China' and its 'high sense of honor to recognize the obligations of her special position and of the confidence which the nations have placed in her as a partner in the organization and maintenance of peace' (OJ 1932d: 383–384).

This appeal to a logic of appropriateness fell on deaf ears as Japan proceeded to impose an ultimatum for China to withdraw its forces on 19 February and announced the independence of Manchukuo. To defend the legality of these actions Satō argued that the preamble of the Covenant stated that its principles only applied to organised peoples. China may have been recognised as such when admitted to the League, he maintained, but it had since descended into 'a state of complete anarchy' due to the wars between its generals. Given that this left the rights and interests of foreigners unprotected by the various treaties and conventions, Japan was merely acting in the interests of all the powers when it infringed on Chinese sovereignty. Claiming the right to 'a method of legitimate defence, or protection', he proposed, was admitted, and recognised as permissible by 'certain other Powers having interests in China'. If the situation in China had been 'normal', he went on, the powers would have appealed to the Council to settle their dispute by pacific and regular methods (OJ 1932a: 363–364).

By portraying Japan as the victim, Satō could present this argument as part of a more general plea that his country had been treated unfairly. Recalling how its appeal for racial equality had been turned down by the League, he complained of being 'subjected to treatment that is derogatory to our dignity and against which we constantly protest'. This included the closure of most countries to Japanese immigration and the expulsion of its traders had been driven from central and southern China. Insisting that Japan had no territorial ambitions in Manchuria, he professed that it was only reasonable 'to preserve in Manchuria a field of action for the Japanese'. He could also cite the precedent of the League's failure to protest the disappearance of Outer Mongolia from the map of China when it had been annexed by the 'Soviet group of countries' (OJ 1932a: 365).

Yen responded to these accusations by complaining that it was not reasonable to expect 'perfect peace and order' in a country with a population the size of Europe's and transitioning from an absolute monarchy to a republic. More ingenious is that he then turned the focus on to Japan's domestic politics by ask whether the government's lack of control over its armed forces and its frequent violation of the promises made by its diplomats meant that it was not an 'organized State' itself. He also pointed out that many Chinese had been massacred in Korea and during the 1923 Great Kantō earthquake in Japan. Moreover, he maintained that it was quite inconsistent for Japan to insist on negotiations with a China that it believed was not 'well-organized'. If there was instability, argued Yen, it was due to Japanese interference. It alone among the powers was striving to keep China weak and divided by supporting one side against another.

Finally, Yen deployed a logic of appropriateness by complaining how Japan's behaviour was in contradiction to the virtue of 'benevolence' that members of the League had displayed when by extending sympathy and aid to forty million people who had been left starving and destitute by floods in central China. This he contrasted with the shame that should be felt by Japanese for going to war and failing to shoulder its responsibilities, which was a betrayal of the chivalry, bravery and courage that it had been known for. He also rejected any equivalence between Outer Mongolia and Manchuria on the grounds that the Manchus were scattered all over China, and that the region had become 'politically, historically and ethnically Chinese' and because Mongolia had separated from China in 'a non-juridical way before the League was founded' (OJ 1932a: 367).

This strategy was reinforced by the mobilisation of various organisations behind a public relations campaign to shame Japan by emphasising the contrast between its aggression and the efforts being taken by other nations to assist the victims of the flooding in central China. Most powerful was a joint telegram submitted by the President of the Chinese Flood Relief Society and the President of the Federation of Universities and Colleges, which recalls:

> Clear and categorical international agreements were entered, first in the Covenant of the League of Nations; secondly in the Nine-Power Treaty; thirdly, in the Locarno Pact of 1925, and, fourthly, but recently, in the Briand-Kellogg Pact, that international aggression shall be deemed a criminal act and that united action shall be taken to preserve as against external aggression the territorial and existing political independence of one another... (OJ 1932e: 405-406).

The telegram then goes on to complain how, despite the bravery of China's patriotic soldiers, the country was militarily too weak to resist whatever Japan demanded and too disabled to champion alone the cause of world peace that Japan threatened to destroy. If the strong in arms were allowed to master the weak, regardless of what was right, there would be consequences for all nations—particularly those with interests in the Far East. Concluding with a list of Japanese atrocities, the authors finish by making the plea:

> Facing the terrible menace of floods, famines, conflagration, untold miseries, inhuman attacks and continual bombardments, and yet with goodwill towards all speaking in the name of justice and humanity, may we not solicit the most serious consideration upon this world question of the Japanese invasions?

It is hard to assess how much such appeals contributed to the decision of the twelve members of the Council (hereafter the Council of Twelve) to demand that Japan should rescind the ultimatum it had laid down for the withdrawal of Chinese troops from Shanghai because their own interests were also directly threatened by the prospect of war. It is clear, though, that the crisis had enhanced the potential for China's representatives to use the League as a forum to influence international opinion. This is shown by the Council President's expression of embarrassment at its apparent powerlessness, which he rather lamely attributed to the seriousness and conscientiousness with which it approached its task and the difficulty of negotiations that 'were not taking place in an exclusively pacific atmosphere...' (OJ 1932a: 368). Moreover, Yen's strategy of shaming Japan was reflected when the President appealed to it to maintain the status as a power that had achieved greatness not only by military and naval strength but also because it had shown 'so great an example of development and progress and as a permanent Member of the Council'. This message was reinforced by the Marquess of Londonderry, who stressed that the appeal from the Council of Twelve '...contained no indictment; it embodied no judgement; it was an appeal to the strength and honour of japan' (OJ 1932a: 369).

That this had some impact can be seen from the response from the Japanese government, which was delivered on 23 February in the form of a statement from Kenkichi Yoshizawa, then foreign minister (OJ 1932f). This portrayed China as the aggressive party, while Japan had tried to use the League's methods of pacific settlement. Insisting again that Japan's actions were defensive and devoid of territorial ambition, he maintained that they were permissible under Article 10. To support this position, he cited the example of the dispatch of reinforcements by the other powers to defend Shanghai five years previously, and the bombardment of Nanjing by American and British forces. The Covenant, he complained, did not '...make China a "chartered libertine", free to attack other countries without their having the right to repel attack'. Even if the Chinese had been considered an 'organized people' in the past, he complained, the fiction could not last forever, and could not be tolerated when the country had become a grave source of real danger. He regretted that the desire to see China happy, prosperous and united had led the world to treat her as united when its authorities had only exercised control within limited areas in reality and its society was divided into various rudimentary nuclei or organisations instead of a single organised people. To defend his country against accusations of militarism, Yoshizawa concluded:

> Japan altogether repudiated the stigma, which is attempted in some quarters to be attached to her, of favoring and desiring war. Her people yield to none in their detestation of war and its inevitable horrors. If the efforts of the Twelve Powers should succeed in bringing about a pacific attitude on the part of China, nowhere will more sincere delight be felt than in Japan.

Sovereignty in the Lytton Report

The early debates in the Council thus set the context in which agreement was reached to try to resolve the dispute over Manchuria by dispatching the Lytton Commission. The details of that project and its recommendations are covered in some detail by Tohmatsu and Mu in this volume (Lytton 1932). Of more concern here is what the Commission's report reveals about the success or failure of the strategies of China's diplomats. Even if their country's political elite did not believe that the League could impose a solution on Japan, the fact that Wellington Koo persuaded Chiang Kai-shek to support the investigation on the grounds that the League could be a useful forum for arbitration—and to have himself appointed as a member of the Commission—indicates that they did at least see an opportunity to use the organisation as a platform for political performance. From this perspective, it was a significant achievement that the report held back from recommending the recognition of Manchuria as the independent state of Manchukuo. More of a setback was the acknowledgement of the validity of Japan's argument that China's fragile domestic order, its claim to 'special interests' and the wishes of the local population were reasons to impose an international administration. A detailed analysis of the document, however, shows that even this conclusion contained elements that reflected China's criticisms of Japan.

If the complexity of the report is symptomatic of the Commission's attempt to meet the demands of both sides of the dispute, it is also a product of the pursuit of the self-interests of the powers. This can be seen when the term 'sovereignty' is first used in the report, in a paragraph in Chapter IX that discusses the importance of 'international interests' as follows:

> It is quite as much in the interests of the Powers now as it was in 1922 [the Washington Conference] to assist the reconstruction of China and to maintain her sovereignty and her territorial and administrative integrity as indispensable to the maintenance of peace. Any disintegration of China might lead, perhaps rapidly, to serious international rivalries, which would become all the more bitter if they should happen to coincide with rivalries between divergent social systems. Finally, the interests of peace are the same the world over. Any loss of confidence in the application of the principles of the Covenant and of the Pact of Paris in any part of the world diminishes the value and efficacy of those principles everywhere.

While this commitment to apply the principles of the Covenant was good for China's case, the intention to assist its construction opened the way for a considerable curtailment of its Westphalian sovereignty by opening the way to intervention in its internal affairs. This was further strengthened by framing the argument with a summary of the empirical findings of the Commission which stresses that the three Manchurian provinces have 'more than once been declared by their rulers to be independent of the Central Government of China, yet no wish to be separated from the rest of China has ever been expressed by their population, which is overwhelmingly Chinese'. Introducing this note of ambiguity makes it reasonable to propose that the government of the region should be modified in such a way as to 'secure, consistently with the sovereignty and administrative integrity of China, a large measure of autonomy designed to meet the local conditions and special characteristics of the Three Provinces'. The addition of the qualification that 'the new civil regime must be so constituted and conducted as to satisfy the essential requirements of good government' makes it clear that China would not be alone in deciding the new political dispensation.

By linking the condition of China's internal governance with international order, this line of reasoning presents a good example of giving priority to a logic of consequences over maintaining the principles of non-intervention and territorial integrity. This is further reinforced by emphasising that the dispute over Manchuria is 'exceedingly complicated' and 'requires an intimate knowledge of all the facts, as well as of their historical background'. In other words, because the crisis is *sui generis*, it can be presented as a case in which only some of the rights and interests claimed by the League's members can be clearly defined by international law. As the report explains:

> This is not a case in which one country has declared war on another country without previously exhausting the opportunities for conciliation provided in the Covenant of the League of Nations. Neither is it a simple case of the violation of the frontier of one country by the armed forces of a neighbouring country, because in Manchuria there are many features without an exact parallel in other parts of the world.

This pursuit of a logic of consequences can certainly be seen as supporting Krasner's view that the meaning of sovereignty is ultimately decided by the most powerful states. This is even more so when the report appears to compromise the legal international meaning of China's sovereignty by observing that although Manchuria is legally an integral part of China, it has 'a sufficiently autonomous character to carry on direct negotiations with Japan on the matters which lay at the root of this conflict'.

Such a conclusion needs to be qualified, however, because China gained some traction for its case by linking these pragmatic arguments to the service of a logic of appropriateness. The rejection of recognition for Manchukuo, for example, is based not only on the pragmatic argument that it would be a threat to 'the good understanding between the two countries upon which peace in the Far East depends' but also because it is incompatible with the fundamental principle of existing international obligations. In this context, moreover, the principle of national self-determination is deployed to strengthen rather than obfuscate Manchuria's relationship with China by observing that the settlement of millions of Chinese farmers had made Manchuria 'in many respects a simple extension of China south of the Wall'.

The combination of the two types of logic can again be seen in the criticism of Japan's claim to have the right to protect its 'special interests' by recognising Manchukuo. This is partly based on the pragmatic argument that recognition would have a negative impact on Japan's interests because it would just perpetuate China's hostility and boycott. However, Japan's argument that the installation of a stable government would serve Manchuria's economic development is also qualified by the more normative comment that such a system would only serve Japan's strategic interests if it was 'in conformity with the wishes of the population and which takes full account of their feelings and aspirations'. This challenge to the more overt colonial elements of Japan's proposals can be considered something of a success for China, even though it is accompanied by a call for the Chinese government to facilitate rapprochement by restraining 'the more intolerant tendencies of her nationalism' and preventing the practice of organised boycotts.

This shift of focus on to the normative character of domestic politics is further developed in China's favour when the report criticises the argument that the invasion of Manchuria was needed to ease domestic political pressures on the Japanese government. Mirroring the position of the Chinese diplomats in the Council, it warns Japan's 'statesmen and military authorities' who spoke of Manchuria as their nation's 'lifeline' that occupation would not only impose a heavy financial burden on their country but also expose their troops to serious embarrassment 'if they were surrounded by a restive or rebellious population backed by a hostile China'. If China was called on to ease rapprochement by reining in its hotheads, therefore, it was equally important to persuade 'young Japan' not to follow the advocates of the 'positive' policy of strong measures. Much better would be to join the process of building the gendarmerie in Manchuria, as described in Tohmatsu's chapter, which would both ameliorate Japan's 'newly awakened nationalism' and sooth China's restive politics by delivering Sun Yat-sen's plan to create a strong central government through the process of internal reconstruction.

The complex implications of such arguments for the meaning of Chinese sovereignty become clearer in the Commission's recommendations to the Council, which are presented in Chapter X of the report. Central to these is the proposal to invite China and Japan to take part in an advisory conference that will enable 'effective and practical measures to be taken to meet the situation in Manchuria as it exists to-day and, at the same time, allow for such modifications hereafter as the changes in the internal situation in China may warrant'. This process, insists the report, will be 'consistent with the sovereignty of China', even though the conference was to be composed of representatives of the two governments. Moreover, two delegations would also represent the local population—one selected in a manner prescribed by China and one in a manner prescribed by Japan. Neutral observers would also be present if the parties agreed, and any deadlocks would be referred to the Council for arbitration.

If the acknowledgement that this process should be 'consistent with the sovereignty of China' can be seen as a nod of approval to the principled arguments of China's diplomats, therefore, it was only a partial victory. The curtailment of domestic and interdependence sovereignty is again made clear when the report goes on to stipulate that foreign advisors would be selected to supervise the constabulary and fiscal administration and to act as a general advisor to the central bank. To allay protests, the report stresses that such measures were in conformity with the policy of the GMD and the national government of China and that 'Chinese opinion' should be able to understand that the exercise of such 'exceptionally wide powers' by foreigners 'merely represents a form of international co-operation'. It even goes so far as to point out that enlisting foreign expertise was not only a long-established practice in China but had also contributed to Japan's successful development. Somewhat ironically, this makes it reasonable to suggest that Japanese advisers could train the civil service, albeit one that would eventually be staffed by Chinese personnel.

The interplay between the various meanings of sovereignty that runs through these recommendations is illustrated above all by the plan for the advisory conference and the Council to be tasked with considering the broad outlines of the form of administration to be agreed between China and Japan. While this stipulates that the maintenance of territorial and administrative integrity should be included in the discussion, it also expects China to grant a large degree of autonomy to Manchuria and allow the creation of the special gendarmerie. Moreover, Manchuria's autonomy would be guaranteed by a binding declaration to limit the central government's role to the control of general treaty and foreign relations, the customs, the post office, the salt gabelle and possibly stamp duty and tobacco and wine taxes. Even the division of income between the central and local governments and the power to appoint the chief executive of Manchuria would be decided by the advisory conference. Most intriguing is that the report floats the possibility of allowing the expression of public opinion through functional bodies such as the chambers of commerce, guilds and other civil society organisations (which sets an interesting precedent for the political system that would be introduced for Hong Kong under British rule after World War Two and consolidated under the 'one country, two systems' formula since the transition of the colony to China in 1997).

China's interdependence sovereignty would also be significantly curtailed by the signing of a bilateral treaty for the management of Japan's interests. These were principally the granting of certain economic rights to Japanese nationals and questions of railway ownership and control. China was supposed to be reassured by the recommendation that such a guarantee for Japan's free participation in the economic development of Manchuria would 'not carry with it a right to control the country either economically or politically'. What this would have meant in practice is left less than clear from the further stipulation that the right to settle and lease land, coupled with some modification of the principle of extra-territoriality, would be granted to Japanese citizens. The Commission believed that such a proposal was viable because China had already granted the right to settle in some parts of Manchuria. It should be willing to extend the policy, therefore, so long as the extra-territorial status it conferred did not create a Japanese state in the heart of Chinese territory. Yet it also acknowledged that the Japanese would not consent to abandon their extra-territorial status until the administration of justice and finance had reached a very much higher standard than had hitherto prevailed in Manchuria.

In other words, the most satisfactory solution to the problem of extra-territoriality was to make the administration of the contested provinces so efficient that it would no longer be needed. To allay any doubts on the part of Japan, at least two foreign advisers would be appointed to the supreme court, one of whom would be of Japanese nationality. Perhaps there is no clearer indication of sovereignty as 'organised hypocrisy' than the addition of the condition that any extension of the rights of settlement for the Japanese would also apply to nationals of all other powers that enjoyed the benefits of most-favoured-nation status.

Overall, then, the Lytton Commission managed to claim that it was respecting Chinese sovereignty while stretching its Westphalian, domestic and interdependence meanings in ways that allowed a considerable degree of foreign intervention. The extent of this is especially stark in the proposal that the League should oversee the negotiation of a bilateral treaty that would establish a board of conciliation that would ensure any threats to Japan's interests would be resolved through arbitration, non-aggression and mutual assistance. Moreover, any disputes between the two governments over the interpretation of the new treaty would be overseen by a tribunal composed of persons with judicial experience and the necessary knowledge of the 'Far East'. The two sides would also agree to turn Manchuria into a demilitarised area and entitle any aggrieved party (or parties in the case of a third-party attack) to take any defensive measures deemed to be advisable against an act of aggression.

To gain the support of the League against Japan's invasion of Manchuria and recognition of Manchukuo, China was thus expected to sign treaties that would allow considerable foreign control of all dimensions of its sovereignty, including a trade agreement in which it promised to take all measures within its power to forbid and repress boycotts of Japanese trade. That the government in Nanjing would still be recognised as the legal body representing China did, however, at least maintain a sufficient degree of international legal sovereignty to maintain its role as something approaching a quasi-state in Manchuria.

The Diplomatic Power of a Quasi-State

The decline of the Sino-Japanese relationship to the point of all-out war in 1937 leaves no doubt that the Lytton Commission failed to achieve the League's primary goal of resolving international disputes through peaceful means in the long term. Despite this, its report (Lytton 1932) and the diplomacy that was involved in its formulation provides a rich resource for gaining insights into how the meaning of sovereignty was shaped by the strategies of diplomatic actors between the wars. It is also useful for exploring a number of broader theoretical issues that have persisted in international politics down to the present day.

One of these is the development of the theory of sovereignty. That the major powers were prepared to oversee gross infringements of China's sovereignty certainly supports Krasner's understanding of the concept as a kind of 'organised hypocrisy' which is given meaning by the pursuit of a logic of consequences on the part of the most powerful states. However, the strategies of China's diplomats also show how a relatively weak state can score some success by following the right strategies. Most significant is that the League continued to recognise China's international legal sovereignty over Manchuria, even while it failed to fully defend its other dimensions. The Lytton Commission's criticisms of Japan's domestic militarism also mirror much of what was said by the Chinese in the Council debates.

A fuller assessment of such issues could be developed by looking in more detail at the reactions of the various audiences to the League's management of the Manchurian Crisis. Although Mu's chapter shows that press coverage in China was highly critical, both he and Tohmatsu also note that the Chinese government found it useful to accept the Lytton Report as the basis for keeping the League engaged in negotiations with Japan. Moreover, Shinohara's chapter emphasises how the near unanimous support for the Lytton Commission's recommendations was seen by leading diplomats in Japan as marking an embarrassing failure of their internationalist ideals. That China's strategy raised the stakes of diplomacy for a small state on the Council is shown by Suputtikin's account of the problems encountered by Siam's policy of 'omnidirectional friendship'. Looking more broadly, China's diplomats also proved adept at using the League to gain public support around the world, although this fell short of universal press support for direct intervention.[7]

This mixed picture does at least show how an international organisation can provide a stage on which the representatives of weak states are not merely the supine victims of the strong, as implied by Krasner's theory. Moreover, although the Manchurian Crisis has been studied at length from the perspective of great power politics, there remains much more to be learned from the sources by applying different theoretical models. A good example that has not been looked at in this chapter is what the Lytton Commission's recommendations for management of the railway systems in Manchuria tells us about the political ramifications of international technical co-operation that is discussed in the first section of this book. This attempt to placate Japan's claim to have 'special rights' involved establishing a joint Sino-Japanese Railway Commission, with at least one foreign adviser, which would exercise functions analogous to those of boards that existed in some other countries. The report presents this amalgamation of the Chinese and Japanese railway interests as the true mark of the Sino-Japanese economic collaboration that would transform a geopolitical flashpoint into a commercial enterprise, that would also allow considerable savings by replacing the forces tasked with its protection with a special corps of the new gendarmerie. From a more critical perspective, however, it illustrates the need for more work to be done on understanding the conditions under which technological co-operation can become a conduit for imperial expansion rather than a facilitator of international stability.

Notes

1. For biographical studies of Wellington Koo see Craft (2004); Chu (1981).
2. This point is made in the autobiography of the Malaysian-born Dr Wu Lien-teh, who represented China at the conference (Wu 2004: 10). Wu would become a leading authority in the emerging international health system, working with the Jewish-Polish epidemiologist, Ludwik Rajchman, who took the leading role in the building the League Health Organisation. For more on Rajchman and the significance of the plague in China for the development of international health co-operation see Belińska 1998.
3. The text originally appeared in May 1917, under the name of Zhu Zhixin, one of the leading ideological thinkers of the nationalist-revolutionary movement at the time. It was published under Sun's name in January 1928 with the explanation by the GMD's ideological expert, Hu Hanmin that Zhu had merely recorded Sun's thinking. Sun's secretary, Dai Jitao, who was entrusted by Chiang Kai-shek with systematising Sun's writings as a coherent ideology saw the text as the most authoritative embodiment of Sun's views on diplomacy.
4. For a detailed discussion of the Soviet offer see Whiting (1951). On the GMD and the Soviet Union see Leng and Palmer (1961).
5. For information on Satō see the chapter by Shinohara in this book.
6. For more details on the Petrich Incident see the chapters by Mu and Shinohara.
7. An analysis of British press coverage in November 1931 shows that opinion in British newspapers was roughly split along partisan lines between left and right-leaning organs. See Society for Socialist Inquiry and Propaganda (1932?).
8. This is of course a reference to Margaret Macmillan's seminal essay, The Rhyme Of History: Lessons of the Great War Macmillan. Macmillan (2013).

References

Asada, Sadao. 2007. *Culture shock and Japanese-American relations: Historical essays*. University of Missouri.

Belińska, M. A. 1998. *For the good of humanity: Ludwig Rajchman medical statesman*. Budapest: Central European University Press.

Chu, Pao-chin. 1981. *V.K. Wellington Koo: A case study of China's diplomat and diplomacy of nationalism, 1912–1966*. Hong Kong: Chinese University Press.

Craft, Stephen G. 2004. *V.K. Wellingtron Koo and the emergence of modern China*. Lexington: The University Press of Kentucky.

Jackson, Robert H. 1993. *Quasi-States: Sovereignty, international relations and the third world*. Cambridge: Cambridge University Press.

Kawakami, K. K. 1928. Manchuria: The crux of Chino-Japanese relations. *Foreign Affairs* (6/3): 379–394.

King, Wunsz. 1965. *China and the League of Nations: The Sino-Japanese controversy*. New York: St. John's University Press.

Krasner, Stephen D. 1999. *Sovereignty: Organized hypocrisy*. Princeton N.J.: Princeton University Press.

Leng, Shao Chuan and Palmer, Norman D. 1961. *Sun Yat-sen and communism*. London: Thames and Hudson.

Lytton. 1932. *Report of the commission of enquiry* (The Lytton Report). Geneva: The League of Nations. https://en.wikisource.org/wiki/Report_of_the_Commission_of_Enquiry/Chapter_1, accessed 31 July 2022.

Macmillan, Margaret. (2013). The rhyme of history: Lessons of the great war. The Brookings Institution. https://csweb.brookings.edu/content/research/essays/2013/rhyme-of-history.html, accessed 20 June, 2022.

Mao, Zedong. 1919a. Manifesto of the founding of the Xiang river review. In *Mao's road to power: Revolutionary writings 1912–1949*, vol. 1, ed. S. Stuart, 318–320.

Mao Zedong. 1919b. 'The waves of strikes in various countries'. In *Mao's road to power: Revolutionary writings 1912–1949*, vol. 1, ed. S. Stuart, 321–324.

Mao Zedong. 1919c. Poor Wilson. In *Mao's road to power: Revolutionary writings 1912–1949*, vol. 1, ed. S. Stuart, 338.

Mao, Zedong. 1919d. For the Germans, the painful signing of the treaty. In *Mao's road to power: Revolutionary writings 1912–1949*, vol. 1, ed. S. Stuart, 357–366.

Mao, Zedong. 1919e. Joy and suffering. In *Mao's road to power: Revolutionary writings 1912–1949*, vol. 1, ed. S. Stuart, 367.

Mao, Zedong. 1925a. Analysis of the classes in Chinese society. In *Mao's road to power: Revolutionary writings 1912–1949*, vol. 2, ed. S. Stuart, 249–262.

Mao, Zedong. 1925b. Propaganda guidelines of the Chinese Guomindang in the war against the Fengtian clique. In *Mao's road to power: Revolutionary writings 1912–1949*, vol. 1, ed. S. Stuart, 239–246.

March, James G., and James Olsen. 1989. *Rediscovering institutions: The organizational basis of politics*. New York: Free Press.

March, James G., and James Olsen. 1998. The institutional dyunamicss of internaitional political orders. *International Organization* 52: 943–969.
OJ. 1932a. 66th session of the Council, January 25–February 20. Part 1. PRO 30/52/580.
OJ. 1932b. First report of the committee appointed at the request of the secretary-general to report on events in Shanghai and the neighbourhood, Dated February 6 1932b, Annex. 66th session of the Council, January 25–February 20, Part 1: 374–376. PRO 30/52/580.
OJ. 1932c. Second report of the Shanghai committee dated February 12, 1932c, Annex. 66th session of the Council, January 25–February 20. Part 1: 379–380. PRO 30/52/580.
OJ. 1932d. Appeal dated February 16, 1932d, Addressed to the Japanese government by the President of the Council in the names of the members of the Council other than the representatives of China and Japan, Annex. 66th session of the Council, January 25–February 20 Part 1: 383–384. PRO 30/52/580.
OJ. 1932e. Communication, dated February 18. From the Chinese delegation to the secretary general of the League of Nations (original message dated Shanghai, February 17, 1932e), Appendix. 66th session of the Council, January 25–February 20. Part 1: 405–4066. PRO 30/52/580.
OJ. 1932f. Reply Dated February 23, 1932f, From the Japanese government to the appeal of the President of the Council, Dated February 16. Annex. 66th session of the Council, January 25–February 20. Part 1: 384–386. PRO 30/52/580.
Shinohara, Hatsue. 2012. *US international lawyers in the interwar years: A forgotten crusade*. Cambridge: Cambridge University Press.
Society for Socialist Inquiry and Propaganda (Manchester Branch). 1932. *The Manchurian dispute: A survey of press reports*. Held in British Library of Economic and Political Science.
Sun, Zhongshan (Sun Yat-sen). 1928. Zhongguo cunwang wenti [The problem China's preservation or demise]. *Sun Zhongshan quanji* [Complete Works of Sun Yat-sen]. Vol. 4: 39–99.
Sze, Sao-Ke Alfred. 1962. *Sao-Ke Alfred Sze: Reminiscences of his Early Years*. Washington D.C: no publisher named).
Whiting, Allen S. 1951. The Soviet offer to China of 1919. The Far Eastern Quarterly (10/4): 355–364. https://doi.org/10.2307/2049007.
Wu, Lien-teh. 2004. *Plague fighter: The autobiography of a modern Chinese physician*. Penang: Areca Books.

Conclusion: Eastern Asia and the League—Shifting to a Global Perspective

Madeleine Herren

Introduction

In March 1933, the German newspaper, *Vossische Zeitung*, reported on Japan's expected official withdrawal from the League of Nations (*Vossische Zeitung* 1933). Interestingly, instead of assuming the end of the international order represented by the League, the paper asked whether the establishment of an 'Asian League of Nations' was to be expected. Founded in the eighteenth century and to be suppressed by the National Socialist regime in 1934, the newspaper offered an astonishingly lucid interpretation of the significance of the League. Thus, the organization located in Geneva was not *the* League of Nations, but *a* League of Nations—a multilateral institution of global governance, of which various forms had already come into existence. The article thus referred to other regional concepts, including the Washington System and the Monroe Doctrine, which was explicitly mentioned in Article 21 of the League

M. Herren (✉)
Institute for European Global Studies, University of Basel, Basel, Switzerland
e-mail: madeleine.herren-oesch@unibas.ch

C. R. Hughes and H. Shinohara (eds.), *East Asians in the League of Nations*, New Directions in East Asian History,
https://doi.org/10.1007/978-981-19-7067-2_13

Covenant. Following this rationale, the *Vossische Zeitung* located the Japanese idea of a '*Grossasiatischer Bund*' ('Federation of Greater Asia') within a number of different versions of multilateralism that had already been established in various forms.

In the reading of modern historiography, the statement of the *Vossische Zeitung* strengthens the assumption that the League represented a contested form of multilateralism, on the one hand, but ultimately shaped an irreplaceable pattern of international order, on the other hand. As research moves to understand the League of Nations as a *structural*, and therefore indispensable, element of the twentieth-century international order, new opportunities for analysis and insights open up. Beyond the elements of failure that have been studied so far (the question of the German reparations, the US decision not to join the League, demise of liberal internationalism), the structural necessity of multilateral co-operation emphasizes the importance of a global approach and—unfortunately—also puts into perspective the notion that multilateral co-operation fundamentally stands for peaceful conflict resolution.

Scholarly research started analysing the League of Nations as an institutionalization of global interconnectedness only recently and thus gained two new thematic foci that have substantially broadened the previous Eurocentric perspective. First, the investigation of the promise to deliver the right of self-determination has expanded into a lively debate on the mandate system (Pedersen 2015). This approach emphasizes the dilemma that arose when the League system strengthened the empires that emerged victorious from World War I, while simultaneously providing anti-colonial national movements with a stage for their concerns. The second new focus has been on the ways in which the global relevance of the League was enhanced by the ways in which international technical co-operation required the use of many tools and instruments and the growth of epistemic communities beyond borders.

These two new areas of research, namely the controversy between colonialism and empire and the relevance of seemingly apolitical technical issues, require new approaches that go beyond the insights that an institutional history of the League can offer. The new global understanding of the League thus transforms this organization from a failed concept to an experiment in global governance, and from a relic of the past to a historical magnifying glass that has the potential to reveal the multilayered tensions of a globally interconnected world in the twenty-first century.

The success of such an approach depends on whether the new history of the League of Nations can be told from a global point of view. The challenge is to avoid summing up the contributions of the non-European member states and adding them to an already Western-framed history of the League. Several contributions to this volume mention the very fact that the history of Asia developed differently compared to the history of Europe. The characteristics of each region do indeed require independent consideration. However, the identified differences describe the complexity and not the absence of multilayered relationships.

It is, therefore, a methodological challenge to combine knowledge of the characteristics of the region with an understanding of its global interconnectedness. This task can be approached in different ways. Among the most convincing approaches are those that analyse the contemporary disputes between universalist and regional concepts of international order (Mogami 2018, 2019). In this context, Carl Schmitt's conservative criticism of the League of Nations has an exemplary function (Mogami 2019: 327). From his point of view, the 'Geneva League' was not a global extension of international law but the abandonment of the territory-based *Jus Publicum Europaeum.* Characteristic of this pessimistic and conservative world view is the conclusion that global interconnectedness has no structural significance in shaping international order, an approach invalidated by innovative methodological analyses in global history.

Between 1919 and 1945, there were numerous disputes between liberal internationalists, old and new imperialists, and authoritarian visionaries. Rather than focus on the success or failure of such arguments, it is more enlightening to understand how territorially based regional claims to power were incommensurable with concepts of global governance and how the two tendencies stood in dynamic opposition to each other due to the specific characteristics that they had acquired in the peacemaking process of 1919. Since then, the international order had provided institutions with global membership, while demands for the right to self-determination also led to a multiplication of the number of actors involved in international decision-making. New political dynamics and movements thus emerged as simultaneous demands for and against self-determination, uniting new groups of actors across borders. The same concept was used just as easily for the justification of totalitarian rule on the basis of racism and for the rejection of social, cultural and political diversity (Herren 2016).

This volume opens up new and thrilling insights from different perspectives. Without doing justice to the fascinating complexity of the contributions, this chapter provides an overview of the most important aspects that the authors have offered for further debate. The first section discusses the shift of the most important key concepts after the end of the Cold War. The following main paragraph focuses on the Manchurian crisis, which came up as *the* global moment in most of the contributions. After analysing different understandings of technical co-operation, a concluding paragraph discusses the consequences and issues raised by the approach presented in this volume.

International Organizations, Multilateralism, Global Governance: The Post-Cold War History of the League

This volume closes a sensitive gap in the existing research by reaching beyond a classical history of the League as an institution in two ways. The contributions focus on the simultaneity of imperialist claims to power and the participation in global networks, and they examine the structural significance of this process in Asia. In doing so, the scholarly debate presented in this volume aims to overcome a Eurocentric interpretation by answering a central question: To what extent was the international order outside of Europe shaped by the inescapability of global networks?

By including Eastern Asian perspectives within this research rationale, the significance of the League of Nations for the present can be demonstrated in multiple ways. As the twenty-first-century world has to deal (again) with a fragmented international order, this historical knowledge is of growing importance. This close relationship with the present is revealed by the development of the historiography of the League. After the end of the Cold War, a new perspective emerged that combined the discourses on international organization(s), multilateralism and global governance. The combined key terms created an interdisciplinary context in which the development of the League came to be observed as a historical metaphor for a globally connected international order. This shows how the way in which the League is discussed goes beyond the interest of historians to reveal the problems of today's world order. The frequency and use of the terms 'multilateralism', 'international organization' and 'global governance' gives some insight into the scale of the specific challenges involved in the three levels of discourse that the League had to face. In this respect, it is interesting to look at statistics from the Google Books Ngram Viewer as presented in Fig. 1. Although this data should be used in a careful and critical manner, they can be taken to show a unidirectional and substantial increase of these three terms after the end of the Cold War, which coincides with the historiographical 'rediscovery' of the League in the optimistic post-Cold War period of the 1990s (Pedersen 2007).

These patterns of interest changed fundamentally between 2008 and 2011. At a time considered by some scholars as a moment of de-globalization due to the economic crisis of 2008, the interest in multilateralism and international organizations seemed to decrease. However, continuing growth in interest in global governance reflects a significant dilemma: Despite a rise in the importance of the pursuit of national interests, the world has remained inextricably intertwined. Whether or not the twenty-first century will be described as the 'Asian century', this contemporary interest in the dynamics of the international order is a strong argument for the need for a newly conceptualized history of the League that considers both its Asian and its global impact.

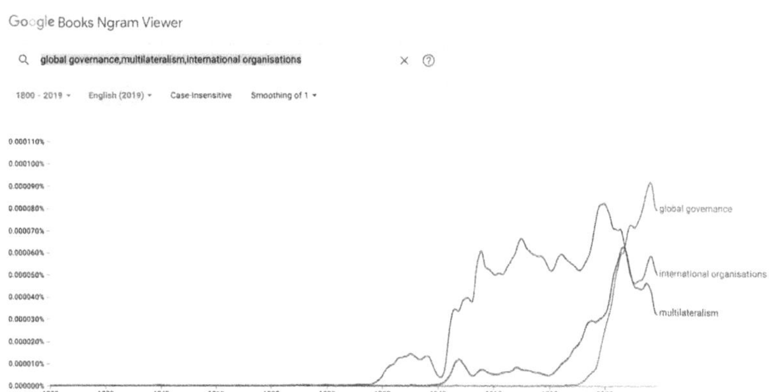

Fig. 1 Use of the terms 'global governance', 'multilateralism' and 'international organisations' 1800–2022[1]

From Global Governance to Empire Building: The Global Momentum of the Manchurian Crisis

For any new interpretation of the League, the Manchurian crisis is a key event which demonstrates much more than the failure of peaceful conflict resolution. As Hatsue Shinohara convincingly explains in her chapter in this volume, the Japanese government was reluctant to accept the organization's version of multilateral order from the very beginning. Instead of emphasizing the differences between various political actors in Japan, this perspective reveals how Japan maintained a consistent policy that remained compliant with the League of Nations as long as its own interests in China and the Pacific were not adversely affected. Both Shinohara and Christopher Hughes, in his chapter, conclusively highlight the importance of this historical context, which is crucial for properly understanding how the actions of the League were justified in contemporary discussions, and whether or not the debates at that time presupposed that the League was a continuation of Western imperialism. The use of concepts of varying scope can be identified in this process. With reference to Krasner, Hughes focuses on the dense interplay of regional, international and Westphalian (i.e., European) conceptions of order. As mentioned by Shinohara, reference to the Japanese experience of European politics in the nineteenth century helped to establish the legitimacy of an imperialist concept in Japan in the 1930s. Both approaches mention how debates on state law and international law in the public sphere were an important and specific characteristic of politics in the post-war period.

The relationship between China and Japan, the two main opponents in Asia, was also influenced from the beginning by a propaganda war fought with different degrees of intensity on both the local and the international levels. In the immediate post-war period, China was much more successful than Japan in spreading its message and engaging in the debate internationally. Hughes demonstrates how this had important consequences for an active public sphere, which could be used as a powerful political instrument to redefine key concepts such as sovereignty by engaging the public with the promise of self-determination. Mu Lunhai's chapter also explores the significance of the League in the emerging public sphere by confirming the awareness and discussion of the Lytton Commission and the Lytton Report in the Chinese media, highlighting how the League ultimately lost not only Japan, but also the support of China. A media-related approach opens the way to a promising agenda for further research gaining historical insights into the increasing importance of the influence of (global) media in international relations and the role of state propaganda.[2]

Whichever challenges the League faced, its mere existence prompted an increase in visions of international order. As colonial and imperialist patterns of domination were deeply embedded in its structure, the development of competitive, illiberal concepts for the use of global networks was an almost unavoidable consequence. In a globally interconnected world, the complete disappearance of the model the League represented was no option in any case. Tomoko Akami's chapter explores the presence of entanglements by elaborating on the structural significance of the inflation of conceptual adoptions, adaptations and (mis)uses of the vocabulary that liberal internationalism had envisioned and started to deploy in the late nineteenth century. In the Asian post-war period, the expansion of this political vocabulary shaped a narrative which overstepped the established scholarly use of simple dichotomies, such as 'Liberals/Utopians versus Realists'.

The contributors to this volume thus confirm from different angles that the political complexity of contemporary internationalisms needs further examination of the relevant practices and concrete actors in international politics. The findings raise the question of whether these actors created new ideological frameworks—such as humanitarianism—or at least brought in new (and more international) mechanics of power. In pursuing such questions, Tomoko Akami highlights the need to pay close attention to those who worked as experts across borders. This contribution points to the increasing importance of expert knowledge beyond diplomacy in the League's system. By including international civil servants in the Covenant, the League added new actors to the stage of international politics. These civil servants were privileged with diplomatic prerogatives and even had access to gender equality, at least in theory.[3] The roles that these experts came to play have been discussed on various occasions in the history of the League, and it seems reasonable to attribute them to the growing importance of technical co-operation across borders. Akami, however, is right to point out that the function of experts is also multifaceted and even contradictory. Indeed, because internationally active experts were interchangeable to a certain extent, their presence in and their impact on the international system is difficult to understand as a specific characteristic of the League of Nations.

The international lawyers are of special interest in this respect. This is because analysis of their historical formation as a group of experts allows for conclusions to be drawn about who shaped the codification of international law and to what extent this project shaped the League system in new ways. Rikiya Takahashi examines the crucial contribution of international law to the League system in this volume. Although decidedly slow, the discussion he traces finally led to the League of Nations Codification Conference in The Hague in 1930. He stresses the significance of the fact that the Japanese community of lawyers used the International Law Association to send a complete draft code to Geneva. By surveying their proceedings and the suggestions they made, it becomes possible to analyse the crucial question of how the League addressed the issue of racial equality from a new and different point of view. Rather than see it as nothing more than a Japanese proposal that was rejected at the Paris Peace Conference, it should be analysed as another element of imperialist continuity that was perpetuated by the League system.

In various contributions to this volume, the Manchurian crisis is treated as a crucial moment for the transformation of notions of international rule into political practice. In this regard, the establishment of Japan's puppet state of Manchukuo is a significant case study that takes research beyond the established agenda of understanding how Asian states were brought into the picture of a modern history of international relations. Through this lens, we can observe not only the clash of different visions and practices of global governance but also how differently modern historiography views the impact of international administration, established in new ways by the League. In my estimation, however, the administrative part also shows how dangerously close those acting in the name of the League came to accepting the ideas of colonial expansion—and the degree to which it was possible to replace the Geneva institution with competing totalitarian visions of global governance.

In this context, it is interesting to note that every League expert in the Lytton Commission (including the American member) drew on the experience that he had obtained while working in national colonial administrations. This is revealed when Haruo Tohmatsu's chapter looks at how the commission's report clearly reflects the dangerous interplay of contradictory concepts, ranging from the attempt to turn Manchuria into a colony under the rule of the mandates system to deliberations on the model of Swiss federalism. The fact the League was obviously unable to envision and apply a concept of international administration for Manchuria based on the models of Danzig and the Saar tells us much about the limitations of its *modus operandi*. Especially interesting is to learn that the question of territorial control in the succession from Qing Dynasty China to the Republic of China has remained an underestimated aspect of the case of Manchuria until now.

The latest scholarly controversy over the League of Nations has been sparked by the question of how it responded to attempts to establish the principle of self-determination. Because the concept had been newly introduced into the international system after World War I, it was inevitably connected closely to the core character of the League. For a number of years, interpreting its positive significance as the starting point for national decolonization movements had been shaped by the notion of Wilsonian internationalism (Manela 2007). More recently, however, the potential contribution of the League to decolonization has been increasingly questioned. Adom Getachew, for example, underlines the unequal position of the few African member states within the League (Getachew 2019). Within this argument, the formally sovereign state of Ethiopia has a position of paradigmatic importance. If the League had indeed remained deeply imbued by European imperialism, the ultimately fruitless sanctions against the Italian invasion takes on a different meaning as a characteristic of inter-war global governance and less as an unwanted tragedy that was the inevitable product of growing political tensions.

In the debate over whether the (hidden) imperialism embedded in the League was the principal source of its weakness, however, the multilateral character of the organization has not yet received the attention it deserves. Its establishment had ended, for better or worse, an international order in which the acting subjects exclusively belonged to the Western great powers. The League stood for the first global order in which member states were accepted as equals, based on the acknowledgement of their sovereignty. So far, however, there has been little discussion of how states without great power status formed coalitions within the League system by using the new possibilities of the League's multilateral system. Little is known, in particular, about how and whether such states used multilateral coalitions when concrete political decisions concerning the national interest took priority over concepts and visions of a new international order.

Much light is shed on this question by Li Chang's chapter on China's policies towards the Ethiopian Question from 1935 to 1938. The findings of his research emphasize the extent to which global connectivity had come to shape international relations by the late 1930s, when World War II had already started in Eastern Asia. When the question arose of whether Japanese recognition of Italy's conquest of Ethiopia could be the prize for Italy's formal recognition of Manchukuo, diplomatic activity was severely challenged by the persistence of traditional power politics. Chinese support for Ethiopia seems obvious due to the fact of both states being the victims of military aggression. However, the Chinese position was made difficult due to the imperative of maintaining its close bilateral relationship with Italy. This situation ultimately resulted in China's refusal to recognize the Italian invasion, while simultaneously asking for the League's support against Japan. In this setting, the fact that the Japanese Ambassador to Italy, Yōtarō Sugimura, was a diplomat intimately familiar with the League is another reminder that imperialist expansion and global governance were conceptually more intertwined in the 1930s than a simple dichotomous interpretation would suggest.[4]

As demonstrated by Teewin Suputtikun's chapter, the case of Siam allows the multilateral character of the League to be investigated from a different angle, namely from the perspective of a small state. In the view of the Siamese government, the optimal strategy for a small state to consolidate its fragile status as a League member was to maintain a position of neutrality in following a policy of 'omnidirectional friendship'. This understanding of neutrality, however, ultimately led Siam to abstain when the League had to make vital decisions on the key issue of Manchuria.[5] Used in the context of an institutionalized international order, this specific understanding of neutrality collided with the concept of collective security. Moreover, it gave rise to substantial misunderstandings and unwanted consequences. The translation of the principle of neutrality into the practice of abstention thus reveals another characteristic of the League system which has received only little scholarly attention until now. In his contribution, Suputtikun explains how the work of Siam's diplomats was complicated by the need to learn the profession of League-style diplomacy in the context of radical political changes at home. When confronted by the case of Manchuria, their actions ultimately did less to develop the principle of neutrality within a universalist form of global governance than to support a new form of Japanese imperialism. It is somewhat absurd that the various choices that could have led to these alternative outcomes were rooted in the fear that the League's guarantee of sovereignty had little to offer against Japan's version of imperialism.

The Political Significance of Technical Co-operation

The institutionalization of the link between security and co-operation may be the most creative of the League's contributions to the shaping of a new international order. The broader benefits of technical co-operation have long been underestimated or downplayed in favour of seeing it as nothing more than a politically innocent exchange of expert knowledge. However, through the inclusion of the Asian member states the political weight of technical co-operation becomes clearly visible. As Harumi Goto-Shibata points out in her chapter, there is no alternative to technical co-operation in a global age. Technical co-operation became a double-edged sword, however. On the one hand, it could enhance the capacity to put pressure on the empires, exemplified by the League's campaign to suppress the opium trade; on the other hand, those who acted in the name of the League's technical co-operation tended to abstain from questioning colonialism. The comparison between China and Japan shows that the decisive factor in making this choice was whether a state received technical assistance, as in the case of the former, or whether engaging with technical institutions was a way to just continue using the League's networks after it had announced its withdrawal from the organization, as in the case of the latter.

Kayo Takuma's chapter on the Far Eastern Bureau in Singapore explores another crucial aspect of the valuable role that international technical organizations can play within the international system. Dealing with the collection and transfer of epidemiological data, this institution of the League had a long-lasting impact and shaped the emergence of the WHO under the UN system during and after World War II. Having put down the first roots of an information service for collecting and disseminating data on infectious diseases, the work of the Singapore Bureau survived a change to its name and the transformation of the framework of multilateral treaties in which it operated. As Takuma shows, this was in large part due to the way in which the Bureau served as an interface to connect regional and international information required in the fight against epidemic diseases. This part of international co-operation specifies a field where states no longer appeared to be the sole and exclusive actors in the emerging international order.

This book reveals in different contributions the political impact of the technical co-operation as a remarkably constant contribution of the

League across a wide range of levels and sectors. As explained by Takashi Saikawa, even the fragile networks and institutions of the League's intellectual co-operation were based on a distinctive political rationale. His comparison of Japan and China is particularly useful for revealing the different degrees of political instrumentality that could be attached to such work. This instrumentalism had a decisive impact on determining whether intellectual co-operation was dedicated to confirming an essentialized authentic national identity, as in militaristic Japan, or was presented as a contribution to world culture *avant la lettre*, as in the case of China that was looking for international recognition and support.

The League in a Global Perspective—Consequences and Questions

A global history of the League of Nations will arrive at the same conclusion as previous literature: The first international and global organization with extraterritorial status ultimately turned out to be a failure. However, there are good reasons to understand this failure by looking at it from a new perspective. The League of Nations was indeed successful in various areas, including public health, communications and transit, social problems, intellectual co-operation, labour and even in economic and financial questions—at least when compared to its handling of the settlement of disputes, armaments, security and minority protection. However, any consideration of technical co-operation will not be able to refrain from assessing the political relevance of such networks within the League's overarching concept of international order. If one takes its principal goal to be the attempt to combine collective security with international co-operation, a Eurocentric institutional history must inevitably fall short. A modern history of the League of Nations is framed in terms of an organization that was the outcome of an increasingly globally interconnected world. It is, therefore, indispensable to pay more attention to all member states worldwide. This approach has to go beyond a simple extension of the list of state actors and must ultimately challenge the historiographical perspective that refers to the 'inter-war period'. For a global historical analysis of the League, it is important to acknowledge the different ways in which the two world wars are referred to as overcoming a terrible past, on the one hand, and as a guarantee for a peaceful future, on the other hand. While World War I had a strong function for legitimizing the invention of the League from a European and Western point of view, from an Asian perspective it was the imminent outbreak of World War II that challenged and tested the League's promise to guarantee a peaceful world order. In addition, a new history of the League of Nations requires considering how regional aspects can be merged with a global research rationale.

From this perspective, it is crucial to consider what Adom Getachew so aptly called 'worldmaking', an approach which suggests an understanding of the League of Nations more as a model of international relations than as a specific and unique institution which was dissolved after World War II (Getachew 2019). A new and more global analysis of the League has its prize. It is no longer enough to understand the League as a liberal, democratic and fundamentally peace-oriented outcome of liberal internationalism, which was unfortunately destroyed by the political and economic crises of the 1930s. Instead, the League should be seen and analysed as an answer to the challenges of global networking which competed with the existence of persistent empires and new ones that were based on fascist and totalitarian ideas of international order.

Contributions to this book understand the significance of the Lytton commission and its report as key element for writing a new history of the League. Indeed, the Manchurian crisis shows how the League dealt with conflicts which were directly related to the Western colonial legacy and were simultaneously located at the core of Japan's rise to imperial power. A global approach thus has the potential to reveal patterns of colonialism in the international system and can tell the story of the League in different ways, including the impact of international public opinion, given that the Lytton Commission and Japan's public exit from the League resulted in a much larger media echo than the Ethiopian conflict.

The contributions in this volume provide new perspectives and demonstrate further research areas. At the same time, they also reveal gaps and blind spots. Among others, the case of Japan clearly shows that non-members could play a crucial role in the League's multilayered networks. To this end, it is necessary to address the role of the Soviet Union, especially since the political marginalization of the newly founded Soviet state led to a remarkable innovation within the international system, the foundation of the International Labor Organization (ILO). Even though the ILO was only loosely connected to the League through the submission of the annual budget, what is today the oldest special agency of the UN contributed considerably to the system of the League and developed an increasing political significance in the 1930s. The inclusion of labour added a new perspective to the League's investigations of global economic questions, but the ILO also began to address a new dimension of globality by referring to slavery and forced labour as critical topics. Moreover, the most recent research discusses the multilateral implementation of labour regulations and sociopolitical norms as a further development of a primarily legally based international order (Fiti Sinclair 2017).

Accordingly, a global history of the League of Nations told from the perspective of its Eastern Asian members shows great potential for further research. Among the many questions to be explored, analysis of the interwar period is particularly suitable for discussing the confrontation between (neo)colonial and multilateral types of international order in new ways.

Notes

1. Results taken from the online search engine Google Books Ngram Viewer, https://books.google.com/ngrams/graph?content=global+governance%2C+multilateralism%2C+international+organisations&year_start=1800&year_end=2019&corpus=26&smoothing=3&direct_url=t1%3B%2Cglobal%20governance%3B%2Cc0%3B.t1%3B%2Cmultilateralism%3B%2Cc0%3B.t1%3B%2Cinternational%20organisations%3B%2Cc0.
2. For the use of the Lytton Commission for Japanese propaganda see: Global Politics on Screen, https://europa.unibas.ch/de/forschung/digital-resources/. Accessed 19 July 2022.
3. Article 7 of the Covenant states: 'All positions under or in connection with the League, including the Secretariat, shall be open equally to men and women'.
4. Sugimura served as undersecretary general of the League of Nations from 1927 to 1933. See LONSEA (League of Nations Search Engine). http://www.lonsea.de/pub/person/5209. Accessed 19 July 2022.
5. For Swiss Neutrality and the League see London Declaration, in Sacha Zala, Marc Perrenoud (ed.), *La Suisse et la construction du multilatéralisme*, vol. 2. Documents Diplomatiques Suisses sur l'histoire de la Société des Nations 1918–1946, Bd. 14, Dok. 18, dodis.ch/1721, Berne 2019.

References

Fiti Sinclair, Guy. 2017. *To Reform the World. International Organizations and the Making of the Modern States*. Oxford: Oxford University Press.

Getachew, Adom. 2019. *Worldmaking After Empire: The Rise and Fall of Self-Determination*. Princeton: Princeton University Press.

Herren, Madeleine. 2016. Fascist Internationalism. In *Internationalisms: A Twentieth Century History*, ed. Glenda Sluga and Patricia Clavin, 191–212. Cambridge: Cambridge University Press. https://doi.org/10.1017/9781107477568.010

Manela, Erez. 2007. *The Wilsonian Moment: Self Determination and the International Origins of Anticolonial Nationalism*. New York: Oxford University Press.

Mogami, Toshiki. 2018. Perpetuum Mobile: Before and After Global Constitutionalism. In *Global Constitutionalism from European and East Asian Perspectives*, ed. Takao Suami, Anne Peters, Dimitri Vanoverbeke, and Mattias Kumm, 29–57. Cambridge: Cambridge University Press.

Mogami, Toshiki. 2019. Japan. In *The Oxford Handbook of International Law in Asia and the Pacific*, ed. Simon Chesterman, Hisashi Owada, and Ben Saul, 320–340. Oxford: Oxford University Press.

Pedersen, Susan. 2007. Back to the League of Nations. *American Historical Review* (112/4): 1091–1117.

Pedersen, Susan. 2015. *The Guardians. The League of Nations and the Crisis of Empire*. Oxford: Oxford University Press.

Vossische Zeitung. 1933. 11 March: 4. http://zefys.staatsbibliothek-berlin.de/list/title/zdb/27112366/.

Appendix: The Covenant of the League of Nations

The High Contracting Parties

In order to promote international co-operation and to achieve international peace and security by the acceptance of obligations not to resort to war, by the prescription of open, just and honourable relations between nations, by the firm establishment of the understandings of international law as the actual rule of conduct among Governments and by the maintenance of justice and a scrupulous respect for all treaty obligations in the dealings of organised peoples with one another, Agree to this Covenant of the League of Nations.

Article 1

The original Members of the League of Nations shall be those of the Signatories which are named in the Annex to this Covenant and also such of those other States named in the Annex as shall accede without reservation to this Covenant. Such accession shall be effected by a Declaration deposited with the Secretariat within two months of the coming into force of the Covenant. Notice thereof shall be sent to all other Members of the League.

C. R. Hughes and H. Shinohara (eds.), *East Asians in the League of Nations*, New Directions in East Asian History,
https://doi.org/10.1007/978-981-19-7067-2

Any fully self-governing State, Dominion or Colony not named in the Annex may become a Member of the League if its admission is agreed to by two-thirds of the Assembly, provided that it shall give effective guarantees of its sincere intention to observe its international obligations and shall accept such regulations as may be prescribed by the League with regard to its military, naval and air forces and armaments.

Any Member of the League may, after two years' notice of its intention so to do, withdraw from the League, provided that all its international obligations and all its obligations under this Covenant shall have been fulfilled at the time of its withdrawal.

Article 2

The action of the League under this Covenant shall be effected through the instrumentality of an Assembly and of a Council, with a permanent Secretariat.

Article 3

The Assembly shall consist of Representatives of the Members of the League.

The Assembly shall meet at stated intervals and from time to time as occasion may require at the Seat of the League or at such other place as may be decided upon.

The Assembly may deal at its meetings with any matter within the sphere of action of the League or affecting the peace of the world.

At meetings of the Assembly, each Member of the League shall have one vote and may have not more than three Representatives.

Article 4

The Council shall consist of Representatives of the Principal Allied and Associated Powers, together with Representatives of four other Members of the League. These four Members of the League shall be selected by the Assembly from time to time in its discretion. Until the appointment of the Representatives of the four Members of the League first selected by the Assembly, Representatives of Belgium, Brazil, Spain and Greece shall be members of the Council.

With the approval of the majority of the Assembly, the Council may name additional Members of the League whose Representatives shall always be members of the Council; the Council, with like approval may increase the number of Members of the League to be selected by the Assembly for representation on the Council.

The Council shall meet from time to time as occasion may require, and at least once a year, at the Seat of the League, or at such other place as may be decided upon.

The Council may deal at its meetings with any matter within the sphere of action of the League or affecting the peace of the world.

Any Member of the League not represented on the Council shall be invited to send a Representative to sit as a member at any meeting of the Council during the consideration of matters specially affecting the interests of that Member of the League.

At meetings of the Council, each Member of the League represented on the Council shall have one vote and may have not more than one Representative.

Article 5

Except where otherwise expressly provided in this Covenant or by the terms of the present Treaty, decisions at any meeting of the Assembly or of the Council shall require the agreement of all the Members of the League represented at the meeting.

All matters of procedure at meetings of the Assembly or of the Council, including the appointment of Committees to investigate particular matters, shall be regulated by the Assembly or by the Council and may be decided by a majority of the Members of the League represented at the meeting.

The first meeting of the Assembly and the first meeting of the Council shall be summoned by the President of the United States of America.

Article 6

The permanent Secretariat shall be established at the Seat of the League. The Secretariat shall comprise a Secretary General and such secretaries and staff as may be required.

The first Secretary General shall be the person named in the Annex; thereafter, the Secretary General shall be appointed by the Council with the approval of the majority of the Assembly.

The secretaries and staff of the Secretariat shall be appointed by the Secretary General with the approval of the Council.

The Secretary General shall act in that capacity at all meetings of the Assembly and of the Council.

The expenses of the League shall be borne by the Members of the League in the proportion decided by the Assembly.

Article 7

The Seat of the League is established at Geneva.

The Council may at any time decide that the Seat of the League shall be established elsewhere.

All positions under or in connection with the League, including the Secretariat, shall be open equally to men and women.

Representatives of the Members of the League and officials of the League when engaged on the business of the League shall enjoy diplomatic privileges and immunities.

The buildings and other property occupied by the League or its officials or by Representatives attending its meetings shall be inviolable.

Article 8

The Members of the League recognise that the maintenance of peace requires the reduction of national armaments to the lowest point consistent with national safety and the enforcement by common action of international obligations.

The Council, taking account of the geographical situation and circumstances of each State, shall formulate plans for such reduction for the consideration and action of the several Governments. Such plans shall be subject to reconsideration and revision at least every ten years.

After these plans shall have been adopted by the several Governments, the limits of armaments therein fixed shall not be exceeded without the concurrence of the Council.

The Members of the League agree that the manufacture by private enterprise of munitions and implements of war is open to grave objections. The Council shall advise how the evil effects attendant upon such manufacture can be prevented, due regard being had to the necessities of those Members of the League which are not able to manufacture the munitions and implements of war necessary for their safety.

The Members of the League undertake to interchange full and frank information as to the scale of their armaments, their military, naval and air programmes and the condition of such of their industries as are adaptable to war-like purposes.

Article 9

A permanent Commission shall be constituted to advise the Council on the execution of the provisions of Articles 1 and 8 and on military, naval and air questions generally.

Article 10

The Members of the League undertake to respect and preserve as against external aggression the territorial integrity and existing political independence of all Members of the League. In case of any such aggression or in case of any threat or danger of such aggression, the Council shall advise upon the means by which this obligation shall be fulfilled.

Article 11

Any war or threat of war, whether immediately affecting any of the Members of the League or not, is hereby declared a matter of concern to the whole League, and the League shall take any action that may be deemed wise and effectual to safeguard the peace of nations. In case any such emergency should arise the Secretary General shall on the request of any Member of the League forthwith summon a meeting of the Council.

It is also declared to be the friendly right of each Member of the League to bring to the attention of the Assembly or of the Council any circumstance whatever affecting international relations which threatens to disturb international peace or the good understanding between nations upon which peace depends.

Article 12

The Members of the League agree that if there should arise between them any dispute likely to lead to a rupture they will submit the matter either to arbitration or judicial settlement or to enquiry by the Council, and they agree in no case to resort to war until three months after the award by the arbitrators or the judicial decision, or the report by the Council. In any case under this Article, the award of the arbitrators or the judicial decision shall be made within a reasonable time, and the report of the Council shall be made within six months after the submission of the dispute.

Article 13

The Members of the League agree that whenever any dispute shall arise between them which they recognise to be suitable for submission to arbitration or judicial settlement and which cannot be satisfactorily settled by diplomacy, they will submit the whole subject-matter to arbitration or judicial settlement.

Disputes as to the interpretation of a treaty, as to any question of international law, as to the existence of any fact which if established would constitute a breach of any international obligation, or as to the extent and nature of the reparation to be made for any such breach, are declared to be among those which are generally suitable for submission to arbitration or judicial settlement.

For the consideration of any such dispute, the court to which the case is referred shall be the Permanent Court of International Justice, established in accordance with Article 14, or any tribunal agreed on by the parties to the dispute or stipulated in any convention existing between them.

The Members of the League agree that they will carry out in full good faith any award or decision that may be rendered, and that they will not resort to war against a Member of the League which complies therewith. In the event of any failure to carry out such an award or decision, the Council shall propose what steps should be taken to give effect thereto.

Article 14

The Council shall formulate and submit to the Members of the League for adoption plans for the establishment of a Permanent Court of

International Justice. The Court shall be competent to hear and determine any dispute of an international character which the parties thereto submit to it. The Court may also give an advisory opinion upon any dispute or question referred to it by the Council or by the Assembly.

Article 15

If there should arise between Members of the League any dispute likely to lead to a rupture, which is not submitted to arbitration or judicial settlement in accordance with Article 13, the Members of the League agree that they will submit the matter to the Council. Any party to the dispute may effect such submission by giving notice of the existence of the dispute to the Secretary General, who will make all necessary arrangements for a full investigation and consideration thereof.

For this purpose, the parties to the dispute will communicate to the Secretary General, as promptly as possible, statements of their case with all the relevant facts and papers, and the Council may forthwith direct the publication thereof.

The Council shall endeavour to effect a settlement of the dispute, and if such efforts are successful, a statement shall be made public giving such facts and explanations regarding the dispute and the terms of settlement thereof as the Council may deem appropriate.

If the dispute is not thus settled, the Council either unanimously or by a majority vote shall make and publish a report containing a statement of the facts of the dispute and the recommendations which are deemed just and proper in regard thereto.

Any Member of the League represented on the Council may make public a statement of the facts of the dispute and of its conclusions regarding the same.

If a report by the Council is unanimously agreed to by the members thereof other than the Representatives of one or more of the parties to the dispute, the Members of the League agree that they will not go to war with any party to the dispute which complies with the recommendations of the report.

If the Council fails to reach a report which is unanimously agreed to by the members thereof, other than the Representatives of one or more of the parties to the dispute, the Members of the League reserve to themselves the right to take such action as they shall consider necessary for the maintenance of right and justice.

If the dispute between the parties is claimed by one of them, and is found by the Council, to arise out of a matter which by international law is solely within the domestic jurisdiction of that party, the Council shall so report and shall make no recommendation as to its settlement.

The Council may in any case under this Article refer the dispute to the Assembly. The dispute shall be so referred at the request of either party to the dispute, provided that such request be made within fourteen days after the submission of the dispute to the Council.

In any case referred to the Assembly, all the provisions of this Article and of Article 12 relating to the action and powers of the Council shall apply to the action and powers of the Assembly, provided that a report made by the Assembly, if concurred in by the Representatives of those Members of the League represented on the Council and of a majority of the other Members of the League, exclusive in each case of the Representatives of the parties to the dispute, shall have the same force as a report by the Council concurred in by all the members thereof other than the Representatives of one or more of the parties to the dispute.

Article 16

Should any Member of the League resort to war in disregard of its covenants under Articles 12, 13 or 15, it shall *ipso facto* be deemed to have committed an act of war against all other Members of the League, which hereby undertake immediately to subject it to the severance of all trade or financial relations, the prohibition of all intercourse between their nationals and the nationals of the covenant-breaking State, and the prevention of all financial, commercial or personal intercourse between the nationals of the covenant-breaking State and the nationals of any other State, whether a Member of the League or not.

It shall be the duty of the Council in such case to recommend to the several governments concerned what effective military, naval or air force the Members of the League shall severally contribute to the armed forces to be used to protect the covenants of the League.

The Members of the League agree, further, that they will mutually support one another in the financial and economic measures which are taken under this Article, in order to minimise the loss and inconvenience resulting from the above measures, and that they will mutually support one another in resisting any special measures aimed at one of their number by the covenant-breaking State, and that they will take the necessary steps to afford passage through their territory to the forces of any of the Members of the League which are co-operating to protect the covenants of the League.

Any Member of the League which has violated any covenant of the League may be declared to be no longer a Member of the League by a vote of the Council concurred in by the Representatives of all the other Members of the League represented thereon.

Article 17

In the event of a dispute between a Member of the League and a State which is not a Member of the League, or between States not Members of the League, the State or States not Members of the League shall be invited to accept the obligations of membership in the League for the purposes of such dispute, upon such conditions as the Council may deem just. If such invitation is accepted, the provisions of Articles 12 to 16 inclusive shall be applied with such modifications as may be deemed necessary by the Council.

Upon such invitation being given the Council shall immediately institute an inquiry into the circumstances of the dispute and recommend such action as may seem best and most effectual in the circumstances.

If a State so invited shall refuse to accept the obligations of membership in the League for the purposes of such dispute, and shall resort to war against a Member of the League, the provisions of Article 16 shall be applicable as against the State taking such action.

If both parties to the dispute when so invited refuse to accept the obligations of membership in the League for the purposes of such dispute, the Council may take such measures and make such recommendations as will prevent hostilities and will result in the settlement of the dispute.

Article 18

Every treaty or international engagement entered into hereafter by any Member of the League shall be forthwith registered with the Secretariat and shall as soon as possible be published by it. No such treaty or international engagement shall be binding until so registered.

Article 19

The Assembly may from time to time advise the reconsideration by Members of the League of treaties which have become inapplicable and the consideration of international conditions whose continuance might endanger the peace of the world.

Article 20

The Members of the League severally agree that this Covenant is accepted as abrogating all obligations or understandings *inter se* which are inconsistent with the terms thereof, and solemnly undertake that they will not hereafter enter into any engagements inconsistent with the terms thereof.

In case any Member of the League shall, before becoming a Member of the League, have undertaken any obligations inconsistent with the terms of this Covenant, it shall be the duty of such Member to take immediate steps to procure its release from such obligations.

Article 21

Nothing in this Covenant shall be deemed to affect the validity of international engagements, such as treaties of arbitration or regional understandings like the Monroe doctrine, for securing the maintenance of peace.

Article 22

To those colonies and territories which as a consequence of the late war have ceased to be under the sovereignty of the States which formerly governed them and which are inhabited by peoples not yet able to stand by themselves under the strenuous conditions of the modern world, there should be applied the principle that the well-being and development of such peoples form a sacred trust of civilisation and that securities for the performance of this trust should be embodied in this Covenant.

The best method of giving practical effect to this principle is that the tutelage of such peoples should be entrusted to advanced nations who by reason of their resources, their experience or their geographical position can best undertake this responsibility, and who are willing to accept it, and that this tutelage should be exercised by them as Mandatories on behalf of the League.

The character of the mandate must differ according to the stage of the development of the people, the geographical situation of the territory, its economic conditions and other similar circumstances.

Certain communities formerly belonging to the Turkish Empire have reached a stage of development where their existence as independent nations can be provisionally recognised subject to the rendering of administrative advice and assistance by a Mandatory until such time as they are able to stand alone. The wishes of these communities must be a principal consideration in the selection of the Mandatory.

Other peoples, especially those of Central Africa, are at such a stage that the Mandatory must be responsible for the administration of the territory under conditions which will guarantee freedom of conscience and religion, subject only to the maintenance of public order and morals, the prohibition of abuses such as the slave trade, the arms traffic and the liquor traffic, and the prevention of the establishment of fortifications or military and naval bases and of military training of the natives for other than police purposes and the defence of territory, and will also secure equal opportunities for the trade and commerce of other Members of the League.

There are territories, such as South-West Africa and certain of the South Pacific Islands, which, owing to the sparseness of their population, or their small size, or their remoteness from the centres of civilisation, or their geographical contiguity to the territory of the Mandatory, and other circumstances, can be best administered under the laws of the Mandatory as integral portions of its territory, subject to the safeguards above mentioned in the interests of the indigenous population.

In every case of mandate, the Mandatory shall render to the Council an annual report in reference to the territory committed to its charge.

The degree of authority, control or administration to be exercised by the Mandatory shall, if not previously agreed upon by the Members of the League, be explicitly defined in each case by the Council.

A permanent Commission shall be constituted to receive and examine the annual reports of the Mandatories and to advise the Council on all matters relating to the observance of the mandates.

Article 23

Subject to and in accordance with the provisions of international conventions existing or hereafter to be agreed upon, the Members of the League:

(a) will endeavour to secure and maintain fair and humane conditions of labour for men, women and children, both in their own countries and in all countries to which their commercial and industrial relations extend, and for that purpose will establish and maintain the necessary international organisations;
(b) undertake to secure just treatment of the native inhabitants of territories under their control;
(c) will entrust the League with the general supervision over the execution of agreements with regard to the traffic in women and children, and the traffic in opium and other dangerous drugs;
(d) will entrust the League with the general supervision of the trade in arms and ammunition with the countries in which the control of this traffic is necessary in the common interest;
(e) will make provision to secure and maintain freedom of communications and of transit and equitable treatment for the commerce of all Members of the League. In this connection, the special necessities of the regions devastated during the war of 1914–1918 shall be borne in mind;
(f) will endeavour to take steps in matters of international concern for the prevention and control of disease.

Article 24

There shall be placed under the direction of the League all international bureaux already established by general treaties if the parties to such treaties consent. All such international bureaux and all commissions for the regulation of matters of international interest hereafter constituted shall be placed under the direction of the League.

In all matters of international interest which are regulated by general convention but which are not placed under the control of international bureaux or commissions, the Secretariat of the League shall, subject to the consent of the Council and if desired by the parties, collect and distribute all relevant information and shall render any other assistance which may be necessary or desirable.

The Council may include as part of the expenses of the Secretariat the expenses of any bureau or commission which is placed under the direction of the League.

Article 25

The Members of the League agree to encourage and promote the establishment and co-operation of duly authorised voluntary national Red Cross organisations having as purposes the improvement of health, the prevention of disease and the mitigation of suffering throughout the world.

Article 26

Amendments to this Covenant will take effect when ratified by the Members of the League whose Representatives compose the Council and by a majority of the Members of the League whose Representatives compose the Assembly.

No such amendments shall bind any Member of the League which signifies its dissent therefrom, but in that case it shall cease to be a Member of the League.

The Council may include as part of the expenses of the Secretariat the expenses of any bureau or commission which is placed under the direction of the League.

Glossary of Names of Individuals Places and Newspapers

Japanese

Adachi, Mineichiro 安達峰一郎
Amō, Eiji 天羽英二
Anesaki, Masaharu 姉崎正治
Emperor Showa (Hirohito) 昭和天皇(裕仁)
Harada, Ken 原田健
Hirota, Koki 広田弘毅
Inukai, Ken 犬養健
Ishii, Kikujiro 石井 菊次郎
Itō Hirobumi 伊藤博文
Kamikawa, Hikomatsu 神川彦松
Kawakami, Tetsutaro 河上徹太郎
Komura, Kinichi 小村欣一
Kuriya, Ken 栗屋謙
Makino, Nobuaki 牧野伸顕
Mantetsu 満鉄
Matsubara, Kazuo 松原 一雄
Matsuda, Michikazu 松田 道一
Matsuoka, Yosuke 松岡洋右
Miyajima, Mikinosuke 宮島幹之助

C. R. Hughes and H. Shinohara (eds.), *East Asians in the League of Nations*, New Directions in East Asian History,
https://doi.org/10.1007/978-981-19-7067-2

Nagaoka, Harukazu (Shun'ichi) 長岡春一
Nitobe, Inazo 新渡戸稲造
Saitō, Makoto 斎藤実
Sakenobe, Nobumichi 鮭延信道
Satō, Naotake 佐藤尚武
Shidehara, Kijyuro 幣原喜重郎
Shigemitsu, Mamoru 重光葵
Shiratori, Toshio 白鳥敏夫
Sugimura, Yōtarō 杉村陽太郎
Tachi, Sakutaro 立作太郎
Tanaka Giichi 田中義一
Tanakadate, Aikitsu 田中舘愛橘
Uchida, Yasuya 内田康哉
Yamada, Saburo 山田三良
Yamakawa, Tadao 山川 端夫
Yokota, Kisaburo 横田 喜三郎
Yokoyama, Masayuki 横山正幸
Yoshizawa, Kenkichi 芳澤謙吉

Chinese

Changchun 長春
Chen, Eugene 陳友仁
Chiang Kai-shek (Jiang Jieshi) 蔣介石
Duan, Qirui 段祺瑞
Fang, Zhi 方稚
Fengtien 奉天
GMD (KMT/Guomindang) 國民黨
Guangdong 廣東
Guowen Zhoubao 國文週報
Hoo, Chi-tsai Victor 胡世澤
Hu, Tianshi 胡天石
Hu, Zushun 胡祖舜
Hukou 湖口
Jiangxi 江西
Jinzhou 錦州
Kong, H. H. 孔祥熙

Koo, Wellington 顧維鈞
King, Wunsz (Jin Wenshi) 金問泗
Li, Yuying (Li, Shizeng) 李煜瀛(李石曾)
Liu, Wendao 劉文島
Luo, Wengan 羅文幹
Mao, Zedong 毛澤東
Minguo Ribao 民國日報
Mukden (Fengtian) 奉天
Nanjing (Nanking) 南京
Peiping (Beijing) 北平/北京
Quo Tai-chi 郭泰祺
Shenyang 瀋陽
Shi, Liangcai 史量才
Shun-Pao (Shen bao) 申報
Soong, T. V. 宋子文
Sun, Fo (Sun Ke) 孫科
Sun Yat-sen (Sun Wen/ SunZhongshan) 孫逸仙 (孫文/孫中山)
Sze Sao-ke, Alfred 施肇基
Ta Kung Pao (Da gong bao) 大公報
Wang, C. T. 王正廷
Wang, Chonghui 王寵惠
Wang, Jingwei (Wang Zhaoming) 王精衛 (汪兆銘)
Weihaiwei 威海衛
Wu, Guozhen 吳國禎
Wu, Lien-teh 伍連德
Wu, Zhihui 吳稚暉
Xinjing 新京

Yan, Huiqing 顏惠慶
Yang, Jie 楊杰
Yen, W. W. 顏惠慶
Yi shi bao, Tientsin (Social Welfare, Tienjin) 益世報 天津
Zhang Qun 張群
Zhang, Xueliang 張學良
Zhang, Zuolin 張作霖
Zhongyang ribao 中央日報

Thai

King Vajiravudh (Rama VI) พระบาทสมเด็จพระมงกุฎเกล้าเจ้าอยู่หัว (รัชกาลที่ 6)
Luang Bhadravadi หลวงภัทรวาที
Phraya Apibarn Rajamaitri พระยาอภิบาลราชไมตรี
Phraya Srivisar Vacha พระยาศรีวิสารวาจา
Prince Chakrapong Phuvanart สมเด็จฯ เจ้าฟ้าจักรพงษ์ภูวนาถ กรมหลวงพิษณุโลกประชานาถ
Prince Charoonsak Kridakorn พระวรวงศ์เธอ พระองค์เจ้าจรูญศักดิ์กฤดากร
Prince Damras Damrong Devakula หม่อมเจ้าดำรัสดำรงค์ เทวกุล
Prince Devawongse สมเด็จฯ กรมพระยาเทวะวงศ์วโรปการ
Prince Pridi Debyabongs Devakula หม่อมเจ้าปรีดิเทพย์พงษ์ เทวกุล
Prince Traidos Prabandh หม่อมเจ้าไตรทศประพันธ์ เทวกุล (พระวรวงศ์เธอ กรมหมื่นเทววงศ์วโรทัย)

Bibliography

Archives

AH—Academia Historica Archives, Taipei

Blakeslee—Papers of George Blakeslee. Worcester, Massachusetts

CHCKS—*Jiang Zhongzheng xiansheng nianpu changbian* [Chronological History of Mr. Chiang Kai-shek]. Taipei: Academia Historica

CKSA—Chiang Kai-shek Archives. Vol. 18. Academia Historica, Taipei

CKSD—Chiang Kai-shek's Diaries. Hoover Archives, Stanford California

DAMOFAJ—Diplomatic Archives Ministry of Foreign Affairs Japan, Tokyo

FO—Foreign Office, National Archives, Kew

JACAR—Japan Center for Asian Historical Records, National Archives of Japan

JCAHR—Japan Center for Asian Historical Records

Koo Papers—Wellington Koo Papers, Butler Library, Columbia University, New York

KW—*Kuo Wen Weekly*

LON—League of Nations Archive, Geneva

Murray—Papers of Gilbert Murray. Bodleian Library, University of Oxford

NGA—Nationalist Government Archives (China). Academic Historica, Taipei

OAS—*Ōsaka Asahi Shinbun*

SLGB.—*Jiang Zhongzheng zongtong dang'an: Shilue gaoben* Vol. 13 [The Chiang Kai-shek collections: The Chronological Events] (33), September–October 1935

SP(S)—*Shun Pao*

C. R. Hughes and H. Shinohara (eds.), *East Asians in the League of Nations*, New Directions in East Asian History,
https://doi.org/10.1007/978-981-19-7067-2

SW(T)—*Social Welfare (Tientsin)* [Tianjin]
TCB—Treaties and Conventions Bureau of the Ministry of Foreign Affairs of Japan
TKP—*Ta Kung Pao*
TKP(T)—*Ta Kung Pao, Tientsin* [Tianjin]
TNA—Thai National Archives, Bangkok
TNA—The National Archives, Kew
UNESCO—UNESCO Archives, Paris
WHOA—World Health Organisation Archives, Geneva
ZYRB—*Zhongyang ribao* [*Central Daily News*]

Official Documents

FRUS—*Foreign Relations of the United States*
LND—*League of Nations Documents, 1919–1946* (*microform*). New Haven: Research Publication
MOFAJ—Ministry of Foreign Affairs of Japan
NGB—*Nihon Gaiko Bunsho* [Diplomatic documents of Japanese Foreign Ministry]
NGB-MJ—Nihon Gaikō Bunsho, Manshū Jihen [Manchurian Incident] dai 3 kan [Volume 3]
OJ—*League of Nations Official Journal*

Works in English and French

Accinelli, Robert D. 1980. Militant Internationalists: The League of Nations Association, the Peace Movement, and US Foreign Policy, 1934–38. *Diplomatic History* (4/1): 19–38.

Acharya, Amitav. 2014. Global International Relations (IR) and Regional Worlds. *International Studies Quarterly* (58): 647–659.

Akami, Tomoko. 1995. The Liberal Dilemma: Internationalism and the Institute of Pacific Relations in the USA, Australia, and Japan, 1919–1942. Ph.D. diss. ANU.

Akami, Tomoko. 2002. *Internationalizing the Pacific: The United States, Japan and the Institute of Pacific Relations in War and Peace, 1919–1945*. London: Routledge.

Akami, Tomoko. 2012. *Japan's News Propaganda and Reuters' News Empire in Northeast Asia, 1870–1934*. Dordrecht: Republic of Letters.

Akami, Tomoko. 2014a. Beyond Empires' Science: Inter-imperial Pacific Science Networks in the 1920s. In *Networking the International System*, ed. Madeleine Herren, 107–132. New York: Springer.

Akami, Tomoko. 2014b. *Soft Power of Japan's Total War State: The Board of Information and Dōmei News Agency in Foreign Policy, 1934–1945*. Dordrecht: Republic of Letters.

Akami, Tomoko. 2016. A Quest to Be Global: The League of Nations Health Organization and Inter-Colonial Regional Governing Agendas of the Far Eastern Association of Tropical Medicine 1910–25. *International History Review* (38/1): 1–23.

Akami, Tomoko. 2017. Imperial Polities and Inter-colonialism in Shaping Global Governing Norms: Public Health Expert Networks in Asia and the League of Nations Health Organization, 1908–1937. *The Journal of Global History* (12/1): 4–25.

Akami, Tomoko. 2018. The Limits of Peace Propaganda: The Information Section of the League of Nations and Its Tokyo office. In *Exorbitant Expectations: Communicating International Organizations in the 19th and 20th Centuries*, ed. Jonas Brendebach, Martin Herzer, and Heidi Tworek, 70–90. London: Routledge.

Akami, Tomoko. 2021. Understanding Trans-Pacific Interactions: The Liberal Inter-Imperial Order in the "Pacific" Region, 1920–1960. In *International Society in the Early Twentieth Century Asia-Pacific: Imperial Rivalries, International Organizations, and Experts*, ed. Hiroo Nakajima, 5–14. London: Routledge.

Akashi, Kinji. 2013. Sakutaro Tachi: A Blend of Scholarship and Practitionership, and Its Fate in Japan. *Japanese Yearbook of International Law* (56): 122–143.

Amrith, Sunil S. 2006. *Decolonizing International Health: India and Southeast Asia, 1930–65*. New York: Palgrave Macmillan.

Amrith, S., and G. Sluga. 2008. New Histories of the United Nations. *Journal of World History* (19/3): 251–274.

Anghie, Antony. 2005. *Imperialism, Sovereignty and the Making of International Law*. Cambridge: Cambridge University Press.

Asada, Sadao. 2007. *Culture Shock and Japanese-American Relations: Historical Essays*. The University of Missouri.

Ashworth, Lucian M. 2002. Did the Realist-Idealist Great Debate Really Happen? A Revisionist History of International Relations. *International Relations* (16/1): 33–51.

Baker, P.J. 1924. The Codification of International Law. *British Yearbook of International Law* 5: 38–65.

Baer, George W. 1976. *The Coming of the Italian-Ethiopian War*. Stanford, CA: Hoover Institution Press.

Bassett, R. 1968. *Democracy and Foreign Policy: A Case History: The Sino-Japanese Dispute, 1931–33*. London: Cass.

Batsan, Benjamin A. 1984. *The End of the Absolute Monarchy in Siam*. Melbourne: Oxford University Press.

Belińska, M.A. 1998. *For the Good of Humanity: Ludwig Rajchman Medical Statesman*. Budapest: Central European University Press.
Berdahl, Clarence A. 1937. The Implications of the Kellogg Pact Concerning American Foreign Policy. *New York University Law Quarterly Review* 15: 82–107.
Birebent, Christian. 2007. *Militants de la Paix et la SDN: Les mouvements de soutien à la Société des Nations en France et au Royaume-Uni, 1918–1925*. Paris: l'Harmattan.
Birn, Donald S. 1981. *The League of Nations Union, 1918–1945*. Oxford: Claredon Press.
Borchard, Edwin O. 1924. The Distinction Between Legal and Political Questions. *Proceedings of the American Society of International Law*: 50–57.
Borowy, Iris. 2009. *Coming to Terms with World Health: The League of Nations Health Organisation 1921–1946*. Frankfurt, Berlin, Bruxelles, New York, and Oxford: Peter Lang.
Brierly, J.L. 1931. The Future of Codification. *British Yearbook of International Law* (12): 1–12.
Brückenhaus, Daniel. 2020. Challenging Imperialism Across Borders: Recent Studies of Twentieth-Century Internationalist Networks Against Empire. *Contemporary European History* (29/1): 104–115.
Burkman, Thomas. 2008. *Japan and the League of Nations: Empire and World Orders*. Hawaii: University of Hawaii Press.
Calichman, Richard F. 2008. *Overcoming Modernity: Cultural Identity in Wartime Japan*. New York: Columbia University Press.
Callahan, Michael D. 2004. *A Sacred Trust: The League of Nations and Africa, 1929–1946*. Brighton: Sussex Academic Press.
Carr, E.H. 1981. *The Twenty Years Crisis 1919–1939: An Introduction to the Study of International Relations*. Basingstoke: Macmillan Press.
Chen, Jerome. 1979. *The Military-Gentry Coalition: China Under the Warlords*. Toronto: University of Toronto.
Chimni, B.S. 2016. International Organizations, 1945–Present. In *The Oxford Handbook of International Organizations*, ed. Jacob Katz Cogan, Ian Hurd, and Jan Johnstone, 113–130. Oxford: Oxford University Press.
Chu, Pao-chin. 1981. *V.K. Wellington Koo: A Case Study of China's Diplomat and Diplomacy of Nationalism, 1912–1966*. Hong Kong: Chinese University Press.
Claude, Inis. 1966. Collective Legitimization as a Political Function of the United Nations. *International Organization* (20): 367–379.
Clavin, Patricia. 2010. Introduction: Conceptualizing internationalism Between the World Wars. In *Internationalism Reconfigured: Transnational Ideals and Movements Between the World Wars*, ed. Daniel Laqua. London: Bloomsbury Publishing.

Clavin, Patricia. 2013. *Securing the World Economy: The Reinvention of the League of Nations, 1920–1946*. Oxford: Oxford University Press.

Clavin, Patricia, and Jens-Wihelm Wessels. 2005. Transnationalism and the League of Nations: Understanding the Work of Its Economic and Financial Organizations. *Contemporary European History* (14/1): 465–492.

Committee on Intellectual Co-operation. 1924. *Minutes of the Third Session*. League of Nations.

Craft, Stephen G. 2004. *V.K. Wellington Koo and the Emergence of Modern China*. Lexington: The University Press of Kentucky.

Crozier, Andrew. 1998. *Appeasement and Germany's Last Bid for Colonies*. London: Macmillan.

Davidann, Jon. 1998. *A World of Crisis and Progress: The American YMCA in Japan, 1890–1930*. Bethlehem, PA: Lehigh University Press.

Dickinson, Frederick R. 2013. *World War I and the Triumph of a New Japan, 1919–1930*. Cambridge: Cambridge University Press.

Dickinson, Frederick R. 2014. AHR Forum: Toward a Global Perspective of the Great War: Japan and the Foundations of a Twentieth-Century World. *American Historical Review* (119/4): 1154–183.

Dickinson, Frederick R. 2018. More Than a 'Moment': 'Woodrow Wilson and the Foundations of Twentieth-Century Japan.' *Japanese Journal of Political Science* (18): 587–599.

Dykmann, Klaas. 2015. How International Was the Secretariat of the League of Nations? *The International History Review* 37: 721–744.

Eagleton, Clyde. 1933. The Attempt to Define War. *International Conciliation* 15: 237–287.

Eloranda, Jari. 2011. Why Did the League of Nations Fail? *Cliometrica* 5: 27–52.

European Commission. European Health Union: Protecting the Health of Europeans and Collectively Responding to Cross-Border Health Crises. https://ec.europa.eu/info/strategy/priorities-2019-2024/promoting-our-european-way-life/european-health-union_en. Accessed 30 June 2022.

Evans, Luther. 1932. The General Principles Governing the Termination of a Mandate. *The American Journal of International Law* (26): 735–758.

Fidler, David P. 2005. From International Sanitary Conventions to Global Health Security: The New International Health Regulations. *Chinese Journal of International Law* (4/2): 325–392.

Fink, Carole. 2004. *Defending the Rights of Others: The Great Powers, the Jews and International Minority Protection, 1878–1938*. Cambridge: Cambridge University Press.

Fiti Sinclair, Guy. 2017. *To Reform the World. International Organizations and the Making of the Modern States*. Oxford: Oxford University Press.

Fitzmaurice, Andre. 2012. Liberalism and Empire in Nineteenth Century International Law. *The American Historical Review* (117/1): 122–140.

Forclaz, Amalia Ribi. 2015. *Humanitarian Imperialism: The Politics of Anti-Slavery Activism, 1880–1940*. Oxford: Oxford University Press.

Franck, Thomas. 1988. Legitimacy in the International System. *American Journal of International Law* (82/4): 705–759;

García, Magaly R., David Rodogno, and Liat Kozma, eds. 2016. *The League of Nations' Work on Social Issues: Visions, Endeavours and Experiments*. Geneva: United Nations.

Getachew, Adom. 2019. *Worldmaking After Empire: The Rise and Fall of Self-Determination*. Princeton: Princeton University Press.

Goto-Shibata, Harumi. 1995. *Japan and Britain in Shanghai, 1925–31*. Basingstoke: Macmillan.

Goto-Shibata, Harumi. 2020. *The League of Nations and the East Asian Imperial Order, 1920–1946*. Singapore: Palgrave Macmillan.

Gram-Skjoldager, Karen, and Haakon A. Ikonomou. 2017. The Construction of the League of Nations Secretariat. Formative Practices of Autonomy and Legitimacy in International Organizations. *The International History Review* (41/2): 257–227

Gordon, Andrew. 1991. *Labor and Imperial Democracy in Prewar Japan*. Berkeley: University of California Press.

Greene, Stephen Lyon Wakeman. 1999. *Absolute Dreams: Thai Government Under Rama VI, 1910–1925*. Bangkok: White Lotus Co. Ltd.

Guieu, Jean-Michel. 2008. *Le rameau et le glaive: Les militants français pour la Société des Nations*. Paris: Presses de Sciences Po.

Guilhot, Nicolas. 2011. Introduction. In *The Invention of International Relations Theory: Realism, the Rockefeller Foundation, and the 1954 Conference on Theory*, ed. N. Guilhot, 1–32. New York: Columbian University Press.

Haacke, Jürgen. 2019. The Concept of Hedging and Its Application to Southeast Asia. *International Relations of the Asia Pacific* (19/3): 375–417. https://doi.org/10.1093/irap/lcz010.

Harootunian, Harry. 2001. *Overcome by Modernity: History, Culture and Community in Interwar Japan*. Princeton: Princeton University Press.

Henig, Ruth. 2010. *The League of Nations*. London: Haus Histories.

Hale, Richard W. 1930. Territorial Waters as a Test of Codification. *American Journal of International Law* (24/1): 65–68.

Hanzawa, Asahiko, ed. 2007. *Japan and the UN in International Politics: Historical Perspective*. Sapporo: Hokkaidō University Graduate School.

Hathaway, Oona, and Scott Shapiro. 2017. *The Internationalists: How a Radical Plan to Outlaw War Remade the World*. New York: Simon & Schuster.

Hau'ofa, Epeli. 1998. The Ocean in Us. *The Contemporary Pacific* (10/2): 392–410.

Hell, Stefan. 2010. *Siam and the League of Nations: Modernisation, Sovereignty and Multilateral Diplomacy, 1920–1940*. Bangkok: River Books Co., Ltd.

Hendrickson, David. 2020. How Many Cheers for the Peace Pact? *American Political Thought* (9): 144–169.

Henri, Rolin. 1970. Louis de Brouckère et l'action pour la paix. *Bulletin de la Classe des lettres et des sciences morales et politiques* (56): 578–590.

Herren, Madeleine. 2016a. Fascist Internationalism. In *Internationalism. A Twentieth Century History*, ed. Glenda Sluga and Patricia Clavin, 191–212. Cambridge: Cambridge University Press. https://doi.org/10.1017/9781107477568.010.

Herren, Madeleine. 2016b. International Organizations, 1865–1945. In *The Oxford Handbook of International Organizations*, ed. Katz Cogan, Hurd Jacob, Ian, and Jan Johnstone, 91–112. Oxford: Oxford University Press.

Hobson, John. 2012. *The Eurocentric Conception of World Politics: Western International Theory, 1760–2010*. Cambridge: Cambridge University Press.

Hoffmann, Stefan-Ludwig. 2011. Introduction. In *Human Rights in the Twentieth Century*, ed. S.-L. Hoffmann. Cambridge: Cambridge University Press.

Hopf, Ted. 1988. The Promise of Constructivism in International Relations Theory. *International Security* (23/1): 171–200.

Hudson, Manley O. 1925. Amendment of the Covenant of the League of Nations. *The Harvard Law Review Association* (38/7): 903–953.

Hudson, Manley O. 1933. The Admission of Iraq to Membership in the League of Nations. *The American Journal of International Law* (27/1): 133–138.

Huntington, Samuel P. 2003. *The Clash of Civilizations and the Remaking of World Order*. New York and London: Simon & Schuster.

International Law Association. 1927. Report of the Codification Committee. *Report of the Thirty-Fourth Conference Held at the Imperial Palace and at the Chamber of Commerce, Vienna*. London: Sweet & Maxwell, Ltd.

Iriye, Akira. 1965. *After Imperialism: The Search for a New Order in the Far East, 1921–1931*. Cambridge, MA: Harvard University Press.

Iriye, Akira. 1997. *Cultural Internationalism and World Order*. Baltimore and London: Johns Hopkins University Press.

Iriye, Akira. 2004. *Global Community: The Role of International Organizations*. Berkeley: University of California.

Jackson, Robert H. 1993. *Quasi-States: Sovereignty, International Relations and the Third World*. Cambridge: Cambridge University Press.

Jackson, Simon, and Alanna O'Malley. 2018. Rocking on Its hinges? The League of Nations, the United Nations and the New History of internationalism in the Twentieth Century. In *The Institution of International Order: From the League of Nations to the United Nations*, ed. S. Jackson and A. O'Malley, 1–21. London: Routledge.

Jennings, Robert, and Arthur Watts. 1992. *Oppenheim's International Law*, vol. 1, 9th ed. Burnt Mill: Longman.

Jerónimo, Miguel Bandeira. 2018. A League of Empires: Imperial Political Imagination and Interwar Internationalisms. In *Internationalism, Imperialism and the Formation of the Contemporary World: The Past and the Present*, ed. M.B. Jerónimo and José Pedro Monteiro, 87–126. Cham: Palgrave Macmillan.

Jerónimo, Miguel Bandeiro, and José Pedro Monteiro. 2018. Internationalism and Empire: The Question of "Native Labour" in the Portuguese Empire, 1919–1961. In *The Institution of International Order: From the League of Nations to the United Nations*, ed. Jackson and O'Malley, 206–233. London: Routledge.

Jolly, Margaret. 2008. The South in Southern theory: Antipodean Reflections on the Pacific. *Australian Humanities Review* 44: 1–20 (downloaded version).

Kaiga, Sakiko. 2021. *Britain and Intellectual Origins of the League of Nations, 1914–1919*. Cambridge: Cambridge University Press.

Kawakami, K.K. 1928. Manchuria: The Crux of Chino-Japanese Relations. *Foreign Affairs* (6/3): 379–394.

Kennedy, David. 1996. International Law and the Nineteenth Century: History of an Illusion. *Nordic Journal of International Law* (65/3–4): 385–420.

King, Wunsz. 1965. *China and the League of Nations: The Sino-Japanese Controversy*. New York: St. John's University Press.

Koo, Wellington. 1937. The Problem of the Pacific and Collective Security. An address by Dr. V.K. Wellington Koo, Chinese ambassador at Paris, at a Meeting of the Academy of Diplomacy, 17 December. In *Japanese Aggression and the League of Nations*, 1938, Vol. 3. Geneva: Press Bureau of the Chinese Delegation, 1937–1940.

Koskenniemi, Martti. 2001. *The Gentle Civilizer of Nations: The Rise and Fall of International law 1870–1960*. Cambridge: Cambridge University Press.

Kott, Sandrine, and Joëlle. Droux, eds. 2013. *Globalizing Social Rights: The International Labour Organization and Beyond*. New York: Palgrave Macmillan.

Krasner, Stephen D. 1999. *Sovereignty: Organized Hypocrisy*. Princeton, NJ: Princeton University Press.

Laqua, Daniel. 2011. Transnational Intellectual Co-operation, the League of Nations, and the Problem of Order. *Journal of Global History* (6/2): 223–247.

League of Nations. 1932. *Appeal by the Chinese Government: Report of the Commission of Enquiry* (signed by the members of the Commission on September 4th, 1932, at Peiping [Beijing]). LON 676809.

League of Nations, 1939. *The Development of International Co-operation in Economic and Social Affairs, Report of the Special Committee* (Geneva: Official No. A.23.1939).

League of Nations. Traffic in Women and Children: Work of the Bandung Conference [of Central Authorities in Eastern Countries]. Geneva: 20 December 1937, C.516.M.357.1937.IV.

League of Nations Advisory Committee of Jurists. 1920. *Procès-verbaux of the Proceedings of the Committee, June 16th–July 24th, 1920: With Annexes.* The Hague: Van Langenhuysen Brothers.

Lebow, Richard Ned. 2008. *A Cultural Theory of International Relations.* Cambridge: Cambridge University Press.

Leng, Shao Chuan, and Norman D. Palmer. 1961. *Sun Yat-sen and Communism.* London: Thames and Hudson.

Lenz, Tobias, and Lora Anne Viola. 2017. Legitimacy and Institutional Change in International Organizations: A Cognitive Approach. *Review of International Studies* 43: 939–961.

Lewis, William Roger. 1977. *Imperialism at Bay: The United States and the Decolonization of the British Empire, 1941–1945.* New York: Oxford University Press.

Liang, Pan. 2017. National Internationalism in Japan and China. In *Internationalisms: A Twentieth-Century History*, ed. Glenda Sluga and Patricia Clavin, 170–177. Cambridge: Cambridge University Press.

Limmoncelli, Stephanie A. 2010. *The Politics of Trafficking: The First International Movement to Combat the Sexual Exploitation of Women.* Stanford: Stanford University Press.

Ling, L.C., K.B. Liu, and Y.T. Yao. 1936. Studies on the So-called *Changch'i*, Part II. *Changch'i* in Yunnan. *Chinese Medical Journal* (50/12): 1815–1828.

Lippmann, Walter. 1922. *Public Opinion.* New York: Harcourt, Brace & Co.

Lippmann, Walter. 1925. *The Phantom Public.* Piscataway, NJ: Transaction Publishers.

Lipscy, Phillip Y. 2017. *Renegotiating the World Order: Institutional Change in International Relations.* Cambridge: Cambridge University Press.

Long, David, and Peter Wilson, eds. 1995. *Thinkers of the Twenty Years' Crisis: Inter-war Reassessed.* Oxford: Clarendon Press.

Lowe, Kimberly. 2017. Reassessing the League of Nations' Humanitarian Assistance Regimes, 1918–1939. In *Decades of Reconstruction: Postwar Societies, State-Building, and International Relations from the Seven Years' War to the Cold War*, ed. Ute Planert and Retallack James, 293–314. Cambridge: Cambridge University Press.

Lytton. 1932. *Report of the Commission of Enquiry* (The Lytton Report). Geneva: The League of Nations. Online version: https://en.wikisource.org/wiki/Report_of_the_Commission_of_Enquiry/Chapter_1. Accessed 31 July 2022.

MacCarthy, Helen. 2011. *The British People and the League of Nations: Democracy, Citizenship and Internationalism, c.1918–45.* Manchester: Manchester University Press.

Macfie, A.L. 1998. *The End of the Ottoman Empire 1908–1923.* London: Longman.

MacMillan, Margaret. 2013a. *The Rhyme of History: Lessons of the Great War*. The Brookings Institution. http://csweb.brookings.edu/content/research/essays/2013/rhyme-of-history.html. Accessed 20 June 2022.

MacMillan, Margaret. 2013b. *The War that Ended Peace*. London: Profile Books.

Mahoney, Joseph O. 2014. Rule Tensions and the Dynamics of Institutional Change: From 'to the Victor Go the Spoils' to the Stimson Doctrine. *European Journal of International Relations* 20: 834–857.

Manderson, Lenore. 1995. Wireless Wars in the Eastern Arena: Epidemiological Surveillance, Disease Prevention and the Work of the Eastern Bureau of the League of Nations Health Organisation, 1925–1942. In *International Health Organisations and Movements 1918–1939*, ed. Paul Weindling, 109–133. Cambridge: Cambridge University Press.

Manela, Erez. 2007. *The Wilsonian Moment: Self Determination and the International Origins of Anticolonial Nationalism*. New York: Oxford University Press.

Mao, Zedong. 1919a. Manifesto of the Founding of the Xiang River Review. In *Mao's Road to Power: Revolutionary Writings 1912–1949*, vol. 1, ed. Stuart Schram, 318–320.

Mao, Zedong. 1919b. The Waves of Strikes in Various Countries. In *Mao's Road to Power: Revolutionary Writings 1912–1949*, vol. 1, ed. Stuart Schram, 321–324.

Mao Zedong. 1919c. Poor Wilson. In *Mao's Road to Power: Revolutionary Writings 1912–1949*, vol. 1, ed. Stuart Schram, 338.

Mao, Zedong. 1919d. For the Germans, the Painful Signing of the Treaty. In *Mao's Road to Power: Revolutionary Writings 1912–1949*, vol. 1, ed. Stuart Schram, 357–366.

Mao, Zedong. 1919e. Joy and Suffering. In *Mao's Road to Power: Revolutionary Writings 1912–1949*, vol. 1, ed. Stuart Schram, 367.

Mao, Zedong. 1925a. Analysis of the Classes in Chinese Society. In *Mao's Road to Power: Revolutionary Writings 1912–1949*, vol. 2, ed. Stuart Schram, 249–262.

Mao, Zedong. 1925b. Propaganda Guidelines of the Chinese Guomindang in the War Against the Fengtian Clique. In *Mao's Road to Power: Revolutionary Writings 1912–1949*, ed. Stuart Schram, 239–246.

March, James G., and James Olsen. 1989. *Rediscovering Institutions: The Organizational Basis of Politics*. New York: Free Press.

March, James G., and James Olsen. 1998. The Institutional Dynamics of International Political Orders. *International Organization* (52): 943–969.

Mason, John Brown. 1946. *The Danzig Dilemma: A Study in Peacemaking by Compromise*. Stanford: Stanford University Press.

Matsuda, Matt. 2012. *Pacific Worlds: A History of Seas, Peoples, and Cultures*. Cambridge: Cambridge University Press.

Matsushita, Masatoshi. 1929. *Japan in the League of Nations*. New York: Columbia University Press.

Mazower, Mark. 2012. *Governing the World: The History of an Idea*. New York: Allen Lane.

Mazower, Mark. 2009. *No Enchanted Peace: The End of Empires and the Ideological Origins of the United Nations*. Princeton, NJ: Princeton University Press.

McCarthy, Helen. 2009. Leading from the Center: The League of Nations Union, Foreign Policy and 'Political Agreement' in the 1930s. *Contemporary British History* 23 (4): 527–542.

Meijknecht, Anna. 2012. The Minority Protection System Between World War I and World War II. In *The Max Planck Encyclopedia of Public International Law*, vol. VII, ed. Rudiger Wolfrum, 275–276. Oxford: Oxford University Press.

Mitrany, David. 1975. *The Functional Theory of International Relations*. New York: St Martin's Press.

Mitzen, Jennifer. 2006. Ontological Security in World Politics: State Identity and the Security Dilemma. *European Journal of International Relations* (12/3): 341–370.

Mogami, Toshiki. 2018. Perpetuum Mobile. Before and After Global Constitutionalism. In *Global Constitutionalism from European and East Asian Perspectives*, ed. Takao Suami, Anne Peters, Dimitri Vanoverbeke, and Mattias Kumm, 29–57. Cambridge: Cambridge University Press.

Mogami, Toshiki. 2019. Japan. In *The Oxford Handbook of International Law in Asia and the Pacific*, ed. Simon Chesterman, Hisashi Owada, and Ben Saul, 320–340. Oxford: Oxford University Press.

Mori, Shigeki. 2006. The "Washington system" and Its Aftermath: Reevaluating *After Imperialism* from the Perspective of the Japanese Historiography. *International Journal of Asian Studies* (3/2): 255–268.

Moyn, Samuel P. 2010. *The Last Utopia: Human Rights in History*. Cambridge MA: Harvard University Press.

Müller, Thomas. 2020. Institutional Reforms and the Politics of Inequality Reproduction: The Case of the League of Nations' Council Crisis in 1926. *Global Society* 34: 304–317.

Murray, Gilbert. 1933. Memorandum on an International Police Force. 20 January. MSS.

Murray, Gilbert. 1948. A League of Nations: The First Experiment (1939). *From the League to U.N.*, 65–83. London: Oxford University Press.

Nish, Ian. 1993. *Japan's Struggle with Internationalism: Japan, China and the League of Nations, 1931–1933*. London and New York: Kegan Paul International.

Noelle-Neumann, Elisabeth. 1995a. *The Spiral of Silence: Public Opinion, Our Social Skin*. Chicago: University of Chicago Press.

Noelle-Neumann, Elisabeth. 1995b. Public Opinion and Rationality. In *Public Opinion and the Communication of Consent*, ed. Theodore L. Glasser and Charles T. Salmon, 33–54. New York: Guilford Press.

Oblas, Peter B. 1971. A Very Small Part of World Affairs' Siam's Policy on Treaty Revision and the Paris Peace Conference. *Journal of the Siam Society* (59/2): 52–74.

Oblas, Peter B. 1972. Treaty Revision and the Role of the American Foreign Affairs Adviser 1909–1925. *Journal of the Siam Society* (60/1): 171–186.

Ogata, Sadako. 1964. *Defiance in Manchuria*. Berkeley: University of California Press.

Ōnuma, Yasuaki. 1986. 'Japanese International Law' in the Prewar Period: Perspectives on the Teaching and Research of International Law in Prewar Japan. *Japanese Annual of International Law* (29): 23–47.

Osterhammel, Jürgen. 1979. "Technical Co-operation" Between the League of Nations and China. *Modern Asian Studies* (13): 661–680.

Paisley, Fiona. 2009. *Glamour in the Pacific: Cultural Internationalism and Race Politics in the Women's Pan Pacific*. Honolulu: University of Hawai'i Press.

Patterson, David S. 1976. The United States and the Origins of the World Court. *Political Science Quarterly* (91/2): 279–295.

Pedersen, Susan. 2007. Back to the League of Nations: Review Essay. *American Historical Review* (112/4): 1091–1117.

Pedersen, Susan. 2015. *The Guardians. The League of Nations and the Crisis of Empire*. Oxford: Oxford University Press.

Petchlertanan, Thamrongsak. 2012a. *1932 Revolution in Siam and Constitutions* (in Thai). Bangkok: The Foundation for the Promotion of Social Science and Humanities Textbooks Projects.

Peters, John Durham. 1995. Historical Tensions in the Concept of Public Opinion. In *Public Opinion and the Communication of Consent*, ed. Theodore L. Glasser and Charles T. Salmon, 3–32. New York: Guilford Press.

Pitts, Jennifer. 2012. Empire and Legal Universalism in the Eighteenth Century. *The American Historical Review* (117/1): 92–121.

Raitz von Frentz, Christian. 1999. *A Lesson Forgotten: Minority Protection Under the League of Nations: The Case of the German Minority in Poland*. New York: St. Martin's Press.

Ranshofen-Wertheimer, Egon F. 1945. *International Secretariat: A Great Experiment in International Administration*. Washington, DC: Carnegie Endowment for International Peace.

Reeves, Jesse S. 1921. International Society and International Law. *American Journal of International Law* (15/3): 361–374.

Reinalda, Bob. 2009. *Routledge History of International Organizations: From 1815 to the Present Day*. London: Routledge.

Root, Elihu. 1925. The Codification of International Law. *American Journal of International Law* (19/4): 675–684.

Rosenne, Shabtai. 1972. Introduction. In *League of Nations Committee of Experts for the Progressive Codification of International Law (1925–1928)*, vol. 1, ed. Rosenne, xxix–cxxiv. New York: Oceana Publications, Inc.

Rosenne, Shabtai. 1992. Codification of International Law. In *Encyclopedia of Public International Law*, vol. 1, ed. Rudolf Bernhardt, 632–640. Amsterdam: North-Holland Pub. Co.

Saikawa, Takashi. 2014. From Intellectual Co-operation to International Cultural Exchange: Japan and China in the International Committee on Intellectual Co-operation of the League of Nations, 1922–1939. Ph.D. diss. The University of Heidelberg.

Schmidt, Brian, ed. 2012. *International Relations and the First Great Debate*. New York: Routledge.

Scott, James Brown. 1931. The Progress of International Law During the Last Twenty-Five Years. *Proceedings of the American Society of International Law* 25: 2–34.

Sealey, Anne. 2011. Globalizing the 1926 International Sanitary Convention. *Journal of Global History* (6/3): 431–455. https://doi.org/10.1017/S1740022811000404.

Secretariat of the League of Nations. 1930. *Ten Years of World Co-operation*. London: Hazel, Watson and Viney.

Sellars, Kirste. 2015. *'Crimes Against Peace' and International Law*. Cambridge: Cambridge University Press.

Semmel, Bernard. 1960. *Imperialism and Social Reform*. Cambridge: Harvard University Press.

Shinohara, Hatsue. 2012. *US International Lawyers in the Interwar Years: A Forgotten Crusade*. Cambridge: Cambridge University Press.

Shotwell, James. 1944. Preface in Kandel, I.L. *Intellectual Co-operation: National and International*. New York: Columbia University Bureau of Publications.

Skinner, Rob, and Alan Lester. 2012. Humanitarianism and Empire: New Research Agendas. *The Journal of Imperial and Commonwealth History* (40/5): 729–747.

Sluga, Glenda. 2015. *Internationalism in the Age of Nationalism*. Philadelphia: University of Pennsylvania Press.

Sluga, Glenda, and Patricia Clavin, eds. 2017. *Internationalisms: A Twentieth-Century History*. Cambridge: Cambridge University Press.

Society for Socialist Inquiry and Propaganda (Manchester Branch). 1932. *The Manchurian Dispute: A Survey of Press Reports*. Held in British Library of Economic and Political Science.

Spencer, John H. 1937. The Italian-Ethiopian Dispute and the League of Nations. *American Journal of International Law* (31/4): 614–641.

Spinney, Laura. 2017. *Pale Rider: The Spanish Flu of 1918 and How It Changed the World*. London: Vintage.

Sze, Sao-Ke Alfred. 1962. *Sao-Ke Alfred Sze: Reminiscences of His Early Years*. Washington, DC: no publisher name.

Teow, Heng. 1999. *Japanese Cultural Policy toward China: A Comparative Perspective*. Cambridge, MA: Harvard University Press.

Thompson, Shamala Kandiah, Karin Landgren, and Paul Romita. 1922. The United Nations in Hindsight: Challenging the Power of the Security Council Veto. Just Security, 28 April. https://www.justsecurity.org/81294/the-united-nations-in-hindsight-challenging-the-power-of-the-security-council-veto/. Accessed 22 June 2022.

Thorne, Christopher. 1972. *The Limits of Foreign Policy: The West, the League and the Far Eastern Crisis of 1931–1933*. London: Hamish Hamilton.

Tohmatsu, Haruo. 2015. Iraq and Manchukuo: State-Building in the Interwar Period. In *History in British History: Proceedings of the Seventh Anglo-Japanese Conference of Historians, Held at Trinity Hall, University of Cambridge, 11–14 September 2012*, ed. Kondo Kazuhiko, 225–247. Tokyo: [s.n].

Tohmatsu, Haruo. 2016. From the Manchurian Incident to Japan's Withdrawal from the League. In *Fifteen lectures on Showa Japan: Road to the Pacific War in Recent Historiography*, ed. Yasutaka Tsutsui and trans. Makoto Noda and Paul Narum, 83–103. Tokyo: Japan Publication Industry Foundation.

van Dijk, Boyd. 2019. "The Great Humanitarian": The Soviet Union, the International Committee of the Red Cross and the Geneva Conventions of 1949. *Law and History Review* (37/1): 209–235.

Vella, Walter F. 1978. *Chiyo! King Vajiravudh and the Development of Thai Nationalism*. Honolulu: The University Press of Hawaii.

Vitalis, Robert. 2015. *White World Order, Black Power Politics: The Birth of American International Relations*. Ithaca: Cornell University Press.

Walters, F.P. 1952. *A History of the League of Nations*. London: Oxford University Press. (1986, Reprint version, Connecticut, MA: Greenwood Press.)

Watenpaugh, Keith David. 2010. The League of Nations' Rescue of Armenian Genocide Survivors and the Making of Modern Humanitarianism, 1920–1927. *The American Historical Review* (115/5): 1315–1339.

Watson, Adam. 1992. *The Evolution of International Society: A Comparative Historical Analysis*. New York: Routledge.

Wertheim, Stephen. 2011. The League That Wasn't: American Designs for a Legalist-Sanctionist League of Nations and the Intellectual Origins of International Organization, 1914–1920. *Diplomatic History* (35/5): 797–836.

Wheaton, Henry. 1846. *Elements of International Law*, 3rd ed. Philadelphia: Lea and Blanchard.

Whiting, Allen S. 1951. The Soviet Offer to China of 1919. *The Far Eastern Quarterly* (10/4): 355–364. https://doi.org/10.2307/2049007.

WHO. 1952. International Sanitary Regulations: Proceedings of the Special Committee and of the 4th World Health Assembly on WHO Regulations No. 2. Geneva: 1–2.

WHO. 2005. US Proposal for Amendments to the International Health Regulations. https://healthpolicy-watch.news/wp-content/uploads/2022/02/C.L.2.2022-IHR-amendments-English.pdf. Accessed 11 June 2022.

Wigen, Kären. 2007. Introduction. In *Seascapes: Maritime Histories, Littoral Cultures, and Transoceanic Exchanges*, ed. Jerry H. Bentley, Renate Bridenthal, and Kären Wigen. Honolulu: University of Hawai'i Press.

Wilde, Ralph. 2008. *International Territorial Administration: How Trusteeship and Civilizing Mission Never Went Away*. Oxford: Oxford University Press.

Williams, John F. 1924. The Geneva Protocol of 1924 for the Pacific Settlement of International Disputes. *Journal of the British Institute of International Affairs* (3/6): 288–304.

Willoughby, Westel W. 1935. *The Sino-Japanese Controversy and the League of Nations*. New York: Greenwood Press.

Wilson, Peter. 1998. The Myth of the "First Great Debate". *Review of International Studies* (24/5): 1–16

Wu, Lien-teh. 2004. *Plague Fighter: The Autobiography of a Modern Chinese Physician*. Penang: Areca Books.

Yamamuro, Shin'ichi. 2006. *Manchuria Under the Japanese Dominion*, trans. Joshua A. Fogel. Philadelphia: University of Pennsylvania Press.

Yasutake, Rumi. 2004. *Transnational Women's Activism: The United States, Japan, and Japanese Immigrant Communities in California, 1859–1920*. New York: New York University Press.

Zachmann, Urs Matthias. 2010. War and International Order in Japan's International Legal Discourse: Attitudes Among Japanese International Lawyers During the 1920s. *Review of Asian Pacific Studies* (35): 103–120.

Zaum, Dominik. 2016. Legitimacy. In *The Oxford Handbook of International Organizations*, ed. Jacob Katz Cogan, et al., 1107–1125. Oxford: Oxford University Press.

Works in Chinese

Chang, Li. 1999. *Guoji hezuo zai Zhongguo: lianmeng jiaose de kaocha 1919–1946* [International Co-operation in China: A Study on the Role of the League of Nations, 1919–1946]. Taibei: Zhongyang yanjiuyuan jindaishi yanjiusuo.

Chang, Li. 2012. *Guoji hezuo zai Zhongguo* [International Co-operation in China]. Taipei: Institute of Modern History, Academia Sinica.

Chen, Hexi, ed. 1933. *Shijie wenhua hezuo: canjia guolian shijie wenhua hezuo-hui di shi ci huiyi zhi baogao* [International Intellectual Co-operation: Report on the Participation in the Fourteenth Session of the ICIC]. Shanghai: Shijie bianyiguan.

Chen, Haiyi. 2021. Jiuyiba shibian hou guolian diaochatuan daibiao xuan-ding yanjiu [Study of Representatives-Election of League Investigation Commission After the 9.18 Incident]. *Shehuixue Jikan* 2: 177–186.

Fang, Zhou. 2005. *Yidai baowang Shi Liangcai* [Shi Liangcai: The King of Journalism of an Era]. Beijing: Zhongguo Wenlian Press.

Furuya, Keiji, ed. 1976. *Jiangzongtong milu: Zhong-Ri guanxi bashi nian zhi zhengyan* [Secret Records of President Jiang. Authentic Account of 80 Years of China-Japan Relations]. Series 8 (translated from Japanese by Central Daily News Press). Taibei: Central Daily News Press.

He, Zuolin. 1926. Guoji zhishijie de hezuo yundong [Movement of International Intellectual Co-operation]. *Dongfang Zazhi* (23/19): 35–42.

Hong, Lan. 2006. Lidun diaochatuan baogaoshu gongbu qianhou Zhongguo shehui gejie de fanxiang [Social Reactions of All Strata Before and After the Publication of Report of the Lytton Commission]. *Shixue Yuekan* (5): 55–59.

Hu, Zushun. 1932. 'Bushihe yu gongduanren hefa xingshi' de Lytton diaochat-uan baogaoshu [League Report as 'Unsuitable Arbitrator of Legal Form']. TKP(T), 25 October.

Hu, Dekun, and Zhigang Luo, eds. 1989. *Di'erci shijie dazhan shigang* [Outline History of the Second World War]. Wuhan: Wuhan daxue.

Kuo Wen Weekly.

Li, Yuying. 1970a. Shijie wenhua hezuo zhongguo daibiaotuan zuzhi dagang chenbao dahui beian Tongqi [The Organizational Outline of the Chinese Delegation to the ICIC Reporting on the Preparatory Notice for the Conference]. *Li Shizeng Xiansheng Wenji* [Collected Works of Li Shizeng], vol. 2, 370–373. Taipei: Zhongguo Guomindang Zhongyang Weiyuanhui Dangshi Weiyuanhui. Originally published 1943.

Li, Yuying. 1970b. Zai di er ci quan guo jiaoyu huiyi jiangyanci [Lecture at the Second National Education Conference]. *Li Shizeng Xiansheng Wenji* [Collected Works of Li Shizeng], vol. 2, 242–249. Originally published 1930.

Li, Yuying. 1970c. Zhongguo guoji xueshu wenti [International Scientific Issues in China]. *Li Shizeng Xiansheng Wenji* [Collected Works of Li Shizeng], vol. 2, 270–276. Originally published 1953.

Li, Yuying. 1970d. Shijie wenhua [World Culture]. *Li Shizeng Xiansheng Wenji* [Collected Works of Li Shizeng], vol. 2, 277–281. Originally published 1954.

Liang, Jingchun. 1995. *'Jiuyiba' shibian shishu: zouxiang lishi yu weilai* [Historical Records of the '9.18 Incident': Towards History and the Future]. Taibei: Shijie shuju.

Liu, Deming. 1935. Guoji wenhua shiye shi shenme? [What Is International Cultural Exchange?]. *Waijiao Yuebao* (6/6): 141–157.

Luo, Jialun, ed. 1984. *Geming wenxian* [Documents on the Revolution]. Series 40. Taibei: Zhongyang wenwu gongying she.

Ogata, Sadako. 2015. *Manzhou Shibian: Zhengce de Xingcheng Guocheng* [The Manchurian Incident: The Process of Policy Formation] (translated from Japanese by Tingjiang Li). Beijing: Shehui Kexue Wenxian Press.

Shen, Zui. 1983. *Wo zhe sanshi nian* [Thirty Years of My Life]. Changsha: Hunan Renmin Press.

SLGB. 2008. *Jiang Zhongzheng zongtong dang'an: Shilue gaoben* [The Chiang Kai-shek Collections: The Chronological Events] (33), vol. 13, September–October 1935.

Social Welfare (Tientsi [Tianjin]).

Song, Jun. 1996. *Shun Pao de xingshuai* [The Rise and Fall of Shun Pao]. Shanghai: Shanghai Shehui Kexueyuan Press.

Sun Pao (Shanghai).

Sun, Zhongshan (Sun Yat-sen). 1928. Zhongguo cunwang wenti [The Problem China's Preservation or Demise]. *Sun Zhongshan quanji* [Complete Works of Sun Yat-sen] 4: 39–99.

Suzuki, Takashi. 1988. *Riben Diguozhuyi yu Manzhou* [Japanese Imperialism and Manchuria] (translated from Japanese by Zhou Qiqian). Taibei: Jinhe Press.

Ta Kung Pao.

Ta Kung Pao (Tientsin [Tianjin]).

Teng, Xia. 1931. Guolian weiquan an zai? [Where Is the Authority of the League?]. *Kuowen Weekly* (8/45), 16 November.

Wu, Yin. 1989. Qianxi Guolian diaochatuan paiqian an de chulong [Simple Analysis of the Formation of the League Commission Dispatch Scheme]. *Waiguo wenti yanjiu* 4: 27–32.

Wu, Tingjun. 2002. *Xinji <Ta Kung Pao> Shigao* [Historical Manuscripts of Xinji Company Ta-Kung-Pao], 9, 144. Wuhan: Wuhan Press.

Yi, Xianshi, ed. 1981. *'Jiuyiba' shibian shi* [History of the 9.18 Incident]. Liaoning: Liaoning Renmin Press.

You, Xiong. 1925. Guoji lianmeng yu xuewen yishu zhi guojihua. [League of Nations and the Internationalization of Arts and Sciences]. *Dongfang Zazhi* (22/19): 44–54.

Yun, Sheng. 1931. Guolian yijin zuida nuli [The League Has Done What It Could Do]. *Kuowen Weekly* (8/49), 14 December.

Zhang, Fuliang. 1927. *Guoji zhishi hezuo yundong shi* [History of the International Intellectual Co-operation Movement]. Shanghai: Shangwuyin shuguan.

Zheng, Dahua, and Liu, Yan. 2009. Zhongguo zhishijie dui guolian chuli 'jiuy-iba' shibian de butong fanying - yi Hu Shi, Luo Longji he Hu Yuzhi weili de kaocha [The Various Reactions of China's Intellectual Circles Towards the Management of the 9.18 Incident by the League of Nations—Focusing on Hu Shi, Luo Longji and Hu Yuzhi]. *Kangri zhanzheng yanjiu* (1): 123–134.

Zhongyang Ribao [Central Daily News].

Works in Japanese

Adachi, Mineichirō. 1930. Kokusai Renmei no hattatsu wa kenzen nariya [Has the League of Nations Developed Well?]. *Kokusai Chisiki* (10/6): 7–17.

Adachi, Mineichirō. 2011. *Adachi Mineichirō: Shokan o chūshin ni shite* [Letters of Adachi Mineichirō]. Yamagata: Adachi Mineichirō Hakase Kenshōkai.

Adachi, Mineichirō. 2019. Junebu giteisho to yo no shusei [The Geneva Protocol and My Proposal]. In *Sekai Bankoku no heiwa o kishite* [For the Peace of the World], ed. Yanagihara Masaharu, 203–207. Tokyo: Tokyo Daigaku Shuppankai.

Banjō, Kenji. 2017. Takokukan kankei no naka no imin mondai to nihon gaikō: Gaikokujin rōdōsha taigū mondai heno kanyo to 'Adachi shūsei' [Japanese Diplomacy and the Multilateral Discussions on Immigration Problems: Japanese Commitment to Equal Treatment of Foreigners and Japanese Amendment of Geneva Protocol in 1924]. *Amerika Taiheiyō Kenkyū* (17): 59–75.

Barry, John M. 2005. *The Great Influenza*, Japanese edition translated by Masao Hirasawa (*Gurēto infuruenza*). Kyōdō Tsūshinsha.

Fujii, Shōzō, 1982. Son Bun no tainichi taido: Shingai kakumei-ki no 'Manshū' soshaku mondai o chūshin ni [Sun Yat-sen's Attitude to Japan, with Special Reference to the Question of Leasing 'Manchuria' During the 1911 Revolution]. In *Ishikawa Tadao kyōju kanreki kinen ronbunshū: Gendai chūgoku to sekai: Sono seijiteki tenkai* [Essays in Honor of the Sixtieth Birthday of Professor Tadao Ishikawa: Modern China and the World: Its Political Developments], ed. Ishikawa Tadao kyōju kanreki kinen ronbunshū henshū iinkai, 127–144. Tokyo: Keiō Tsūshin.

Goto-Shibata, Harumi. 2005. *Ahen to Igirisu teikoku: Kokusai kisei no takamari 1906–43* [The International Control of Opium and the British Empire, 1906–43]. Tokyo: Yamakawa Shuppansha.

Goto-Shibata, Harumi. 2016. *Kokusaishugi to no kakutō: Nihon, Kokusai Renmei, Igirisu Teikoku* [Grappling with Internationalism: Japan, the League of Nations, and the British Empire]. Tokyo: Chūō Kōron Shinsha.

Goto-Shibata, Harumi. 2017. Adachi Mineichirō to Kokusai Renmei no hanji senkyo [Mineichiro Adachi and the Election of the PCIJ Judges at the League of Nations]. In *Adachi Mineichirō* [Mineichirō Adachi and International Legal Order], ed. Masaharu Yanagihara and Hatsue Shinohara, 193–214. Tokyo: Tokyo Daigaku Shuppankai.

Hamaguchi, Yūko. 1996. *Nihon tōchi to higashi Ajia sekai* [Japanese Rule and the East Asian World]. Tōkyō: Keisō Shobō.

Hatano, Ribō, and Hajime Terasawa. 1983. Yokota Kisaburō sensei ni kiku (dai-ikkai) [An Interview with Professor Kisaburō Yokota (First session)]. *Hōgaku Kyōshitsu* (28): 6–17.

Inoue, Tatsuo. 2004. Jiyū shugi, Liberalism, Liberalismus/libéralisme [Liberalism]. In *Iwanami tetsugaku shisō jiten*, ed. Hiromatsu Wataru, et al. Tokyo: Iwanami Shoten.

Ikō, Toshiya. 2002. *Kindai nihon to sensō ihōka taisei: Daiichiji sekai taisen kara nicchū sensō he* [Modern Japan and Outlawry of War: From the First World War to the Sino-Japanese War]. Tokyo: Yoshikawa Kōbunkan.

Ishii, Kikujirō. 1930. *Gaikō yoroku* [Diplomatic Commentaries]. Tokyo: Iwanami Shoten.

Ishijima, Noriyuki, and Tōru Kubo, eds. 2004. *Jūkei Kokumin Seifu shi no kenkyū* [History of the Chongqing National Government]. Tokyo: Tokyo Daigaku Shuppankai.

Japanese Association of International Law. 1930. Furoku: Nihon kokusaihō gakkai ketsugi kokusai hōten-an (dai-ni) [Appendix: The Second Draft Code Adopted by the Resolution of the JSIL]. *Kokusaihō Gaikō Zasshi* (29/3): 1–12.

Kamikawa, Hikomatsu. 1932a. Manshū inin tōchiron' [On the Manchurian Mandate]. *Gaikō Jihō* (650), January.

Kamikawa, Hikomatsu. 1932b. Ritton hōkoku ni okeru kaiketsuan no hihan [Criticism of the Proposed Settlement in the Lytton Report]. *Kokka Gakkai Zasshi* [The Journal of the Association of Political and Social Sciences] (46/11): 1608–1622.

Kamiyama, Akiyoshi. 2000. 'Mayaku Seizō Seigen Jōyaku' hijyun mondai: Kokusai Renmei dattai no ichimen [Progress in the Ratification by Japan of the Convention for Limiting the Manufacture and Regulating the Distribution of Narcotic Drugs: One Aspect of the Japanese Withdrawal from the League of Nations]. *Gaikō Shiryōkan Pō* (14): 51–56.

Katō, Yōko. 2007. *Manshū Jihen kara Nicchū Sensō he* [From the Manchurian Incident to the Sino-Japanese War]. Tokyo: Iwanami Shoten.

Kawakami, Tetsutarō, and Yoshimi Takeuchi, eds. 1979. *Kindai no chōkoku* [Overcoming Modernity]. Tokyo: Fuzanbō.

Kawashima, Shin. 2009. *Chūgoku kindai gaikō no keisei* [The Formation of Chinese Modern Diplomacy]. Nagoya: Nagoya Daigaku Shuppankai.

Kurasawa, Aiko, et al. 2005. Kankō ni atatte [On Publishing This Work]. In *Ajia taiheiyō sensō*, vol. 2, ed. Kurasawa Aiko, et al. Tokyo: Iwanami Shoten.

Makino, Masahiko. 2020. *Fusen Jōyaku* [The Pact of Paris]. Tokyo: Tokyo Daigaku Shuppankai.

Makino, Nobuaki. 1990. *Makino Nobuaki nikki* [Diary of Nobuaki Makino], ed. Itō Takashi, et al. Tokyo: Chūō Kōronsha.

Matsubara, Kazuo. 1931. Kokusai hōten hensan kaigi o kaerimite [The Hague Codification Conference]. *Kokusai Chishiki* (11/3): 7–15.

Matsuo, Takayoshi. 1966. *Taishō demokurashī no kenkyū* [The Research of Taishō Democracy]. Tokyo: Aoki Shoten.

Miyazaki, Shigeki. 1964. *Zāruranto no hōteki chii* [The Legal Status of the Saarland]. Tokyo: Miraisha.

MOFA, Japan. 1926. Gaimu-shō jōyaku-kyoku [Treaties and Conventions Bureau of the Ministry of Foreign Affairs of Japan]. *Nihon kokusaihō gakkai oyobi kokusaihō kyōkai nihon shibu kokusai hōten hensan jigyō* [The Codification Project by the JSIL and the Japanese Branch of the ILA]. Tokyo: Gaimu-shō.

MOFA, Japan. 1966. *Nihon gaikō nenpyō narabini shuyō bunsho* [Japanese Foreign Policy: Chronological Tables and Major Documents], vol. 2. Tokyo: Hara Shobō.

NCIC (National Committee on Intellectual Co-operation). 1928. *Gakugei no kokusai kyōryoku* [International Intellectual Co-operation]. Tokyo: Kokusai Renmei Kyōkai.

Nihon kokusai seiji gakkai Taiheiyō sensō genin kenkyūbu, ed. 1963. *Taiheiyō sensō e no michi: Kaisen gaikōshi*, vols. 1–7, and Bekkan [The Roads to Pearl Harbor: Diplomatic History Towards the War and Appendix]. Tokyo: Asahi Shimbunsha (new edition in 1987–88; select English translation in 1976–1994).

Nishimura, Shigeo, Noriyuki Ishijima, and Nobuo Tajima, eds. 2011. *Nicchū Sensō no kokusai kyōdō kenkyū 4 kokusai kankei no naka no Nicchū Sensō* [International Cooperative Study on the Sino-Japanese War, Vol. 4: The Sino-Japanese War in International Relations]. Tokyo: Keiō Daigaku Shuppannkai.

Satō, Naotake. 1963. *Kaiko 80 nen* [Looking Back at My Eighty Years]. Tokyo: Jiji Tsūshinsha.

Satō, Naotake. 1947. Kokusai Renmei no keiken to Kokusai Rengō [The Experience of the League of Nations and the United Nations]. *Hitotsubashi Ronsō* (18/1): 1–5.

Satō, Naotake, ed. 1972. *Nihon gaikoushi* [Japanese Diplomatic History], vol. 14, 453–454. Tokyo: Kajima Kenkyūjyo Shuppankai.

Saya, Makito. 2015. *Minzoku gaku, Taiwan, Kokusai Renmei* [Folklore, Taiwan, the League of Nations: Kunio Yanagida and Inazō Nitobe]. Tokyo: Kōdansha.

Shinohara, Hatsue. 2010. *Kokusai Renmei: Sekai heiwa he no yume to zasetsu*, [League of Nations: Dream and Frustration of World's Peace]. Tokyo: Chūō Kōron Shinsha.

Sun, Zhongshan (Sun Yat-sen). 1929. *Sanmin shugi* [The Three Principles of the People], trans. Into Japanese by Kanai Kanzō. Tokyo: Kaizōsha. English translation (1975) *San Min Chu I: The Three Principles of the People*. Boston: Da Capo Press.

Tachi, Sakutarō. 1914. Kokusai hōten hensan [Codification of International Law]. *Kokusaihō Gaikō Zasshi* (12/10): 834–837

Tachi, Sakutarō. 1922. Heiji kokusai hōki ni kansuru kokusai-teki rippō jigyō no hitsuyō [The Necessity for the Project of Codification in the Field of Laws of Peace]. *Gaikō Jihō* (428): 583–590.

Tachi, Sakutarō. 1930. Kokusai renmei no kito suru kokusaihō no kaishin-teki hōten hensan [The Progressive Codification of International Law Proposed by the League of Nations]. *Hōritsu Jihō* (2/3): 27–30.

Tachi, Sakutarō. 1931. Senji hōki hensan no hitsuyō [The Need of the Codification of Laws of War]. *Gaikō Jihō* (627): 1–7.

Takeuchi, Yoshimi. 1979. Kindai no Chōkoku [Overcoming Modernity]. In *Kindai no chōkoku*, ed. Kawakami and Takeuchi, 273–241. Tokyo: Fuzanbo.

Taoka, Ryōichi, 1941. *Inin tōchi no honshitsu* [Essence of Mandate Administration]. Tokyo: Yūhikaku.

Tochigi, Toshio, and Banno, Ryōkichi. 1997. *Chūgoku kokumin kakumei: Senkanki higashi Ajia no chikaku hendō* [The Chinese Nationalist Revolution: Tectonic Shifts in Interwar East Asia]. Tokyo: Hōsei Daigaku Shuppankyoku.

Tohmatsu, Haruo. 2011. *Nihon teikoku to inin tōchi: Nanyō guntō wo meguru kokusai seiji 1914–1947* [The Japanese Empire and Mandates: International Politics on the Former German Islands North of the Equator 1914–1947]. Nagoya: Nagoya Daigaku Shuppankai.

Tomizuka, Kazuhiko. 2003. 'Renmei dattai no konpon gi' to Nihon gaikō ni okeru 'Tōa' gainen no keisei [The Meaning of the 'Withdrawal from the League' and the Making of the Concept of 'East Asia' in Japanese Diplomacy]. *Kokugakuin Daigaku Nihon Bunka Kenkyūjo Kiyō* [Bulletin of the Institute of Japanese Culture, Kokugakuin University] (92): 147–172.

Unno, Yoshirō. 1972. *Kokusai Renmei to Nihon* [The League of Nations and Japan]. Tokyo: Hara Shobō.

Usui, Katsumi. 1995. *Manshūkoku to Kokusai Renmei* [Manchukuo and the League of Nations]. Tokyo: Yoshikawa Kōbunkan.

Yamada, Saburō. 1926a. Kokusaihō-jō kokuseki no tokusō ni kansuru gensoku (ni) [Principles Concerning the Acquisition and Loss of Nationality (2)]. *Kokusaihō Gaikō Zassh* (25/6): 18–38.

Yamada, Saburo. 1926b. Kokusai renmei to gakugei kyōryoku [League of Nations and Intellectual Co-operation]. *Kokusai Chishiki* (6/6): 2–11.

Yamada, Saburō. 1929a. Gakugei kyōryoku kokunai iinkai daihyōsha kaigi no gaikyō [Overview of the General Conference of Nations Committees on Intellectual Co-operation]. *Kokusai Chishiki* (9/11): 54–65.

Yamada, Saburō. 1929b. Kokusai renmei to kokusai hōten hensan [League of Nations and the Codification of International Law]. *Kokusaihō Gaikō Zassh* (28/2):1–31.

Yamada, Saburō. 1929c. Waga kokusaihō gakkai ni taisuru renmei sōkai no sanji [Acknowledgement from the Assembly of the League of Nations to Our Society of International Law]. Kokusai renmei to kokusai hōten hensan

[League of Nations and the Codification of International Law]. *Kokusaihō Gaikō Zasshi* (28/2): 92–93.

Yamada, Saburō. 1957. *Kaiko-roku* [The Memoir]. Tokyo: Yamada Saburō Sensei Beiju Shukuga-kai.

Yamakawa, Tadao. 1962. *Watashi no ashiato* [My Footprints]. Self-published book. Available in Tadao Yamakawa Papers (Private Collection), Modern Japanese Political History Materials Room, National Diet Library, Tokyo.

Yanagihara, Masaharu. 2014. Kindai nihon to kokusai saiban: 'Saiban girai' wa shinwa nanoka ? [International Adjudication and Modern Japan: Is the Reluctant Litigant a Myth?]. *Kokusaihō Gaikō Zasshi* (113/3): 1–24.

Yanagihara, Masaharu, and Shinohara, Hatsue, eds. 2017. *Adachi Mineichiro* [Adachi Mineichiro]. Tokyo: Tokyo Daigaku Shuppankai.

Yasuda, Kayo. 2014. *Kokusai seiji no naka no koksai hoken jigyou: Kokusai Renmei hoken kikan kara sekai hoken kikan, Yunisefu he* [International Health Work in International Politics: From the League of Nations Health Organization to the WHO and UNICEF]. Tokyo: Minerva Shobō.

Yokota, Kisaburo. 2016. Kokusai minshu seikatsu no genri [Principles of International Democracy-Life]. In *Heiwa kokka no aidentity* [The Identity of the Pacifist Country], ed. Tetsuya Sakai, 3–20. Tokyo: Iwanami Shoten.

Yu, Xintun. 1989. *Son Bun no kakumei undō to Nihon* [Sun Yat-sen's Revolutionary Movement and Japan]. Tōkyō: Rokkō Shuppan.

Works in Thai

Chanthima, ed. *Nayobai tangprathet Thai bon thang phraeng* [Thailand's Foreign Policy in Dilemma]. Bangkok: Thammasat University Press.

Duke, Pensri. 1999. *Kan tangprathet kap ekkarat lae athippatai khong thai: tangtae samai ratchakan thi 4 thueng sin samai chomphon p. phibunsongkhram* [Thailand's Foreign Affairs and Her Independence and Sovereignty: From King Rama IV to the End of the Phibunsongkhram Administration]. Bangkok: Text and Journal Publication.

Nuchpiam, Theera. 2016. *Tua ton mai khong sayam nai loka: Kan tangprathet nai samai ratchakan thi VII* [Siam's New Identity in the World: Its Foreign Affairs During King Rama VII]. Bangkok: Prajadhipok-Rambhai Barni Foundation.

Numnonda, Thamsook. 1981. *Kanmueang lae kan tangprathet nai prawattisat Thai* [Politics and Foreign Affairs in Thai History]. Bangkok: Thai Watana Panich Press Co., Ltd.

Petchlertanan, Thamrongsak. 2012. *Patiwat 2475 lai ratthathammanun* [1932 Revolution in Siam and Constitutions]. Bangkok: The Foundation for the Promotion of Social Science and Humanities Textbooks Projects.

Prachachart. 1933. Rao mi sitthi khrai cha rusuek yangrai mai tong wan [We Have Our Right, Do Not Fear for Others' Feelings] (in Thai), March 3. TNA, KT 96.1.6.2/9: 28.

Sattayanurak, Attachak. 2012. *Kan plianplaeng lokkathat khong chonchan phunam thai tangtae ratchakan thi IV- phoso 2475* [Changes in Perception of Thai Elite Class from King Rama IV to 1932], 3rd ed. Bangkok: Chulalongkorn University Press.

Suntarawanit, Chalong. 1990. *Prathet Thai kap kanmueang lok: kan khaosu songkhramlok khrang thi nuen* [Thailand and World Politics: Entry into the World War]. In *Nayobai tangprathet Thai bon thang phraeng* [Thailand's Foreign Policy in Dilemma], ed. Chanthima Ongsurak. Bangkok: Thammasat University Press.

Index

C. R. Hughes and H. Shinohara (eds.), *East Asians in the League of Nations*, New Directions in East Asian History,
https://doi.org/10.1007/978-981-19-7067-2

WHOAI. 1949. Bird to Kuhl, 11 March. 452-6-5.
Yasuda, [illegible]. 2017. [illegible] [illegible] [illegible] [illegible] [illegible] [illegible] [illegible] [illegible] [illegible] [illegible] [illegible] [illegible] [illegible] [illegible]. Historical and [illegible] [illegible] [illegible] on the League of Nations Health Organisation in the 1920s and 1930s. Tokyo: [illegible].

Müller, Thomas. 2020. Institutional Reforms and the Politics of Inequality Reproduction: The Case of the League of Nations' Council Crisis in 1926. *Global Society* 34: 304–317.

New York Times. 1941. Julius Arnoldson Dies in Amsterdam. 28 December.

Shih, Lu. 2004. [illegible]

Q

R

S

T

The manufacturer's authorised representative in the EU is Springer Nature Customer Service Centre GmbH, Europaplatz 3, 69115 Heidelberg, Germany. If you have any concerns regarding our products, please contact ProductSafety@springernature.com

Printed and bound by CPI Group (UK) Ltd, Croydon, CR0 4YY

30/09/2026

02225243-0011